MU00779319

Readers will find themselves pausing t
wearing or to take a mental stock of ~~... ... .~~ ~~..... . ...~~
member the last time I read something that made me think so profoundly
about my own fashion choices and how they're influenced by generations
before me.
—Dolores Inés Casillas, University of California, Santa Barbara, author of
Sounds of Belonging: U.S. Spanish-language Radio and Public Advocacy

As I read *meXicana Fashions* I thought of my mother—a second-generation
thrift store queen seamstress artist—and grandmother—a soft-spoken
woman from Monterrey who still loves a velour track suit at age 70—and
of my own color-coded closet filled with rococo ensembles. I felt all of us
situated and witnessed, challenged and archived, in these pages. From the
politics of donning rebozos to what Stacy I. Macias calls "racialized rasquache raunch," this book thoughtfully examines an important array of
questions: What is fashion? What does it do? How do we articulate dissent
through what we wear? What stories are we telling? Who are we? Where
did we come from? But it does more than that. All the contributors bring
reverence and affection to this subject as well as to the family members,
television characters, historical figures, activists, artists, and colleagues
they invite into their chapters. This book is a meXicana "look" in its own
right—fashioning memories and stories from here and there, hybridizing
the academic with the vernacular. This book is as much a rigorous examination of the politics of meXicana fashions as it is an homage to the people
who give these aesthetics life.
—Virgie Tovar, author of *You Have the Right to Remain Fat*

meXicana Fashions is a welcome scholarly investigation—by Xicanas, Chicanas, and Latinx scholars—into the construction of an identity that (contrary to mainstream views on both sides of the border) is defiant, original,
proud, and trendsetting. From Frida to the 1940s, pachucas to the cholas
featured recently in *Vogue*, everything about the meXicana identity says,
¡Presente!
—Ana Castillo, author of *So Far from God*, *Black Dove*, and many other
works.

meXicana Fashions makes a unique and compelling argument about the ways in which fashion, self-adornment, and dress contribute to the making of social identities. This wide-ranging and imaginative collection explores the layered border aesthetics of meXicanas across multiple identities, bodies, nationalities, and cultural geographies. In *meXicana Fashions*, the authors deftly examine the cultural processes enacted in everyday practices of self-adornment and fashion and capture Chicanas' complicated engagements with the fashion industry. Informed by theories and methodologies of feminist border thinking, mestiza consciousness, and intersectionality, *meXicana Fashions* explores the complex dynamics of fashion aesthetics at the heart of meXicana creativity and cultural politics of belonging and resistance. An engaging read for anyone interested in border aesthetics and feminist cultural politics!
—Rosa-Linda Fregoso, professor emerita, University of California, Santa Cruz, and author of *meXicana Encounters: the Making of Social Identities on the Borderlands*

This book is long overdue as both a document and an analysis of the creative aspects of meXicana dress. In discussions ranging from the unique personal style to the social group identity of our dress, the authors have brought to bear a theoretical and aesthetic perspective on style. The Indigenous, the political, and the process of ethno-adornment are all examined in multiple essays. Analyzing clothing from the huipil to the urban chola, the authors have broken ground in presenting the ethnic aesthetic of creative resilience and cultural identity. Bravo!
—Amalia Mesa-Barnes, professor emerita, California State University at Monterey Bay, and MacArthur Fellow

meXicana Fashions

Politics, Self-Adornment, and
Identity Construction

EDITED BY AÍDA HURTADO AND NORMA E. CANTÚ

University of Texas Press ⟠ *Austin*

Chapter 9 originally appeared in Laura E. Perez, *Eros Ideologies: Writings on Art, Spirituality, and the Decolonial* (Duke University Press, 2019); © Duke University Press; used by permission.

Requests for permission to reproduce material from this work should be sent to:
  Permissions
  University of Texas Press
  P.O. Box 7819
  Austin, TX 78713-7819
  utpress.utexas.edu/rp-form

♾ The paper used in this book meets the minimum requirements of ANSI/NISO Z39.48-1992 (R1997) (Permanence of Paper).

Library of Congress Cataloging-in-Publication Data

Names: Hurtado, Aída, editor. | Cantú, Norma E., 1947– editor.
Title: MeXicana fashions : politics, self-adornment, and identity construction / edited by Aída Hurtado and Norma E. Cantú.
Description: First edition. | Austin : University of Texas Press, 2020. | Includes bibliographical references and index.
Identifiers: LCCN 2019010289 | ISBN 978-1-4773-1958-1 (cloth : alk. paper) | ISBN 978-1-4773-1959-8 (pbk. : alk. paper) | ISBN 978-1-4773-1960-4 (library e-book) | ISBN 978-1-4773-1961-1 (nonlibrary e-book)
Subjects: LCSH: Mexican American women—Clothing. | Mexican American women—Ethnic identity. | Clothing and dress—Political aspects—United States. | Clothing and dress—Social aspects—United States. | Fashion—Social aspects—United States. | Group identity—United States.
Classification: LCC E184.M5 M534 2020 | DDC 305.48/86872073—dc23
LC record available at https://lccn.loc.gov/2019010289
doi:10.7560/319581

Contents

Introduction

AÍDA HURTADO AND NORMA E. CANTÚ

*The term ... "meXicana" draws attention to the historical, material, and
discursive effects of contact zones and exchanges among various communities
on the Mexico-U.S. border, living in the shadows of more than 150 years
of conflict, interactions, and tensions. "me-Xicana" references processes of
transculturation, hybridity, and cultural exchanges—the social and economic
interdependency and power relations structuring the lives of inhabitants on
the borderlands.*
ROSA-LINDA FREGOSO, MEXICANA ENCOUNTERS

In her book *meXicana Encounters: The Making of Social Identities on the
Borderlands,* the cultural critic Rosa-Linda Fregoso describes the inextri-
cable ties that Mexicanas and Chicanas have in the construction of their
social identities, cultural production, and in the visual representation of
self and others. The term *meXicana* exalts the hybridity produced by la
mezcla, the mixture, as essential to all that is Mexican-ness and references
chicanismo to highlight resistance and creativity. *meXicana* encompasses
the Indigenous roots of Mexico while simultaneously recognizing mestizaje—the inheritance of the Spanish conquest and other colonizations,
including the French and other cultural insertions from the Asian and the
African. It is at these crossroads, esta bocacalle, that the self-fashioning
of meXicanas is born. Catherine Ramírez highlights the process of re-
mezclando (the re-mixing)—of genres, genders, outlaws, urban/non-
urban—when she writes about the pachucas' reclamations of the male
zoot suit as their own. Similarly, the contributors to *meXicana Fashions*
underscore the effects of border crossings between Mexican, US, Latin
American, and European aesthetics as they put together a visuality que no
es ni de aquí ni de allá, neither from here nor from there—a phenomenon

1

that occurs whenever two or more cultures meet. The result is an aesthetic that is a confluence, a mezcla, a cultural mestizaje.

In *meXicana Fashions*, we take up Fregoso's call to examine meXicanas' social identities, and we do so in the realm of fashion and dress. Here fashion is defined broadly as a "code" of communication, as Roland Barthes noted in *The Fashion System*, in which he developed an analysis of dress and fashion using De Saussure's linguistic structuralism. Similarly, Fred Davis writes, "We know that through clothing people communicate some things about their persons, and at the collective level this results typically in locating them symbolically in some structural universe of status claims and life-style attachments" (5). Capable of individual style, meXicanas also have a repertoire of fashion vocabularies that emanates from the histories, social existences, and aesthetics derived from their cultures and their standing in the sociopolitical order. Notably, there is not one uniform and constant meXicana aesthetic in fashion. As Davis points out, fashion is "an incipient or quasi-code, that although it must necessarily draw on the conventional visual and tactile symbols of a culture, does so allusively, ambiguously, and inchoately, so that the meanings evoked by the combinations and permutations of the code's key terms (fabric, texture, color, pattern, volume, silhouette, and occasion) are forever shifting or 'in process'" (5). For Baudrillard, fashion "exists only within the framework of modernity . . . in a schema of rupture, progress, and innovation" (89). For meXicana fashion codes to be "read" (Barthes), they require "meanings that are sufficiently shared within one or another clothes-wearing community" (Davis 5). Broader fashion codes communicate across Latina/o nationality groups in the United States, with strong connections to fashion codes and aesthetics in the rest of Latin America. In a consumer society, meXicana fashion both adheres to and defies the dictates of fashion to change and persist.

In this book we focus primarily on meXicanas to highlight specific constituencies that are defined by regional aesthetics (Tejana style, L.A. style), age groups (homie style, gangsta style, chola style), and social class (haute couture; for example, Carolina Herrera, Oscar de la Renta, and Narciso Rodriguez). Of course, these styles are not mutually exclusive but rather commingle to create a layered, complex aesthetic that includes other Latina/o nationalities. Thus, the authors in this edited volume use an intersectional lens to consider meXicana fashions and styles in their analyses of sex, age, class, occupation, origin, personality, tastes, sexual desires, and current fads.

The Aesthetics of Self

In our analysis and approach to fashion, we make the social-psychological theoretical distinction between personal and social identity, which taken together compose an individual's integrated sense of self (Baumeister). Tajfel posits that personal identity is that aspect of self composed of psychological traits and dispositions that give rise to personal unique-ness. In contrast, social identity is defined as "that part of an individual's self-concept which derives from his *knowledge* of his membership of a so-cial group (or groups) together with the *value* and *emotional* significance attached to that membership" (Tajfel 92). Social psychologists argue that although personal identity and social identity are not entirely indepen-dent of each other, neither are they one and the same (Tajfel).

Personal identity is derived from intrapsychic influences, many of which are socialized within family units (however the families are defined) (Hur-tado, "Understanding" 309). From this perspective, human beings have a great deal in common precisely because their personal identities comprise universal processes such as loving, mating, doing productive work, and self-adornment. However, these universal components of self emerge fil-tered through language, culture, historical moment, social structures, and social context (Reicher). For example, although infinite variations in the constellation are considered appropriate for raising children—from a vil-lage, to a nuclear family, to foster care—most societies consider children as belonging to their biological parents, not to neighbors, aunts, uncles, or other relatives (Hurtado and Silva).

Similarly, all societies consider self-adornment to be indicative of group memberships, and most societies have elaborate rules about the types of self-adornment that are appropriate based on their intersectional identi-ties based on gender, class, sexuality, and other significant groupings. An addendum to note is the tie between self-adornment and social occasions, rituals, public versus private displays, and acceptable aesthetics. The con-tributors to *meXicana Fashions* write eloquently about the various dimen-sions of self-adornment—from quinceañera attire to huipiles worn inside and outside the academy—as well as self-adornment as signifier and refer-ent to current and past class belongings.

Tajfel considers personal identities as less socially salient and there-fore more fluid than social identities because they are less socially moni-tored. An individual is permitted, without a perception of incoherence, to be happy and effervescent one day and gloomy and depressed another. Furthermore, those emotional variations require social interaction for an evaluation to take place. In contrast, an individual's intersectional identi-

ties based on the social identities of gender, race, ethnicity, and socioeconomic class are relevant in most social contexts, regardless of some or no
social interaction. Therefore, the presentation of self is regulated through
these group belongings such that coherence is a necessary prerequisite for
social functioning. For example, an individual categorized as a man cannot dress as a woman one day and as a man the next without social (and
sometimes violent) consequences. According to Tajfel, personal identity is
for the most part a private sense of "me-ness" that is not necessarily negotiated or challenged in every social interaction (325–326). For instance,
people generally consider themselves kind and open-minded; until someone or some incident challenges this self-assessment, there is no reason to
doubt this judgment. In the ordinary course of social events, the unchal-
lenged personal self-assessment does not motivate the person to reevalu-
ate the personal self.

As stated earlier, social identity is that aspect of self derived from the
knowledge of being part of social categories and groups, together with the
value and emotional significance attached to those group formations. Tajfel
argues that the creation of social identities is the consequence of three
social-psychological processes. The first is social categorization. Nationality, language, race and ethnicity, skin color, and other social or physical
characteristics that are meaningful socially, and many times meaningful
politically in particular social contexts, can be the basis for social categorization and thus the foundation for the creation of social identities. Self-
adornment in the form of clothing, jewelry, and hairstyle often serves as a
proxy for social categorization into gender, race, ethnicity, sexuality, and
class groups. On the other hand, self-adornment can be used to challenge
the social categorizations that are often taken for granted (Rodríguez).

Another process underlying the construction of social identities is social comparison. In this process, the meaning of an individual's group affiliations, group status, degree of affluence, or other characteristics achieve
significance *in relation to* perceived differences and their value connotations from other social formations in the environment. The contributors
to this volume address this social comparison directly when they choose
to wear huipiles, the traditional dress of Indigenous women in the Americas, to professional conferences while others of their stature wear business
suits. Huipiles have gained significance and political relevance through the
social-psychological process of intergroup social comparisons.

The third process for developing a social identity involves psychological work, both cognitive and emotional, which is prompted by what Tajfel
claims to be a universal motive: the achievement of a positive sense of self.

When different values are attached to different group affiliations, individuals have to do psychological work to come to terms with their social identities. As Tajfel posits, individuals of a group strive to be different from other groups, but the difference has to be positive. The social groups and social identities that present the greatest obstacles to a positive sense of self are those that are disparaged (including "invisible" identities, such as physical challenges that are not evident), those that have to be negotiated frequently because of their visibility (physical attributes, such as dark skin), those that have become politicized by social movements, and so on. Moreover, these social identities become especially powerful psychologically; they are easily accessible and dwelt on, likely to be salient across situations, and likely to function as schemas, frameworks, or social scripts (Gurin, Hurtado, and Peng; Hurtado and Gurin). For example, a poor, lesbian, Latina adolescent with a physical disability is more apt to reflect on her social identities than a middle-class, heterosexual, white male adolescent with no physical impediments. Reclaiming the right to self-adornment to highlight previously derogated social identities, such as being Mexican or lesbian, is a scheme to restitute the self on positive terms rather than the stigma assigned by society. For instance, "fat fashion" is now available in major retail outlets and included in runway shows. Social media has provided a platform for "fatshionistas" to talk back to hegemonic aesthetic standards that exclude large women and men, as well as queer aesthetics of self-construction (Munoz; Taylor; Tovar).

Unproblematic group memberships—that is, ones that are socially valued, accorded privilege, or indistinguishable to others—may not even become social identities. For instance, until the emergence of whiteness studies, being racially white and male was not considered a problematic category and is still not widely thought of as a social identity[1] (Fine et al.; Hurtado and Stewart; Phinney). Although there may be different groups of whites (for examples, varying by class—poor whites versus middle-class whites), the privileges accrued because of the racial benefits of whiteness are not easily articulated by its possessors, regardless of class, because white race privilege is considered the norm in the United States (McIntosh).

Intersectionality

Hurtado (*Voicing*, "Multiple Lenses," "Intersectionality") locates a link between social identity theory (Tajfel) and intersectionality where intersectionality refers to the particular constellation of social identities that are based on what sociologists call "master statuses" (Hughes)—that is, class, race, sexuality, ethnicity, physical challenges, and gender. Master statuses are the primary basis for power distribution, stigmatization, *and* subordination. Master statuses are also the basis for significant social identities because individuals must psychologically negotiate their potentially stigmatizing effects. Conversely, if these master statuses confer privilege and that privilege becomes problematized, then the individuals holding such privilege must negotiate the psychological effects of devalued group membership. In the United States, as in many other countries, master statuses are used to make value judgments about group memberships and to allocate political, social, and economic power (Reicher). Furthermore, these master statuses affect all measures of inequality, such as education, income, and accumulated wealth. Tajfel's theory of social identity, which has been elaborated upon by others (Gurin, Hurtado, and Peng; Hogg and Reid; Hurtado, "Understanding"; Reicher and Hopkins), provides a framework for understanding both unproblematic and stigmatized group affiliations, especially those based on master statuses.

Given the powerful effects of master statuses on social identity formation (Reicher), it becomes important to distinguish social identities that are based on master statuses from other social categories. Individuals can construct multiple group identities that are not based on master statuses, and multiple identities do not necessarily refer to master statuses. According to Tajfel, "nonstigmatized social memberships" are part of an individual's multiple identities. For example, a person may identify with a political party (Democrat or Republican), a geographical area (California or Texas), and a profession (architect or teacher). These multiple group memberships are significant to people and have social consequences, but from a Tajfelian perspective they do not constitute an individual's social identity, primarily because they have no consistent stigmatizing effects. They are not used systematically to assign political, social, and economic power; membership can be changed; and membership does not intersect in significant ways to produce any of the delineated consequences ascribed to social identities (Turner and Onorato). We include sexuality as a master status because any divergence from heteronormativity (lesbian, gay, transsexual) is used to stigmatize individuals. Sexuality can also have oppressive consequences when it intersects with other master statuses such as race, class, and ethnicity.

The Social Self and Intersecting Identity Constellations

Social identities are tied to significant group memberships, which together form a constellation that constitutes a whole and integrated sense of the social self (Turner and Onorato). Even if an individual belongs to several significant social categories or master statuses (say, being a woman, Chicana, and poor), these group belongings do not operate psychologically and socially as separate categories but as an integrated sense of the social self (Turner and Onorato). Thus, individuals' social identity constellations compose their overall social identity because human beings experience themselves as whole, not as independent social categories. When individuals are asked "What is most important to you, being a woman or being Chicana?," most have difficulty creating a hierarchy because they experience these social identities as integrated social categories. If pressed, individuals can indeed rank their social categories, but this ranking is cognitively created, not one that is naturally occurring in the social world.

Although individuals may not necessarily rank their social identities, the salience of different affiliations varies according to social context—that is, which stigmatized social identities gain significance is largely context-dependent. As Reicher and Hopkins indicate, "the particular social identity that is salient in a given context will determine who is seen and treated as similar and who is rejected as an alien" (385–386). Indeed, Turner and Onorato argue that the meaning of particular social categories can be fully understood only in context because the meaning will change if the circumstances vary. When stigmatized social identities intersect in particular contexts, they become intersectional identities.

Intersectional social identities can therefore be conceptualized as fluid and amorphous amoebae that change shape as they move through their surroundings, making one (or more) social identities especially salient depending on the context. Each social category is porous, overlapping others, with boundaries that are not rigid or fixed. From a social-psychological point of view, as proposed by Hurtado ("Intersectional Understandings") intersectionality refers to this particular constellation of social identities, which is the primary basis for stigmatization and allocation of privilege. Because personal identity is not entirely independent of social identities, individuals cannot completely override the negative and oppressive effects of their stigmatized social identities on their personal identity. For example, a poor, Latina lesbian with a physical disability will be treated in many social contexts according to her visible stigmatized social identities rather than her personal identity, which quite possibly may include being a kind, gentle, and intelligent human being. Intersectionality as embodied in stigmatized social identities allows for an agile analysis of the different social contexts in which certain stigmatized social identities are more salient and likely to be used to impose oppression (Hurtado and Cervantez). This framework also facilitates the examination of the social process of external intersectional social identity assignations by others versus the private self-perceptions of an individual's personal identity. Individuals use self-fashioning through clothing and accessories — such as jewelry, shoes, and hair ornaments — to declare allegiance to particular intersectional identities or to refute them. Individuals can also use intersectional identities to create disjunctures between what we expect visually between social categories and dress. A man wearing a skirt not only creates a fashion statement but also destabilizes the expectation that men should not wear skirts, unless it's a kilt. Self-adornment can be used to complicate the gender binary, as seen in the case of queer aesthetics (Clarke and Turner).

Intersectional Identities, Social and Political Spaces, and Temporality

Stigmatized social identities intersect and form alternating constellations in various social spaces. Consequently, the significance and relationship between these social identities (such as class, race, ethnicity, and sexuality) vary from social sphere to social sphere and across time. In some circumstances, one particular group membership or set of memberships may be more salient than others; when functioning within a group that is homogeneous with regard to its significant social identities, that particular social identity (or identities) may be much less relevant than it would be in a situation where many groups interact with each other. For example, a Chicana professor who wears a huipil during an ethnic studies conference may not think about her self-fashioning, but she may become acutely aware of her ethnic, class, gender, and sexual identity when she wears the garment in her college classroom, where many students may have never encountered a Chicana professor and for whom the huipil is an unknown marker.

As mentioned earlier, intersectionality can also illuminate contradictory intersections of subordination and privilege: for instance, the joint identities of being a professor and a Chicana. Because master statuses can confer privilege, personal identity also benefits from the freedom of stigma if an individual's master statuses protect her or him from subordination. Intersectionality can also be applied to study the consequences of privilege when master statuses are aligned to benefit individuals. The application of intersectionality to the problematics of privilege, however, has yet to be fully developed. In sum, the concept of intersectional social identities allows the examination of this complexity in various social spheres, in different life cycles, and across historical moments.

Intersectional Social Identities, Identification, and Consciousness

While Tajfel's social identity theory provides a sophisticated framework for understanding individual responses to desirable and undesirable group affiliations, Gurin, Miller, and Gurin provide a different theoretical bridge between group affiliations and awareness of the values attached to the group's status. According to their perspective, most people are aware of their social identities when they are tied to master statuses. For example, individuals can almost universally articulate if they are female or male; Chicana or white; poor, middle-class, or wealthy; and physically challenged or not. But Gurin and colleagues believe that individuals are less likely to be aware of how the entire group of individuals in that category rank in relation to other social formations in the same "life space" (Lewin)—that is, individuals may be highly identified with particular social formations and may be aware of whether that affiliation is desirable or not, but they may not be at all conscious of the status of their entire stratum. According to Gurin and colleagues,

> Identification and consciousness both denote cognitions: the former about a person's relation to others within a stratum, the latter about a stratum's position within a society. Identification refers to the awareness of having ideas, feelings, and interests similar to others who share the same stratum characteristics. Consciousness refers to a set of political beliefs and action orientations arising out of this awareness of similarity. (30)

Through identification, then, individuals see themselves belonging to certain social formations—for example, ethnic, gender, and class groups. Through consciousness, they become aware that the social formations they belong to hold a certain status (either powerful or not powerful) in society, and they can decide (or possibly feel compelled) to take action to change this status, not just for their own benefit but also for that of others in the group. Thus, having a characteristic that could potentially become a social identity, such as being a woman, does not necessarily mean that the individual develops such a social identity; an awareness of what that particular category signifies socially and politically is necessary for identity constructions to become conscious and result in political mobilization. The contributors to this volume are highly conscious about their meXicanness and claim self-adornment as a weapon to combat negative perceptions of meXicanas/os in the United States and abroad. Several contributors have used meXicana aesthetics strategically to reclaim the positive aspects of their ethnicity, working-class backgrounds, and racial memberships. As this volume's second section proclaims, the contributors are "Saying It Loud / Saying It Clear" that there is nothing wrong and much that is right with meXicana self-adornment.

Hurtado ("Intersectional Understandings") contends that Gloria Anzaldúa's Borderlands theory helps explain a particular type of consciousness (as defined by Gurin and colleagues) in which border crossings or multiple social subjectivities (Hurtado, "Multiple Subjectivities") contribute to political understandings of various group statuses and thus influence an individual's intersectional social identities.

Intersectionality and Borderlands Theory

Since the late 1980s, Chicana feminist scholars have been working at the forefront of intersectionality by proposing feminisms that take into account culture, class, sexuality, race, ethnicity, and, most recently, masculine gender (Hurtado and Sinha). A pivotal theoretical addition to Chicana feminisms has been the work of Gloria Anzaldúa—a writer and public intellectual, and one of the first Chicanas to openly claim her lesbianism (Moraga and Anzaldúa). Anzaldúa wrote extensively on Borderlands theory, as scholars in the humanities call it, before her untimely passing at the age of sixty-one. Borderlands theory expands on W. E. B. DuBois's concept of double consciousness, applying it to the experiences of Chicanas growing up in South Texas along the Mexican border (Martinez). According to Anzaldúa, the border between the United States and Mexico is a metaphor for multiple types of crossings—crossings between geopolitical boundaries, sexual transgressions, social dislocations, and those necessary to exist in multiple linguistic and cultural contexts. Anzaldúa locates that geographical border as the source of her theorizing. As Hurtado (*Voicing*) summarizes:

The history of conquest, which basically layered another country over a preexisting nation, gave Chicana feminisms the knowledge of the temporality of nation-states. . . . The political line dividing the United States from Mexico did not correspond to the experiential existence on the border. Chicana feminists declare the border as the geographical location (lugar) that created the aperture for theorizing about subordination from an ethnically specific Chicana/mestiza consciousness. (18)

According to Anzaldúa, the borderlands create a third space between cultures and social systems; living within this space leads to coherence by embracing ambiguity and holding contradictory perceptions without conflict. La frontera (the border) is also the geographical area most susceptible to hybridity, being neither fully of Mexico nor fully of the United States. As Anzaldúa claims, la frontera is where you "put chile in the borscht / eat whole-wheat tortillas / speak Tex-Mex with a Brooklyn accent" (195). The word *borderlands* denotes that space in which antithetical elements mix and combine in unique and unexpected ways rather than being obliterated or subsumed by a larger whole (Hurtado, *Voicing*). Several of the contributors to this volume explicitly refer to crossing borders, actual and metaphorical, in the choices they make in self-adornment. Several of them reference their families and upbringing, and describe how they influenced their aesthetic choices — from learning to sew with their grandmothers, to living in two countries, Mexico and the United States.

Living between two countries, two social systems, two languages, and two cultures results in understanding experientially the contingent nature of social arrangements (Martinez). Anzaldúa asserts that living in the borderlands produces a special knowledge derived from being within a system while also retaining the knowledge of coming from outside the system. This "outsider within" status produces a layered complexity within Chicanas' sense of self that is captured in Anzaldúa's concept of mestiza consciousness, as summarized by Hurtado (*Voicing*):

It was at the border that Chicanas/mestizas learned the socially constructed nature of all categories. By standing on the U.S. side of the river they saw Mexico and they saw home; by standing on the Mexican side of the border they saw the United States and they saw home. Yet they were not really accepted on either side. Their ability to "see" the arbitrary nature of all categories but still take a stand, challenges Chicana feminisms to exclude while including, to reject while accepting, and to struggle while negotiating. . . . The basic concept involves the ability to hold multiple social perspectives while simultaneously maintaining a center that revolves around concrete material forms of oppression. (18)

The application of mestiza consciousness to self-fashioning is reflected in the contributors' multiple aesthetic vocabularies, which are influenced by a variety of styles in the United States and Mexico and numerous geographical and cultural experiences encountered in their travels and education. Visual "codes" can be informed by a cultural mestizaje that arises through an array of aesthetic vocabularies.

Although Anzaldúa developed Borderlands theory by examining her experiences as the daughter of farmworkers living in extreme poverty in South Texas, the theory also applies to many social, economic, sexual, and political dislocations. Her insights help us understand and theorize about the experiences of individuals who are exposed to contradictory social systems and who then develop what she terms la facultad (the gift)—the ability of individuals (primarily women) who are exposed to multiple social worlds as defined by cultures, languages, social classes, sexualities, nation-states, and colonization—to develop the agility to navigate and challenge linear conceptions of social reality. Other writers have called this ability "differential consciousness" (Sandoval), perception of "multiple realities" (Alarcón), "multiple subjectivities" (Hurtado, "Multiple Subjectivities"), and a state of "concientización" (Castillo).

Another application of Borderlands theory appears in the analysis of intersectionality through the concept of social identities. The fluidity and context-dependent nature of social identities result in "social travel" between social systems, cultural symbols, and cognitive understandings, ultimately creating a non-normative consciousness of the arbitrary nature of social reality. Following the logic inherent in Borderlands theory, stigmatized social identities based on master statuses are not additive: they do not result in increased oppression with an increased number of stigmatized group memberships. Instead, the group memberships of individuals are conceptualized as intersecting in a variety of ways, depending on the social context (Hurtado and Gurin).

Anzaldúa's work integrates Aztec beliefs and epistemologies into Borderlands theory to circumvent linear positivist thinking, which does not allow for hybridity, contradiction, and, ultimately, liberation from existing social arrangements (Hurtado, *Voicing*; Martinez). As Martinez states:

The "borderlands" signify Anzaldúa's family of oppression, her memory of brutal backbreaking work, and her knowledge of border history. The "borderlands" are the site of her worst struggles with racism, sexism, classism and heterosexism: "*La mestiza* undergoes a struggle of flesh, a struggle of borders, an inner war. . . . The coming together of two self-consistent but habitually incompatible frames of reference causes *un choque*, a cultural collision" (Anzaldúa 1987, 28). Yet, this crossroads is also the site of her greatest strength. This "floundering in uncharted seas," this "swamping of her psychological borders" (79), creates the other ways of coping and seeing the world. It forces the mestiza consciousness into existence in a psychic birthing and synthesis to become a reflection of the "borderlands" themselves— a juncture, a crossroads, and a consciousness of multiple voices and paradigms. (559–560)

The contributors to this volume have experienced a similar "consciousness of multiple voices and paradigms." They discuss at length the clash between their internal desires for an aesthetic that honors and highlights their various social identities, history, and culture, and the external reactions from dominant group members who may not understand the aesthetic or who associate it with the stereotyped representation of lo mexicano. The general public lacks the cultural and visual understandings of the hybridity inherent in meXicana aesthetics. A lack of knowledge on the part of producers of fashion can result in a carnivalesque display of lo mexicano. In chapter 7, Hurtado describes a "Mexican" fashion layout in *Vogue* with European-looking models who clap and dance in a Spanish style, thus homogenizing two aesthetics—from two different continents with two different histories—that represent two national identities. The ironic twist is that "Spanish clapping" (with hands held high) is the style of the colonizers who tried to obliterate a Mexican aesthetic. The meXicana fashion aesthetic represents resistance and reclamation of that which has been appropriated by mainstream media and colonizing cultures.

Through Borderlands theory, Anzaldúa provides the experiential documentation for Tajfel's social identity theory. In his writings, Tajfel does not address extensively what it means for individuals, let alone women, to carry the burden of stigma from others' categorization of them into social groups. Furthermore, he does not explore how individuals cope with the incongruence between their private self-perceptions (say, as a competent, intelligent, and logical person) and others' negative perceptions shaped by stigmatized social identities. Anzaldúa proposes that one possibility, among many, is to use the contradiction to one's advantage, rising above the negative assignation to develop a complex view of the social self, or what Gurin, Miller, and Gurin term *consciousness* about one's intersectional identities. One potential type of consciousness, according to

Borderlands theory, is a mestiza consciousness. In many ways, Anzaldúa's work exemplifies the poetics of political resistance and rescues Chicanas (and other Latinas) from potential stigma derived from their derogated social identities. meXicana self-adornment can become a strategic weapon of public self-presentation, challenging the visual expectations of those who do not value the complexity and visual play of a meXicana aesthetic.

Fashioning the Aesthetics of the Body

Transnational embodied social signifiers based on intersectional identities lead to the disruption and, simultaneously, homogenization of beauty standards and rules of adornment. The irony is that increased globalization has also increased the availability of visual codes for self-adornment. At the same time, hegemonic Western capitalist standards of visual display are reinscribed as most desirable. meXicana fashion adheres to these global dynamics at the same time that it subverts, modifies, co-opts, and appropriates them. There is no doubt that meXicana fashion is as subject to domination as any other form, including fat fashion, but the contributors to this volume argue that meXicanas are exposed to more fashion and aesthetic vocabularies than those floating in the hegemonic sea of fashion. Among these are the border existence between two nation-states, the United States and Mexico, which includes historical events; political movements; Indigenous cultures; dual language systems; distinct but overlapping popular cultures; exposure to art, film, and architecture; geographies; and personal narratives of struggle and resistance—all of which influence self-adornment, both consciously and unconsciously.

The body provides a space for various forms of self-expressions reflecting a cultural aesthetic and identitarian codes; furthermore, it allows for the articulation of a narrative of representation based on shared aesthetic modalities. Thus, for a Chicana, wearing a huipil may fulfill the function of adornment while also communicating various intersectional identities, which can include gender, class, ethnicity, and sexuality, among others. The display of intersectional identities, as discussed above, and the disruption of the various intersections are at the core of the essays gathered in *meXicana Fashions*. The authors explore the landscape of dress and adornment from a number of vantage points, constituting a complex and multifaceted whole that offers various ways of entering the discussion for further reader engagement.

The Structure of This Book

While self-definition takes its expression from the embodied manifestation of personal identity, it is the social identities that find visual articulation among the authors contributing to this book. Hence, the contributions naturally fall within three sections based on the social self: section 1,
"Rendering of Self: Personal Narratives / Personal Adornment"; section 2,
"The Politics of Dress: Saying It Loud / Saying It Clear"; and section 3, "The
Politics of Entrepreneurship: Making (It) / Selling (It)." Of course, some of
the approaches and content overlap and apply to each of these categories.
Nonetheless, we provide an initial structure from which readers can identify the themes and rearrange the discussions in a recursive process according to their purposes. The richness of the analysis provided by the
authors allows for multiple ways of organizing the materials for course-
work and class discussion. Below is an overview of the three sections and
the chapters in each of them.

Section I. Rendering of Self: Personal Narratives / Personal Adornment

The five chapters in this section address meXicanas' desire to wear their
personal identities in the public sphere for all to see. As Davis points out,
"Dress . . . comes easily to serve as a kind of visual metaphor for identity" (25). The authors provide subjective narratives constructed to accompany discussions of chosen adornments as a public manifestation of
their identification processes. Through their dress, these authors claim
personal validation and identity construction, wearing clothing and accessories that may otherwise be viewed as ethnic or even inappropriate for
their social and economic status. In chapter 1, "Wearing Identity: Chicanas
and Huipiles," Norma E. Cantú explores her personal connection to wearing huipiles, as well as that of other Chicanas who occupy various social
spheres and identities. She surveyed and interviewed a number of huipilistas (women who wear huipiles) in San Antonio, Texas, to inform her
analysis and conclusions. She finds that among the motivations for wearing the garment is the desire to claim a sense of self that acknowledges
and honors the Indigenous roots of meXicana culture. As Cantú states,
from the late nineteenth century (or possibly earlier), rebozos, huipiles,
and other garments have signaled Mexican-ness. She notes that at least
one scholar traced the practice of women's coverings to the Arab tradition,
which arrived via Spain (Bourke 83–85). The huipil is an identitarian signifier that suggests not only Indigeneity but class position.

In chapter 2, "Con el huipil en la mente: The Metamorphosis of a Chicana," Josie Méndez-Negrete also assesses the significance of the huipil in building her identification with her Indigenous origins. She claims that the piece of clothing is a protective shield against identity dispersion. Like the colorful threads of the huipil, Méndez-Negrete weaves memories into a tale of her early childhood in Mexico, where she spent time with aunts who taught her to sew and encouraged her creativity. Eventually, she left her aunts' home, which she considered a magical place, to reunite with her parents in the United States. Méndez-Negrete develops the tools provided by her aunts to protect herself and her siblings from the harsh realities experienced in and out of her nuclear family. Designing, sewing, and wearing the huipil allowed her to survive and thrive, and become the accomplished writer and professor she is today.

For chapter 3, "Rebozos, huipiles, y ¿Qué?": Chicana Self-Fashioning in the Academy," author Micaela Díaz-Sánchez interviewed Chicana faculty to explore their commitment to wearing huipiles, rebozos, and Mexican jewelry. Her analysis, which is based on the faculty responses, identifies four themes: honoring past ancestors, the implications of self-fashioning on classroom pedagogies, the use of iconic Mexican figures to adorn their attire, and the general academy's reaction to faculty members' self-adornment. Díaz-Sánchez observes that the visual intervention made by the Chicana faculty's meXicana attire disrupts the uniformity found in institutions of higher education and honors the faculty's transnational ethnic and racial heritage, which is often obfuscated in the pervasive whiteness of the academy.

In chapter 4, "'Por la facha y por el traje, se conoce al personaje': Tales about Attire as Resistance and Performativity in a Chicana's Life Trajectory," Gabriella Gutiérrez y Muhs provides an auto-ethnography from a developmental perspective, exploring the meaning of wearing huipiles, rebozos, and other Mexican and Indigenous clothing throughout her life. Gutiérrez y Muhs's extensive travel in other countries is part of her education, profession, and life trajectory; she conveys her identity in her chosen garments, which display her mexicanidad and allegiance to her Indigenous roots.

In chapter 5, "A Familial Legacy of meXicana Style," Domino Renee Perez also relies on auto-ethnography. She combines this approach with a historical and poetic retracing of her family's meXicana style and the influence it has had on her current construction of self. The analysis in this chapter employs the new and developing method of excavating a family's and meXicanas' complex social history through the practices of dress and adornment. Perez's narrative presents the immigration history of her family, the class divisions among meXicanas/os at the turn of the twentieth century, and the buying patterns of meXicanas/os as they struggle with constructing identity through self-adornment and intersectional oppression through the impositions of social class, ethnicity, gender, and race.

Section II. The Politics of Dress: Saying It Loud / Saying It Clear

While the authors in section 1 focus on the personal importance of dress for identity construction, the chapters in section 2 explicate the social, economic, and political significance of meXicana style, thus highlighting their intersectional identities. For the racialized and ethnicized body, self-adornment is a political act, both of compliance to existing hegemonic standards for decorum and resistance against homogenization into the mainstream (and everything in-between). Self-adornment can be a political placard for a person's ideologies and political commitments as embodied in their social identities. The authors in this section are saying their politics loudly and clearly by analyzing the political and social messages manifested in dress.

In chapter 6, "Buying the Dream: Relating 'Traditional' Dress to Consumer Practices within US Quinceañeras," author Rachel Valentina González-Martin highlights the commercialization of the quinceañera tradition as manufacturers and corporations take control of the production of the essentials for the celebration. González-Martin highlights the variations in the ritual and addresses the overwhelming choices available today to quinceañeras and their families as they enter the new consumer market for everything related to a young woman coming of age within a Mexican as well as Latin American tradition.

In chapter 7, "Visuality, Corporality, and Power," author Aída Hurtado explores from a transnational perspective the common racialization that women of Color are subjected to in fashion magazines. This chapter highlights the racialization of femininities in an effort to exalt whiteness. Hurtado provides a case study of a pictorial layout in an issue of *Vogue* from Spain, titled "Buscando a Frida" ("Looking for Frida"), in which the Mexican artist Frida Kahlo is portrayed by a white model, and the visual display reads as an appropriation of Mexican art, folklore, culture, and the legacy of the artist. The political act of appropriation and distortion reinscribes the centrality of whiteness regardless of the national origins of its possessors.

In chapter 8, "Black, Brown, and Fa(t)shionable: The Role of Fat Women of Color in the Rise of Body Positivity," Jade D. Petermon addresses blogging practices among "fatshionistas" (women of Color who are considered "plus size" by the fashion industry) as a form of resistance to homogenous standards applied in the fashion world. We include this chapter as an acknowledgment of the diversity in meXicana racial identifications, such as Latinas who consider themselves as Afro-Latinas and may identify with a wide range of phenotypes, including Black aesthetics.

In chapter 9, "Fashioning Decolonial Optics: Days of the Dead Walking Altars and Calavera Fashion Shows in Latina/o Los Angeles," Laura Pérez provides a rich and textured history of the art walk designed around the Day of the Dead celebration by artists in Los Angeles. She explores the cultural, philosophical, aesthetic, and spiritual motivation for the calavera fashion shows and the intervention they provide in creating a community for artists and residents in the area.

In chapter 10, "'Fierce and Fearless': Dress and Identity in Rigoberto González's *The Mariposa Club*," Sonia Alejandra Rodríguez argues that certain types of dress, such as that deployed by Trinidad Ramos—one of the main characters in the novel, a queer Latino teen who often dresses in drag—serves to disrupt hetero-patriarchal structures. Rodríguez argues that self-adornment can punctuate how the novel's characters create and assert their queer identity.

Section III. The Politics of Entrepreneurship: Making (It) / Selling (It)

While meXicanas are creating personal identity and embodying social identities by making political statements through their choices in dress and style, they have also entered into the sphere of fashion commerce and entrepreneurship. The chapters presented in section 3 represent a beginning in the mapping of the contours of meXicanas' entrepreneurial activities.

In chapter 11, "Lydia Mendoza, 'Reina de la Música Tejana': Self-Stylizing Mexicanidad through China Poblana in the US-Mexico Borderlands," Marci McMahon analyzes the intense attention to detail and economics required to become an icon. McMahon argues that the Tejana musical icon Lydia Mendoza constructed her self and her art while developing her artistic performance and remaining loyal to her artistic intent. From the costumes she designed and sewed herself, to the booking of her own performance dates, Mendoza was dedicated to the process of making artistic performance an integral part of economic survival.

In chapter 12, "(Ad)Dressing Chicana/Latina Femininity: Consumption, Labor, and the Cultural Politics of Style in Latina Fashion," Stacy I. Macías challenges the dichotomy between fashion as the weapon of the state to impose subordination, and fashion as the "weapons of the weak" (Scott) to reestablish agency. Instead, Macías recognizes that the dance that oppressed subjects perform within the limitations offered by neoliberalism contains spaces of resistance and reinvention. She proposes that the economic acquisition of fashion is reconstructed by Chicanas/Latinas to provide a sense of identity and an assertion of a racialized rasquache aesthetic as one of many possibilities for the reconstitution of self.

In the final chapter, "Urban Xican/x-Indigenous Fashion Show AR-Tivism: Experimental Perform-Antics in Three Actos," Chela Sandoval, Amber Rose González, and Felicia Montes narrate in detail the labor involved in staging alternative fashion shows by Chicana and Indigenous artists to reconstitute the visual. In this process, the workers at the fashion show—including the designers, models, and others involved in the staging—visually create a Xicana Indigeneity that summons those aspects of culture relevant to reasserting a cultural heritage combined with a spiritual vision of self-adornment. These fashion shows, which are economically self-sufficient and staged without corporate sponsorship, facilitate the vending of alternative fashion, jewelry, and other cultural products, such as drawings and paintings, making them sites of self-affirmation and economic independence. Structured around a three-act play, the chapter explores global Indigenous fashion focusing on a local Xicana-Indígena fashion show as a co-created textual spectacle. The three actos that constitute this chapter weave together the voices of feminist urban Indigenous and Xicanx organizers, curators, designers, re-fashioners, students, supporters, advisers, and audiences. Within the meXicana identity, the Xicana-Indígena identity is useful in this particular analysis of the women involved in political, educational, and cultural work that serves to raise Indigenous consciousness and support the social justice struggles of people of Indigenous American origins, North and South.

We trust that the contents of this book will ignite further exploration into the significance of fashion, self-adornment, and the economics of self-fashioning among meXicanas, as well as other women of Color whose femininities and sense of style have not informed or been informed by the mainstream fashion industry. Readers will find that the authors offer thought-provoking and informative analyses of meXicana fashion that will undoubtedly initiate discussion and further questioning and exploration of the topic. There are many more technologies of adornment that are waiting to be explored—tattooing, piercing, cross-dressing, drag shows, and emerging aesthetics yet to be labeled. All of the contributors hope our book on meXicana fashions will open new avenues of exploration and create an aperture for further theorization, documentation, and advancement of the role self-adornment plays in creating identities and resistance.

Note

1. Except for the emerging white nationalist movement.

Works Cited

Alarcón, Norma. "The Theoretical Subject(s) of This Bridge Called My Back and Anglo-American Feminism." *Making Face, Making Soul: Haciendo Caras*, edited by Gloria Anzaldúa, Aunt Lute Books, 1990, pp. 356–369.

Anzaldúa, Gloria. *Borderlands/La Frontera: The New Mestiza*. Aunt Lute Books, 1987.

Barthes, Roland. *The Fashion System*. Translated by Matthew Ward and Richard Howard, U of California P, 1967.

Baudrillard, Jean. *Symbolic Exchange and Death*. Translated by Ian Grant, Sage, 1993.

Baumeister, Roy F. "The Self." *The Handbook of Social Psychology*, vol. 1, edited by Daniel T. Gilbert et al., Oxford UP, 1998, pp. 680–740.

Bourke, John G. 1896. "Notes on the Language and Folk-Usage of the Rio Grande Valley. (With Especial Regard to Survivals of Arabic Custom.)" *Journal of American Folklore*, vol. 9, no. 33, Apr.–June 1896, pp. 81–116.

Castillo, Ana. *Massacre of the Dreamers: Essays on Xicanisma*. U of New Mexico P, 1995.

Clarke, V., and Kevin Turner. "Clothes Maketh the Queer? Appearance and the Construction of Lesbian, Gay and Bisexual Identities." *Feminism and Psychology*, vol. 17, no. 2, 2007, pp. 267–276.

Davis, Fred. *Fashion, Culture, and Identity*. U of Chicago P, 1994.

DuBois, W. E. B. *The Souls of Black Folk*. McClurg, 1903.

Fine, Michelle, Louise Weis, Linda Powell Pruitt, and April Burns, editors. *Off White: Readings on Power, Privilege, and Resistance*. Routledge, 2004.

Fregoso, Rosa-Linda. *meXicana Encounters: The Making of Social Identities on the Borderlands*. U of California P, 2003.

Gurin, Patricia, Aída Hurtado, and Tim Peng. "Group Contacts and Ethnicity in the Social Identities of Mexicanos and Chicanos." *Personality and Social Psychology Bulletin*, vol. 20, 1994, pp. 521–532.

Gurin, Patricia, Arthur H. Miller, and Gerald Gurin. "Stratum Identification and Consciousness." *Social Science Quarterly*, vol. 43, 1980, pp. 30–47.

Hogg, Michael A., and Scott A. Reid. "Social Identity, Self-categorization, and the Communication of Group Norms." *Communication Theory*, vol. 16, 2006, pp. 7–30.

Hughes, Everett C. 1945. "Dilemmas and Contradictions of Status." *American Journal of Sociology*, vol. 50, no. 5, 1945, pp. 353–359.

Hurtado, A[ída]. "Intersectionality." *Bloomsbury Handbook of 21st-Century Feminist Theory*, edited by Robin T. Goodman, Bloomsbury, 2019, pp. 159–170.

Hurtado, Aída. "Intersectional Understandings of Inequality." *Oxford Handbook of Social Psychology and Social Justice*, edited by Phillip L. Hammack, Oxford UP, 2018, pp. 1–24.

———. "Multiple Lenses: Multicultural Feminist Theory." *Handbook of Diversity in Feminist Psychology*, edited by Hope Landrine and Nancy Russo, Springer, 2010, pp. 29–54.

———. "Multiple Subjectivities: Chicanas and Cultural Citizenship." *Women and Citizenship*, edited by Marilyn Friedman, Oxford UP, 2005, pp. 111–129.

———. "Understanding Multiple Group Identities: Inserting Women into Cultural Transformations." *Journal of Social Issues*, vol. 53, no. 2, 1997, pp. 299–328.

———. *Voicing Chicana Feminisms: Young Women Speak Out on Sexuality and Identity*. New York UP, 2003.

Hurtado, Aída, and Karina Cervantez. "A View from Within and from Without: The Development of Latina Feminist Psychology." *The Handbook of U.S. Latino Psychology: Developmental and Community-based Perspectives*, edited by Francisco A. Villarruel et al., Sage, 2009, pp. 171–190.

Hurtado, Aída, and Patricia Gurin. *Chicano/a Identity in a Changing U.S. Society: ¿Quién Soy? ¿Quiénes Somos?* U of Arizona P, 2004.

Hurtado, Aída, and Janelle M. Silva. 2008. "Creating New Social Identities in Children through Critical Multicultural Media: The Case of Little Bill." *The Intersections of Personal and Social Identities*, special issue of *New Directions for Child and Adolescent Development*, vol. 120, 2008, pp. 17–30.

Hurtado, Aída, and Mrinal Sinha. *Beyond Machismo: Intersectional Latino Masculinities*. U of Texas P, 2016.

Hurtado, Aída, and Abigail J. Stewart. "Through the Looking Glass: Implications of Studying Whiteness for Feminist Methods." *Off White: Readings on Power, Privilege, and Resistance*, edited by Michelle Fine et al., Routledge, 2004, pp. 315–330.

Lewin, Kurt. *Resolving Social Conflicts: Selected Papers on Group Dynamics*. Harper and Brothers, 1948.

Martinez, Theresa A. "Making Oppositional Culture, Making Standpoint: A Journey into Gloria Anzaldúa's Borderlands." *Sociological Spectrum*, vol. 25, 2005, pp. 538–570.

McIntosh, Peggy. "White Privilege: Unpacking the Invisible Knapsack." *Peace and Freedom*, July–Aug. 1989, pp. 9–10.

Moraga, Cherríe, and Gloria Anzaldúa, editors. *This Bridge Called My Back: Writings by Radical Women of Color*. Kitchen Table, 1981.

Muñoz, José Esteban. *Disidentifications: Queers of Color and the Performance of Politics*. U of Minnesota P, 1999.

Phinney, Jean S. "When We Talk about American Ethnic Groups, What Do We Mean?" *American Psychologist*, vol. 51, 1996, pp. 918–927.

Ramírez, Catherine. *The Woman in the Zoot Suit: Gender, Nationalism, and the Cultural Politics of Memory*. Duke UP, 2009.

Reicher, Stephen. "The Context of Social Identity: Domination, Resistance, and Change." *Political Psychology*, vol. 24, no. 6, 2004, pp. 921–945.

Reicher, Stephen, and Nick Hopkins. "Psychology and the End of History: A Critique and a Proposal for the Psychology of Social Categorization." *Political Psychology*, vol. 22, no. 2, 2001, pp. 383–407.

Sandoval, Chela. *Methodology of the Oppressed*. U of Minnesota P, 2000.

Scott, James C. *Weapons of the Weak: Everyday Forms of Peasant Resistance*. Yale UP, 1987.

Tajfel, Henri. *Human Groups and Social Categories: Studies in Social Psychology*. Cambridge UP, 1981.

Taylor, Sonya Renee. *The Body Is Not an Apology: The Power of Radical Self-Love*. Berrett-Koehler, 2018.

Tovar, Virgie, editor. *Hot & Heavy: Fierce Fat Girls on Life, Love & Fashion*. Seal, 2012.

Turner, John C., and Rina S. Onorato. "Social Identity, Personality, and the Self-Concept: A Self-categorization Perspective." *The Psychology of the Social Self*, edited by Tom R. Tyler et al., Lawrence Erlbaum Associates, 1999, pp. 11–46.

RENDERING OF SELF: PERSONAL NARRATIVES/ PERSONAL ADORNMENT

CHAPTER 1

Wearing Identity: Chicanas and Huipiles

NORMA E. CANTÚ

My mother, an accomplished seamstress, taught me to sew on my Grandmother Celia's old Singer sewing machine when I was seven or eight years old. As I grew older, I sewed garments for myself and my siblings as well as for friends. By the 1960s, I was also embellishing my clothing with intricate embroidery. In the 1970s, attracted by the textile art and design of the embroidered garment that has been worn by Indigenous women in the Americas for centuries, I began wearing handwoven huipiles. Ever since then, I have worn them—at first simply because I liked them. As I learned more about the traditional garb, I realized that by wearing the huipil, I honor the "artists" who make the pieces while I am also reclaiming my Indigenous identity. I was unprepared, however, for what happened in the mid-1990s at a restaurant in Washington, DC. I was having dinner with friends and wearing a huipil I had bought in Oaxaca. An anthropologist I had just met through a mutual friend chastised me, claiming that by wearing a huipil, I was insulting Indigenous women. While I took exception to such a claim, I was unprepared to offer a proper defense. I was simply stumped. This incident awoke in me issues of identity and race that led me to question the subject position of Chicanas like myself, mestizas whose Indigenous roots have been erased but who would identify, not disidentify,[1] with Indigenous women.

By wearing the garment, Chicanas become part of the narrative of the Indigenous peoples of this continent, for in some ways, wearing huipiles is a kind of storytelling, a narrative that tells the tale of the wearer and the weaver at once. Seeking a theoretical framing for the analysis of such a narrative led me to testimonio as theory, and plática as methodology. When working on the Latina Feminist Research Group's book *Telling to Live*, one of the goals identified by the eighteen collaborators was to create new research methodologies that worked for us as Chicanas and Latinas, research that breaks free of the restraints inherent in our own disciplines' scholarly approaches. We came upon testimonio (testimony) as the way to create that new methodology. Through testimoniando we claimed our own process of creating a theory; as a result, a research praxis emerged.[2] Later in my discussion, I address how through identifying a piece of clothing, in this case the huipil, as the narrator of a story—a testimonio, as it were—we can then speak of the narrative communicated, of the story it tells. In addition to using testimonio as the methodology for exploring the narratives of huipiles and huipilistas (the women who wear them), my research is based on pláticas (informal conversations) rather than on strict ethnographic interviews.[3]

I have been documenting and studying traditional culture in South Texas for over thirty years, so when faced with questions about my wearing of huipiles, I eagerly set forth to explore other Chicanas' practice of wearing huipiles. Initially, I approached friends and asked for their stories about wearing the garment. Our pláticas were sporadic and spontaneous. Later, I formally scheduled pláticas with certain individuals. This chapter, based on selected pláticas, seeks to present the findings as well as analyze the way huipiles function as identitarian markers.

My central argument focuses on the wearing of the garment and the many spaces it occupies in the Chicana imaginary in terms of culture and identity. Specifically, the chapter focuses on my pláticas with three Chicanas living in San Antonio, Texas (Rosemary Catacalos, Graciela Sánchez, and Larissa Mercado-López). I first provide a historical context and define some key terms, then I unpack some of the issues raised in the pláticas. Finally, I explore the pláticas/narratives and analyze the salient points made by the huipilistas themselves. A core premise of this chapter is that for Chicanas whose cultural ties to Indigenous ways of being may still exist in culinary and folk belief practices, whose Western ways place us more in the realm of non-Indigenous, we still self-define what part of the mestiza world we inhabit through wearing huipiles and thus establish a link to Indigenous cultural practices.

History and Definitions

The term *huipil*, according to Ellen Riojas Clark, a professor of Mexican American studies, is a derivation of the "Náhuatl word 'huipoopi' meaning blouse. The huipil can be worn loose or tucked into a skirt . . . called a cueitl and to say skirt and blouse, one said 'cueitl huipilli,' which is also a metaphor for woman." The huipil, as an Indigenous garment of Meso-america, is easily recognized as a marker of Indigenous identity. As Carlos Romero Giordano claims, "each ethnic group has its own type, and while there are similarities in the ways they are woven . . . their symbolism and the techniques of weaving, dying, and decoration give each a special character" (22).

Historically, the huipil's existence precedes the arrival of the Spanish; in the earliest codices, the glyphic writings of the Indigenous peoples of the Americas, women wear them as they perform daily tasks. Moreover, remnants have been located in some archeological sites. Various scholars have scoured the codices to describe the way clothing marked status in Aztec society (Ludden 10; Sayer 60; Ruiz Chávez 47). George C. Vaillant, in *Aztecs of Mexico*, mentions that clothing marked "sex, age, group, occupation, rank, and even [the] character of its wearer" (136). In 1948 Laura Start described the huipil in Mexico and Guatemala, and noted how already "the rapid spread of commercialism and easier contact with the outside world is resulting in the adoption of western types of garment" (68). Jacques Soustelle, the famed French scholar of Aztec civilization, similarly noted the way clothes marked status in Aztec society (131–132). Patricia Anawalt explores not only huipiles but also other items of clothing, such as the quechquemitl, which is also worn by Chicanas and others (844–846). In my own exploration conducted in December 2014 at the exhibit *Códices de México: Memorias y saberes* at the Museo de Antropología in Mexico City,[4] I viewed codices that indeed portrayed women wearing huipiles throughout Mesoamerica. Among the main items on display was the early painting *Lienzo de Tlaxcala*. In various depictions, La Malinche[5] wears a huipil as she acts as translator for the Spanish conqueror Hernán Cortés (fig. 1.1).

The one-piece cotton, or sometimes wool, garment is handwoven on a back-strap loom and is given an opening for the head; sometimes it is sewn together to shape armholes. But most often it is left open so the two flaps are draped. The history of the garment notwithstanding, we can claim that it is an essential garment for Indigenous women of Meso-america even today, despite the fear that it may be a vanishing tradition (Romero Giordano 24). Mexican anthropologist Marta Turok's work on Mexican textiles is noteworthy for her examination of the origins of cotton and the natural dyes used since before the European contact (64–67). Her work also includes explorations into the rebozo, the traditional shawl-like garment from Tenancingo, and the danger the tradition faced of disappearing ("Rebozos").

1.1. *Lienzo de Tlaxcala.*

Many of the artists who create huipiles are facing increasingly difficult circumstances that are in some ways forcing them to abandon their
centuries-old art form. In some cases, it is the convenience of access to
Western apparel that supplants traditional garb. One particular study includes an analysis of the impact of tourism on the sale of huipiles and
found that the two towns at the center of this study, Santa Catarina and
San Antonio, competed for customers and that both laid claim to the
weaving tradition (Little 215–216). While this is not the focus of this chapter, it bears mentioning that the Chicanas who participated in this study
collect most of their huipiles from Mexico and Guatemala, directly from
weavers and collectors, and thus indirectly influence the tradition, albeit
often unknowingly.

Many weavers bemoan the fact that their dress is being commodified
and their traditional ways are being challenged; there is fear for the future
of the tradition even as scholars assert that the huipil will survive and
remain a visual and signifying marker of the group, especially for special occasions (Romero Giordano 24). In a *New York Times* article by Larry
Rother, ethnographer and professor Cherri M. Pancake expresses her fear

that the tradition is changing and that "we are going to lose the richness and variety of huipiles." She adds, "That is not the same thing as saying they are dying out entirely. But it's becoming less a form of daily dress and more of a badge, and I don't see how a tradition can flourish when it is relegated to export and special occasions." In the article Rother points out that "the tradition is in jeopardy" due to decades of war and notes the changes in the tradition among the Guatemalan women who have moved to the urban centers. In her survey of Oaxacan textiles, Ruth Lechuga also notes the shift, pointing out that some communities have abandoned the huipil for blouses (81–83). Even as there are fewer huipilistas making the garment, there is a proliferation of huipilistas among young Chicanas. I tend to agree that the huipil may suffer transformation, but I am heartened because that is how traditional textiles seem to survive; anthropologist Marta Turok holds that another traditional textile, the rebozo, has undergone innovation while retaining the traditional elements (personal communication).

In Texas, a San Antonio group of huipil-wearers and/or collectors call themselves "mujeres del huipil" (women of the huipil) or huipilistas.[6] The contemporary use of the term among the participants in this study applies to women who have decided, con conciencia—with consciousness— to wear the garment, and believe that by doing so they are in some way affecting the way it is viewed by society at large. In my initial inquiry, I interrogated friends and acquaintances who wear huipiles, but not all of them were part of the formal pláticas presented here. Many recounted poignant stories of how as Chicanas they identify with the Indigenous part of their heritage and feel impelled to wear a huipil as a signal of who they are. One of these women, attorney Frances Herrera, tells of strategically wearing the piece of clothing in professional circles to make a statement. As a former dancer with a local Aztec dance troupe, she wears a huipil as a reference to her Indigenous identity. In César Martínez's film *Huipiles: The Fabric of Identity*, several huipilistas, led by Ellen Riojas Clark, present their views on the matter. Just as every Chicana who chooses to don the garment has a story to tell of her experiences, so do the items themselves; as one of the huipilistas claims in the film, "Every huipil has a story." I would add that every huipilista has a story as well. The fact that it is a so-called traditional piece of clothing adds to the complexity of the matter, for as part of the discussion, we must also deconstruct the very idea of what is traditional.

I call for a self-reflection that will also explain how the adjective *traditional* connects with the noun *tradition* and how these contend with the fact that the very concept of what is tradition or traditional has changed over time; indeed, these terms may seek to solidly freeze things in time, but the reality is that everything evolves and changes.[7] Thus, the annual celebration for a saint's day or for a secular event like Memorial Day is ever-evolving and changing. The concepts of traditional knowledge and cultural imperialism surface as key ideas in a discussion of dress as an identity marker. The huipil as a traditional garment may suffer the fate of so many other traditional dress traditions around the world, especially those in Europe.[8] Traditional knowledge that informs worldviews and belief systems likewise is at risk. Dress, an artifact that signals identity, may be relegated to service as a nationalist symbol to be displayed at a town's fiesta or for national celebrations and not for daily wear.

The dresses of folklórico dancers is a case in point; they are based on traditional dress but have become stylized markers worn only for folklórico performances.[9] In many European settings and in Asia, traditional garments have given way to contemporary global market ideas of dress; blue jeans, for instance, appear as apparel across the world, in what some scholars may call cultural imperialism, as discussed by John Tomlinson (2)—a signifier of what I liken to the "soft power" that influences popular culture and ways of assimilating the values and ideas of culturally hegemonic cultures.[10] These concepts—cultural imperialism and soft power—in my mind work hand in hand to shift identities away from the regionalist or nationalist and toward globalized markers of progress. Such ideas merit scrutiny for they are at the core of why many Chicanas choose to wear huipiles as a signifier of resistance and empowerment.

Joanne B. Eicher, editor of a collection of essays on dress and identity, writes that the authors of the essays she included do not see ethnicity as "primordial or circumstantial," but rather rely on dress as a "visible mark of ethnicity" (301). Traditional dress then becomes the site of contested identities that shift and more often than not displace the specific and place-bound markers that situate subjects in time and place. Thus, the Chicanas who wear the traditional huipil are in like fashion performing their identity and reclaiming the link to their past, their traditions. Their sense of community and who belongs to such a community can be further explained using Werner Sollors's ideas. In his book *Beyond Ethnicity*, he claims that there are two ways of imagining community. He uses the terms *descent* and *consent* to explain how one either belongs to a group by descent—having been born into the group—or by consent, having chosen to join the group.

Serious critical scholarship on Mexican traditional dress has been mostly descriptive or historical, and some scholars, such as Marta Turok, have focused on the function of Indigenous dress; however, hardly any scholarship that deals with traditional dress in Chicanx traditional culture exists. Yet, an increased interest in the analysis of dress in Chicanx culture and performance, and some forays into theorizing, do exist. Folklorist Dorie S. Goldman, in an article on the T-shirts worn by Chicano youth, claims that they are "artistic expressions designed to enable or facilitate Chicano self-determination" (123), and she further examines how the images on the T-shirts tell three "(hi)stories: a cultural (hi)story, a (hi)story aesthetic, and a (hi)story of resistance against hegemonic Euro-American culture" (124). Similarly, Robert Neustadt examines the use of wrestling masks in performance to conclude that "masked anonymity allows Mexican and Chicano performance artists to conjugate collective (non)identities that face, and performatively efface, the masks of nationalism" (429). Chicanx theater scholars Jorge Huerta and Yolanda Broyles-González have looked at the use of masks and costume in the plays by El Teatro Campesino. So, the discussion has often been relegated to particular performances, particular items—such as the use of masks—or particular events.

Academic analysis of dress has also appeared as part of a larger analysis of dance—folklórico, for example—or of popular culture dress codes, as discussed in Goldman's article, but such studies have not focused on the performance of Chicana identity that is the wearing of clothing itself, nor on the complexity of that identity. Since the earliest mention of dress in the Mexican community in the late nineteenth century, little if any scholarly analysis has been done.[11] One particular essay, however, does bring in the relationship between huipiles and Chicanas. In her memoir, *A House of My Own: Stories from My Life*, Sandra Cisneros writes about her personal relationship to the garment (55–65).

The foregoing discussion of key terms, concepts, and previous work on dress introduces my subsequent analysis of the wearing of huipiles by Chicanas in San Antonio. As I mentioned earlier, my initial research goal centered on the question "Why do Chicanas choose to wear huipiles?" However, this initial inquiry spawned a series of other intriguing questions around identity and the role of dress in creating one's identity. When did these Chicanas start collecting and wearing the garments? How do they feel when they wear huipiles, and how do others receive or perceive their doing so? I sought answers to these questions by going to the huipilistas themselves and engaging them in informal pláticas. By delving into what the practice of wearing huipiles signifies for Chicanas, we can explore the multifaceted signifier that is the huipil itself.

Wearing Huipiles: The Body as Contested Space

Traditional dress has been at the core of much of my folklore work during the last thirty years or so. My research has focused on the traditional
fifteenth-birthday celebration, the quinceañera; on the dress worn by the
matachines dancers; and on the wearing of hábitos, modeled on the special clothes worn by Catholic saints and other holy icons.[12] In "Costume
as Cultural Resistance and Affirmation," which focuses on the latter, I examine how traditional cultural actions often affirm an adherence to traditional practices rooted in faith belief. Clearly, the use of hábitos is tied
to folk belief and to a way of negotiating the very real material condition
of illness. Similarly, my work on Chicanas and traditional dress, specifically my research on the wearing of certain colors for the quinceañera, reveals significant shifts as people reterritorialize and settle in the United
States. Both of these studies provide a backstory for my current research
on huipiles.

Folklore studies of dress and identity—such as the work of Jennifer
Michaels on dress in Arles, France, and Dorothy Noyes's on dress in a Catalan town, as well as others such as Alicia Arrizón's—are useful in considering my focus on the representation of Chicana identity. Michaels specifically looks at a European town's identity and its costume in terms of
Sollors's notions of descent and consent, translating the notion of the
imagined community to that of identity. Michaels's work is useful because
she deconstructs the ideas of who should wear a community's costume,
tracing use of the local costume as a shibboleth in the French town of
Arles from the nineteenth century to today. While Michaels focuses on
dress, Noyes does not. Yet in her study of the Patum, the Corpus Christi
festival in the Catalan town of Barga, Noyes also disentangles the complex
relationships in communities between locals and outsiders, especially in
chapter 3 of her book, where she explores the idea of belonging (81–107).

The notion of belonging is at the center of my discussion about how huipiles mark identity. For the huipilistas in San Antonio, the garment functions as a kind of shibboleth to signal belonging. I venture to say that the
same is true outside of San Antonio and in wider circles where Chicanas
celebrate their Indigenous roots. Studies of traditional dress in Indigenous
communities help to explore the phenomenon that is the subject of this
chapter—that is, Chicanas wearing huipiles. Diana Crane opens her book
on gender and fashion by stating, "Clothing, as one of the most visible
forms of consumption, performs a major role in the social construction of
identity" (1). The use of artifacts of clothing as a signifier to send a num-

ber of messages concerning gender, class, and ethnicity has been clearly noted in the case of Highland Maya women in Guatemala, whose huipiles are signifiers of their identity. As J. Claire Odland notes:

> From the wearer's apparel, one can deduce age, education, worldliness, financial and social standing, as well as the function—utilitarian or festive—of the occasion. Impulses toward change are counterbalanced by the intensity of conservative values and a strong sense of community identity and pride, expressed in traditional dress. (10)

For many Indigenous women in Oaxaca, Mexico, and in Guatemala, the wearing of huipiles constitutes an identifiable link to their place of origin, as Morgadanes describes in her "note" from 1940. During the 1980s, when Guatemala was in the midst of a civil war and Indigenous populations were persecuted, this practice became a dangerous act.[13] Many Chicanas, coincidentally, began wearing these garments around the same time, albeit for a different purpose. For Chicanas, the act of wearing huipiles became identified with political ideology and solidarity with Central American women. There is a similarity between Chicanas' impetus to perform a political ideology and the T-shirts worn by the youth that Goldman studied. For Chicanas, such an act constitutes a claim on a recovered identity that transcends boundaries and is not place-bound. It signals an alliance and solidarity with Indigenous women in the Americas, a political and ideological action that establishes a bond across borders. As Patrisia Gonzales notes in *Red Medicine*, the Indigenous people among us are often erased and their knowledge negated. By choosing to wear traditional clothing, Chicanas reclaim an identity that has been erased—the Indigenous. Through their clothing, they tell a story of who they are and affirm their sense of belonging to a group, to a community of women that is rooted in ideological and aesthetic narratives of identity. In a sense, the personal becomes political: everyone wears clothes, but not everyone chooses to wear certain items of clothing with a consciousness to make a political statement. The wearing of a huipil nurtures and feeds Chicanas' sense of self even as it serves to signal political and ideological subjectivity.

Perhaps one of Mexico's most famous non-Indigenous wearers of huipiles is Frida Kahlo, who, as Henestrosa points out, "wanted to portray her mexicanidad, or Mexican cultural identity. She wants to feel part of the *pueblo*, of the people," and she did this through her clothing, mostly donning the Tehuana traditional attire (qtd. in Oatman-Stanford). Upending the traditional notion of why people choose to dress as they do, Diana

Crane notes how Simmel sees fashion change "as a process of imitation of social elites by their social inferiors." (6–7). Chicanas choose the dress of those most marginalized, of those occupying the lowest rung on the social ladder, the Indigenous women in Mesoamerica (Crane 7).

The huipil's specific uses in Mesoamerica differ from its uses as a garment in the United States. As anthropologist Néstor García Canclini notes in his book *Consumers and Citizens*, the differences between Latin American and US globalized societies extend to notions of what is popular culture and how consumers, including tourists, shape what is considered traditional.[14] I offer one example of how the huipil has gained recognition outside of Indigenous communities: as a referent for Mexican identity in the city of San Antonio, Texas. At a fundraising event in 2001, Hispanas Unidas, a nonprofit social justice organization that supports programs for young Chicanas to raise cultural awareness and pride, used the huipil precisely to raise awareness and celebrate cultural pride. As Elda Silva reported in the *San Antonio Express-News*:

> For centuries, Indigenous women in Mexico and Central America have created huipiles, using the means at hand to weave and embroider the traditional garment as a form of expression and economic survival. In part, that's why the huipil is an apt metaphor for what Hispanas Unidas is trying to accomplish, says Selina Catal, executive director. ("Fund-raiser")

I agree and further note that the huipil may be used in various ways once it leaves the confines of an Indigenous village, where it signals a number of subject positions, including group membership. Morgadanes observes that "it is . . . easy to recognize Indians from the different villages" in Guatemala because of the women's distinctive huipiles (360).

For centuries, the huipil continued to serve the same function and have the same meanings as it did in the pre-Columbian world, but during the twentieth century it became something else when it was picked up by figures in the arts, including Frida Kahlo. For Chicanas, the decision to wear the huipil is not just a result of aesthetics; theirs is a more conscious decision to reclaim their Indigenous roots. To better understand this behavior and to support the idea that it is a conscious and decidedly political statement, I turn to the primary method of my research, testimonio. As explained above, I was led to this methodology by the topic itself because the narratives coming from the wearers, the huipilistas, and from the garments themselves seem to be narrating a life story.

Theory and Testimonio

At the core of folklore studies are the narratives we collect around artifacts, and the narratives we construct to theorize around all traditional
cultural performances. If we identify a piece of clothing, in this case the
huipil, as a narrator of a story—a testimonio, as it were—we can then
speak of the narrative communicated. The narrativeness of a piece of clothing, as Goldman and Michaels show in their works, can signal inclusion as
well as exclusion. The testimonios that the huipilistas tell become one with
the garment itself. The complication arises in how Mesoamerican huipiles
have been strongly identified with Indigeneity—mostly in Chiapas and
Oaxaca, Mexico, and in Guatemala. But Chicanas—as mestizas, and therefore detribalized—can fall within the category or be left out of it. We are,
at the core, a people whose cultural ties to Indigenous belief systems may
still exist in our culinary and folk belief practices but whose Western ways
place us more in the realm of the non-Indigenous, the mestiza world. The
erasure of our Indigenous identity at the level of cultural knowledge can be
severe for some of us, but the desire to reclaim it persists, for we are aware
that, as Anzaldúa points out,

> this land was Mexican once
> was Indian always
> and is.
> And will be again. (25)

As noted above, Sollors claims that there are two ways of imagining community: consent (having chosen to join the group) and descent
(having been born into the group). Obviously, if there is no descent claim,
the situation becomes more complex, and the charge of appropriation becomes more relevant. The non-Indigenous woman wearing a traditional
dress is choosing to perform an identity that is not hers by descent but
by her own volition, or by consent. Goldman also uses Sollors's ideas in
her discussion of the T-shirts worn by Chicano youth, but she shifts the
categories to fit her analysis. Similarly, I find that Sollors's neat dichotomy
does not work quite as nicely when applied to Chicanas wearing huipiles.
We are on one level *choosing* to wear a traditional marker of identity that
places us within a community that is not necessarily ours, but at the same
time we carry an inherent connection to that community that would place
us within that group. That is, we do belong to the Indigenous community
by descent, but as detribalized Indigenous people. Thus, we *choose* to iden-

tify by wearing the garment since we do not belong to the group culturally or geographically. A discussion of how detribalized Chicanas fall within the various ethnic categories of Indigeneity can serve as a segue to the next section of this chapter. In explaining this dance between Indigenous and mestiza identities, I use Anzaldúan philosophical views on belonging and exclusion from the hegemonic centers of Mexico and the United States. By focusing on the representation of the garment in official public spaces, such as museums, and in fashion shows, as well as the ways that individual women wear the garment, we can begin to discern the dual role the huipil has come to play in the imagination of the community and of the women who wear them.

The Pláticas: Method and Practice

I now turn to a discussion of the pláticas[15] held in San Antonio, Texas, with my huipil-wearing friends Rosemary Catacalos, Graciela Sánchez, and Larissa Mercado-López.[16] Although I spoke to other huipilistas, I chose these individuals based on my personal acquaintance with them and my knowledge of their practice of wearing huipiles.[17] There was no compensation for their participation, and we met informally. The pláticas, all but one of which were scheduled and conducted in a place of their choice, were recorded digitally. The conversation with my then-graduate student Larissa Mercado-López happened serendipitously when she was in my office; as we were talking about the project, she began telling me the story of her first huipil.[18] Her participation added a dimension to the study that I had not previously considered: age. The other participants were in their fifties and sixties; here was a younger Chicana who had just been initiated into the practice and therefore, in my view, represented hope for the future. The pláticas took place in locations where the women felt most comfortable and that had been previously agreed to by both of us. I met with Rosemary Catacalos and Graciela Sánchez at their place of work. Catacalos was at the time the director of Gemini Ink, a literary arts center in San Antonio, and Sánchez is the director of the Esperanza Peace and Justice Center, also in San Antonio.

All three participants identify the wearing of huipiles with mexicanidad; they also invariably identify huipiles as markers of Indigeneity, and all mentioned their solidarity with the artists who make them. Four central questions helped us stay grounded on the topic, even as we meandered and engaged in reflexive conversation:[19] When did you first start consciously wearing huipiles? What does your family say about you wearing huipiles? What do your peers or colleagues say about your choice of wearing huipiles? Why do you wear huipiles?

These very basic touchstone questions spurred other questions as the pláticas ensued. All of the women claim there is something very special about wearing a huipil; they referred to the feelings elicited by wearing them and to the sense of identity that wearing the garment brings. It makes them feel powerful, connected to their identity. In the following section, I analyze the huipilistas' answers individually.

Rosemary Catacalos

Rosemary Catacalos (fig. 1.2), who identifies with both her ethnicities, Chicana and Greek, said,

> As a child, my family would send me the tiny huipiles from Yucatan. My grandmother was always teaching me Mayan[20] and stressing that part of who we are . . . but consciously? Not until the seventies, I think. Obviamente [obviously] we were political at that point, and it served as an identification, visually representing who we were. But it gets complex for me, because of the Greek. I was also wearing traditional dress from Greece, doing traditional Greek folk dances.

For Catacalos, then, wearing huipiles was a practice that preceded her consciously choosing the garb for identitarian purposes. The fact that she was also doing traditional Greek folk dances raises the issue of how mixed ethnicity plays out in many Chicanas' lives.[21] In terms of what wearing the huipil means for her, Catacalos said it means connection to her maternal family; she strategically wears the garment.

> It's a protective garment for me. Very strong connection to my grandmother I feel I have with me when I wear traditional dress. If I am unhappy or down on a particular day, I put on the huipil. When I need strength, for example, I wear a red huipil. It's more about an internal relationship than with what is out here.

It is not unusual to have clothing and color provide a sense of well-being. Catacalos strategically uses the garment to empower herself emotionally by identifying with her grandmother, and by finding the right color, she adds to the emotional benefit. She also expressed a desire to talk more

1.2. Rosemary Catacalos. Photo by Jasmina Wellinghof.

about what her huipiles have been used for: "Curtains, tablecloths, throws on the bed or couch, as art work hung on the wall." She does not judge it inappropriate to use the huipiles in such a way, adding, "They are women's work. It's a comment on . . . the reusing of pieces of things. Made by women's hands."

In discussing why she wears the garment, Catacalos returned to a common theme expressed by most huipilistas: their fascination with textiles. "All textiles fascinate me in the most profound way. It is women's work," Catacalos explains. She also referred to an exhibit she saw. "A while back el Banco de Mexico . . . had a show of women's huipiles, and the women had embroidered their stories on the huipiles." The idea of narrative attracted her because it connects to her keen interest in textiles and words. As a writer, she can identify with the need to transmit a story.

Talking about why she wears huipiles, she brought up a point for discussion: "Another thing is how gringas wear them."[22] She then went on to discuss the appropriation of the garment by outsiders, non-Indigenous and non-Chicana: "It's a long tradition of gringas who grew up in a certain class level back in the sixties. It felt less inauthentic for them to wear them." To deconstruct all of the issues that Catacalos raised, especially regarding who wears huipiles and how they are appropriated, we can begin with the idea of what is being called "cultural plagiarism"—that is, the borrowing of traditional cultural artifacts by designers for their own lucrative ends. Unlike the cultural imperialism that imposes the developed world's fashions onto developing nations, in this case fashion houses are using traditional designs for haute couture. What comes to mind is the controversy surrounding the use of the design from the Indigenous Mixes in Oaxaca by French designer Isabel Marant for a dress in her 2015 Etoile collection. The issue is not just the "taking" of a product that is closely identified with an Indigenous group whose identity is bound to the design, but that it is commodified and exists in the marketplace, far removed from the community of origin and for the profit of those who have no intention of honoring the original creators of the design. Unlike the controversy caused by the appropriation by celebrities such as Selena Gomez of the bindi, the ornamental dot placed on the forehead of Hindu women to signal marital status, the use of huipil-inspired fashion has monetary consequences. Catacalos also spoke of her predilection for the huipil as daily wear at work and for social functions, claiming that wearing it gives her a sense of self, a connection to her cultural antepasados, her ancestors.

Graciela Sánchez

Graciela Sánchez (fig. 1.3) also wears huipiles with a definite political intention and often wears garments that men would wear. She acquired her first huipil while traveling in Mexico, and that is where she still gets them, from the actual weavers, the artists. She speaks of her allegiance to these artists and how through her purchases she ensures that the tradition remains a vital part of life for them; she also acknowledges that she has received some huipiles as gifts.

Sánchez reiterated a sentiment I heard repeatedly: "We honor the women whose labor produces such beauty." She also mentioned that through purchasing and wearing the huipiles, she is resisting the mass-produced items that create sweatshops. Furthermore, she expressed her solidarity with Indigenous and marginalized communities. When she wears her huipil to a city council meeting or when she appears before TV

1.3. Graciela Sánchez. Photo by Al Rendón, © 2014.

cameras during a press conference, she feels that the huipil sends a visual message of what her work as an activist is all about. I was not surprised to learn that as a queer Chicana whose life's work has been to confront social justice issues in San Antonio, she often wears men's huipiles, or tops, and thus also expresses a critique of gender and sexuality through her clothes. Most huipilistas, not just the ones in this brief study, feel that wearing the garment is an affirmation of their identity in all its complexity; they use it as a signifier of that identity and wear it con conciencia, with awareness, of what it means. Sánchez's response is emblematic of how most women who wear huipiles respond when asked why they wear them — that is, they cite the beauty and the aesthetic quality of the garment as well as its significance as a marker of identity.

Sánchez further discussed its appropriation. She sees "the concept of cultural genocide" playing a role in "undermining Chicanas' sense of self." For her, the garment as exhibited or worn plays a role in what she observes is the result of a hegemonic critique of Latinas, the "hating [of] ourselves as women of Color, as dark-skinned women, as Indigenous-looking mujeres, as women with accents—and of course the mestizaje of all of us." The hegemonic powers in fashion and elsewhere normally erase the traditional practices unless they can be adapted, appropriated, for commercial purposes. The social contexts where the huipil exists—in Indigenous communities, the marketplace, and the fashion industry—determine the relative value given to the garment. Moreover, all of these factors impact the value given to the creator or artist whose work—the weaving and embroidering—results in the unique creations. Chicanas, by choosing to wear huipiles, impact their creation as well as the artists. They claim the garment as a signifier of Indigenous identity, and they choose to wear it as a referent to their ethnic identity, albeit one that has been often denied them as mestizas.

Larissa Mercado-López

Larissa Mercado-López (fig. 1.4) was a doctoral student at the time of our plática and had just received her first huipil as a gift from a fellow student. She loved it and said she planned to buy more, and she spoke of her admiration for the weavers and the art involved. I followed up with her recently to find out if she has indeed acquired more huipiles and if she still wears them. I also posed the same questions from our first plática, and she responded with some updates, especially regarding her current position in academia. Mercado-López brought up an important point, one that no doubt impacts the purchasing choices of young Chicanas, especially students: huipiles are often sold for hundreds of dollars. She mentioned their cost in the "touristy shops in the hypercommercialized Mexican Mercado" in San Antonio as a deterrent to not having bought one herself before.

I was not surprised to learn that when Mercado-López wore her huipil to the mall in San Antonio, she was met with "a few curious looks," because huipilistas often experience that reception. In fact, almost all of the participants in my study told of similar reactions, especially from people who do not recognize the garment. Further, when Mercado-López wears her huipiles—and the Mexican blusas (blouses) she likes to wear—her family thinks they are "cute." She further clarifies this comment by positioning her own identity within her family and their acceptance of her politics and identity: "I think that I am not questioned because they have always

1.4. Larissa Mercado-López. Photo by Larissa Mercado-López, © 2018.

known me to be invested in my culture, so for them, the huipiles seem to be more about asserting an ethnic identity." As to wearing the garment at work, she said,

> My peers and colleagues are in women's studies and Chicano studies, so they are very complimentary when I wear huipiles, as they have more of a consciousness about the politics. There are very few of us who wear them at Fresno State—in fact, besides me, I can only think of one other Chicana in literacy and a white woman in anthropology. Fresno is politically conservative, so I imagine that there may be a resistance to wearing huipiles because of the imagined stigma.

Underscoring that Fresno is politically conservative obviously signals that the spaces where one wears a huipil affects how it is received.

Similar to Sánchez's comment about strategically wearing the garment, Mercado-López also wears huipiles "as a form of resistance to colonization, imperialism, and capitalism." She adds, "I wear them when I am going into meetings . . . so that my politics are understood immediately. I feel that the huipiles disrupt the space in ways that encourage people to be conscientious in their words and ideas." In addition to this, she wears them to teach, and, like others, she claims that the mere act of donning the huipil empowers her. She said, "When I know that I will be teaching a particularly rough subject, I will wear a huipil for strength and to remind me to teach in ways that decolonize."

A close examination of Mercado-López's forceful statement reveals that even though she shares sentiments expressed by the others, especially Sánchez, she seems to be more aligned with the political identity that the garment signifies as a Chicana feminist. Regarding when she wears huipiles, she said, "Though I wear regular clothing most of the time, I most often wear huipiles to teach, to cultural events, and to community meetings." She added, "I also wore the gauzy Mexican blusas when I was pregnant and nursing because they allowed for more room."

Mercado-López, like the other participants, is fully aware of the impact her clothing choices have on the way she is perceived and further establishes that wearing a huipil affords her a sense of power vis-à-vis the situations where she must negotiate her identity as a Chicana.

Conclusion

While the huipil remains grounded in its more traditional meaning in the Indigenous communities of origin, it also has morphed and shifted into signification in a new terrain—in this case, the United States, as many Chicanas claim it as their own. García Canclini asserts that "globalization diminishes the importance of the foundational events and territories that supported the illusion of ahistorical and self-absorbed identities" (80). I contend that, indeed, the complexity and shifting identities of the women who wear huipiles in a globalized world can be destabilizing. He continues, noting that in the late twentieth and early twenty-first centuries,

> identitarian references are shaped not by the arts, literature, and folklore— which for centuries gave nations their distinctive features—but by textual and iconographic repertoires furnished by electronic communications media and by the globalization of urban life. (80)

While I concur with his general assessment, I underscore the fact that huipiles, rooted in folk tradition, are still woven on back-strap looms and are still signaling messages of identity. In this instance the referent arising from the folk textile tradition shifts into "textual and iconographic repertoires" for Chicanas in the United States. The women who participated in the pláticas all agreed that the garment fulfills a need for them—the need for comfort, for beauty, for a way to wear their identity. It is indeed functioning as a marker of identity, and as Riojas Clark says in the film *Huipiles: The Fabric of Identity*, "They identify the garment as a connection to their heritage."

The huipil has traveled along a path diachronically and thus has transcended the class borders that confined it to a particular segment of society and a particular geographic region. Yet it remains synchronically tied to that earlier space and retains the visual semantic value to signal the Indigenous in spaces far from its villages of origin. We can assess its trajectory. By focusing on the Chicanas who wear the garment, I sought to find answers as to the "text" of their self-authoring. Indeed, in all instances, the pláticas revealed that the huipilistas not only care about their own subject position allied to their cultural bonds to Mexico and all things Mexican, but also that they see a link between the Indigenous women who weave the huipiles and their own wearing of the garments as Chicanas in the United States. Further, they affirm that wearing the huipil is a political act.

After considering the ways that the huipil functions for Chicanas, including the very personal and identitarian use, it seems clear that the garment is not about to die out, as some fear, and that, at least for the time being, huipiles will continue to be made and worn. As anecdotal evidence, I submit the phenomenon I observed recently at the annual meeting of the Mujeres Activas en Letras y Cambio Social (MALCS), the professional organization for Chicana and Latina feminist scholars. A quick head count at the opening ceremony in the courtyard outside the meeting place at the University of New Mexico in Albuquerque revealed that well over 50 percent of the hundred or so attendees were wearing some kind of blusa or huipil that signaled mexicanidad. Granted that the venue and the circumstances—after all, MALCS members tend to be students and academics who work in the field of Chicana studies—would tend to draw huipilistas who don the garment as a piece of daily wear. Perhaps the oldest member in attendance, octogenarian Inés Talamantez, a professor of religious studies at the University of California, Santa Barbara was wearing a beautiful huipil de fiesta from Chiapas. The huipil was obviously also a favored garb of many of the young scholars, students, and community members in attendance. In addition, huipiles were being sold in at least two of the nearby vendor booths throughout the conference. Such a public and symbolic use of traditional garments by Chicanas affirms my thesis that the huipil functions as a signifier of identity and that Chicanas choose to wear it for very specific reasons, con conciencia.[23]

Will the huipil survive the onslaught of inexpensive, ready-made Western clothing in its home communities? The market that Chicanas constitute may not be the decisive factor in the survival of the tradition, but just as collectors' interest has influenced the production of the garment, the fact that Chicanas are buying and wearing huipiles may also positively impact the industry. In a lecture delivered at the Mexican Cultural Institute, Turok noted a similar impact on the rebozeros[24] in Tenanczingo in central Mexico. The huipil, like the rebozo, will survive as it has for at least a century and will continue to be worn by the women in Indigenous communities as well as by those of us who seek to reclaim our Indigenous identity. For now, I predict that weavers will continue to sell to tourists and others who favor handmade natural-fiber textiles over machine-made, mass-produced fabrics. But given all this, one question remains: What will happen when the weavers' children move to the urban centers, or perhaps even to the United States, and stop weaving the fabric in the traditional way? Who will weave the cloth for the garment? Who will carry on the tradition?

Notes

1. I adopt the term *disidentify* that José Esteban Muñoz uses in his book *Disidentifications* to mean the denial of a close relationship. The erasure of Indigeneity I experienced as a child growing up in South Texas includes the hidden and often blatant messages that discouraged any identification with our Indigenous past. If we walked around barefoot, for instance, we were behaving como indias.

2. The process of telling one's testimonios. Perhaps heeding the charge of Chicana feminist philosopher Gloria Anzaldúa to create our own theories, we decided the goal was to use testimonio as a specific theorizing project using a kind of autohistoria, another term from the Anzaldúan canon.

3. For a discussion of plática as a method and a methodology, see Fierros and Delgado-Bernal's essay "Vamos a platicar."

4. The exhibit was curated by María Teresa Franco and had over 400,000 visitors. It closed in early 2015 but remains accessible through the Instituto de Antropología e Historia website.

5. Also known as Malinali Tepenal or by her Spanish name, Marina, La Malinche was the translator who has been deemed a traitor and is maligned by many Mexican people. Chicanas, on the other hand, often see her as a savior whose intervention undoubtedly lessened the casualties among the Indigenous. Many scholars have grappled with this historical figure who remains controversial to this day. See Octavio Paz, "The Sons of Malinche"; Norma Alarcón, "Traddutora, Traditora"; Alicia Gaspar de Alba, "Malinche's Revenge"; and Mary Louise Pratt, "'Yo Soy La Malinche.'" In 2015 I attended the exhibit of forty-three codices from around the world curated by the Instituto de Antropología e Historia and exhibited at the museum in Mexico City. I was moved by the beautiful "texts" but upset because no mention was

made of the role of La Malinche in the signage even though she was certainly visible at the side of Hernán Cortés, especially in the *Lienzo de Tlaxcala*.

6. This circle of friends who wear huipiles use the term *huipilistas* to refer to themselves and whoever wears huipiles on a regular basis. Among them are Catacalos, Sánchez, and Mercado-López as well as Luz María Prieto, Gloria Uribe Ramírez, Ellen Riojas Clark, Antonia Castañeda, Frances Herrera, and others featured in the documentary *Huipiles: The Fabric of Identity.* For a discussion of the tradition in San Antonio, see Elda Silva's article "Huipil Appeal." The most senior and most devoted collector is María Luisa Camacho de López, who owns a comprehensive collection of huipiles from various regions of Mexico. Following their practice, I use the term *huipilistas* when referring to women who wear the garment and the women who weave and create them.

7. See Peter Boyer's ideas on tradition and theories of the traditional in his book *Tradition as Truth and Communication.*

8. Under UNESCO's program on intangible cultural heritage the "Recommendation on the Safeguarding of Traditional Culture and Folklore" was approved by the General Conference in 1989. Since then, the definition of what is traditional has been understood to be part of the world's intangible cultural heritage.

9. Ballet folklórico dance troupes perform traditional dances outside of their original context that are highly choreographed. One particular dress worn in folklórico performances, the Mexican Revolution–inspired "Adelita" dress, is also worn in the escaramuza, the female horseback riding performance at the rodeo-like event of Mexican ranching culture; in both instances the dress represents a period in Mexican history.

10. I borrow the term from Joseph Nye, who coined it in his book *Bound to Lead.* He writes that "when one country gets other countries to want what it wants—might be called co-optive or soft power in contrast with the hard or command power of ordering others to do what it wants" (188). He explores the concept further in his book *Soft Power.*

11. The clothing worn by Mexicans in the late nineteenth century was described by John Bourke in 1896.

12. The now almost forgotten practice of wearing hábitos was common in South Texas and Mexico up to about the mid-1980s (Cantú 118). The tradition involved an individual wearing an hábito in fulfillment of a promesa as a form of thanksgiving for a prayer answered. For instance, a child that is sick might be "promised" to Saint Francis. If she recovers, the child wears a brown tunic similar to that worn by the saint for a prescribed period of time as an action of thanksgiving. It was customary fifty years ago or so that many in that region still wore hábitos, but the practice has fallen into disuse. In particular, the belief that one may gain health if wearing a saint's hábito for a prescribed length of time led wearers to seek seamstresses who were adept at designing and sewing the very specific prescribed garments.

13. See Larry Rohter's *New York Times* article "Maya Dress Tells a New Story, and It's Not Pretty." See also Hilary E. Kahn, "Respecting Relationships and Día de Guadalupe: Q'eqchi' Mayan Identities in Livingston, Guatemala." Kahn notes that "in Guatemala many criollos and latinos celebrate the Día de Guadalupe by dressing their children in huipile and corte" (5–6).

14. See chapter 2, "Mexico," where García Canclini explores how the megacity in-

corporates identity markers through communitarian practices such as rituals and celebrations.

15. I refer to my chats with the participants as pláticas following the methodology used by various scholars who shun the use of the term *interview* in an attempt to establish a more culturally relevant methodology. See *Three Decades of Engendering Work*, especially the introduction by co-editors Linda Heidenreich and Luz Maria Gordillo (15, 25–32).

16. All subsequent quotations from these three participants are from our pláticas in the spring of 2007 unless otherwise noted.

17. I had identified other participants, but time and travel constraints prevented interviews with these other huipilistas, including Ellen Riojas Clark, Carmen Tafolla, Luz María Prieto, Gloria Uribe Ramírez, and Frances Herrera. I also had a brief plática with Sra. Camacho de López, but I was not able to return for a more comprehensive conversation on the subject and consequently did not include her in my study.

18. When Larissa informed me that she had just acquired her first huipil, I immediately whipped out my digital recorder and began to record—of course, only after she signed the University of Texas at San Antonio's Internal Review Board forms, like those that most university research offices require.

19. Fierros and Delgado-Bernal discuss "researcher reflexivity" as an integral feature of pláticas (114–115).

20. Her grandmother spoke the Indigenous language from southern Mexico, the region of Yucatan.

21. This kind of mestizaje, which is not necessarily Indian and European (and in this case is Greek and Mexican) has been studied in literature by Venetia June Pedraza.

22. The term *gringa* as used in Texas refers to Euro-American women, although in Laredo a student once told me that she was called a gringa, even though she is Mexican American, because she had been living in Austin. I was called a gringa by some Indigenous people near Monte Albán in Mexico, so it is an elusive term. In general, though, it refers to a white person or someone who belongs to the dominant Anglo world in the United States. The common etymology offered for the word that holds that the term comes from "green gold," in reference to dollars, is unsupportable, for the term existed in Spain to denote *foreigner*, or someone who spoke Spanish with an accent.

23. I have not included a discussion of non-Chicanas wearing the garment in San Antonio as it is outside the purview of this study. However, at least one white woman told me how the garment became de rigueur at the Night in Old San Antonio (NIOSA) celebration held in April during the 1960s. According to her, it is due to the white women who began NIOSA that the garment has become a staple and has garnered so many followers among both white and Mexican/Chicana San Antonians.

24. The rebozeros are the weavers of the shawl-like wrap called a rebozo that women wear in Mexico. Like the huipil, the rebozo is woven on a back-strap loom and has a rich history.

Works Cited

Alarcón, Norma. "Traduttora, Traditora: A Paradigmatic Figure of Chicana Feminism." *Cultural Critique*, vol. 13, 1989, pp. 57–87.

Anawalt, Patricia Rieff. "Costume Analysis and the Provenience of the Borgia Group Codices." *American Antiquity*, vol. 46, no. 4, 1981, pp. 837–852, www.jstor.org /stable/280110?seq= 1#page_scan_tab_contents. Accessed 11 Apr. 2007.

Anzaldúa, Gloria. *Borderlands/La Frontera: The New Mestiza*. 3rd ed., Aunt Lute Books, 2007.

Arrizón, Alicia. *Latina Performance: Traversing the Stage*. Indiana UP, 1999.

Ávila, Alejandro de. "Tejidos que cuidan el alma." *Artes de México*, vol. 35, 1996, pp. 39–53.

Ayala, Elaine. "Sharing Culture or Stealing It." "Latino Life," *San Antonio Express-News*, 25 Sept. 2007, blog.mysanantonio .com/latinlife/2007/09/sharing-culture -or-stealing-it/. Accessed 12 Apr. 2017.

Blum Schevill, Margot. "Museum Collections as Oracles for Research," *Museum Anthropology*, vol. 12, no. 1, 1988, pp. 3–7, anthrosource.onlinelibrary.wiley.com.

Bourke, John G. "Notes on the Language and Folk-Usage of the Rio Grande Valley. (With Especial Regard to Survivals of Arabic Custom.)" *Journal of American Folklore*, vol. 9, no. 33 (Apr.–June 1896), pp. 81–116.

Boyer, Peter. *Tradition as Truth and Communication: A Cognitive Description of Traditional Discourse*. Cambridge UP, 1990.

Broyles-González, Yolanda. *El Teatro Campesino: Theater in the Chicano Movement*. U of Texas P, 1994.

Cantú, Norma E. "Costume as Cultural Resistance and Affirmation: The Case of a South Texas Community." In *Hecho en Tejas*, edited by Joe S. Graham, U of North Texas P, 1991, pp. 117–130.

Catacalos, Rosemary. Personal interview. 8 Mar. 2007.

Cisneros, Sandra. *A House of My Own: Stories from My Life*. Knopf, 2015.

Códices de México. Exhibit at the Instituto de Antropología e Historia, Oct. 2015, codices.inah.gob.mx/pc/index.php.

Crane, Diana. *Class, Gender, and Identity in Clothing*. U of Chicago P, 2000.

de Orellana, Margarita, et al. "Hilos que son palabras"; "Técnicas de tejido"; "Mirando los textiles Oaxaqueños"; "Anatomía de una tradición textil"; "Tejidos que cuidan el alma"; "Imaginación bordada de palabras"; "De fibras, gusanos y caracoles"; "Vidas hiladas en Teotitlán"; "Tejidos paralelos." Translated by Jennifer Clement. *Artes de México*, no. 35, 1996, pp. 81–96.

Eicher, Joanne B., editor. *Dress and Ethnicity: Change across Space and Time*. Berg, 1995.

Fierros, Cindy, and Dolores Delgado Bernal. "Vamos a platicar: The Contours of Pláticas as Chicana/Latina Feminist Methodology." *Chicana/Latina Studies*, vol. 15, no. 2, 2016, pp. 98–121.

García Canclini, Néstor. *Consumers and Citizens*. U of Minnesota P, 2001.

Gaspar de Alba, Alicia. "Malinche's Revenge." *Feminism, Nation, and Myth: La Malinche*, edited by Rolando Romero and Amanda N. Harris, Arte Público, 2005.

Goldman, Dorie S. "'Down for La Raza'; Barrio Art T-Shirts, Chicano Pride, and Cultural Resistance." *Journal of Folklore Research*, vol. 34, no. 2, 1997, pp. 123–138.

Gonzales, Patrisia. *Red Medicine: Traditional Indigenous Rites of Birthing and Healing.* U of Arizona P, 2012.

Heidenreich, Linda, and Luz Maria Gordillo, editors. *Three Decades of Engendering Work: Selected Works of Antonia I. Castañeda.* U of North Texas P, 2014.

Huerta, Jorge. *Necessary Theater: Sixth Place about the Chicano Experience.* Arte Público, 1989.

Huipiles: A Celebration. An exhibit at the Museo Alameda in San Antonio, 19 Sept. 2007–20 Jan. 2008.

Huipiles: The Fabric of Identity. Directed by César Martínez, vimeo.com/101329181. Accessed 20 Oct. 2015.

Kahn, Hilary E. "Respecting Relationships and Día de Guadalupe: Q'eqchi' Mayan Identities in Livingston, Guatemala." *Journal of Latin American Anthropology*, vol. 6, no. 1, 2001, pp. 2–29, doi.org/10.1525/jlca.2001.6.1.2.

Latina Feminist Research Group. *Telling to Live: Latina Feminist Testimonios.* Duke UP, 2001.

Lechuga, Ruth D. "Mirando los textiles oaxaqueños." *Artes de México*, vol. 35, 1996, pp. 11–23.

———. *El traje indígena de México: Su evolución, desde la época prehispánica hasta la actualidad.* Panorama Editorial, 1982.

Little, Walter E. "Common Origins / 'Different' Identities in Two Kaqchikel Maya Towns." *Journal of Anthropological Research*, vol. 59, no. 2, 2003, pp. 205–224, scholarsarchive.library.albany.edu/cgi/viewcontent.cgi?article=1011&context=cas_anthro_scholar. Accessed 11 Apr. 2007.

Mercado-López, Larissa. Personal interview. 7 Feb. 2007.

———. Personal communication. 16 Sept. 2018.

Michaels, Jennifer. "(Ad)Dressing Shibboleths: Costume and Community in the South of France." *Journal of American Folklore*, vol. 111, no. 440, 1998, pp. 146–172.

Morgadanes, Dolores. "Similarity between the Mixco (Guatemala) and the Yalalag (Oaxaca, Mexico) Costumes." *American Anthropologist*, vol. 42, no. 2, 1940, pp. 359–364, www.jstor.org/stable/663129.

Muñoz, José Esteban. *Disidentifications: Queers of Color and the Performance of Politics.* U of Minnesota P, 1999.

Neustadt, Robert. "Studies in 20th Century Literature." *New Prairie Press*, 1 June 2001. Accessed 19 Jan. 2014.

Noyes, Dorothy. *Fire in the Plaça: Catalan Festival Politics after Franco.* U of Pennsylvania P, 2003.

Nye, Joseph. *Bound to Lead: The Changing Nature of American Power.* Basic Books, 1990.

———. *Soft Power: The Means to Success in World Politics.* BBS/Public Affairs, 2004.

Oatman-Stanford, Hunter. "Uncovering Clues in Frida Kahlo's Private Wardrobe." *Collectors Weekly*, 1 Feb. 2013, www.collectorsweekly.com/articles/uncovering-clues-in-frida-kahlos-private-wardrobe. Accessed 15 Oct. 2015.

Odland, J. Claire. "Fashioning Tradition: Maya Huipiles in the Field Museum Collections." *Fieldiana Anthropology*, vol. 38, no. 1, 2006, p. 1, www.bioone.org/doi/abs/10.3158/0071-4739%282006%2938%5B1%3AFTMHIT%5D2.0.CO%3B2. Accessed 25 Oct. 2015.

Paz, Octavio. "The Sons of Malinche." *The Labyrinth of Solitude*, translated by Lysander Kemp et al., Grove, 1962.

Pedraza, Venetia June. *Third Space Mestizaje as a Critical Approach to Literature*. U of Texas at San Antonio, PhD diss., 2008.

Pratt, Mary Louise. "'Yo Soy La Malinche': Chicana Writers and the Poetics of Ethno-nationalism." *Callaloo*, vol. 16, no. 4, 1993, p. 859.

Rohter, Larry. "Maya Dress Tells a New Story, and It's Not Pretty." *New York Times*, 13 June 1997, www.nytimes.com/ 1997/06/13/world/maya-dress-tells-a-new -story-and-it-s-not-pretty.html. Accessed May 2011.

Romero Giordano, Carlos. "The Death Agony of Indigenous Mexican Textiles." *Voices of Mexico*, vol. 34, 1994, pp. 20–24.

Ruiz Chávez, Glafira. *Monografía de la Indumentaria Femenina del Estado de México*. Dirección de Turismo, Mexico, 1970.

Sánchez, Graciela. Personal interview. 22 Feb. 2007.

Sayer, Chloe. *Costumes of Mexico*. U of Texas P, 1990.

Silva, Elda. "Fund-raiser Stars Practical, Expressive Huipil." *San Antonio Express-News*, 29 Mar. 2001, /Fundraiser_stars_ practical/San_Antonio_Express-News /p1F.pdf. Accessed 11 Apr. 2007.

———. "Huipil Appeal: Women Love Ease of Traditional Garment—and What It Symbolizes." *San Antonio Express-News*, 12 Oct. 2000, /Huipil_appeal_Women _love/San_Antonio_Express-News p1F%20(1).pdf. Accessed 11 Apr. 2007.

Sollors, Werner. *Beyond Ethnicity: Consent and Descent in American Culture*. Oxford UP, 1986.

Soustelle, Jacques. *Daily Life of the Aztecs on the Eve of the Spanish Conquest*. Stanford UP, 1961.

Start, Laura E. "Indian Textiles from Guatemala and Mexico." *Man*, vol. 48, 1948, pp. 67–68.

Tomlinson, John. *Cultural Imperialism: A Critical Introduction*. Bloomsbury, 2002.

Turok, Marta. "Rebozos: The Threads That Bind Us Historically and to the Present." Lecture at the conference "Handmade Tradition/Tradición Hecha a Mano," at the Mexican Cultural Institute, San Antonio, Texas, 22 Sept. 2018.

———. "Rebozos from Tenancingo." Lecture at the conference "Handmade Tradition/Tradición Hecha a Mano," at the Mexican Cultural Institute, San Antonio, Texas, 21 Sept. 2018.

———. "Trama Natural de Fibras, Gusanos y Caracoles." *Artes de México*, vol. 35, 1996, pp. 62–69.

Vaillant, George C. *Aztecs of Mexico*. Allen Lane, 1975.

CHAPTER 2

Con el huipil en la mente:
The Metamorphosis of a Chicana

JOSIE MÉNDEZ-NEGRETE

In this chapter I navigate cultural memories framed inside the values and norms of a Mexican society that shaped my own sense of identity. I came of age in a Mexico where mestizaje was celebrated and served the nation's master narrative. Mestizaje romanticized the mestizo heritage of the country, while ignoring the realities of poverty, illiteracy, and lack of social and economic integration of Indigenous populations. This was the context in which I learned to understand myself as an ethnic person. Marked as a Mexican Indian, from a peasant background, once in the United States I became a Chicana.

To begin, I reflect on a cultural memory that speaks to a process of endurance as I navigated misogynist, patriarchal, classist, and racist environments, whereby I learned to rely on my cultural practices to survive (Anzaldúa 60–61). I build on those early Mexican cultural memories that gave me options to isolate, merge, contest, and challenge the ways in which I was perceived as a young girl in transition to becoming a woman. Toward that end, I engage a discussion of identity and cultural memory within what Vicki L. Ruiz has called cultural coalescence. This is premised on the notion that "*cultures* are rooted in generation, gender, region, and personal experience" (50). As an active agent, I reflect on the ways in which I understood and engaged the social world as a means of keeping, rejecting, and subverting who I could be by exploring the differences with which I contended as a mexicana del otro lado—a Mexican from the other side of the border.

These recollections have their foundation in Tabasco, Zacatecas. During my upbringing, I was socialized to become a domesticated woman defined by traditional Mexican cultural norms; I was not prepared to become an educator. In the context of that traditional landscape, as a girl I had limited options: marriage or the convent. At the same time, under the tutelage of my paternal great-aunts Hermelinda and Rosenda Méndez, independent women who were widowed at an early age, I learned to become a strong and self-reliant person who believed she could realize her dreams. I could speak: I had a voice, and when expressing ideas, my community and those who loved me valued me for my ability to think. My siblings and I were barely four, seven, and eight when our parents went to el norte, later taking my sister Mague with them and leaving Felisa and me behind with our two elderly aunts.

We were supported by remittances from our parents, who were working the fields of South Texas. It was under the care of my tías that I learned about privilege—entitlement by income—because they were well-off and we never lacked a thing. My great-aunts provided love and nurturance, replacing Amá, who left us to follow my father. Mague, who had been born in the United States, joined our parents when our brother was born, before she turned eight. Mague's legal status as a US citizen made her the likely choice to accompany and help Amá.

My upbringing emphasized a national identity that erased my Indigeneity. México's national narrative promotes its citizens' mestizaje as part of its mexicanidad, while simultaneously deriding lo indio—the Indian in us. In Mexico it is not uncommon to commercialize the Indigenous population for consumption by tourists. Because our aunts had money and were nurturing, we experienced living inside the safety of a loving, stable home. Before too long, we grew accustomed to our mother's absence, and it was in those early years that I learned to value myself through an active process of identity negotiation among strong women. My aunts could support themselves with the livestock Tía Hermelinda owned, coupled with the income from a convenience store. Tía Hermelinda, who had inherited wealth from her departed husband, hired vaqueros to tend to the livestock, and with the profits she was able to finance her son's university education. Supplemented by remittances sent from our parents, the income from the convenience store kept all of us in a comfortable lifestyle.

Our great-aunts ensured we valued our history and ethnic origins. From them I learned the surnames of seven generations of my ancestors on both lines of my family, thus establishing the foundation for a genealogy of empowerment. My aunts also taught me to be fearless. They taught us to value all peoples without judgment or criticism. Tías Hermelinda and Rosenda practiced their beliefs; children, for them, were complete human beings who should use their imagination and creativity to make their mark on the world. From their perspective, everything was connected to the sanctity of life.

All this changed upon my arrival in the United States. Still, I held on to the cultural practices I had learned to value as a young child. It was the domestic cultural practices I was taught when I lived with my aunts in Mexico, such as sewing and embroidering, that compelled me to reclaim the huipil.[1]

Recycling Others' Old Clothes to Create New Ones

From a very early age I was taught to create new objects or works of art from what others considered waste, such as used clothes and discarded material, otherwise known as rasquachismo.[2] My creativity was cultivated inside my tías' home. For example, bottle caps became the building blocks of furniture I would make for the dollhouses I created from empty boxes that had contained the goods sold at Tía Hermelinda's convenience store. She gave me the beer and soda caps, and loaned me the tools to reshape them into tables, benches, chairs, or stools for my doll box-houses. I diligently painted my creations to represent the vibrant colors of the streets in our village—Mexican rose and green, purple, watermelon red, and orange. Later, these bottle caps became bases of the earrings that honored saints or other Mexican and Chicana/o cultural icons. The store, which was adjacent to their home, became a safe place and a site where I learned and heard stories about the colorful lives of the people of our town—those who had left and those who remained behind. In that precious space, we learned some of life's greatest lessons.

It was with my tías that I began to design patterns for miniature dresses using vintage materials and make rag dolls from women's discarded nylons. I shaped each doll's face and body using my imagination to create different looks and expressions. By filling the nylons with balls of white thread to flesh out their bodies, I could carefully carve out and embroider features on their faces. In addition to miniature dresses, my rasquache sensibilities—my ability to create something from nothing—were further enhanced with macramé and crochet doilies that became the cushions for the chairs and sofas of my doll furniture made from bottle caps.

Some of my fondest memories are of the magical times my Tía Hermelinda spent working on my tiny chair, peddling the sewing machine while she put together the clothing she designed. I learned to value the uniqueness of clothing produced by sewing and embroidering the garments I made for my dolls. By her side, watching her piece together her creations, I imagined decorating my own dresses with hand-stitched flowers and other images, inadvertently developing my Mexican aesthetic: nopales,

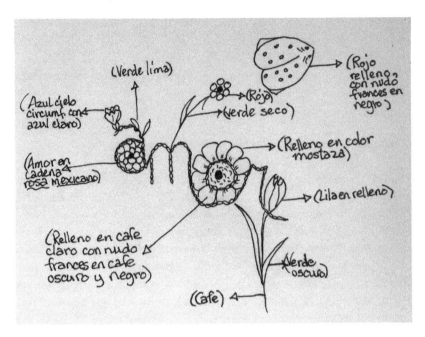

2.1. Sketch for pillowcase under the tutelage of Tía Hermelinda.

magueyes, sombreros, and even burros adorned those early pieces. I soon began to sketch ideas for embroidery projects.

In my experience, domestic duties were not limited to women. Surrounded by lo indio—my maternal tíos were matachines, or Indian dancers, who made their own ceremonial vestments for cultural celebrations in which they held central roles—I learned that both men and women could create art with textiles and thread. While some may assume these activities were in preparation for domestic life, I was taught that sewing, embroidering, and patterning were skills that any man or woman could learn to fashion or create something from scratch. Thus, when my aunts called me to bring my small wooden chair with its woven textile seat of fiber from maguey leaves, I was only too glad to embroider the vistas I had sketched (fig. 2.1).

Those drawings guided me as I began creating art. I labored over kitchen towels and pillowcases made from local cotton that I would later give away as gifts. In those embroidery projects, every stitch I created was a challenge, but none was more difficult than the cross-stitch: front and back had to be perfectly executed and ready for inspection. Tía Hermelinda scrutinized every piece. It was not her intent to chastise, but to ensure I learned to embroider the best possible way. Up for the challenge and proud of my endeavors, I made sure to do it just right so that Tía would not make me redo my work. Furniture and dolls were not the only projects we learned to make with the remnants rescued from the outfits and dresses made by Tía Hermelinda; I also designed and hand-sewed many clothes for my dolls. Depending on the material, the dresses could be huipil style or blouses with embroidery on the collar or arms.

Luckily, when I left Mexico to join my parents in the United States, I did not forget the practices I had learned under the tutelage of my Tías Hermelinda and Rosenda. They encouraged me to retain the knowledge and skills without associating them as part of my class or race background, or as indicative of gender subjugation. In the sanctuary my tías created, I was protected. Since my father had not lived with us for most of our lives, we were not exposed to a patriarch who would have kept us in our place; his absence allowed me to grow into the person I was capable of becoming. In that town of single women, old men, and children who had lost their parents to el norte, I was able to live an idyllic childhood. Storytelling, dancing, singing, sewing, and other types of creative expression became part of my daily life and eventually the tools of survival once I, too, left my tías for el norte. When the rest of the children in my family and I emigrated, I would use these cultural memories to keep at bay the violence I encountered at home.

Because my childhood experiences were positive, there was little to forget and much to cherish. It was this early socialization that provided me the means to endure domestic and sexual violence. In el norte my sisters and I learned to contend with a misogynist patriarch who saw us only as chattel, who beat and abused us on a whim as he controlled and subordinated the useless girls whom he thought were good for nothing. Art, music, and writing were the cultural salve to my soul—places of refuge that later became healing practices in my recovery from psychological, physical, spiritual, and sexual trauma. Such cultural expressions created possibilities, sites of imagination, alternative ways of living for a young immigrant who had left México against her will.

From Eden to Hell

We were finally brought to the United States by our parents when I was eleven and Felisa almost four. After years of refusal, Amá finally wore our father out. It was during the late 1950s, at a time when immigration policies were most restrictive, that they brought us with them. Rather than post a bond in the amount of $1,500 for each of us, a sum we simply could not afford, our father brought us into the country without documents. We joined our US-born sister when our entire family entered the migrant stream that worked the fields in South Texas until we settled in Northern California. Emigrating was not a choice given to us; Amá wanted her family together.

With nearly a sixth-grade education in México, when I came to this country, I already had been socialized into a national Mexican identity. I was proud of who I was, even when wealthy Mexicans in my town and peers in my new environment perceived me as una india pata rajada, a shoeless Indian with cracked feet from walking barefoot—a term mestizos and people with money bandied about when referring to anyone who looked Indian. It was through my social relationships in California that I learned to rethink and negotiate my Mexican identity. As a child, although I considered myself Mexican, I also learned to engage a racialized ethnicity that marked me as inferior based on my Indigenous identification and appearance.

At the age of twelve, now living in my adopted country, my identity shifted. Instead of encountering people of Mexican descent who carried their culture with pride, as my siblings and I had been taught, I found myself interacting with Mexican and Mexican American children who claimed Portuguese, Italian, or Spanish heritages. It was also during this time that my home life became a dangerous and traumatic place in which to exist. My father, Juan, ruled our household with a strong and violent hand. Every opportunity he had, he told us without hesitation that we were worthless—no servíamos pa' nada—that we were of no use to anyone or anything. As women-in-the-making, our only value came from knowing how to serve men.

From México to the United States, and from within the in-between spaces of the borderlands, my identity has continued to unfold inside notions of rasquachismo and domesticana.[3] I have continued to hone my artistic ability to create something from nothing and to value the expressive work of a domestic environment as having cultural merit. My allegiance to mi tierra is nuanced in my childhood memories. The Mexican aesthetic expressed in my clothing as a child persisted into my adolescence and shaped my identity to claim both my Mexican-ness and my US experience when I eventually identified as a Chicana. It was an identity in opposition to dominant forces that communicated assimilation into the US mainstream was the only acceptable cultural adaptation. However, many of my peers called me a fake Chicana because I was not born in the United States and therefore could not claim the colonized status central to a Chicana identity. Thus, when the time came to dress in Indian clothing, I was first in line because I already owned or knew how to make the requisite attire. This aesthetic had been part of my everyday practice as a child, and I reclaimed it and took up the domestic customs my great-aunts first taught me, which were also practiced by my mother. These domestic abilities became strategic sites of relating rather than cultural practices of being Chicana in terms of the nationalist and patriarchal notions of the time. They framed my coming of age as a woman, not in preparation for marriage and motherhood, but as a path to the community and social relationships I craved.

It was through these domestic practices that I created a community of support for myself and my sisters in the new environments we inhabited. Our cultural knowledge and skills gave us entry into the rituals and celebrations of our community. The ways in which I merged these practices—creating something from nothing or from other people's discards, using embroidery and sewing as artistic creations—yielded a culture of survival for me. This was where I could be myself inside an ethnic cultural identity and find value as a person. Up to this point I had only sewed as a creative outlet.

Once we settled in Santa Clara, California, having left field work behind, I began to repurpose used clothing because I had to make clothes for my sisters and me. Rather than rely on the discarded clothing my father picked up on his rounds as a garbage collector, I chose another route. With the knowledge of textiles I had acquired from Tía Hermelinda, I sought expensive material at second-hand stores. If we were going to wear used clothing, it would be garments I made with the finest material. It was in Santa Clara that I found my treasure trove. It was also then that embroidering became a creative outlet for fashioning the skirts and blouses I constructed from pre-owned clothing that would become our very own.

A New Home: Change in Name Only

Our family home in Santa Clara was at the corner of Fremont Street and the Alameda; it was the second to the last house, located between the tax preparer/notary's office at the corner, whose daughter Jessica was my friend, and Mr. Luigi, our next-door neighbor on the opposite side. My ability to access and create community began with the rag dolls I made, which I later shared with Jessica, who also loved to play with dolls. She had a collection of them that my sisters and I envied. At the same time, I realized my dolls came from the traditions I learned from my aunts.

Our family home was only two and a half blocks away from my fantasy store—a segunda, or second-hand, store that raised funds for the Veterans of Foreign Wars (VFW). Those Santa Clara days brought changes for my siblings and me. Amá had always sewn. She often relied on the cotton material from the Harina La Piña flour sacks to create what we wore, such as the sleeveless purple and blue plaid baby doll dresses we wore to our first and only visit to the San Francisco Zoo (fig. 2.2). Unlike me, Amá repurposed the clothes that came from Juan's dumpster diving so she no longer had to rely on the material from the flour sacks.

During the early 1960s, just before the beginning of the Chicano Movement, my family was living in the same neighborhood as Chicano writer Jose Villarreal—that place that inspired his 1950s coming-of-age story about Mexican Americans, *Pocho*. Located immediately behind our house, Villarreal's home on Alviso Street was en route to the VFW store, the segunda that I frequented to create our new attire.

By 1965 I was going to the segunda three to five times a week searching for the largest dresses and the most interesting fabrics to make clothes in the mod styles of the day for me and my sisters. Aware that colors and styles come and go with the seasons, something I learned from Tía Hermelinda, I looked for material that was similar to those in vogue. Paisley, plaid, linen, brocade, dotted Swiss, and solids in all types of fabrics. Among the materials for our flexible baby doll and tent pattern dresses that became the rage in the mid-1960s were cotton, peau de soi satin, and silk. From four patterns with sleeves and two without, cut onto newspaper print—it was the easiest style to craft—I sewed seventeen such dresses for one of my friend's fifteenth-birthday celebration. Because of my sewing abilities, my sisters and I participated in many quinceañeras—the coming-of-age ritual for every young woman who is presented to the community. The only condition was that I make the dresses; sometimes it was fifteen, other times twenty, depending on the number of madrinas or sponsors. With this practice in design and pattern-making, I would later create huipiles, peasant blouses, and ethnic skirts.

My favorite pattern to sew, however, was the linen baby doll dress, with a white collar and an added layer of pleats at the bottom to give it flair. The basic form of the dress was that of a huipil, a loose-fitting garment (fig. 2.3.), In this dress, together with white mesh nylons and Mary Jane shoes, we were as much in style as the most popular girls at our high school, who purchased their clothing in high-end department stores.

2.2. Josie Méndez-Negrete, *Harina La Piña Days*, detail. Watercolor on paper, 14″ × 11″.

In the late 1960s and early 1970s, Chicana-style creations—embroidered blouses; slit, wide bell-bottoms with embroidered or crocheted seams; and peasant skirts made of ethnically identified cloth—became all the rage among my friends. When I was in high school in the late 1960s, I began to design flared bell-bottom pants with zippers on the side, vests, and rumba sleeve blouses that simulated wasp-like waists. My sisters and friends were the beneficiaries of my skills, but contrary to what some per-

Marinera 1965

2.3. Josie Méndez-Negrete, *Marinera*, 1965. Ink and pencil sketch, 14″ × 11″.

ceived, because we dressed alike, we were not a gang. We dressed the way we wanted to because we could, primarily wearing black and white. The only color other than the blush on our cheeks and lipstick was the embroidery I boldly stitched on our blouses. Sometimes I embroidered the outer side of our flared pants, fanning the legs with accordion-like folds of colorful fabric that identified us as a group of girls from Santa Clara High School who hung together—but the Santa Clara gang we were not.

Impressed by the baby doll dresses I had designed for my sisters and best friends, those who invited us to be in their quinceañeras begged me to transform this pattern into something that would allow them to dance freely. I came up with a tea-length dress with an A-line flare and a split on the side that gave them the room to skip and kick along with the "temptation walk"—our soul dance at the time, created by the group it was named after. My knowledge of fabric and pattern-making came in handy as a means to raise funds and gave us access to events we would not have been invited to otherwise.

It was also in the late 1960s that Indigenous clothing reappeared as part of the Chicano Movement. It recalled the ancestral land of Aztlán, the imaginary nation of our origins. Nationalist notions of womanhood meant wearing the attire expected of a mythical huipil-wearing Aztec princess, and embroidered peasant shirts became all the rage for men. Maylei Blackwell discusses "the gendered struggles over the iconography of nationalism . . . not just as 'representations' . . . [but] rather as political and cultural practices that played a constitutive role in the domain of culture" (92). How we talked, what we called ourselves, and the ways in which our clothing represented the imaginary Aztlán were all part of a political statement of who we were in the context of the time. As Blackwell notes, it was in the tension of idealized gendered spaces that Chicano nationalists imagined women in an "idealized femininity largely by conflating a conservative cultural construct of 'tradition' with a particular version of family" (98). In her analysis of the Chicano Movement, she provides an intellectual framework in which to analyze the huipil as a garment representative of a changing, progressive identity for Chicanas. Her notion of retrofitted memory, or "a practice whereby social actors read the interstices, gaps, and silences of existing historical narratives in order to retrofit, rework, and refashion older narratives" (102), allows us to understand the huipil as exemplifying the feminine and traditional, as well as a counter aesthetic of revolutionary chic.

During this time many tall, skinny, and light-complexioned Chicanas chose to dress in Tehuana and Chiapaneca styles paired with bell-bottom jeans or peasant skirts. I did as well. However, I could not afford the elaborate pieces of Indigenous clothing my peers wore, so I relied on the practice of embroidering taught to me by my tías. I began to make my own peasant blouses and skirts to match. On my body, the attire affirmed my Mexicanness, but it did not provide me with the legitimacy of Chicanismo. I did not pass the litmus test: my birth in Mexico denied me the right to call myself a Chicana.

During those hippie, peasant blouse–wearing days, I fit in with the United Farm Workers (UFW) Movement, many of whose members lacked the resources to buy the huipiles that had become the uniform of the day for those affiliated with the UFW. Activists and teatristas—cultural workers and theater activists—also opened up spaces for me to gain a sense of belonging and creativity; I became one in their troop of actors. Thus, it was through the UFW that my initiation into Chicanisma began—my own way of thinking about being one in a collective of people who were beginning to reclaim their Aztec cultural past and the imagined nation of Aztlán. With an origin story in the United States and the rhetoric of the imagined nation of Aztlán, those of us who had felt excluded for too long could now claim ancestral ties to our Indigenous past in the context of the United States.

You Are Not Always What You Wear

My cultural activist friends Rosie, Laura, and Elisa best reflect the Chicana iconography of those days: tall, slim, huipil-wearing, with unrestrained long hair that fell to near waist length unless it was braided to perform folklórico dances. More of a uniform reflecting the politics of the day, the huipil was understood by very few of my contemporaries because they had not been exposed to the history and geographical origins of the dress. Understandably, most of us were a product of US schooling, which emphasized an Americanization that urged us to whitewash our ethnicity. During those early days of the Chicano Movement, we reappropriated huipiles to reflect a Chicanisma-chic aesthetic. With our identity displayed on our bodies, we allied with those who were fighting for Chicano civil rights—not just the United Farm Workers, but also with those who expressed cultural autonomy as a nation of people connected to the land and who affirmed the rights that had been promised through the Treaty of Guadalupe Hidalgo, the document that ceded more than 50 percent of Mexico's land.

My fashion changed when I became employed. Even though I continued to wear embroidered cotton blouses with jeans and skirts at activist events such as marches and protests, at work I more often dressed in professional suits and high heels, almost as if to contest those Mexican-hating peers who had previously derided me for wearing ethnic clothes as a reflection of what the critics perceived and despised as my chuntara Mexican Indian ancestry. As I retrieved my memories, I realized that I limited my use of huipiles to disassociate with those who cast stones, but strategically used it in the context of my activism—UFW support, youth work, and teatro days—to mark my association with the movement and my coming of age as an activist and cultural worker.

For me, identity and clothing articulated fluid notions of self and the

ways in which I expressed my allegiance to Mexican culture. My early upbringing in México gave me knowledge about traditional Indian clothing
as well as an awareness of racist and classist ideas held by many Mexicans
about who could and should wear such clothing. I did not have to learn
about huipiles, unlike my US peers who had been pushed to assimilate and
dismiss that which was Mexican. Rather than participate in a silent war of
contention about who could be Chicana or whether I was Chicana enough,
I began conversations with friends about their image as huipil-wearing
women: Where is your huipil from? Is it embroidered in handwoven textile? From what region of Mexico does it come? Is it a festive or common
garment? What meaning do the colors convey, the embroidery? Do women
in all regions of Mexico dress in huipiles? What I found was that they did
not know or understand the garment's origins. They only recognized that
wearing huipiles gave them a sense of belonging and participating in the
Chicano Movement.

Clothing and Body Image

For me, the loose-fitting huipil became another way to cover my violated
and sexualized body. In those early days of my recovery from sexual and domestic violence, huipiles suited me fine. After about seven years and much
personal work, I began to overcome my injuries. This was during the time
when San José, California, became known as the feminist capital of the nation because it had the first female mayor and very active supporters of the
Equal Pay for Equal Work Movement and the Equal Rights Amendment.[4]
In 1972 I began to display my healing body as a braless young woman who
wore painted or embroidered sleeveless tees, which had become the craze
during those days of *Raging Bull*, the film that gave the garments the de-
risive name "wife-beaters." Despite being a survivor of domestic violence,
I did not contest the garment's name. I was most concerned with embracing my body and my sexuality as my own, so I continued to create clothing
that would not only display my mexicanidad, but also accentuate my body.
I had learned to embrace my sexuality—trauma and all.

Creating My Own: Huipiles Contemporáneos

Nowadays I seldom dress for anyone other than myself. The huipil—
traditional or my own creation—allows me to express my cultural prac-

tices as I reproduce the arts and crafts of Mexico. For me, color and textile are integral to the garment, as it reflects who I am. An example of this is a huipil grande I designed, Lillie's Dress, which I made with Vietnamese raw silk purchased from textile vendors in east San José on one of my trips to visit family (fig. 2.4). It is embroidered with a tree of life in the tradition of Maestro Alfonso Castillo Orta, as drawn by Verónica Castillo, master clay artists from Izúcar de Matamoros, Puebla.

Huipil-wearing practices continue. In the late twentieth century, the Zapatista Movement made huipiles visible as garments of revolutionary women. Salma Hayek did as much with her film biography and portrayal of Frida Kahlo. In my own community, another example of how the huipil achieved renewed interest took place through an art exhibition that opened July 15, 2007, in San Antonio, Texas. It was sponsored by Mexicans and Americans Thinking Together (MATT), a sociopolitical group organized by Lionel Sosa, who also underwrote Kathy Sosa, his wife, for the show, *Huipiles: A Celebration.*

Among the activities organized in conjunction with the exhibit was a videotaped panel discussion featuring local women who were in some way identified with the garment. Invited speakers included Ellen Riojas Clark and Luz María Prieto, two members of Las Mujeres del Huipil, so called because they consistently wear the garment; writers Sandra Cisneros and Norma E. Cantú, who sometimes don huipiles; and the artist and designer Veronica Prida, who uses these textiles in her design projects. The focus of the discussion was each woman's involvement with the huipil.

Reflecting on that discussion, Cristina Sosa Noriega, in an editorial that appeared in MATT's newsletter, notes that there is "a strong uniting factor in the pride they feel when they wear a huipil. They also described how wearing huipiles allows them to connect with their cultural heritage in a powerful way." Elaborating on the reasons for their use of huipiles, Riojas Clark, from San Antonio, and Cisneros, who grew up in Chicago, provided their rationales. Riojas Clark said the huipil made her feel connected after having grown up "in a white neighborhood," and Cisneros said she sees wearing the huipil as "a part of holding onto your culture," of being "legitimate here."

For Cantú, at the time a professor of English at the University of Texas at San Antonio, wearing huipiles is more an aesthetic or artistic expression. She explained,

> The woman who creates a huipil is telling her story, her life. It becomes part of her life having made the huipil, and the woman who wears the huipil is

2.4. Lillie's dress. Vietnamese raw silk huipil embroidered with silk thread in the style of the huipil grande, designed and made by Josie Méndez-Negrete.

also adding to the story. The artist creates it, but the person who appreci-
ated the art, they are connected in very intimate ways, especially when you
wear the art.

Clearly, Cantú links our use of huipiles with the valuation of the garment.
For Prida, the huipil becomes a tool for creating art. She explained, "I don't
wear them like most people do. . . . I change them." She transforms huipiles
by adding her design touches with other embellishments to the garment
and showcases them as furniture or purses. Interestingly, for Cantú and
Cisneros the issue of class (and race, although nuanced) became a point of
contention in their decision to wear huipiles. Cantú recalled that at first
her relatives did not understand her use of the garment; thus, she educated them to its meaning. For her, the huipil reflects her persona in the
public readings and presentaions of her literary work. She said, "When I
do a reading and wear them, it's already a signifier to the audience; they
want to know why I am wearing it. I think it is a political act, a political statement." For Cisneros, the garment is associated with servants and
poverty in the context of Mexico, yet it also links her to the Mexican past
that she often writes about in her work.

Riojas Clark also associates the garment with the village of Yaxchitlan,
Chiapas, Mexico, AD 75, and Lady Xoc, a member of the nobility in Mayan
culture. In a historical retrospective she wrote for the now-defunct website *Huipiles*, we learn about the huipil and other regions of Mexico and
Guatemala where it may be found. She concludes,

> The huipil is an important dress not only historically, but important for the
> work and social life of today's woman who will maintain the importance of
> the huipil throughout subsequent generations. The huipil will continue to
> reflect femininity, identity, strength, tradition, values, and, of course, cul-
> ture throughout time.

Riojas Clark's analysis lends fluidity and change to the garment.

In contrast, Bárbara Renaud González critiqued the San Antonio huipiles exhibit in her blog *Las True Stories of San Antonio*. Her entry includes
a photograph of a mask-wearing "Comandante Ramona" in a huipil. The
caption reads: "This is the kind of woman you're not going to see [at the
exhibit]" (boldface in the original). Gonzalez's intent is to mark the Indigenous as she questions Sosa's right to render the cultural practice of
preserving our expressions in textiles and paintings, maintaining that
the heritage of Indian women was absent from the event. But clearly the

panel participants' use of the huipil is not one of authenticity but of aes-thetic—one of wearing art on our bodies. All the women who participated in the discussion are not easily perceived as originating in Indigenous cul-ture; most can afford the costly garments and do not hesitate to purchase and display them on their bodies or incorporate them as accents in their homes.

In my view, the San Antonio exhibit evidenced a type of cultural imperi-alism. Consumerism and money merged to support the development of an artist, art designer, and gallery owner who lives outside of San Antonio. Kathy Sosa—who has a track record of rendering Mexican art in her own image, without fully acknowledging the creators of the original art or the cultural practice she emulates—was center stage. My response to the ex-hibit, which until now has remained private, was to write a poem dedi-cated to the huipil, a calavera: a type of poem that critiques sociocultural practices that may aggrieve others. That poem is the narrative I carry about huipiles.

CALAVERA A LOS HUIPILES
Otra vez la burra al maíz
Teaching us del mestizaje
Le dijo un Chicano al otro
Al fisgar la exhibición

Según lo habían chismorreado
Son de la millonaria Sosa
Que rescata la cultura
De nuestras mismitas manos.

If my memory don't fail me
Eso fue en el dos mil siete
En YouTube ya la enseñaron
Con sus huipiles pintados

Muy satisfecha quedó
Y sin importarle un comino
Explota ella el patrimonio
De artesanas y bordadoras

Ignora o no quiere saber
Que las prendas dibujadas

Hechas por humildes manos
Apenas dan pa' comer.
JOSIE MÉNDEZ-NEGRETE

Both Sosa and I have traveled the huipil path. However, access to the same garments is prohibitive for me, as we do not fall into the same socioeconomic class or have the same racial ethnic background: she is a wealthy woman with a Euro-American background. While I wear the garment as a sign of solidarity and to display my Indigeneity, Sosa commodifies and profits from the works of women whose creative expressions are at risk of extinction. I recognize that she provides a venue for displaying the work of weavers and textile makers of Mexico, but as she does this, she is also appropriating and distorting the work of Indigenous women, making invisible those creators of art who barely eke out a living from their labor-intensive work.

Huipiles for Life

For me, the huipil has a nuanced meaning that goes beyond artistic representation. It has been a living, inspiring, and protective garment: it gives me freedom to be the person I am and allows me to reclaim an Indigenous historical legacy. It also gives me license to wear whatever color I desire, regardless of the season, for it is in the layering and dressing of the garment that I become my own creation. In a huipil I am forever comforted, as I honor generations of women who came before me and who inspire the creation of the garments I make.

As in the past, my aim is to continue designing huipiles and wear them when I perform readings or when invited to present my work, with a garment of my choice as it connects to the event. For example, for the reading of my book *Las hijas de Juan: Daughters Betrayed* in San Antonio in 2002, I made a huipil from Guatemalan silk, which I adorned with crocheted borders of emerald green to complement one of the four main colors in the textile—yellow, green, black, and gray. The textile linked me to my Indigenous roots, and the garment allowed me to dress in a color (yellow) that called attention to my message. Tías Hermelinda and Chenda taught me "El color amarillo significa sabiduría, inteligencia y el éxito" ("Yellow is the color of wisdom, intelligence, and success"). I wanted my presentation to get its message across and to honor the wisdom of women.

Sadly, because of our immigration status, returning to our aunts was not feasible, even after Felisa and I were given permits to remain in the United States; it was a restrictive document that did not allow us to travel beyond its borders. Felisa and I finally visited Tía Hermelinda in 1991. Our beloved aunt passed away March 31, 2005, the same day Selena Quintanilla-Perez was murdered by Yolanda Saldívar. We visited Tía Herme only once, and never saw Tía Chenda again; she died a few years after we left for the United States as children.

In my presentations, but also in what I wear, I carry the knowledge of sage ancestors, including my great-aunts who taught me the skills to create something from nothing and to value domestic practices to create cultural artifacts that speak to our experience and link us to our histories. In the accessories I wear—rebozos, earrings, bracelets, and necklaces—I carry a remembrance of these women and the gifts they gave me. I honor every one of them who has been part of my formation, as I make visible the creativity of my people.

Notes

Without the amazing encouragement and support of our students Sandra D. Garza, Jennifer Ojeda, and Jesus Jaime-Diaz, who continue to inspire us, this essay would have not been completed. To Aída Hurtado and Norma E. Cantú, who continue to create venues in which we can express our ideas, thank you.

1. A huipil is the top garment of a two-piece embroidered and embellished traditional garment crafted and worn by Indigenous women in Mexico and Central America.

2. According to Holly Barnet-Sanchez, this term was coined by Tomás Ybarra-Frausto, who defined it as "the aesthetic sensibility of los de abajo, of the underdog," as well as a "visceral response to lived reality that began as a strategy of survival among working-class Mexicans and Mexican Americans and was later transformed into an overarching attitude expressed in much Chicano/a activist art-making" (92). Furthermore, it was defined as an "attitude rooted in resourcefulness and adaptability, yet mindful of stance and style," as stated in "Rasquachismo, a Chicano Sensibility," which was published in *Chicano Art: Resistance and Affirmation* (Richard et al.). This cultural practice I learned from my great-aunts, who served as interim mothers in the absence of Amá, who had immigrated to Chicago to be with her husband.

3. Amalia Mesa-Bains uses the term *domesticana* to refer to a sort of Chicana rasquache, the process of creating culture from discards or giving alternative uses to others' discards, that affirms culture and domestic expression as a way to value contributions by Chicanas. Jennifer Gonzáles, quoting Mesa-Bains, states that domesticana is "the affirmation of cultural domestic values in combination with an emancipation from traditional feminine roles" (86); furthermore, Mesa-Bains writes that "domesticana characterizes the activity of taking the space of the feminine and

transforming its isolation into a powerful representation of lived experience" (qtd. in González p. 5), as it adds value to domestic work by bringing it to public viewing.

4. Most recently San Jose State University documented this designation with its "Guide to the South Bay Second Wave Feminist Oral History Project," which covers the years 2006–2010. During this era we saw increased political involvement, the election of Janet Gray Hayes as mayor of the city of San José, pop. 500,000, and stories in *Time, People,* and *U.S. News and World Report.* With an emphasis on equal rights and equal participation, these women opened up the political process, as well as advanced the Equal Rights Amendment. See the project description at scholar-works.sjsu.edu.

Works Cited

Anzaldúa, Gloria E. *Borderlands/La Frontera: The New Mestiza*, 3rd ed., Aunt Lute Books, 2007.

Barnet-Sanchez, Holly. "Tomás Ybarra-Frausto and Amalia Mesa-Bains: A Critical Discourse from Within." *Art Journal*, vol. 64, no. 4, 2005, pp. 91–93.

Blackwell, Maylei. *¡Chicana Power! Contested Histories of Feminism in the Chicano Movement.* U of Texas P, 2011.

Frida. Directed by Julie Taymor, performances by Salma Hayek, Alfred Molina, and Antonio Banderas, Miramax, 2002.

Gaspar de Alba, Alicia. *Chicano Art: Cultural Politics and the CARA Exhibition—Inside Outside the Master's House.* U of Texas P, 1997.

González, Bárbara Renaud. "This Is the Huipil You Won't See at the Museo Alameda's 'Huipiles: A Celebration.'" *Las True Stories of San Antonio: Stories, Journalism, Confessions,* www.barbararenaud.blogspot.com. Accessed 22 Sept. 2007.

González, Jennifer A. "Rhetoric of the Object: Material Memory and the Artwork of Amalia Mesa-Bains." *Visual Anthropology Review,* vol. 9, no. 1, 1993, pp. 82–91.

Griswold del Castillo, Richard, editor. *Chicano Art: Resistance and Affirmation.* U of Arizona P, 1991.

Méndez-Negrete, Josie. "Calavera a los Huipiles." N.p., 2012.

———. *Las hijas de Juan: Daughters Betrayed.* Duke UP, 2002.

Mesa-Bains, Amalia. "Domesticana: The Sensibility of Chicana Rasquache." *Aztlán: A Journal of Chicano Studies,* vol. 24, no. 2, Fall 1999, pp. 157–167.

Noriega, Cristina Sosa. *Dialogue & Culture: US-Mex Relations.* MATT, www.matt.org /english/editorial/395_new_documentary_explores_the_modern_women_who _wear_huipiles.htm. Accessed 15 July 2007.

Raging Bull. Directed by Martin Scorsese, performances by Robert De Niro, Cathy Moriarty, and Joe Pesci, United Artists, 1980.

Riojas Clark, Ellen. "Historical Essay." *Huipiles,* huipiles.org. Accessed Oct. 2012.

Ruiz, Vicki L. *From Out of the Shadows: Mexican Women in Twentieth-Century America.* Oxford UP, 2008.

CHAPTER 3

"Rebozos, huipiles, y ¿Qué?": Chicana Self-Fashioning in the Academy

MICAELA DÍAZ-SÁNCHEZ

Several years ago I was asked to be a bridesmaid in the wedding of a good friend with whom I had navigated the hallways of an Ivy League college as a woman of Color in the late 1990s. My friend is a Native Alaskan woman — Iñupiaq from the circum-Arctic Inuit people to be exact — and she was marrying a man from two Indigenous communities in New Mexico. The ceremony took place in a picturesque, iconographic, and sacred site in a northern New Mexican pueblo. The other bridesmaids included an Iñupiaq woman, a Navajo woman, and a Native Hawaiian woman. When I inquired about what I should wear, she replied, "Micaela, just wear your traditional garb." As a third-generation Chicana born in Albuquerque, New Mexico, and raised in San Antonio, Texas, the notion of what constitutes "traditional garb" was an ambiguous mandate informed by hemispheric colonial legacies. Yet her request operated as an opportunity to critically examine my own meXicana self-fashioning practices.

This chapter focuses on the self-fashioning practices of Chicanas[1] in the academy, particularly cis-gendered women who wear huipiles, rebozos, Indigenous-centric clothing, and other culturally specific adornments in professional contexts.[2] Employing performance as the critical lens, I interrogate the making of social and political identities by Chicana professors who perform a particular body politic that operates as both culturally specific and politically subversive while navigating academic institutions across disciplinary and geographic contexts. In attending to these self-fashioning practices, I engage Ramón Rivera-Servera's theorization of performance functioning as both "a social situation and a set of expressive techniques" (32). In *Performing Queer Latinidad: Dance, Sexuality, and Politics*, Rivera-Servera approaches performance as "a social situation always already embedded in the political and a technology for achieving political interventions" (32). This analytic of performance as a "series of expressive techniques" propels my argument that when Chicana profesoras wear Indigenous clothing and jewelry, they make political interventions in multiple institutional settings. The deployment of performance as a theoretical framework is particularly effective in illuminating how these self-fashioning practices make legible complex constructions of social and political identities as we navigate systems of power and knowledge production.

Having informally theorized about the political and semiotic significance of these aesthetic practices during the decades that I myself have navigated multiple academic institutions while wearing such clothing and jewelry, this chapter presents an opportunity to formally conceptualize how these practices operate. I asked Chicana-identified professors about their decisions to wear clothing and accessories that are culturally specific in the classroom and in other professional settings, particularly dress rooted in hemispheric Indigenous aesthetic traditions (e.g., huipiles, rebozos, beaded earrings, etc.). This research, ethnographic in its approach, is propelled by three major inquiries: How do these embodied practices operate in relation to pedagogical methodologies? How do they operate in relation to individual research projects? And how do they operate in professional settings outside the classroom (e.g., departmental meetings and meetings with administrators)? The examination of their responses illuminates broader analytic frameworks about the political directives enacted by wearing such clothing in institutional settings and the implications of those practices. The critical reflections are in direct conversation with this anthology's mandate to explore "self-adornment, identity constructions, and political self-presentations" in relation to a repertoire of MeXicana fashions.

In their introduction to *Chicana Traditions: Continuity and Change*, the first anthology dedicated to Chicana expressive culture, Norma E. Cantú and Olga Nájera-Ramírez resist static ways of understanding what constitutes "tradition" and instead address "the ever-evolving landscape of our field of study, for as we can see in many of these essays, the traditional production has changed and continues to change even as it shapes the ways that Chicanas experience their lives" (6). It is critical to interrogate the ways that these fields of study inform everyday lived experiences, thus constantly shifting the intellectual landscapes on which we theorize and create. In turn, this "ever-evolving" scholarly terrain propels mandates for collective knowledge-making processes that respond to political exigencies. Employing Emma Pérez's foundational theoretical framework of the "decolonial imaginary," which operates as a "theoretical tool for uncovering the hidden voices of Chicanas that have been relegated to silences, to passivity, to that third space where agency is enacted through third space feminism" (xvi), I interrogate how self-fashioning practices are rooted in decolonializing paradigms.

While acknowledging that fashion operates as a profoundly personal articulation of identity, I theorize about this culturally specific self-adornment as a practice rooted in a collective consciousness among self-identified Chicanas in the academy (of which there are very few). In this sense these embodied practices operate as an expression of what Aída Hurtado articulates as a "social identity" linking personal self-fashioning with broader communitarian affiliations. Hurtado conceptualizes social identity as an aspect of "the knowledge of being part of social categories and groups, together with the value and emotional significance attached to those group formations" (112). Hurtado asserts that this social identity operates as an aspect of "an individual's group affiliations and emotional attachments to those group memberships" (114). While the profesoras featured in this chapter teach at different institutions, they share the sentiment of being "the only one" or "one of few" dressed in "traditional" garb at their institution while belonging to a larger community of Chicana academics across the country.

In tracing prominent Chicana fashion trends, scholars have situated these practices in discourses of political resistance operating at particular historical moments. Most prominently, Catherine S. Ramírez examines the pachuco/pachuca and zoot culture of the 1940s as an articulation of "politicization of Mexican Americans . . . in the creation of an oppositional, rather than assimilationist, Chicano cultural identity" (1). She makes a feminist intervention by focusing on pachucas as figures who deviated from the "confines of domesticity" (13). The increased presence of Mexican American women in the public sphere due to the labor demands of World War II fueled an escalation in the policing of particular racialized and gendered bodies. Ellie Hernández traces Chicana/o fashion trends through iconographic characters, beginning with the trope of "la señorita" and ending with what she identifies as "revolutionary chic."[3] Hernández asserts that throughout the twentieth century Chicanas "have exhibited an inventiveness of style, a sense of community, cultural defiance, and definitive political standpoint against traditionalism and conventional attire" (119). What constitutes "traditional" in the self-fashioning and self-adornment of the professors profiled in this chapter becomes critical given that they teach material rooted in analytical ethnic and gender studies; as these fields are under attack at this particular historical moment, the professors' dress practices are acts of political intervention. These political self-representational articulations operate as affirmations of a particular body politic that emblematizes the political as personal and vice versa.

Propelled by these personal and political mandates, I conceptualize this chapter according to five thematic frameworks that emerge from ethnographic analysis: "'I Know Where It Comes From': The Politics of Location"; "'Honoring the Antepasadas': Invocations of Indigeneity"; "'The Classroom as a Borderlands': Pedagogical Implications"; "'Por el amor de Frida': Embodied Iconographies"; and "'They Function Like Armor': Chicana/Indígena Adornment in Institutional Settings."

As previously stated, performance operates as a foundational methodological framework exploration of how lived experiences shape Chicana self-fashioning practices in academic settings. This chapter does not look at these items of clothing and jewelry as objects of study. For example, one approach to this study might be a close reading of specific patterns of huipiles, given the complex symbolism and regionally specific weaving traditions of hemispheric Indigenous communities.[4] Instead this chapter examines self-adornment as performance, a choreography enacted by Chicana academics in the navigation of academic institutions, a repertoire of embodied articulations. I turn to musicological scholarship for an analytic model of performance to conceptualize the self-fashioning practices among the women in this study; their carefully crafted steps register as legible to some and illegible to others. The musical structure of "call and response," in particular, offers a frame with which to theorize descriptive practices of personal aesthetic expression as choreographic iterations. As women of Color in the academy, these profesoras face a series of complex institutional challenges, with their self-fashioning practices operating as embodied responses or, as Rivera-Servera states, "expressive techniques" (32). Anita González theorizes "call and response" as a series of movements between the dancers' feet on the tarima[5] that employ a "subtle use of syncopated rhythms to fill in and respond to musical breaks, and the use of gesture and body positioning to communicate beyond the actual dance steps" (57). The critical responses of these teachers/scholars/activists provide us with rich discursive material with which to weave an intersectional tapestry, an embodied performance of meXicana fashions.

"I Know Where It Comes From": The Politics of Location

The circulation of culturally specific clothing and jewelry is a foundational point of entry, particularly in the neoliberal economic relationship between Mexico and the United States. All of the professors included in this chapter teach at colleges and universities in the United States, and the acquisition of clothing and jewelry is imbricated in a complex system of exchanges across multiple borders framed by these neoliberal policies. Dr. Sandra Pacheco, an associate professor of interdisciplinary studies at the California Institute of Integral Studies in the Bay Area, states that transactions illuminate "the uncomfortable relationships between the impact of colonialism, globalization, and tourist-dependent economies," which operate as critical in her own self-fashioning practices.

Several of the professors noted the self-reflexive processes that expose the connection between the economic and cultural implications of donning meXicana clothing. Dr. Jennie Luna, an assistant professor of Chicana and Chicano studies at California State University, Channel Islands, states,

> I am thinking about what feelings it might evoke for an Indigenous woman who sees a Xicana wearing traditional clothing of her community. I also discuss this in class in the context of examining the maquiladora industry and thinking about where our clothes come from. I discuss that part of why I like wearing my huipil blouses is because I am conscious of where they come from and where the money is going.

Luna's comments expose a critical acknowledgment of privilege in purchasing this clothing while simultaneously offering a pedagogical opportunity to address hemispheric Indigenous identities in a neoliberal context. Her statements also illuminate the contradictions of being able to purchase these items while teaching at a "first-world" college or university.

This manner of acquisition emerged as a central point of entry in the exploration of these self-fashioning practices. Pacheco states, "Most of my rebozos and huipiles are purchased from women's collectives in Mexico or small communities developing fair trade practices. The process holds energy in the material and in the construction." She goes on to clarify, "I only wear items that I have personal, cultural, or spiritual connection with that is tangible." Pacheco's research and personal spiritual practices enable her to cultivate close relationships with these communities in Mexico, thus maintaining equitable exchanges.

Echoing these sentiments, Dr. Lilliana Saldaña, an associate professor of bicultural-bilingual studies at the University of Texas at San Antonio, comments:

> The textiles that I have carefully preserved over the years are treasures and remind me that I can honor the culture and knowledge of my ancestors and continue to support the work of present-day artesanas and artesanos who continue to create these precious garments in the face of neoliberal policies that crush their way of making a living.

Saldaña illustrates the material reality that frames these exchanges, often informed by the impossibility of knowing the person who made the huipil or pair of earrings. Having worn this clothing and jewelry myself for many years, I can say that I have not always known the town of origin or even the state of origin of the purchased garments. These experiences signal a kind of privilege: the ability to travel back and forth between the United States and Mexico with a knowledge of the origins of these regionally specific items of self-adornment.

"Honoring the Antepasadas": Invocations of Indigeneity

The body of scholarship linking Chicana and Indígena identities elucidates frameworks with which to explore a breadth of embodied practices, with particular attention to personal articulations of spirituality.[6] These inter-subjective identities are also propelled by activist mandates for social justice in multiple geographical and institutional contexts, illustrating spaces in which the spiritual operates as political. In tracing the intersectional linkages between scholarship, spirituality, and activism as personal praxis, Norma Cantú states,

> My activism springs directly from my spiritual practice, since I am drawn to work on projects and to exercise certain tasks with a sense of mission. Knowing that I am here on this Earth reality for a purpose, knowing that my work in academia is intimately tied to my work on Earth allows me to live my life *con conciencia*, exercising *la facultad*, and doing work that matters. (215)

Cantú invokes the Anzaldúan theoretical framework of "la facultad" as a strategy with which to traverse the multiple realms of her labor. She enunciates this personal praxis as a testament to her work as an influential and prolific scholar/activist, but ultimately as a spiritual being with work to do on this planet. Enabled by her facultad, Cantú enacts these multiple elements of subjectivity necessary for transformative political and spiritual work inside and outside the academy.

Acknowledging the wearing of huipiles, rebozos, and jewelry as a spiritual embodiment of "the sacred" emerged in many of the professors' responses. Pacheco explicitly states, "What I wear serves as a mobile, fluid, and embodied altar." As Pacheco embodies a living altar, she performs a spiritual and political site that shifts according to the landscape. In Laura Pérez's discussion of "altar-installations" and "altar-inspired art," she writes that Chicana artists "articulate presently meaningful, hybrid forms of spirituality and spiritually conscious art making" (92). In this way, each of the profesoras interviewed for this chapter asserts herself as an altar-maker, with her body acting as decolonial topography on which to map multiple spiritual and political ideologies.

These individually embodied altars express spiritual and political systems of self-adornment that simultaneously enact feminist ideologies. Saldaña asserts that wearing huipiles facilitates

> a way of remaining connected to my Indigenous antepasadas [ancestors] on an everyday basis (esas mujeres indígenas campesinas who raised families on their own . . . solitas), as a way of redefining non-Western notions of femininity in a world that constantly imposes White, hetero-patriarchal, and middle-class ideals of femininity.

This self-representation illustrates a critical intervention linking hetero-patriarchal and colonial legacies enacted in contemporary gendered identities. She continues, "Wearing huipiles, rebozos, blusas, beaded necklaces with sacred stones, and other handmade jewelry is a way of honoring the sacred and labor intensive textile making techniques that are thousands of years old." Saldaña's comments resonate with what has been a personal assertion driving central inquiries in this study: that the clothing and jewelry circulate as energized matter. With origins predating Spanish colonization, these items are sacred on multiple levels, from the iconography woven into the textiles to the process of weaving itself.[7]

The transformative potential of this clothing elucidates a spiritual register to the self-fashioning practices discussed in this chapter. Propelled by Anzaldúa's positing of "spiritual mestizaje" as a methodology, Theresa Delgadillo expands upon this approach, referring to "the transformative renewal of one's relationship to the sacred through a radical and sustained multimodal and self-reflexive critique of oppression in all its manifestations and a creative and engaged participation in shaping life that honors the sacred" (1). Each huipil and necklace carries with it a genealogy traversing hemispheric routes of remembrance, and as these profesoras wear their revered pieces, they transform the spaces that they traverse.

Yolanda Broyles-González critically acknowledges Indigenous identities in relation to the lived experiences of Chicanas. She writes,

> The institutions within which we labor—be they church, university, school, hospital, beauty salon, or home—are all linked to the political economic order of the society that devalues native women. However, as native women, Chicanas are not lacking in a rich legacy of sociospiritual practices and affirmations in our image. These sustaining practices, and the class-, gender-, race, and region-based social visions they embody, continually prefigure and inspirit a different order of things, domains of freedom, equality, dignity and self-affirmation. (130)

Broyles-González links these "sociospiritual" practices with those that sustain Chicanas as they navigate the multiple contexts in which they labor. And in the embodiment of these self-fashioning practices, the profesoras create decolonial topographies on which to interrogate these systems of power. Professor María Figueroa-Chacón, who teaches English, literature and humanities at MiraCosta College in San Diego County, states, "Part of my conscious and unconscious inclinations are to wear huipiles, rebozos, bright beaded earrings as praxis. As living Chicana theory . . . to colorize, decolonize and breathe." These "inclinations" echo what Rivera-Servera deploys as "expressive techniques." Figueroa-Chacón enacts this personal praxis as a collective decolonizing process as an educator. She continues,

> When wearing the culturally specific clothing, I feel like it also validates them (Chicanx and Latinx students) and their families, especially their mothers. Some students will strike up conversations during or after class to share how in their home pueblos the women wear these or how their mothers wear these during specific fiestas. Then the conversation leads into Indigenous identity often, Indigenous language, traditions among other things. Other students of color will comment on their traditional wear as well (Samoan for example). We begin to make connections over our indigeneity.

Figueroa-Chacón asserts the embodiment of this praxis not solely as a personal set of self-fashioning practices, but as one that facilitates a discussion of global Indigenous identities in the classroom.

The concept of nepantla, which is prominently articulated in the theoretical offerings of Gloria Anzaldúa, is central to many Chicana feminist pedagogical mandates inside and outside of the classroom. In Anzaldúa's conceptualizations of borderlands consciousness, nepantla functions as an "in-between" space, a third space. This interstitial site facilitates knowledge-making processes foundational to Chicana feminist methodologies. Figueroa-Chacón declares,

> There is just so much power in the symbol of the huipil. . . . What does it say when one wears an intricately woven huipil or silky rebozo with jeans and boots? It's that bicultural, constant state of negotiation as Xicana Indígenas. We are not only nepantla in the flesh, but creating and wearing nepantla outfits as well.

Figueroa-Chacón performs an enunciation of borderlands consciousness with the intricate pairing of a huipil with a pair of jeans. This embodiment of nepantla functions as an extension of borderlands consciousness into pedagogical practices.

"The Classroom as Borderlands": Pedagogical Implications

A driving inquiry for this chapter was an exploration of how self-fashioning practices operate in relation to pedagogical methodologies. Several of the profesoras enunciated direct correlations between what they wear and the political mandates of the material they teach. Figueroa-Chacón comments, "It's interesting. Sometimes I consciously choose the huipil according to the audience of students, or the course context of the day." She said that in one particular classroom scenario,

> I was teaching Gaspar de Alba's novel *Desert Blood*, which examines the Femicides of Juarez through the mystery novel genre. It does many other things too. . . . Anyhow, I have a black huipil that has pink embroidered letters saying "Ni una más" under a pink cross. Pink and black, but more specifically the pink crosses against a black background, have been the visual symbol for educating and consciousness-raising around this issue. So I wore this huipil, which also had other traditional symbols embroidered along the neck and sleeves, on one of the days we were discussing the novel. Without bringing attention to the huipil (yet), one young Chicana student looks at me and then at her friend, and says, "Mira, she's wearing a pink cross on her blouse. It's about the novel we're reading." This was such a memorable

moment for me as a great teaching moment. My dress, the huipil, became a teaching tool. So I seized the opportunity to address her comment with her and the larger class. I shared the story of the huipil with them, where I purchased it and that it had been made by the Zapatista women's collective in Chiapas who were in solidarity with mujeres and madres de Juarez. We talked about the visual power of the pink crosses.

Figueroa-Chacón's self-fashioning practices function as an explicit peda-gogical process of hemispheric consciousness-building among her stu-dents. As is the case with many of the other profesoras, Figueroa-Chacón illustrates the political mandate and responsibility of wearing this cloth-ing beyond systems of self-adornment.

These pedagogical mandates are rooted in ideological approaches to the labor of teaching and, by extension, the spaces in which we facilitate knowledge production as Chicana professors. Pacheco writes,

> The space I create in my classroom also reflects my work. There is always a central class altar that each student is invited to contribute to, and when I have challenging groups, I invite them to join me on the rooftop garden to be smudged prior to the start of the weekend intensive.

Pacheco connects her personal research of spiritual practices with Indige-nous Mexican communities with her work as a profesora in northern Cali-fornia. She configures her classroom spaces into a decolonizing landscape in which to honor the multiple experiences of her students.

"Por el amor de Frida": Iconographic Invocations and Aesthetics

The discussion of iconographic figures in Chicana and Mexicana popular culture offers an opportunity to theorize about personal self-adorning practices rooted in transnational aesthetics. In Laura Pérez's critical theo-rizing of art practices by Chicanas across genres, she writes, "Dressing and other forms of decorating the body (cosmetics and other forms of body painting, tattooing, piercing, and scarification) are cultural practices that produce, reproduce, interrupt, or hybridize (and thus produce new) cul-tural values" (50). While Pérez focuses on the employment and representa-tion of dress in Chicana art practices, I extend her work, applying it to the daily self-fashioning practices of the Chicana professors in this chapter.

One of the most prominent figures reproduced in these Chicana/Mexicana transnational aesthetic expressions is Frida Kahlo. Dr. Anita Revilla, an associate professor of gender and sexuality studies at the University of Nevada, Las Vegas, is a self-proclaimed "Frida lover." She states,

> Her image and intensity resonated with my reality in a way that no other piece of art or person has done. Her thick eyebrows and hairy upper lip looked like mine. Her pride, resilience and pain felt like mine. I yearned for the pride she exhibited in her Mexicana and Indigenous identity. As a multi-generation Tejana, I was not taught to be proud of my Mexicanness or my brownness.

Kahlo's image offers a liberatory reclamation of simultaneous beauty and pain. Revilla continues,

> I don't go two consecutive days without wearing something that has Frida on it. I have Frida earrings, t-shirts, sweaters, socks, a phone case, wallet, and purse. In my house, I have a wall adorned by images and paintings of Frida. In my bedroom, I have a huge airbrushed painting of her facing my bed, and I wake up every morning to her intense gaze.

Through Kahlo's image, Revilla has cultivated and asserts a self-representational practice rooted in radical politics. Kahlo's identity as "an activist, a socialist, a queer, bisexual woman" propels Revilla's aesthetic practices in both public and private spheres. While the mass reproduction of Kahlo on everything from T-shirts to placemats is imbricated in systems of cultural appropriation, I argue that profesoras like Revilla resist this commodification and instead employ Kahlo's image with a more personal mandate situated in Chicana political consciousness and intersectional identities.

"They Function Like Armor": Chicana/Indígena Adornment in Institutional Settings

In recent years there has been a growing body of scholarship focusing on the institutional racism facing women of Color in the academy.[8] In this final section I briefly focus on the ways that the wearing of huipiles, rebozos, and jewelry function as practices of resistance and political intervention in academic settings. These practices are not only aesthetic choices but also operate as politically charged performances in an institutional space that is still largely white, male, middle-class, and hetero-patriarchal. The title of this section is a direct quote from Figueroa-Chacón, who states,

> My huipiles and rebozos are like a regalia when I go into professional meet-ings and in my context, mostly made up of white middle-aged women.
> I often pray when I go into meetings for protection and to speak my truth if I need to speak — my prayer summons my ancestors, my abuelitas who are the original huipil and rebozo-wearing women. So they function like armor.

In addition to operating as protective garments in these institutional spaces, wearing this clothing facilitates the embodied practice of claiming space. Saldaña echoes this reclamation of space: "Every single day when I wake up, I make the intentional and politically conscious decision to self-fashion as a way of creative resistance." This creative resistance demon-strates a powerful embodied intervention in academic spaces in which women of Color occupy the paradoxical position of being simultaneously invisible and hypervisible. Figueroa-Chacón wears this clothing to "stand out, make a statement and be seen in a professional setting that will often want to make me invisible and silent, non-existent." She says, "The rebozo es como el ombligo, it's what connects you to yourself and to the life force . . . when we need to feel protected during a meeting or even in the class-room setting."[9] Figueroa-Chacón powerfully connects ancient hemispheric cosmological frameworks with contemporary strategies for protecting oneself while navigating these institutional spaces, rooting these practices in the feminine and matriarchal.

It is critical to interrogate the wearing of self-fashioned clothing in re-lation to the embodied labor of teaching in these institutions that strate-gically invoke our presence at particular moments. Revilla states:

> As a first generation academic (college student), queer muxer, from a working-class Tejana home, I realize that many spaces in higher education are not inhabited by people like me — in fact, these institutions were not intended for people like me. With this knowledge, it's important for me to claim my space, remind people of my distinct reality and origin, and teach people about my political alignment with a radical vision for social justice, all while trying to be my most authentic self. I believe that my clothing and jewelry says this as loudly as my words and actions.

For Revilla, wearing her clothing and jewelry functions as an expressive technique deployed as an embodied intervention in predominately white and hetero-normative institutions that have historically rendered her invisible—a radical claiming of space.

As these profesoras negotiate systems of professional promotion, these self-fashioning practices shift. Pacheco, who was promoted to an advanced administrative position, chose to continue wearing culturally specific clothing as an act of defiance. She states:

> The context simply did not lend itself to anything but "professional" attire. Nonetheless, I was inclined to wear my studded cowboy boots and silver turquoise jewelry with my suits, a very intentional subversive statement to being told I needed to dress more professionally within the first few months of my employment. The cowboy boots were a nod to my Juarez and El Paso family ties where custom boots made by a family in Juarez were easy to come by, even for lower income families. Y pues, a Chicana wearing boots is also a "don't fuck with me" energy.

Resonating with Revilla's earlier statement, Pacheco's performance of defiance is about the claiming of space in multiple institutional contexts. Luna asserts a similar strategic practice: "I make sure that every day I have something that explicitly claims space . . . if not a huipil, then earrings or some kind of jewelry or rebozo. It has very much become part of my identity and style." She adds, "Even in all my job interviews . . . I would wear a huipil blouse with my suit jacket or a broach of an Indigenous symbol. I wanted to be very clear about my identity, where I stand and who I am." Of course, a consequence of these practices is the reaction of colleagues who fetishize this clothing and jewelry; several of the profesoras mentioned invocations of words like "costume" and "exotic" by colleagues within their institutions, a reaction that I have also experienced.[10] Despite these occasional untoward comments, the reflections of the profesoras illustrate a powerfully complex repertoire of expressive techniques that operate strategically according to their personal, pedagogical, aesthetic, and political directives.

Conclusion: The Choreography of MeXicana Self-Adornment in the Academy

In closing, I return to musicological scholarship as a point of analysis, positing the self-fashioning practices of the women in this study as enacting a choreography that enables them to navigate multiple institutional stages. The academic institutions in which we labor are fraught with colonial legacies of racism, sexism, homophobia, and classism; thus, navigating these spaces requires a kind of syncopation, a series of movements that challenge institutional rhythmic structures. In our work we make critical interventions in building programs and departments, conceptualizing leading-edge research projects, creating innovative curriculum, and advocating for underrepresented students, faculty, and administrators. As we mobilize for structural transformation, we adorn ourselves with carefully crafted clothing and jewelry representative of ancient and hemispheric histories. With the donning of intricately woven huipiles, handmade beaded earrings, and brightly colored rebozos, we articulate a cadence that is central to our interventions in the academy, defiantly marking syncopated steps essential to our survival and success in this profession.

Notes

1. I recognize the multiplicity of gendered identities articulated by spellings like "Chican@" and "Chicanx" as a critical intervention in discourses of gender binaries. In the context of this chapter I am discussing the self-fashioning practices of Chicanas who identify as cis-female.

2. In recognizing the multiple genders that exist outside of a male/female gender binary, *cis-gendered* refers to a person who performs an expression of traits associated with the gender they were assigned at birth.

3. Hernández continues, "Chicana/o fashion codes, frequently marked by social alienation, delinquency, criminality, romantic hyperbole, historical pastiche, hypersexuality, and cosmopolitan chic, maintain the community's oppositional stance and retain a measure of political significance in the image production of the community" (110).

4. In her essay on huipiles, Rebecca Nelson Jacobs writes,

Seemingly subtle characteristics of the dress, ranging from the color scheme or motifs within the cloth to the garment shape or wrapping technique, can signal the wearer's ethnicity, geographic origin, marital status, socioeconomic status, community organization membership, age cohort, ceremonial roles, and personality. (153)

5. A tarima is a wooden platform used by dancers to amplify percussive footwork in Son Jarocho, a musical tradition from southern Veracruz.

6. It is also critical to problematize this inherent correlation between Chicana articulations of Indigeneity and spirituality. See Sheila Marie Contreras, *Blood Lines*; and María Josefina Saldaña-Portillo, "Who's the Indian in Aztlán?"

7. For example, "the neck opening may represent the sun at the center of the four cardinal directions" (Jacobs 153).

8. *Presumed Incompetent: The Intersections of Race and Class for Women in Academia* (2012), edited by Gutiérrez y Muhs et al., offers a recent example of scholarship that critically examines the experiences of women of Color in the academy.

9. Figueroa-Chacón states,

> I come from a long line of rebozo wearing women so using them and always carrying one is a must for mostly practical reasons. I wrapped rebozos around my belly when pregnant to dance or when I felt I needed support (like a faja), I wrapped my children in them when they were babies and wore them on my body, and they were the best nursing blankets around. So, rebozos and I have a great relationship.

Figueroa-Chacón refers to the practice of wearing the rebozo as a girdle-like belt in the post-partum period referred to as the cuarentena, or the approximately 40-day period during which mothers focus entirely on caring for their infants and themselves.

10. I wear handwoven blusas and huipiles very often, and in the weeks leading up to Santa Barbara's annual "fiesta" (which is a very complicated celebration of a Spanish heritage [read: fantasy], complete with rodeos and reenactments of events leading to the colonization of the area), I have been approached consistently with statements like "Oh, you're getting in the mood for fiesta!" To which I steadfastly respond, "No, I wear blouses like this on a daily basis, thank you."

Works Cited

Anzaldúa, Gloria. *Borderlands/La Frontera: The New Mestiza*. Aunt Lute Books, 1987.

Broyles-González, Yolanda. "Indianizing Catholicism: Chicana/India/Mexicana Indigenous Spiritual Practices in Our Image." *Chicana Traditions: Continuity and Change*, edited by Norma E. Cantú and Olga Nájera-Ramírez, U of Illinois P, 2002.

Cantú, Norma E. "Living *La Vida Santa*: My Chicana Spirituality and Activist Scholarship." *Fleshing the Spirit: Spirituality and Activism in Chicana, Latina, and Indigenous Women's Lives*, edited by Elisa Facio and Irene Lara, U of Arizona P, 2014.

Cantú, Norma E., and Olga Nájera-Ramírez. Introduction. *Chicana Traditions: Continuity and Change*, edited by Norma E. Cantú and Olga Nájera-Ramírez, U of Illinois P, 2002.

Contreras, Sheila Marie. *Blood Lines: Myth, Indigenism, and Chicana/o Literature*. U of Texas P, 2008.

Delgadillo, Theresa. *Spiritual Mestizaje: Religion, Gender, Race, and Nation in Contemporary Chicana Narrative*. Duke UP, 2011.

Figueroa-Chacón, María. Personal correspondence, Feb. 2016.

González, Anita. *Jarocho's Soul: Cultural Identity and Afro-Mexican Dance*. UP of America, 2004.

Gutiérrez y Muhs, Gabriella, Yolanda Flores Niemann, Carmen G. González, and Angela Harris, editors. *Presumed Incompetent: The Intersections of Race and Class for Women in Academia*. Utah State UP, 2012.

Hernández, Ellie. *Postnationalism in Chicana/o Literature and Culture*. U of Texas P, 2009.

Hurtado, Aída. *Voicing Chicana Feminisms: Young Women Speak Out on Sexuality and Identity.* New York UP, 2003.

Jacobs, Rebecca Nelson. "Huipil." *Ethnic Dress in the United States: A Cultural Encyclopedia*, edited by Annette Lynch and Mitchell D. Strauss, Rowman & Littlefield, 2015.

Luna, Jennie. Personal correspondence. Feb. 2016.

Pacheco, Sandra. Personal correspondence. Feb. 2016.

Pérez, Emma. *The Decolonial Imaginary: Writing Chicanas into History.* Indiana UP, 1999.

Pérez, Laura. *Chicana Art: The Politics of Spiritual and Aesthetic Altarities.* Duke UP, 2007.

Ramírez, Catherine S. "Crimes of Passion: The Pachuca and Chicana Style Politics." *Meridians: Feminism, Race and Transnationalism*, vol. 2, no. 2, 2002, pp. 1–35.

Revilla, Anita. Personal correspondence. Feb. 2016.

Rivera-Servera, Ramón. *Performing Queer Latinidad: Dance, Sexuality, and Politics.* U of Michigan P, 2012.

Saldaña, Lilliana. Personal correspondence. Feb. 2016.

Saldaña-Portillo, María Josefina. "Who's the Indian in Aztlán? Re-writing Mestizaje, Indianism, and Chicanismo from the Lacadón." *The Latin American Subaltern Studies Reader*, edited by Ileana Rodríguez, Duke UP, 2001.

CHAPTER 4

Por la facha y por el traje, se conoce al personaje: Tales about Attire as Resistance and Performativity in a Chicana's Life Trajectory

GABRIELLA GUTIÉRREZ Y MUHS

I will never forget my friend Ariel, one of our students at Cabrillo College in the 1990s. His life trajectory had led him to believe that his attire had to become who he was performing in that period of his life: born and raised for ten years in Oaxaca as an Indigenous Zapotec, he then spent eight years living in Mexico City as a mestizo, followed by a few more years in Santa Cruz, California, as a Bay Area surfer—with the chameleonic capacity to adapt his dress to each particular milieu. For him, as is often the case with members of ethnic minority populations and immigrant communities, fashion represents a performance of self, the creation of an assimilationist or else an oppositional cultural ethnic identity, often in direct response to historical and social pressures of the time. In the history of Chican@s and Latin@s in the United States, clothing, appearance, and accessories have mattered immensely in the formation, maintenance, resistance, and (re)formulation of identity. As Ellie D. Hernández maintains in her analysis of the political significance of fashion choices among Chican@s, "The political use of clothes or fashion elicits a 'stylization' of ethnicity and captures Chicanas/os' subject formation across the vast historical and intersectional political moments of identity play" (109). For Chican@s, fashion has not only served as a shield that at different times has represented nationalism, identity, culture, and creativity, either separately or combined, but also a certain savoir faire and savoir vivre entrenched with wisdom that has come to represent the familial culture.[1]

In Mexican anthropologist Fernando Benítez's renowned work on Indigenous communities in Mexico, one of the Mexican campesinos (peasant-farmers) and hat-makers he interviewed in the 1960s asserts that "el sombrero es la sustancia de nosotros" ("The hat is our substance")

(417). For this man, his hat serves not only as a symbol of his essence—indeed, an essential element to his persona that physically protects and shelters him—but also an accessory that symbolically embodies him, and which allows him to earn subsistence by providing shade when toiling the land under the scorching sun.[2] In a similar fashion, traditional Mexican aesthetics, from clothing items to jewelry and other accessories, have become the palpable markers of identity for Chicanas and other Latinas. For many of us, these have become symbols of resistance, culture, and solidarity with our Othered subjectivities, which at times have simply characterized us, while at other times have further racialized us in the white gaze of dominant US society. In my own journey, my style of Mexican clothing, hair, shoes and other accoutrements have almost taken on a life of their own in regard to my own identity and my personal history as a Chicana/Latina living in the United States in the twenty-first century.

It is clear to me that I would not have felt compelled to dress in Mexican traditional dresses—colorful dresses sold mostly to tourists nowadays, or huipiles woven by Indigenous women from Oaxaca for themselves—had I not participated in school dances in a Mexican grammar school as a child.[3] The nuns who educated me in a parochial school in Mexico, on and off as my family migrated in and out of the United States to work in the fields, instilled the empowerment of ethnicity and culture in my life at a very early age.[4] My earliest memories of the distinctiveness of Mexican clothing are from those early years of watching folklórico dancing and observing the way women in my family would dress. Indeed, would I be so attached to the rebozo if it did not remind me of the shawl my grandmother wore every day of her ninety-six years of life? In 1959, the sociologist C. Wright Mills first wrote, "The sociological imagination enables us to grasp the connection between history and biography" (4). Sociologists agree unequivocally that what we do or don't do during those first ten years of life in regards to culture, identity, gender, and social class affects the rest of our lives.[5] Renato Rosaldo, in *Culture and Truth*, has clearly indicated that the Chican@ is one of the first Native informants who is able to go back and report on his/her life trajectory.

> When people play "ethnographers and natives," it is ever more difficult to predict who will put on the loincloth and who will pick up the pencil and paper. More people are doing both, and more so-called natives are among the ethnographer's readers. . . . One increasingly finds that Native American Tewas, South Asian Sinhalese, and Chicanos are among those who read and write ethnographies. (45)

In the spirit of a Native informant who witnessed an indoctrination of nationalism in Mexico and a rejection of Mexican ethnicity and cultural practices in the United States, I explore the evolution of my conscious-ness through attire by sharing autobiographical accounts and personal anecdotes.[6]

The 1970s and 1980s: The Soles of My Huaraches— A Journey to the Tour Eiffel and Back

Huaraches, Mexican leather sandals, are often associated with Mexico's underclass, having been worn by Indigenous and mestizo peasants throughout most of Mexico's colonial and recent history (DeMello). Still widely popular, huaraches represent an emblematic social class symbol in Mexican popular culture. In the following song, "Par de Huaraches," the Mexican indie reggae band La Celestina uses the huarache as a metaphor to denote class stratification in Mexican culture by juxtaposing the use of huaraches to that of high heels and rhetorically asking "What's there to class differences anyway?"

> ¿Pero qué es eso de las clases sociales?
> Prefieres una discoteca
> Y yo el reggae
> Tú prefieres un glamour allá en París
> Y yo en la playa mi libertad
> Prefieres un rico con carro
> Y yo un habano, en el bar
> Y ahora comprendo por que no somos iguales[7]

Consider also the popular Mexican song "Cuando los huaraches se acaban":

> Con los huaraches que traigo yo
> muchas veces te he venido a ver.
> Tú no me quieres corresponder
> y eso a mi dentro me va doler. . . .[8]

As a child living at times in rural México and the migrant fields of the US Southwest, I witnessed the importance of leather and rubber-soled huaraches, the latter still worn by children, especially girls, whose parents cannot afford to buy or make the leather ones. I was one of them. We were proud that, like cars, we got to wear tires under our sandals. My mother would always say that I was "a fire"—"Eres una lumbre"—and when she could, she would buy me huaraches with tire soles because all my other shoes would wear out so quickly. In the 1960s and 1970s, especially for those who were part of the Chican@ Movement, wearing huaraches was a sign of resistance and affirmation of one's culture as well as a statement about social class, especially among those who attended university. These intellectual rebels, as one might call them, wore Mexican clothing (rebozos, embroidered blouses, ponchos, huaraches, and huipil dresses), dressed up for Cinco de Mayo, and danced folklórico. It is widely known that Cinco de Mayo has become a symbolic holiday for Chicanos and that it is celebrated much more and with much more significance in the United States than in México. This holiday celebrates the underdog Mexicans winning a battle with the highly trained French army in a major war. Initially it was a celebration of the Mexican Indigenous people preventing the French Napoleonic armies from fully invading and controlling Mexico in the 1860s during the French invasion. But in Mexico it is not the major holiday; that is September 16, which celebrates the Grito de Dolores—independence from Spain. Nonetheless, Cinco de Mayo in the United States has become a metaphor for untrained and unimportant people winning a victory over sophisticated and rich foreigners.

During the 1970s the most common regional dances performed in universities and even high schools were from Jalisco and Veracruz. Jalisco is where mariachis and their outfits come from: the charro outfit for men and long, colorful, flowing skirts with ribbons of all colors stitched at the bottom for women. The Veracruz outfit, on the other hand, has a long, flowing white skirt that cools and refreshes the woman as she dances in the extreme heat and humidity of the region. María Herrera-Sobek wrote about this practice: "During the Chicano movement, wearing Indigenous types of clothing was popular; many Chicanas wore embroidered blouses and the men wore Mexican ponchos" (58). We were at that time making people conscious that we existed and were proud of our ancestry and our cultural icons, including the clothes made and worn by our ancestors. However, as Herrera-Sobek notes, the majority of Chican@s then and now wear typical American clothes. As the times evolved, many Chican@s did not feel it was necessary for them to affirm their culture through their clothing, and unless it is for a holiday such as Cinco de Mayo or Día de Muertos (Day of the Dead), college-educated Chican@s no longer wear traditional Mexican clothing as an everyday garment.

However, I was not an exception in feeling that rural Mexican sandals affirmed my identity and ethnicity. In *Cultural Suicide*, author Julián Camacho Segura shares a personal account of why he chose to wear huaraches as a young adult from California: "The truth is that I wore them because it made me feel more Mexican, at a moment in my life when I felt I did not belong. . . . At least in those huaraches I was somebody even if that somebody was still nobody" (42). Camacho Segura clearly understands that he was wearing huaraches as an ethnic signifier that empowered him and others like him.[9] Very much in the same vein as Mexican writer Octavio Paz states in *The Labyrinth of Solitude*, that pachucos in Los Angeles were wearing larger clothes in order to occupy more space because they were being rendered socially and politically invisible, Camacho Segura tells us how his huaraches came to possess a life of their own in his testimony.[10]

Huaraches are so entrenched in Mexican/Chican@ culture that they are essential for understanding Mexican Spanish. There are countless sayings, expressions, and even offensive language that use the word *huarache* or a variation of it. In Mexican parlance, "No dar paso sin huarache" is a very common saying with a cautionary message. It warns people to not go anywhere or do anything without being prepared or aware, anticipating a result. To be left "con el huarache en la mano" means to be left worried or preoccupied about something. Another popular saying is "Al que no ha usado huaraches, las correas le sacan sangre" ("If you've never worn huaraches, the straps will make [your feet] bleed"). This expression suggests that if someone has never experienced something, she can expect some sort of challenge that she will not be able to overcome without struggle. Because of the strong association of huaraches with the working poor of Mexico, especially Indigenous peasant-farmers, the expression also alludes to the rough life they live and how their bodies, particularly their feet, adapt to it and have grown both callous and calluses, something someone who wears other types of shoes does not understand. In that sense, it also seems to suggest that for those who have not lived a challenging life, perhaps in a more materially deprived sense, when faced with some type of difficulty, small as it may be, it becomes a rather tremendous challenge to them since they are unaccustomed to dealing with the harshness of life.[11]

Similarly, there are just as many songs that point out the Westernizing of Mexican clothing. In some, huaraches are taken off in favor of Western footwear such as closed shoes and high heels, describing the treacherous aspect of assimilation both in ethnic and class terms. A common trope is exemplified in the songs that open this section: a young person comes up against a socially stratified world and feels he has to give up his huaraches in order to fit in with a higher class—that is, assimilate into mainstream Mexican society—in order to be accepted by the object of his affection, presumably a middle- or upper-class woman.

Renowned Mexican anthropologist Guillermo Bonfil Batalla has long given a name to this particular phenomenon in Mexican colonial legacy, referring to it as "desindianización," or the process through which Mexicans have been historically and systematically stripped away, at times quite literally, from any signifier of Indigenous ethnic identity. The majority of the Mexican population has now come to internalize these oppressive social expectations by adopting a national (read as mestizo) identity regardless of their actual racial makeup. Hence, shoes, sandals, or the lack thereof tell stories not only of possession, poverty, style, fashion, and socioeconomic circumstances but also of cultural resistance.

Hernández, in analyzing fashion trends among Chican@s, asserts that "Read against the historical context of race and ethnic formation, fashion serves as a semiotic sign system that informs and disassembles normative race politics" (110). This is precisely why wearing huaraches during the Chican@ Movement was such an important political counter-cultural statement; it not only underscored Chican@s' pull toward claiming their Indigenous ancestry and strengthening their collective ethnic identity in the process but also aligned Chican@s with the working poor of Mexico and Latin America. As a result of the Mexican Revolution, whose cultural symbols finally hit the Southwest in the 1960s and 1970s, huaraches have been popular in dance troupes for children in folklórico groups, partly because they also represent a turn toward visual signs of Indigeneity. In California in the 1970s, Los Angeles gang members wore huaraches with colorful socks as a way of claiming their "mexicanismo," especially as other Central American groups of Latinos arrived in the United States. In urban areas, the huaraches became specific markers of Chicanism@.[12]

Another rural Mexican song attests to this phenomenon:

Llegaste el año pasado,
yo te vi llegar descalza
traías un morral cargado,
cuando venías de tu casa,
y ahora andas apantallando
y alborotando a la raza. . . .
Ya no escuchas el pitido de mi carro de camote,
tal vez algún individuo te pase pitando el coche,
ya cambiaste el morralito por una bolsa de broche. . . .[13]

This song is titled "La del Morral" ("The One Who Wears a Morral"). There are several versions of this song, although it is usually sung in the banda/

norteño and traditional mariachi style. In this case the woman subject of this song does not even have enough money or status to wear huaraches. She then is portrayed as climbing the social ladder, along the way exchanging her morral (a bag usually carried by Indigenous people) for a "bolsa de broche," a Western purse. I must also note that this song has clear sexist undertones, which become more evident later in the lyrics as it equates the woman protagonist's Westernization—that is, her mestizo assimilation, exemplified by her choice of wearing shoes and short skirt, carrying a purse, and sporting short hair instead of braids—with sexual decadence and promiscuity, tropes the male narrator uses to ridicule and discredit her, and to paint her as an "interesada" (gold digger).[14]

As a student at Occidental College in the early 1980s, I too carried a morral and wore a traditional Mexican dress when I studied abroad in France. Today I found my identity again, imbued in a Kodak snapshot of me at the Tour Eiffel: the "verde bandera" (bright green) embroidered Mexican dress I wore to Paris that defined me at age eighteen is a dress I would still wear today, a dress that erases eras and periods. The fashion it represents is timeless.[15] Looking at this photo, I am transported back to France: as a newly arrived US foreign exchange student with a Mexican sweater at hand, the Mexican (from Mexico) students at the Instituto de Estudios Mexicanos in Perpignan view my usual garb suspiciously. They question me, ask for my address in Mexico simply because to them there is something just not right about me. I give them my grandmother's address in the state of Durango, knowing that in nationalistic terms Mexican identity is ascribed geographically.

However, the interrogation continues. They ask for my genealogy: Am I a full Mexican, or is one of my parents a gringo? How did I get to France? Why do I wear Mexican clothes, an embroidered blouse, to the university? Yes, Mexican academics, particularly anthropologists, might wear one in the 1970s and 1980s, and lefty public intellectuals and performers, but not respectable middle- or upper-class Mexicans. Those who would most often wear such clothes, working-class or rural Mexicans, well, how could they possibly end up in France? It took me some time to understand that unapologetically wearing an embroidered Mexican dress in France was not only atypical of a Mexican teenager abroad who is there as part of an American university program but, in fact, made me suspect.

A full dress in bright green becomes the white elephant in the room; the huaraches do not help either, or the braids worn like Rosita Quintana in Mexico's Golden Age movies.[16] All these aesthetic markers of mexicanidad were considered unacceptable, and not how the Mexican study-abroad students wanted Mexicans to be perceived. But not only would I identify myself as Mexican, which I was, but I also called myself a Chicana, which I was too. And as such, I stood alone among all the other international students in the program. Looking back, I realize that my choice of clothes not only defined me as a Chicana but also, unknowingly at the time, affiliated me with the intellectual class of Latin Americans who emerged from the post-revolutionary movements. In the case of Mexico, they are often known as indigenistas: people proud of the country's Indigenous roots and mestizo identity, including Kahlo, novelist Rosario Castellanos, and writer and public intellectual Elena Poniatowska.[17]

During university holidays while I was a student abroad, I would take the train to Paris to make a little money. I danced folklórico to the rhythms of Veracruz and Jalisco outside the Georges Pompidou Centre with my partner, Manuel, guitar in hand. He was a Chicano I'd met at a youth hostel. We made enough money to remain in Paris, hailed by Parisians who loved Mexican folk songs such as "Jarabe Tapatío," "La Negra," "Canelo," and "La Bamba," and anything else that has stereotypically come to define Mexico abroad. Yet I was thrilled to be Mexican and to have taken my outfits with me, which allowed me to perform a dance that became the representation of an entire culture, served as my passport to reaffirming my cultural identity overseas, and allowed me to perform Mexico for nostalgic French people who had mostly experienced Mexico as part of the Golden Age of Mexican cinema.

Back in the United States, as I finished my studies at Occidental College, I was reminded of the fact that for every type of performance, there is a tradition and an evolution. In the early 1980s, while dancing with a folklórico group in Los Angeles, I met mexicanistas on campus, women for whom their middle-class life in Mexico had been central.[18] Two sisters who had come to the United States to attend college, and whose parents were middle-class professionals in Mexico, ran the folklórico group I danced with. These two women were quite condescending toward the mostly working-class Chican@s in the dance group and claimed that we did not know "enough" about Mexican folklore. This was extremely controversial and frustrating for us, American-born Mexicans who saw the traditional folklórico practices as ageless signifiers of mexicanidad for generations of American-born Mexicans. According to Chicano historians, in the 1930s and 1940s nationalist organizations had folklórico groups in most schools in the Southwest where the majority of the population were Chicanos. There were then three very different factions represented in our troupe, including the well-meaning professors who wanted to dance as a form of exercise but who were also interested in carrying out field research. In fact, one of these professors later wrote a book about folklórico based on participating in our Occidental College group. Nevertheless, we were largely a Chican@ group, working on formulating our individual and group identities, at times by comparing ourselves to the condescending mexicanas who did not yet know they had more in common with some Mexican Americans than they ever acknowledged.

After graduating from college in the mid-1980s, when I was working at a high school and dancing with the Mexicas troupe from the University of California, Santa Cruz, I found similar patterns in who was represented within the group. Dancing folklórico to me meant you establish that, first of all, you want to be Mexican, and not simply someone with a monolithic, almost homogenous, pan-Latino identity. Those in the group of dancers I performed with were usually working-class, except for the teachers who wanted to learn a dance or two to teach their students. This latter group was the exception to the rule in all the groups I danced with in the central coast region. It is generally the working-class children of rural Mexican parents who are interested in showing their mexicanidad in this manner of performance-based identity, or, as stated previously, it might have to do with experience, exposure, and socialization. People interested in learning more about Mexican culture were also adept at this type of hands-on representation of mexicanidad, song and dance, since this was a common practice in their place of origin. Today, no longer living in California and almost two decades later, I sometimes join the White Hawk dancers when I visit California, a group whose members used to be mostly First Nation peoples with a few Chican@s here and there in the 1980s. Currently the members are mostly Chican@s and Mexicans, but some are Central Americans and Indigenous Mexicans wearing feathers—writing identity, consciousness, and cultural practices with feathers without ink, the future of American identities. These shifting positionalities signal the fact that identity formation is gelatinous and porous regarding the element of Indigeneity. Because of the shifting positive attitudes toward Indigenous populations, White Hawk now can be a more inclusive group.

1990s: The Sisterhood of the Traveling Rebozos—Fashion as Hybridity and Questions of Cultural Appropriation

In the 1990s, as I was working toward earning my MA and PhD at Stanford University, I saw how mariachi jackets, popular among Mexican pop stars like Thalia and Paulina Rubio, made their way across TV screens. These customized jackets were, however, no revelation to the many Chican@s who had long adapted these items of clothing to form part of their fashion repertoire. Early in the decade, Tejana singer Selena had already transformed the Chican@/Mexican aesthetic imagination with her own creations. Perhaps most representative of her fashion style were her famous low-cut rhinestone bustiers, which she herself designed, partly inspired by the flashy attire worn by American pop icons such as Janet Jackson. Today another Mexican American singer, Lila Downs, has combined her Mixteca background, reflected in the embroidered modern miniskirts and fashion pumps she wears in her concerts, sometimes of her own creation. She has also adapted Indigenous garments to her individual fashion sense in the same tradition of Chicanas who have long combined and designed their outfits to create a hybrid or what I would call a mestiza fashion style.

Many Chicana public figures bank their image on some of the iconic items I have mentioned so far, such as huipiles, huaraches, Mexican boots, Mexican jewelry, and most iconic of them all, the rebozo.[19] Ellen McCracken discusses Sandra Cisneros's fashion style in her public appearances and how she deliberately works to construct a particular image of herself as the embodiment of the artistic persona she has created through her writing career. She offers the following detailed description of Cisneros in some of her most iconic pictures:

> Chicana writer Sandra Cisneros poses under a hot-pink parasol for a picture outside her purple house in San Antonio, wearing a flowered Mexican blouse, black short-shorts, and a red *rebozo*. For other appearances she wears Virgin of Guadalupe earrings, an ornate antique Oaxacan skirt, or a *china poblana* costume. She poses in a Mexican folkloric dress in a publicity photo for an appearance at the University of Southern California in 2002, and in a *rebozo* for the back cover of the first edition of *Woman Hollering Creek*. She remakes herself as a Chicana vamp on earlier book covers such as *My Wicked Wicked Ways* and *Loose Woman*, and for Angel Rodríguez-Díaz's "Portrait of Sandra Cisneros" housed in the Smithsonian Museum. In another photo, she lowers her *rebozo* to display her "Buddahlupe" tattoo on her upper arm. Her bright red truck has *zarape* seat covers and a license plate reading "AY TU." (167)

McCraken then goes on to assert that "these visual displays of ethnicity are part of a larger constellation of semiotic performance through which Cisneros deploys hundreds of ethnic signifiers to define and individualize herself" (167).

Prolific Mexican Jewish author and literary critic Ilan Stavans has long been openly critical of Cisneros—and not only of her work. He has at times harshly criticized her persona as well, using a different voice when speaking about her appearance. In *The Riddle of Cantinflas* he references Cisneros's fashion style as a way of further criticizing her. He contends that Cisneros's "cowboy boots, tiny miniskirts, idiosyncratic Mexican shawls, and hairbands inject the needed exoticism into her ethnic roots" (81). He then offers, almost in a tone of mockery, "She proudly parades around under a hybrid façade, part nativist Spanish and part anti-establishment American" (81). These statements seem to be aligned with Stavans's views on Frida Kahlo, herself a Chicana/Mexican feminist, cultural, and fashion icon:

> And yet, as part of the Europeanized minorities who have ruled Mexico since colonial times, Frida Kahlo is pure fake: a hybrid, a consummate actress. She mastered the art of adapting native costumes to her labyrinthine personality, and then resold the package to their contemporaries and the world at large. . . . [and] imitations of her idiosyncratic dresses and colorful hairbands, ubiquitously on sale, have become a corrosive fashion. (54)

Stavans's criticism seems to stem not from a concern with issues of cultural appropriation per se, particularly around the use of Mexican Indigenous attire by, in both cases, mestizas, but rather his focus is on the ways in which Mexican ethnic signifiers are allegedly used by Cisneros and Kahlo deliberately to give themselves a level of "exoticism," particularly before a Western/US audience.[20] Through his descriptions of Cisneros as a "hybrid façade" and Kahlo as "a pure fake: a hybrid"—and his further denunciation of what he calls a commercialized, ubiquitous "corrosive fashion"— Stavans seems to ascribe to a rather traditionalist view of Mexican fashion that renders it one-dimensional and belonging only to an ill-conceived past romanticization of Mexican Indigenous culture. For a literary critic, Stavans seems to forget that fashion style, like language style, is not static but rather is always evolving and available for multiple interpretations and uses—even contradictory ones. Fashion is, indeed, a hybrid; it is in continuous (re)formulation and stands as an expression of a community's identity and legacy, which often takes on different meanings depending on the social and historical context in which it (re)appears.

Moreover, long before Cisneros or Kahlo, the image of the Mexican woman as a wearer of rebozos and huipiles, Mexican dresses, blouses, and huaraches was inscribed into a narrative of what it meant to be Mexican.

Rebozos have just recently become popular attire for those who pull them out as a testament of their culture and ethnicity, as well as by those who have also worn them all along. In Mexico, rebozos have also reemerged as part of an important sign of culture, even among middle- and upper-class women, who now wear them to weddings and other social events. In the United States, Chicanas—and now even some queer Chicanos—wear rebozos as scarfs, belts, a necklace, or a shawl, but mostly as an accessory that constitutes a piece of their identity.

Among Chicana writers, scholars, activists, cultural workers, and public intellectuals, rebozos stand out as a deeply valued piece of clothing that many of them wear in public and which at times brings them together. In one of my interviews with writer Helena María Viramontes, she referred to her rebozo as a type of "security blanket" that cloaks her with confidence. She said, "It hides my body, it makes me feel like I'm encased in a shell like a turtle or I can hide myself in it or at the same time I feel it's a part of me" (qtd. in Gutiérrez y Muhs, *Communal Feminisms* 124). In the same interview, Viramontes shared how Cisneros, a close friend of hers, used to take orders for rebozos from their network of friends before her visits to Mexico since "she knew exactly where to go, what place, what colors and she was just good about buying them" (125). This last statement exemplifies how there is a whole subculture around wearing rebozos and an entire system to acquiring one, which is of great importance to Chicanas. I have written extensively about the meaning of the rebozo in Viramontes's and Cisneros's work, and in particular about the meaning of the rebozo to Chicanas in "Rebozos, Our Cultural Blankets."

The 2000s: Saris and Huipiles—A Chicana Academic in the Globalized Twenty-First Century and Questions of Authenticity

Today I wear saris for Mexican holidays, but for non-holidays I still wear huipiles. For me, being Mexican still means passing the time by listening to music and a threading pen, sewing, and crocheting, with a Mexican dress by my side. For my mother, being Mexican meant being a Guadalupana, dressed up at la Villa as a china poblana, and taking a picture next to an image of Our Lady of Guadalupe.[21]

Socorro Favela, my mother, was born in the 1920s, right after the Mexican Revolution. She was marked by a nationalistic period that imbued both her religious views and her cultural essence. Many Chicana authors, including Erlinda González Berry and Norma E. Cantú, and performers such as Lila Downs explore the use of traditional dress in their literary, artistic, and (in the case of Downs) musical presentations as a maker and marker of identity.

As a professor at Seattle University, which is predominantly white, I have experienced moments of agony when my clothes have made some of my students and colleagues uncomfortable. In one of my classes, a couple of students brought to my attention that one of the deans of a teaching program at the university once commented to them that neither I nor the other Latina in our building should be wearing Indigenous clothing, mainly rebozos, because we were not Indigenous. This occurred around the time I appeared in a photo wearing a huipil for an article I wrote about desprendimiento, which was published by the *National Catholic Reporter*. In this article I was attributing the beautiful act of giving something material to someone, simply because you felt that they would enjoy it more than you did, as a spiritual practice. *Desprendimiento* means "detachment"; nonetheless, I attribute this type of detachment to the Indigenous peoples of Oaxaca, Mexico, who believe that if you like something so much, you should own it, and they should detach themselves from it, thus the picture of me wearing the Indigenous huipil/dress that the woman I had just met gifted to me. According to this administrator, even though the other Latina professor and I might claim to be mestizas, we had no right to wear rebozos. Married to an upper-class Spanish woman and himself of Californio Spanish ancestry, he was making assumptions about our cultural roots and the ways we were manifesting our identity. In an attempt to counter his misinformation, I explained to my students that I grew up seeing my grandmother wear an ikat rebozo every day of her long life in northern Mexico, and that many Mexicans are, in fact, if not fully Indigenous, at least mestizos having emerged from a specific Indigenous group—in my family's case the Tepehuanos from the mountains of Durango—and that as a feminist I believe that no one has the right to tell me how I should dress. If we extrapolate a bit, we could make the case that Mexicans, like most Latin Americans, are culturally mestizos, even the European(ized) minorities. Chilean novelist and critic Jorge Guzmán suggests the controversy stems from the tendency to confuse racial content with cultural connotations; for him, all Latin Americans are cultural mestizos, and the creative energy behind the best artists emerges from this "mestizaje" (qtd. in Vicuña and Grossman xix). So Latin Americans and US Latinos may not necessarily be hybrid racially, but are definitely mestizos culturally.

Another incident serves as evidence of the politics of dress in a multiracial nation of immigrants. The week after the Twin Towers collapsed,

I was crossing the street from our university to the local IHOP to meet a colleague. On my way there, I was confronted by a truck driver who yelled at me from his high car seat, "Go back to where you came from!" Undoubtedly his verbal attack was prompted by my clothes. On that day I was wearing a Triqui huipil from Oaxaca, which marked me as an outsider to the hegemonic white establishment, a potential "illegal alien," and suddenly an imminent threat to national security. My clothes became more of a symbol of Otherness, an easy bull's-eye target amid the rise of anti-immigrant (read "anti-Mexican") hysteria in the United States, especially since 9/11. Yet perhaps it may have worked in my favor in those rare times when immigrants and Chican@s/Latin@s were also embarking on deconstructing my accessories as signifiers of a shared identity. Last year, when my teenage son had a court date, the presiding Chicano judge recognized me by my earrings from Guanajuato and my gauze scarf, which I wear as a diadem over my head. He and I alone in the entire courtroom of the Northwest knew who we really were, the "your honor" courtesy and the "Dr. G" from one of my students who now works as a lawyer, already too much formality among us, and he was especially kind to us, perhaps because — or so I like to think — he could read into my fashion style and know who I was, and where my son and I came from, all by looking at my earrings and my headband.

The Mexican dresses in my closet — my huipiles made by Rosalía and Mercedes, two Indigenous Triqui women I met in Oaxaca — await the pre-winter wash, because they will be worn in Seattle to keep me from the real cold. The women who made them, weaving at their looms or sitting on the floor outside a mercado, would perhaps be happy to know that their creations are still being worn in another country, and admired, and that they still are the banner of both owners and producers. From pre-Columbian times when both the Maya and Aztecs had a goddess of textiles and crafts — Ixel and Xochiquetzal, respectively — to the present time, weaving has been an intrinsic part of Mexican culture and civilization.

Among Indigenous women, particularly in south-central Mexico and Central America, the patterns and colors they weave into their huipiles and rebozos represent their ethnic affiliation and place of origin, which can then be deciphered and interpreted by other Indigenous people. Virginia Tilley, in her analysis of Indigenous communities in El Salvador — a country where Indigenous people are "invisibilized" in the dominant mestizo imaginary — elaborates on the meaning of the huipil among Mayan women of Guatemala: "Requiring months to weave, a fully embroidered huipil therefore serves as a woman's deeply personal expression of her identity. These meanings, especially the spiritual ones, may not be perceived by ethnic outsiders at all" (66). She also shares the following account by Beverly Gordon from *Identity in Cloth: Continuity and Survival in Guatemalan Textile*:

> Given the meaningfulness of these handmade garments and the highland Indian women's personal involvement with them, it is not surprising that they often saw their own garments as extensions of themselves. . . . It was on cloth destined to become a huipil that weavers generally did their most inspired and involved work, and once they had constructed and worn the garment, it embodied their very essence. . . . At the end of their lives, they were typically buried in their best huipiles; their spirit went with them to the grave. (qtd. in Tilley 2–3)

Those of us who are ethnic outsiders to these communities can only abstractly and at best marginally comprehend the deep cultural and spiritual meaning instilled in a Maya huipil. I, however, believe that Indigenous clothes carry an equally immense value for Chicanas, serving as a deeply personal expression of our identity and an embodiment of our essence — one that similarly symbolizes our ethnic group, our place of origin, and our clan affiliation as part of the Chicana tribe, which can be "read" only among us and remains indistinctive and unintelligible to outsiders, even to other Chican@s and Mexicans, especially those of the middle and upper classes.

When my close friends visit Mexico, they know they must bring me something I will wear that will make that item even more Mexican than it already is, because the object they carry back from Mexico for me will become an extension of my identity. It is no longer about proving anything about who I am to anyone but merely about not proving anything, about not boring my students and friends with the same Mexican attire — which is me, whether in Mexico, the Northwest, or even India. In 2011 I had the pleasure of experiencing India, where many cultural practices reminded me of Mexico. I wrote the following short poem, paralleling the rebozo and the sari, of utmost importance to Mexican and Indian women.

¿SARI OR REBOZO?
Our
fabric
could
cover

it
all,
or
lay
it
all
bare.

In India, for the Kritya International Poetry Festival, I wore huipiles and Mexican dresses. The country of textiles did not seem overly impressed with my huipiles, but still I wore them because in a global forum, they made a statement about the part of the world I hailed from. The East Indians perhaps preferred me dressed in saris; those they could judge as to the quality of the thread or textile, but they were unaccustomed to verifying the quality or precedence of a rebozo or huipil. To them embroidery, in a country of dexterous hands, did not seem as relevant as in Mexico or the United States. The real silk rebozos I showed them did not seem to impress them either; the handiwork in my Mexican outfits was simply not eye-catching to them. And yet they loved me, and welcomed me, and wanted me to wear their saris, as much as I wished they would try my rebozos on. I reminded myself that I was in a country of long traditions in designing sophisticated embroidery projects and complicated weaves. I understood that in India, embroidery could be seen as common as owning a loom. In a country where each sari is at least seven yards long, an expression of exclusivity and originality, huipiles are not a complex codex to be deciphered. The colors are what we share in common. The use of color combinations within one garment is what binds us. What also binds us is that for them textiles are obviously tied to memory, as is a huipil or a rebozo for women in Oaxaca and other parts of Mexico and the United States.

Notes

Many thanks to Aldo Ulisses Reséndiz for assisting me in completing this project by conducting research, providing thoughtful comments, and editing the final version of this chapter. It would not have been published without his invaluable professional assistance.

"Por la facha y por el traje, se conoce al personaje" is a well-known Spanish saying that translates to "By the appearance and the outfit, one will know the character" or, simply, "You know who they are by their physical appearance" (my translation), referring to the fact that you can change what or who a person is by solely changing his/her vesture. The opposite message is captured in another popular saying: "El traje no hace al monje," or "The habit does not make you into a monk." The English equivalents of these expressions would be "You can't make a silk purse out of a sow's ear" and "You can't put lipstick on a pig." Both of these popular sayings also remind us that aesthetics do not shape the entirety of the emergent elements of identity complexities and schisms that come about in daily life. However, in the first saying the affirmation is strong in stating that appearance is what fully represents a person. These sayings are so important given that Latin American countries emerged out of a strong physical and cultural colonizing philosophy, especially socially and spiritually.

1. Within the realm of cultural production, Chican@ theatre has put appearance front and center in its representations of archetypical Chican@ subjectivities. I am thinking here of the plays *Los Vendidos* and *Zoot Suit* by Luis Valdez and Cherríe Moraga's theatrical productions.

2. With my example of what a sombrero means to a Mexican campesino, I am purposely using an accessory that in global popular imagination has been histori-cally construed to represent Mexican-ness. In the United States, in particular, the early twentieth-century large straw hat, popular during the Mexican Revolution, has become a value-laden item that embodies racist stereotypes of the caricaturistic "lazy Mexican" who uses a significantly large sombrero to cover his face while rest-ing on a cactus in the middle of the desert, taking a siesta under the hot sun. Case in point, controversy broke out in 2012 when—in what has become a trend among col-lege fraternities and sororities, yet almost always goes unnoticed by US mainstream media—members of a Chi Omega sorority chapter at Penn State came under fire after posting photographs on Facebook of a "Mexican-themed" party they hosted. The pictures showed a group of mostly white college women wearing stereotypically racist "Mexican" costumes while holding offensive and degrading signs. Most salient of all the accessories they chose to wear in their representation of Mexicans was the infamous big sombrero. This sombrero image is perhaps more prevalent in the US imaginary than that of Mexico, where for many, especially in the central and north-ern parts of the country, the word *sombrero* today conveys images of a cowboy hat also known as a Tejana, mostly worn by men from rural areas in northern Mexico and the US Southwest. See Baker for more on the Penn State Mexican-themed party controversy. See also note 20 on the use of Mexican Halloween customs.

3. *Huipil* is a word of Nahuatl origin, the language of the Mexica (or Aztecs) and the second most widely spoken language in Mexico today, and refers to a traditional handwoven pullover blouse or dress of elaborate and intricate embroidering, most often worn by Indigenous women in central and southern Mexico as well as in Cen-tral America. The Maya huipil, for example, resembles a sleeveless knee-length tunic and is very popular in the Yucatan Peninsula and Guatemala, not only among Mayan women but also mestizas. To a lesser extent, this is also true in other parts of central and northern Mexico where huipiles are worn by women of immediate Indigenous ancestry or by those known to be indigenistas. See also note 17.

4. I attended school in Mexico every year until the age of nine, when I was in the third grade, which is when I first entered a school in the United States. Thereafter, my family worked in the fields in the Southwest and then would return to Mexico in the winter or for the rest of the school year. I also spent my fifth and eighth grades

in US schools. Otherwise I was in Mexico until I went to high school in Chicago and Watsonville, California. I still vividly remember how, as a child, I aspired to be the Indigenous-looking woman holding the Mexican flag depicted on the cover of every free governmental textbook distributed by Mexico's secretaría de educación to public school children in the 1960s. Frantz Fanon made the case in *The Wretched of the Earth* that for former colonial subjects, a national and cultural identity and a reverence for their Native past—in Mexico's case, this was more of a romanticization, especially at that time—serve as a rehabilitating mechanism that validates their own existence and helps them resist further European colonization. See also note 6.

5. James M. Henslin analyzes Mills's statement and further explains, "By *biography*, Mills referred to the specific experiences that give individuals their orientations to life. . . . In short, the society in which we grow up, and our particular location in that society, lie at the center of what we do and how we think."

6. I am well aware of the level of the patriotic/nationalistic/essentialist indoctrination that takes place in rural Mexican school classrooms, which many children internalize at a very young age. However, in my case I do not completely write off the outcome of this process since I realize that, as a child living in the United States, I must have held on to some of the positive values of self-affirmation in relation to my ethnic and cultural identity that were fomented in me while in school in Mexico. To some extent, I attempted to survive Othering and the otherwise almost inescapable threat of internalized racism by, at the very least, holding on to alternative counter-narratives to US hegemony, which, in turn, perhaps limited the extent to which I was indoctrinated in US public schools. My claim today could be further complicated when analyzed through the lens of post-nationalism theory, especially when it comes to the historical intersections of identity between Chicanas and Mexicanas, otherwise known as meXicanas. For more on this, see Fregoso and Hernández.

7. "What's there to class differences anyway? / You prefer a night club / And I, reggae / You prefer the glamour of Paris / And I, freedom on the beach / You prefer a rich man with a car / And I, a cigar at the bar / And now I understand why we're not equals."

8. "With the huaraches that I wear / I came to see you many times. / You don't want to love me back / and that makes me suffer inside."

9. Camacho Segura focuses in his writings on US-born Mexicans of northern Mexican heritage and strongly identifies as an "Apache-Californian" or "norteño Apache" having been born and raised in California.

10. Paz is, however, notorious among Chican@s for his otherwise negative and Othering descriptions of pachucos.

11. The number of popular Mexican sayings that conjure up the image/metaphor of the huarache is extensive. "No dar paso sin huarache" ("Do not take a step without [wearing] huaraches" or "Look before you leap.") An additional subversive meaning would be "Don't leave your identity of origin behind when you move forward." "Dar un huarachazo" means to either slap or hit someone (not necessarily with a sandal), usually as a form of defense. It is sometimes used in a metaphorical way, meaning to get someone who's "out of line" to behave or act appropriately; it also takes on another very different meaning, similar to "hit the dance floor," when referring to dancing. "Huaraches" is also the name of a popular corn-based dish that is thick and oblong, made in the same way handmade tortillas are, and then layered with a

variety of toppings. The dish is particularly popular in central and southern Mexico. This is another example of how the concept (in this case, image/metaphor) of the huarache is so ubiquitous in Mexican vernacular.

12. We also wore jorongos, or what some call in English ponchos, because just like huaraches, they were a symbol of identity, icons of Mexican culture.

13. My translation:

> You arrived last year.
> I saw you arrive barefooted.
> You were wearing a morral
> when you came from home,
> and you are now showing off [trying to impress]
> and arousing people. . . .
> You no longer pay attention to my camote [sweet potato] cart.
> Maybe there's some guy who now honks his car horn at you.
> You've exchanged your morral for a purse. . . .

The sixth line, "Y alborando a la raza," can also be translated as "And [sexually] arousing men." The colloquial use of the verb *alboratar* can be interpreted as "to arouse" in both the sense of stirring up or provoking someone, and the sense of stimulating sexual desire. "La raza" does not mean "race"; among Mexicans/Chican@s it can be interpreted as "the people." Among rural Mexican men from places like Sinaloa on the Pacific coast of Mexico or the northern region, *la raza* can also mean "a group of young guys" with whom one shares similar characteristics, depending on the social location of the speaker, gender, or age, but most often it refers to those of a common working-class, rural background. Not coincidently, the term is often associated with people who have a similar taste for banda/norteño music.

14. Equally popular among Chican@s of the 1960s and 1970s, and still today, is the morral, a handwoven shoulder bag with a long strap, traditionally worn by Indigenous people, young and old, throughout Latin America. Many rural Mexican children grew up carrying their textbooks in a morral, making its most common use similar to that of a satchel. In response to the Zapatista Movement, many Chican@s/Xican@s are still drawn to carrying morrales; exceptionally popular are those available through co-ops in autonomous Indigenous communities in Mexico's southernmost state of Chiapas. Most recently, carrying a morral has become trendy among white college students and others who travel to Latin America, raising questions of cultural appropriation and making the morral a contested accessory item. This parallels—with similar neo-colonial/racial dynamics, yet significantly less politically charged—the recent controversy surrounding the commercialization and appropriation of the Kufiyyeh (Palestinian scarf) as a fashion statement in the United States.

15. I have long been fascinated by the richness of the Mexican color palette, perhaps only obvious to a connoisseur. The bright green of my dress is known in Mexico as "flag green," in reference to the first of three blocks of color on the Mexican flag. Similarly, there is a "loud," bright purplish-pink color known as "rosa mexicano" (Mexican pink), most often found in fabric. This unique hue captures the Mexican national imagination as a color associated with popular working-class aesthetics, an iconic element of Mexican visual idiosyncrasy, but it is often rejected and mocked

by the upper classes, and by those with upper-class aspirations, as a poor choice of a color that to them is "de mal gusto" ("in bad taste").

16. Rosita Quintana was an actress during the época de oro del cine mexicano. Born in Argentina, she was a Mexican national who performed in several classic movies, including *El mil amores* (1954), in which she starred with a Latin American idol, the Mexican heartthrob Pedro Infante. She played some of her most well-known roles alongside comedian-turned-actor Germán Valdés, known as Tin Tan. In movies such as *Soy charro de Levita* (1949), she wore two braided loops on either side of her head, tied at the ends with long, thick ribbon bows. Also worn by Frida Kahlo and immortalized in several of her paintings, this is the hairstyle I wore back then.

17. In the Mexican popular imagination, indigenistas are individuals with some formal education who are drawn to support and take on the causes of Indigenous people.

18. I use the term *mexicanista* to describe an ethnocentric Mexican essentialist and nationalist: at best, someone who holds tight to her national/ethnic identity while abroad; at worst, someone who claims to be an authority on Mexican culture and uses her assumed Mexican birthright to delegitimize everything and everyone who does not ascribe to or come close to resembling what she considers to be "authentically" Mexican. I do not employ the term as it is used in US academic circles to refer to individuals who study Mexico and specialize in Mexican culture, history, and society.

19. Rebozos are a pre-Columbian icon, a shawl worn by Mexican and Chicana women in Mexico and the United States. For over a decade now, I have theorized and written extensively on the rebozo. For a comprehensive analysis and additional commentary on the significance of the rebozo in Chican@ life and culture, see my articles "Sandra Cisneros and Her Trade of the Free Word" and "Rebozos, Our Cultural Blankets." Also see Heredia for an expanded discussion of the rebozo in Chicana literature.

20. The fetishization of Frida Kahlo and Indigenous Mexican clothing is nonetheless a relevant issue. A colleague recently asked to borrow some of my clothes because she wanted to dress as Kahlo for Halloween. In her eyes, my fashion style was a custom, not an integral and deeply valued part of my identity. Cultural appropriations of clothing and grotesquely stereotypical portrayals of communities of Color through their customs, especially during Halloween, are a far too common sight across the United States. This seems, at times, more pervasive in so-called liberal (read "pretentiously 'colorblind' and 'post-racial'") white enclaves such as Seattle.

21. The feminist theologian Jeanette Rodríguez has analyzed this particular picture of my mother, underlining the importance of the links among attire, spirituality, and identity, as well as gender, faith, and social class. My poem about the evolution of the image of the Virgen de Guadalupe, "She's Come out of Bakery Calendars," addresses this journey from a 1950s rural Catholic Mexican woman's imaginary, in which young Catholic women of this time felt that they had to visit the Villa in Mexico City, as if it were a Mecca, at least once in their lifetime, to the evolution of Virgin tattoos in the United States in 2000. This poem appears in my collection *A Most Improbable Life.*

Works Cited

Baker, Katie J. M. "Penn State Sorority Girls Dress Up as Mexicans Who Will 'Mow Lawn for Weed and Beer.'" *Jezebel*, 4 Dec. 2012, jezebel.com/5965675/penn -state-sorority-girls-dress-up-as-mexicans-who-will-mow-lawn-for-weed-and -beer. Accessed 5 Dec. 2012.

Benítez, Fernando. *Los indios de México.* Mexico City: Ediciones Era, 1967.

Bonfil Batalla, Guillermo. *México profundo: Una civilización negada.* Mexico City: Grijalbo, 1987.

Camacho Segura, Julián. *Higher Education as Ignorance: The Contempt of Mexicans in the American Educational System.* Hamilton, 2008.

———. *Societal Suicide.* Hamilton, 2006.

DeMello, Margo. *Feet and Footwear: A Cultural Encyclopedia.* Greenwood/ABC-CLIO, 2009.

Fanon, Frantz. *The Wretched of the Earth.* Grove, 1965.

Fregoso, Rosa L. *meXicana encounters: The Making of Social Identities on the Borderlands.* U of California P, 2003.

Gordon, Beverly. *Identity in Cloth: Continuity and Survival in Guatemalan Textiles.* U of Wisconsin P, 1993.

Gutiérrez y Muhs, Gabriella. *Communal Feminisms: Chicanas, Chilenas and Cultural Exile: Theorizing the Space of Exile, Class, and Identity.* Lexington Books, 2007.

———. "Rebozos, Our Cultural Blankets." *Voces: A Journal of Chicana/Latina Studies,* vol. 3 (2001), pp. 134–149.

———. "Sandra Cisneros and Her Trade of the Free Word." *The Rocky Mountain Review of Language and Literature,* vol. 60, no. 2 (Fall 2006), pp. 23–36.

———. "Touched by Mexico's Unrandom Acts of Kindness." *National Catholic Reporter,* 27 Sept. 2002, p. 23.

Henslin, James M. *Essentials of Sociology: A Down-to-Earth Approach.* Allyn and Bacon, 2010.

Hernández, Ellie D. *Postnationalism in Chicana/o Literature and Culture.* U of Texas P, 2009.

Heredia, Juanita. "Sandra Cisnero's 'Caramelo' (2002): Translating Gender and Genealogy across the US/Mexico Borderlands." *Transnational Latina Narrative in the Twenty-first Century: The Politics of Gender, Race, and Migrations,* Palgrave Macmillan, 2009, pp. 25–60.

Herrera-Sobek, María. *Chicano Folklore: A Handbook.* Greenwood, 2006.

McCracken, Ellen. "The Postmodern Continuum of Canon and Kitsch: Narrative and Semiotic Strategies of Chicana High Culture and Chica Lit." *Analyzing World Fiction: New Horizons in Narrative Theory,* edited by Frederick Luis Aldama, U of Texas P, 2011.

Mills, C. Wright. *The Sociological Imagination.* Oxford UP, 1959.

Moraga, Cherríe. *Heroes and Saints & Other Plays.* West End, 1994.

Paz, Octavio. *The Labyrinth of Solitude: Life and Thought in Mexico.* Grove, 1961.

Rodriguez, Jeanette. "Latina Popular Catholicism." *The Encyclopedia of Women and Religion in North America,* edited by Rosemary Skinner Keller et al., Indiana UP, 2006, pp. 168–178.

Rosaldo, Renato. *Culture and Truth: The Remaking of Social Analysis.* Beacon, 1993.

Stavans, Ilan. *The Riddle of Cantinflas: Essays on Hispanic Popular Culture*. U of New Mexico P, 1998.

Tilley, Virginia. *Seeing Indians: A Study of Race, Nation and Power in El Salvador*. U of New Mexico P, 2005.

Valdez, Luis. *Luis Valdez—Early Works: Actos, Bernabé, and Pensamiento Serpentino*. Arte Público, 1990.

———. *Zoot Suit and Other Plays*. Arte Público, 1992.

Vicuña, Cecilia, and Livon Grossman. *The Oxford Book of Latin American Poetry*. Oxford UP, 2009.

CHAPTER 5

A Familial Legacy of meXicana Style

DOMINO RENEE PEREZ

Mija, style is not about what you have on. It's about how you carry yourself.
It's how you tell the world you matter without saying a word.
TÍO NICOLAS ORTIZ

I am envious of people who have photographic histories of their families stretching back for generations. Androgynes dressed in high-necked collars adorned with cameos and their heads covered in black lace, thick-fingered men in shirtsleeves standing in front of prized vehicles, and cherubic babies with dark eyes peering out of bonnets. Images such as these and others are a visual record of the past for which I once longed. The absence of such a collection in our family is a direct result of an economic reality. For migrants, photographs were a non-portable luxury, easily damaged, lost, or ruined.

As limited as our visual archive from previous generations may be, we are fortunate to have three pictures of my maternal grandmother, Eugenia, who died when she was still in her twenties. She left behind a husband and seven surviving children, the three youngest of which her parents raised, including my mother. In fact, I grew up believing that my bisabuelos were actually my abuelos, a misapprehension no one bothered to correct until I was much older.[1] Never entirely sure about the identity of the woman in the photos, what I did know was that something about her seemed familiar. After learning about Tati Eugenia,[2] I spent hours staring at an oversized, oval-framed, sepia-toned photo, trying to make out the faded details of her life. Years later I would learn about her decision to leave behind the luxury of her parents' house with the wraparound porch and ornate parlor in Beeville, Texas, where everything had its place, to live in a one-room abode on the edge of a cotton field with the man she loved

5.1. "Eugenia Ortiz." Photographer unknown; courtesy of Domino Renee Perez.

FLYING

Eugenia, standing in a cluster of feather-leafed palms, her arms stretched wide as if to steady herself or take flight. The trees conspire to mask her intent, obscuring the shape and position of the white-gloved hands that are holding on or letting go. Head cocked slightly to the right, she looks directly into the camera. The side bow of the cloche hat with a black satin band rests on the fur collar of her camel-colored coat, which is open from neck to knee, revealing a loose-fitting shift with a drop waist and a gathered skirt. Heavy white stockings and a thoughtfully placed scarf tied intricately around her neck offset the boldness of her pose and youthful style. She does not yet know she will leave the safety of the big house for a one-room shack. She does not know she will give birth to eight children. She does not know she will fail to survive the next decade. She does not know she will be buried in an unmarked grave. She does not know that as a child I will spend hours staring at her picture, wondering what she is trying to tell me with her eyes.

in Yorktown, Texas.[3] What fear, what courage, what resolve must she have possessed to make such a choice? The pictures held no answers for me. Puzzling images of her convey a social and economic standing that do not reflect the reality of her life married to a man who labored in the fields of others. The incongruity has always fascinated me.

In contrast to the scant record of Tati Eugenia and her life with Tito Lalo, their children and grandchildren have extensive visual archives, and it is through them that I learned much of my family history. Although we became adept as a family at documenting our lives in pictures, we were never as enthusiastic about organizing them. As a result, the pictures ended up in a cardboard box simply marked "FOTOS." Many an afternoon was spent shuffling through the images and grouping them based on subject, year, event, or any other category my child's mind could devise. When the game was complete, back they would go in piles, more disorganized than the time before. Each adventure into the box would yield a new treasure, a new tale. I remember finding the photo that first occasioned one of my favorite stories. It was of a glamorous woman in oversized sunglasses with a floppy hat, saluting into the sun. Though I would not have described her as such at the time, she looked like a meXicana Audrey Hepburn but was even more beautiful, more chic because she was my Tía Felita, the refined lady with the porcelain tchotchkes married to my mother's hardworking uncle Raul. They complemented each other perfectly, her refinement and his roughness, and did until their last days.

When I was growing up, my mother's Tía Felita was one of the most stylish people I knew. With her taste in fashion leaning toward timeless rather than trendy, she favored clean lines and great accessories. Always graceful, always impeccably dressed, no matter the occasion, Tía Felita once helped me move out of a third-floor apartment, outfitted in white linen pants, a navy boat-neck top, and a pair of micro-strapped sandals adorned with decorative leather flowers. At the end of the day, despite hauling boxes down three flights, not to mention also sweeping floors and wiping down baseboards, she was spotless. She took as much care in maintaining her appearance as she did in taking care of me. Her wardrobe was never vast, but always held items that could be mixed and matched with at least three or four other clothing essentials, a lesson she learned from her career in high fashion.

Before she was my great-aunt Felita, she was Ofelia, head seamstress for a Houston-based designer whose looks were made famous in the 1950s when he created a dress for a then well-known Hollywood starlet, or so they say. Ofelia's professional life was filled with glamour, flowing like the silk and chiffon she sewed into works of art bearing the designer's name. They had a familiar, if not unspoken, agreement: she oversaw the quality of the garments, and he stayed out of her way. Occasionally, though, he would swagger into Ofelia's studio and make some outrageous request to remind her who was boss. My favorite of these stories was the time he walked into the studio early one morning, picked out a bolt of iridescent navy taffeta, heaved it over to the design area, and dropped it onto her table like an animal carcass. After much harrumphing, he ordered her to create a one-of-a-kind masterpiece for his daughter by five o'clock that afternoon. He made sure to punctuate his ultimatum with a less-than-subtle threat about losing her job if she failed. Knowing full well that he would never fire her and accustomed to his bad behavior, at no time did Ofelia acknowledge he had been in the room. Instead, she began to sew one of the dresses she had always imagined making for herself. At precisely five o'clock, a strapless, A-line masterpiece, with yards of material cascading over the straight skirt and gathered on the left side of the waist, was hanging on the dress form, along with a lined matching bolero jacket that Ofelia added to remind him who was *really* the boss. The designer arrived shortly thereafter, surveyed her work, and simply muttered, "Good." And while his daughter appeared in the society pages wearing another one of her father's "original designs," my aunt remained an unacknowledged source of genius behind the brand. She worked at the design studio for more than twenty years, until it was sold. Afterward she vowed never to sew commercially again. Over the years my tía has maintained the habit of turning a retail garment inside out to examine the stitching and "machine work." To this day, it is the rare piece of apparel that meets with her exacting standards.

Together with her daughters, Alisa and Yolanda, who as teenagers were accomplished dressmakers in their own right, my tía and cousins wrapped me until I was around seven years old in frothy, frosty creations: tiered organza dresses with appliqué flowers, fitted velvet bodices with flair skirts, eyelet jumpers, tulle ballet skirts with satin bloomers. My brother Michael had endured a similar fate as a toddler, dressed in heavy velvet shorts, vests, lined jackets, knee-high socks, Buster Brown black-and-white flats, and leather-soled lace-ups, but graduated to a more casual rough and tumble style. Photos from my childhood reveal that from birth I was immaculately outfitted and accessorized: ruffled diaper covers, lace-trimmed socks, bows, ribbons, tiny hooped earrings, hinged gold baby bangle bracelets, and miniature Mary Janes in black, red, and white.[4] What could not be made, Ofelia bought at great expense from Neiman-Marcus, Sakowitz,

Battelsteins (later Frost Bros.), or, on rare occasions, Saks Fifth Avenue, and only after she had scrutinized its quality or decided it was not worth the expense to duplicate.[5] Equally notable as these unbelievable ensembles is the utter disregard I appeared to have for them, snagging, ripping, or spilling on the delicate material. Dresses instantly became arrugados (wrinkled). Bows ended up on the floor next to shoes. Socks were misshapen from being pulled off by the toe. Undaunted by my antics, year after year the women in my family persisted, and I resisted: what I wanted more than anything was to be in possession of my own body, to run with my shirt off, to feel the sun on my back without the stickiness of material, to squat instead of sit, to sprawl, to hang upside down, to be too loud, to be more like my brother.

During the 1940s and 1950s, a steel mill, oilfield, and railroad yard just minutes away from downtown Houston served as the economic life of a small community known as Cottage Grove. Overshadowed by its wealthy geographic neighbor The Heights, the more humble Cottage Grove was a working-class, surprisingly diverse neighborhood that included businesses owned by Anglos, Mexicans, Czechs, and Chinese. Around 1950, much of my family lived in this Cottage Grove community, where we too would eventually take up residence on 5633 Petty. My father's parents lived one block north on Kiam; my mother's grandparents' house sat on the corner of Kansas and Arabelle, a mere two blocks away; my Tío Raul and Tía Felita lived on the same street two blocks east. Aunts, uncles, and cousins, who were never more than a quick stroll away on Larkin or Leroy, surrounded us. Because both of my parents worked, one of our many relatives often looked after my brother and me. Most often, the responsibility fell to my father's mother, the Big Grandma, because of her flexible schedule: she cleaned houses on the weekends or worked at night.

One afternoon while the Big Grandma sat watching her telenovelas or, as she called them, her "stories," I wandered about the house and came across my mother's plastic, pink-bottomed sewing box. Underneath the clear lid sat an array of colored thread, wooden spools, and crystal buttons that looked like diamonds. The deep compartment below the removable tray held even more wonders: twists of lace, batting, scraps of satin ribbons, an odd assortment of appliqués, and a pair of pinking shears. Unlike memories built on a photo, I remember the details of that afternoon with great clarity: the weight of the black-handled scissors, the cool of the heavy steel, the difficulty of opening and closing the hungry mouth with my small hands, and the overwhelming urge to put them to use. I walked the short distance down the hall to the room I shared with my brother.

I opened the closet door, stepped into the darkness, and reached for my dresses. One by one, I watched the jagged teeth of the shears bite effortlessly through the material again, and again, and again. The crunch of cotton and the whisper of silk yielding to the instrument in my hand were spellbinding. I sought out other materials: a rubber band, a leather shoe, the plastic shade on my baby buggy purchased only weeks before with S&H green stamps. Of everything I cut through that afternoon when I was five, my hair was the most inspired choice. Shingled in zigzagged patterns around my head, patches of my scalp peeked through the haphazard design. The Big Grandma was concerned that I might have dulled the scissors' blades by using them to cut vinyl and hard plastic, and seized them from me once she discovered what I had done. Conversely, my mother was crestfallen upon seeing my self-styled hair design. I left her no option but to crop the remaining hair into a pixie cut, which produced a most unexpected result. It made me look exactly like my brother. For an instant, I pictured my new life free of frilly fashion confections: Bermuda-length shorts, fitted tanks, wide-collared shirts, and Toughskin jeans.[6] Before I could fully imagine joining my brother and male cousins in their outdoor escapades, Mami had already begun to devise ways to make sure that no one would mistake her short-haired daughter for a boy. For the next year, I endured a barrage of hair ornamentation, bows and barrettes. When my hair grew long enough to wrap around pink sponge rollers, a ringlet bob told the world I was a girl. I cannot even remember being punished for my cutting adventure — looking back, the crocheted dresses and sausage curls were punishment enough.

In 1958 my mother graduated from high school. The one advantage she was given by being separated from her father and brothers was that she and her younger siblings could stay in one place with their grandparents in Houston and receive an education instead of traveling with their father and older brothers on the migrant trail. When my Mexican American mother was in high school, her classmates called her Cat Eyes, Mary, or güera (light-skinned or white girl). Penned throughout her senior yearbook in hasty scrawl are messages of remembrance: "Mary, don't forget crazy times in gym." "Cat Eyes, you were always a really nice girl." "Hey, güerita! ¿Sabes que? Ha! Ha!"[7] When she was seventeen, she sat for a portrait at Ayers-Kipperman Photographers, located at 1504 Main Street in Houston. The 12 × 14 image conveys a youth and innocence made familiar to me only through pictures, though her beauty remained the same. Pincurled hair flattened down into black waves of silk. Light skin, eyes the color of an amber sunburst floating in a sea of green. From the delicate

5.2. "Siblings." Photo by Maria Perez; courtesy of Domino Renee Perez.

MEDITATION IN BROWN

Coffee, camel, beaver, fallow, chamoisee. Floor, furniture, fixtures, my brother's short-sleeved button-down, plaid pants, loafers, our skin. Brown, brown all around. My basket and I disrupt the earthy palette: a robin's egg blue Easter basket filled with electric pink grass, me in a glacial hue. Light from the camera flash reflects off the satin bow affixed above five tiers of organza, white alternating with ice blue. My shorn hair and smile suggest that on this day I don't mind the ribbed, itchy cotton tights or white Mary Janes that bite my heels. I am about to laugh or suppressing the urge to do so.

5.3. "Eugenia dressed for travel." Photographer unknown; courtesy of Domino Renee Perez.

IN TRANSIT

A finger-wave hairstyle peaks out beneath the edge of the same cloche hat, and the wrap-over coat is now fastened. Hands positioned at the waist are tucked inside an oversized black fur muff that matches the trim on the collar and cuffs. She is traveling. Pushed to the edge of the frame, she is upright, tall, the world behind her plunging down out of the frame at an impossible angle. With the left side of her body in full light, the right in afternoon shadow, she uses the position of the hat to shield her eyes so she can look directly into the camera. The face is fair, the downturned eyes uneven. The painted lips give only a hint of a smile. I tell myself she was at a train station, posing beside a railway car or perhaps the ticket booth, the unfamiliarity of its gently sloping exterior a novelty worth capturing in the frame. But this cannot be right, not in Texas and not in the early 1920s. Her light skin and fine clothes would not have been enough to get her admitted to the passenger coach. Where were you going, and how did you steady yourself when the world around you seemed so out of balance?

floral-patterned lace collar and the arch of her perfectly penciled brow to the position of her hands and the shape of the twin pearl ring, a gift from Tía Felita, I have made a study of the image. The schoolgirl in the print is and is not my mother.

I first came across the portrait during a game of hide-and-seek with my brother when I was eight. The portrait and I shared the dusty space beneath my parents' bed. Later, when I asked my mother why she kept the picture hidden away, she said, after scolding me for getting into her things, "That was a long time ago, and besides it's ruined." When I told her a frame would hide the worn edges, she replied, without heat, "Déjalo." In other words, I was told rather plainly to leave the issue alone. I had seen the twin strands of pearls. I had seen the matching bracelet. I had seen that her fingers appeared elongated. I had not seen the state of her nail polish, jagged lines receding from the tips exposing the whiteness beneath. My brother assured me that this was the "flaw" in the picture, but it did not change my opinion of her or the photo. She still looked like one of those stars in the old issues of the celebrity fan magazine *Photoplay*.[8]

I eventually learned the photograph was taken on the eve of a big senior dance, not the local Baile de Graduación (graduation dance) for Mexican American teenagers held in the Emerald Room of the Shamrock Hilton, where the Orquestra de Luis Casca played, and my mother waltzed all night in the green fishtail dress that brought out the color of her eyes. This was the end-of-year prom, held in the Reagan High School gymnasium, where she wore the ivory-colored dress made of tiered lace.[9] The prom where she and her friends Velen, Jimmy T, Angel, Mary, Tacho, Rudy, Spider, Chico, El Killer, and Frankie were made to feel unwelcome as Mexican Americans in a predominately white school. The expectation on the part of their white classmates, according to the late 1950s racial politics of Texas, was that the "Mexicans" would self-segregate or self-exclude by either holding their own event or staying away. With heads held high and arms linked, my mother and her friends walked—pressed, pouffed, and pompadoured—into the gym to bop and stroll because, after all, it was their school too. Everyone told El Killer, who earned the name for his painfully handsome good looks and short fuse, he had better not start any trouble, though they had failed to exact the same promise from Jimmy T; so when Rufus Evans, a popular football player, called the pretty redhead in the group, Angel Cooper, a spic lover, Jimmy T slugged him. What few outside of the neighborhood knew was that Angel was half Mexican. Her father was Irish and her mother was Mexican, but that made no difference to Rufus, who condemned Angel for the company she kept.

The friends were not looking for trouble, but trouble found them soon enough. After being kicked out of the prom for "starting the fight," the group headed over to a field on Maxroy to dance in crisscrossed headlight beams to music from their car radios. Before long, more than a third of the prom-goers found their way to that open field, though no one was sure how, and brought with them reports of things "going square" after the fight. Under the night sky, they willingly admitted Rufus was "bad news," a "closet case" (slang for "unstable"), and most certainly "had it coming." Classmates who had never uttered a single word to each other over the years sang and swayed as the song "At the Hop" by Danny and the Juniors pulled them up from their trunks, hoods, or bumpers to their feet again and again. Few in the field that night gave thought to the fleeting nature of their fellowship, which would begin to erode as soon as they climbed into their cars to drive home across the interstate and forever vanish with the rising sun. So when the Platters, a popular doo-wop group of the era, reminded the revelers of "Twilight Time," the dawn that was quickly approaching, and the title of their number-one song that year, my mom quietly slipped away to watch the merrymaking from a distance: the small group gathered around Jimmy T reenacting the fight, Spider and Chico pulling on the creases of their pants, Tacho and Frankie laughing with some pachucos my mother did not recognize, and El Killer living up to his name by dancing with three girls at once. Satisfied with the scene, my mother pulled her wrap over her shoulders, looped her fingers into the toe boxes of her satin stilettos, and walked the three blocks home.

Two years later, in 1960, Rufus and Billy Simms were driving down the corridor between Houston and San Antonio. Some say they were going too fast or horsing around. Others say they were drunk or that it was raining. What the police report confirmed was that Billy, who was driving, somehow lost control of the car and slammed into the back of a semi parked on the shoulder. Both were killed instantly.

I once offered to have the picture of my mother taken on the eve of that memorable night retouched for her so that she might display the photo as a remembrance. She flatly refused, saying, "I don't need to have it out or hanging up to remember." When she received the invitation to her fiftieth class reunion, included in the envelope was a handwritten personal note addressed to my mother from Nancy Pittman, Rufus's prom date and a woman who had never spoken a kind word to my mother in high school. Pittman expressed her hope that she would attend so they could "visit and catch up."

The old circle of friends had not kept in touch, but my mother knew that Jimmy T and Chico died in Vietnam; Rudy and Velen were married right after high school and moved to the Rio Grande Valley; Angel died of cancer; Mary still lived in the old neighborhood with her mother; Tacho became a professor; Spider had been imprisoned on burglary charges; and no one knew the whereabouts of El Killer and Frankie, though it was rumored that El Killer was a doctor somewhere in Arizona. At the reunion, there would be no razor-sharp creased slacks, no layers of silk or chiffon, but more importantly, there would be no interlaced arms woven together in a show of strength and courage. I found the invitation and Pittman's message at the bottom of the recycling bin. The note had been torn in two.

The early 1980s saw the rise of designer literacy, a trend that reached its full strength by the middle of the decade. Before that, however, in my freshman year of high school, I wore a Hefty garbage bag to school. It was my first real attempt at social commentary. My act was prompted in part by an unexpected change in clothing priorities, namely the idea of belonging made manifest through designer labels. A few years before, I'd thought nothing of trying on shoes at the grocery store or selecting clothes mid-summer that were held on layaway until the fall, and the only prior knowledge I had about clothing labels was matching Garanimals tags.[10]

In preparation for high school, I tried to approximate styles and trends depicted in *Seventeen*. Through careful thought and selection, my freshman-year wardrobe was appropriately fashionable. But somehow priorities had changed between middle and high school, and no one, not even my teen fashion magazine, had bothered to tell me, at least not in words. The ads, in retrospect, were a portent of what was to come: Jordache, Sasson, Calvin Klein, Izod, Ralph Lauren, and Guess. Quality and style had given way to name recognition. I learned this too late, not that it made any difference because in my family, school clothes were purchased once a year. Additional necessities (socks and underwear, primarily) were gifted at Christmas.

All at once, in my first year at high school, I had to navigate six classes on two floors, wend my way through upperclassmen, and also learn to read the clothing labels on my classmates' rear ends and pecs. Although I could not remember the location of my locker, in a matter of days I could distinguish designers at a glance, based on iconography, the shape and placement of a label, and pattern of the stitching on the pocket. I watched the popular girls clad in costly apparel move in comfortable packs. Those on the outside tried to buy their way into relevance by quickly acquiring and donning one or even two treasured brands. These poseurs were relegated to second- or third-tier status, for they soon learned that it was not only the names but also the number and assortment of labels that mattered. And it wasn't just jeans; it was K-Swiss shoes, Louis Vuitton purses, Swatch watches, and Giorgio perfume. The rest of us would have to wait for Christmas, each brightly wrapped package holding the promise of a pair of turquoise velvet Gloria Vanderbilt pants or some other label that might help salvage our social standing and free us from the hell of our Levi's and Lee jeans. But Christmas was four months away.

Deprived of the cultural currency of conspicuous consumption, I made the temporary decision to hide. In truth, there was nothing to be done about my situation. I could not approach my parents with such nonsense, and if I had discussed the issue with them, they would have most certainly told me it was nonsense, though it didn't feel that way to me. So while I contemplated my options, I donned my own version of an invisibility cloak, a hunter green sweatshirt zipper jacket that I wore over dresses, pants, skirts, and jeans. It became a part of my unofficial uniform during the first month of school as I watched longtime friendships dissolve and reform around clubs, organizations, and activities. As an athlete, more specifically a volleyball player, I too had forged new friendships but found that court camaraderie did not always extend into the hallways or classrooms. Unhappy and confused, I hid in plain sight while I searched for a solution. Just when it seemed likely that I would still be wearing the coat four years later at senior prom, two things happened: Mark Douglas's mood swing and Halloween.

Of all the peripherally popular freshman boys, Mark was the most kind. He was also the shortest. We were eye level only when he sat perched on his lab stool. I enjoyed being partnered with him in biology for lab assignments because we worked well together, and he made me laugh. On that particular day, though, he seemed solemn, distracted. Still I was not prepared for the questions that finally broke his silence: "Why do you always wear that jacket? I mean it's like eighty-five degrees outside. Aren't you hot?" Suddenly I felt very exposed, and what followed struck with unexpected accuracy. "It's like you're hiding. And, I guess . . . why would you do that? Did something happen?" Although I cannot recall my response or what we said after that, I do remember the concern in his voice and getting an A on the assignment. The fate of the zipper coat remains a mystery to this day, for it simply vanished.

Around this same time, excitement was building in certain circles for the school-wide Halloween contest. The principal announced that we were going to be allowed to wear costumes to class, which was unprecedented in the high school's history. Uncertain about what to wear or whether or not

5.4. "Kindergarten graduation performance." Photographer unknown; courtesy of Domino Renee Perez.

PORTRAIT OF A LADY

Kindergarten graduation. With hats sitting squarely on our heads, dress-up skirts pulled over celebration clothes, and tacones on socked feet, we march in the "Mommy Parade." I do not smile coquettishly like the girl over my shoulder. The other miniature mommies in their pillbox hats with netted veils appear maternal, sweet, yet there is something lacking in my performance. Round and round, we navigate plastic infants in strollers about the stage, passing a businessman, milkman, reporter, doctor, teacher, secretary, fireman, policeman, and nurse, all seated along the back wall. These are the children waiting to perform their skit called "The Jobs in Our Town." When the parts were announced for the graduation program, I raised my hand high for a chance to be the reporter but was told there were only three girls' jobs—teacher, secretary, and nurse. Instead of a notepad, starched white shirt, pencil skirt, and loafers, I was offered a doll and an elastic-waist overskirt. The first day of rehearsal, when the other girls ran to pick the best buggies and babies, I focused my attention on the shoes and accessories, selecting a rose-colored saucer hat, with its wide bow fixed across the brim, and champagne-tinted satin stilettos for my self-styled costume as a "doctor." Making my way across the stage, the stroller with its bent frame and lopsided wheels hampers my stride. The blonde, barefooted baby rattles in her seat. Stage left, the nurse eyes me nervously and marks my contempt.

to even participate in the contest, my fellow volley baller Lisa Reyes and I discussed our options one night as we sat up late watching *Times Square* (1980), a film about two young women—one poor, the other rich—who meet in and escape from a mental hospital. While fleeing from parents and authorities, they form a punk rock duo called the Sleez Sisters, whose antiestablishment, anticonformity message resonates with the city's disaffected youth. The action culminates in a rooftop concert attended by a legion of Sleez Sister devotees, identifiable by their crimped hair, painted-on black eye masks, and heavy-duty garbage bags belted over brightly colored shirts with tights. Suddenly inspiration hit.

Times Square played round-the-clock on cable television and would go on to become a cult classic, and its soundtrack—a mixture of punk and New Wave, featuring such artists as Patti Smith, Roxy Music, and Suzi Quatro—is hailed for capturing the mood of a generation. But we didn't know that. What *we* knew was that people we had played with as kids would no longer talk to us, that jocks and band nerds didn't mix, that cheerleaders only dated football players, that losers like us rode the bus or had their parents drop them off, that lunch was for talking not eating, and that unless we wore the right clothes and looked the right way, we would never belong. The morning of the contest, we dressed in the locker room, where we stored a change of clothes just in case we lost our nerve. With our garbage bags affixed firmly around our waists, masks perfectly penciled in place, and zigzagged hair bunched in brightly colored bands, we added one final flourish to complete our outfits: designer tags. On white envelope labels, I wrote Hefty in flowing cursive and Lisa printed GLAD in block script. We affixed the stickers hip-level on our backsides and made our way into the hallways past the lockers with combinations we couldn't remember, past the gawkers and onlookers, past the popular students who decided en masse not to dress up, past the teachers who shook their heads in disbelief, past everything, past them all.

Located in DeWitt County and situated in the south-central part of Texas, Yorktown has a population of approximately 2,300.[11] The most famous person to ever come out of Yorktown was Harlon Block, one of six World War II soldiers immortalized in Joe Rosenthal's iconic photograph *Raising the Flag on Iwo Jima*. Depicted planting the base of the second flag on Mount Suribachi on February 23, 1945, Block died a month later in Iwo Jima.[12] This, however, does little to explain why my Tío Joe chose Yorktown in which to settle, marry, and have eleven children, but he did, and he is buried in San Luis Catholic Cemetery outside of town.

In a small, quartered cherry frame in the corner of my mother's living room sit the only pictures of my uncles from their youth: Tío Eduardo (Lalo), a teenager in a white T-shirt and khakis, leg hiked up, calf exposed, eye squinting against the smoke curling up from a cigarette perched in the corner of his mouth, head tossed back defiantly; Tío Ovidio in a tight close-up, hair piled loosely into a pompadour, shoulders rolled forward, the sleeves of his button-down tight against hard triceps, his light eyes staring directly into the camera; Tío Nicolas, a small boy in an oversized field shirt hanging about his waist, facing forward with his chin pointed in the direction of the photographer; and Tío Joe, the oldest, in a long, billowy sleeved white shirt, broad pinstriped pants cuffed at the ankle, sitting casually, his arms loosely draped about his legs. My mother's older brothers posed in front of the same backdrop in some unknown studio in Yorktown.

Because all of my mother's older brothers at one time lived in or near the tiny town, it was a gathering place for weddings, quinceañeras, funerals, christenings, and other family events. As time passed, we congregated less frequently and only saw each other during Yorktown's annual three-day event known as Western Days, a celebration that includes a multi-county parade, fair, and barbecue cooking contest.[13] Year after year, my Tío Joe, a fierce competitor, sacrificed sleep to stoke the fire on his 100-gallon smoker that held his competition-worthy ribs, brisket, and chicken. For all of his labor and devotion, he never won a ribbon, though he succeeded in bringing together his family for more than forty years. Family members came from all over to attend Western Days and visit with Tío Joe, some staying for only a few hours, others for an entire week. While attending graduate school out of state, I did not join my family for Western Days, and only resumed the annual trek after my son was born. I wanted him to have the joyfully chaotic experience of being surrounded by scores of second, third, fourth, and fifth cousins.

In advance of one of our last trips, Mami asked me to print copies of the photos I had of Tati Eugenia and Tito Lalo, as well as those of her older brothers, José, Lalo, Ovidio, and Nicolas. I was asked to bring them to Western Days so she could share them with my cousins who had no pictures of their grandparents or of their fathers as young men. We arrived in Yorktown Saturday morning during the parade and made our way over to the barbecue competition area to find the Ortiz family booth. After wandering among lavish RVs, boat-sized smokers, team booths and tables, we stumbled upon a familiar sight. My Tío Nicolas, whom I had not seen for some time, was seated among a cluster of folding chairs, holding court with some of my older primos. In years previous, the spot would have be-

5.5. "Mother and son." Photographer unknown; courtesy of Domino Renee Perez.

MADONNA AND CHILD (1930)

The tight-fitting light cotton bodice accentuates a woman's small frame. A plunging neckline exposes smooth, flawless skin. She is seated in a straight-backed chair, which peeks out behind the slender shoulder and gathered folds of her skirt. Bare arms protectively, gracefully encircle the boy outfitted in a pinstriped shirt. Unexpectedly large hands that have been concealed, gloved, muffed, here rest against the child's leg. The fingers arch, long and delicate. A hint of calf is exposed beneath the crème-colored clutch purse positioned against her body to hide the naked leg. But it's the au courant hat, a dark bucket cloche, or perhaps a soft felt bonnet, pushed back on her head that commands attention. The curving brim with a basket-weave pattern frames a handsome face and eyes filled with uncertainty, staring at an unknown point only she can see. Gone is the elegant sophistication of her parents' home. Gone is the fox fur. Gone is the hint of a smile. My Uncle Joe's bare feet dangle at her side as he gazes disapprovingly into the camera.

longed to my Tío Joe; instead, family members from four generations surrounded Nicolas, the oldest surviving brother.

As my family and I approached to offer our saludos, I recognized the strand of an oft-told tale about Tío Feliciano's search for his lost siblings. After Eugenia's death, her children were separated because their father, Eduardo, could not take care of all seven children on his own. The four oldest boys, José, Lalo, Nicolas, and Ovidio, went north with their father to work in the fields, while the three younger children, Maria (my mother), Ofelia, and Feliciano (Freddy), were sent to live with their maternal grandparents. Time passed, and the three younger children saw their father and brothers with less frequency until one day, they stopped visiting altogether. When Freddy was old enough, he set out alone, following obscure leads that might direct him toward his older brothers, and eventually found Joe in a Yorktown bar. Having heard the story countless times as a child, I wanted my son to know that my tío's determination helped to reunite his family.

While my husband and son were lured away by the Ferris wheel and Octopus ride, I stayed behind to visit with arriving family members. Before long our easy way of talking returned, and in between reminiscences we made sure the children and elders had food, drinks, or whatever else they needed. After a while, my Uncle Nick called me over and patted the seat beside him. Moving to the edge of his chair, he leaned forward and told me in Spanish-inflected English with a distinct Texas twang, "I was watchin' you earlier."

I laughed a little uncomfortably at the thought of having been studied without my knowledge and replied, "Oh, yeah?"

With his eyes fixed on my face, he slowly nodded. "Umm hmmm, your mama and I want to tell you somethin', but she's busy helpin' your brother Michael fix the contest plates, and I don't want to wait." This time he laughed at what I imagined was his own impatience.

"Okay, tío," I said. "So what is it that you want to tell me?"

"Yo estaba aquí mirando a la gente, familia, people I hadn't seen in years.[14] Your mama was sittin' beside me and we was talkin' about people, some we didn't recognize, some who were gone." Here his accent thickened. "I was thinkin' about my brotha Jo and Big Ed, and then all of a sudden, I turn to your mama and say, 'Look, there's Amá Eugenia.'"

Sensing my confusion, he explained, "Your mama looks at me and I can tell she thinks I'm talkin' about you because she says, 'Yes, mija's fixing lunch.'"

"Pero, that's not what I meant. So I say to her again, 'There's Mami.' Y mi hermana me dice, 'Que estás pensando?'"[15] at which point he pulled his shoulders forward and laughed with his tongue between his teeth, a gesture that made him seem younger and mischievous.

"I says to her," he continued, though this time more emphatically, "'Amá Eugenia.'" He paused for effect. "Your mama thought I was, you know . . ." and he twirled his index finger at his temple. "She looked at me, como asi";[16] he lowered his chin while peering over the top of his glasses in a perfect imitation of my mother. "Then you mama says, 'Nicolas, Amá died a long time ago.'"

"I tole her, 'I know that. I'm talkin' about Domino.'" Shifting in his seat, he turned to address me directly. "You remind me of her. I just wanted you to know that, hijita,"[17] and with that he sat back.

I reached out and placed my hand on his in a manner that suggested absolute certainty in what I was about to say. "Tío, I've looked at the pictures tantas veces. I scanned them. Hice cópias.[18] I've spent hours looking at and working con las fotos de Tati Eugenia. If we looked the same, I would have noticed. Mira, I have pictures of her right here." I got up and retrieved the folder with the photos from the corner of the table and handed it to him. As he sat the file on his knees, I walked around to the back of his chair to point out from over his shoulder that I was, in fact, correct. When he opened the folder, the top photo was of Eugenia with her fur muffler.

"That one is of her at a train station," I said.

"A boat," he offered gently. "She's on a boat." I leaned in closer, and suddenly the shoreline was so unmistakable that my inability to discern it previously seemed baffling. Other details of the photo began to swim in front of me—the metal railings of the ship's skeleton, the white sandy beach, and Eugenia's mien. Cradling the photo gently in his calloused hand, he pointed to his mother and said, "See, the same face, the same eyes. You and Mama, the same."

Notes

I would like to thank my mother, María Pérez, and my Tía Ofelia Ortiz for sharing their stories with me. Both passed away in 2017, months apart.

1. "Bisabuelos" refers to great-grandparents, and "abuelos" to grandparents.
2. "Tati" and "Tito" are family designations for grandmother and grandfather, respectively.
3. The details surrounding my grandparents' meeting and marriage are shrouded in mystery. It is clear that some family members have information that they do not

wish to share. However, the silences most likely have to do with class conflicts: Tati Eugenia's family was financially well off, and my grandfather Eduardo (Lalo) was from a poor migrant family. My grandparents married without the consent of their families.

4. Like every meXicana in my family, my ears were pierced almost as soon as I exited the womb. My paternal grandmother—a skilled practitioner of magia blanca (white magic), or curanderisma, focused on the healing arts—pierced my ears with a heavy sewing needle and used an ice cube to anesthetize the lobe. She then stuck strands from a straw broom into the holes and covered them with Mercurochrome. (I learned only recently that the red medicine had mercury as its main ingredient and was taken off the market for "safety issues.") The practice of infant ear piercing is ongoing, but I am told that it is now done by meXicana-serving pediatricians in sterile environments. The Big Grandma (my father's mother) would not approve because she believed doctors were for keeping people sick, not for serving the community.

5. The upscale Houston retail chain Battelsteins was reorganized under the name Frost Bros. in the late 1970s. Specializing in high fashion and offering exclusive services such as personal shoppers and consultants, Frost Bros. closed in 1989. Mark Tatge, "Frost Bros. to Begin Liquidation," *Dallas Morning News*, 25 Apr. 1989.

6. Making their first appearance in 1971, Toughskins jeans were a brand exclusive to Sears department stores. Constructed from "a new blend of materials, including Dacron Type 59 polyester, DuPont 420 nylon, and cotton," the pants were designed to be durable, a trait parents identified as "most important" when making their purchasing decisions. Along with the unusual sheen of the material, another trademark feature was the "reinforced" knee area, a patch-like rectangle affixed to the inside of the pant leg, intended to extend the life of the jeans by protecting the vulnerable area from tears. "Toughskins: 1971-present," *Sears Archives*, www.searsarchives.com /brands/toughskins.htm. Accessed 25 June 2012.

7. "Hey, little white girl! What do you know?"

8. The magazine *Photoplay* was first published in 1911 and ran until 1980. In its heyday during the 1930s and 1940s, it was the premiere Hollywood celebrity magazine and used as a promotional vehicle by most of the major Hollywood studios. Its emphasis on the personal lives of actors and screen idols and their romances makes it a forerunner to modern celebrity magazines.

9. The Shamrock Hilton, née Shamrock Hotel, in Houston opened on St. Patrick's Day in 1949. With more than 150 film industry types—including celebrities such as Ginger Rogers, Errol Flynn, and Robert Preston, flown or brought in by rail from Hollywood—the opening day event has become the stuff of legend. The larger than life hotel, and to some extent its famed opening celebration, was fictionalized in Edna Ferber's novel *Giant* (1956) and later featured in George Stevens's film adaptation of the same name. Referred to as "Houston's Riviera," the eighteen-story, 1,100-room hotel boasted state-of-the-art amenities, including air-conditioning in every room, as well as televisions and push-button radios. The Shamrock also had a 5,000 square foot lobby and the "largest outdoor swimming pool" (big enough to hold waterskiing exhibitions), with a diving platform three stories high and an open spiral staircase. Oilman and owner Glenn McCarthy, whose Irish ancestry was celebrated throughout the interior design, particularly in the color palette (sixty-two shades of green), imagined the resort hotel as the centerpiece of a grand shopping and enter-

tainment complex. In 1955, the hotel was sold to the Hilton Corporation, and in 1985, forty years to the date from its grand opening, the hotel was razed. Stephen Fox, "Shamrock Hotel," *Handbook of Texas Online*, Texas State Historical Association, www.tshaonline.org/handbook/online/articles/ccs05. Accessed 25 June 2012.

10. Introduced by Garan Inc. in 1972, Garanimals was a color-complementary line of clothing that allowed children to coordinate outfits by pairing animals on the tags; for example, a giraffe-tagged yellow shirt with a giraffe-tagged pair of brown pants or a monkey-tagged pink striped shirt with a monkey-tagged fuchsia skirt, etc. According to the company's history, the idea was to foster independence and self-confidence in children by drawing on "the idea that there is a positive connection between how children dress and how they feel about themselves." The brand has been reintroduced in discount retail chains. "History of Garanimals," www.garanimals.com/history.htm. Accessed 25 June 2012.

11. The county is named after Green DeWitt, the founder of an early Texas colony. According to the 2010 census, DeWitt County had a population of 20,097. The majority of the town's residents are Anglos, with Mexican Americans and Latinos making up 27 percent of the population.

12. There was some controversy surrounding Block's participation in the second flag planting. Originally identified as Sergeant Hank Hanson of Boston, Block's identity was not rightfully acknowledged until later. Fellow flag-raiser Ira Hayes was instrumental in confirming Block's role in the historic event, hitchhiking 1,300 miles from his Pima community in Arizona to Weslaco, Texas, to deliver the news to Block's parents. See James Bradley with Ron Powers, *Flags of Our Fathers*, Bantam, 2000, pp. 528–529.

13. Western Days is held on the third weekend of October in the city park downtown. The event begins with a Saturday morning parade through town. In addition to the carnival and cook-off, the event includes a street dance, horseshoe and washer tossing tournament, a pig scramble, and a quilt show, as well as booths with commercial vendors.

14. "I was here looking at the crowds and family, people I hadn't seen in years."

15. "But, that's not what I meant. So I say to her again, 'There's Mami.' And my sister says to me, 'What are you thinking?'"

16. "Like this."

17. *Hijita* is a term of endearment that literally means "little daughter."

18. "I made copies."

THE POLITICS OF DRESS: SAYING IT LOUD/SAYING IT CLEAR

CHAPTER 6

Buying the Dream: Relating "Traditional" Dress to Consumer Practices in US Quinceañeras

RACHEL VALENTINA GONZÁLEZ-MARTIN

El vestido es el protagonista en tu quince.
RAFAEL AGUAYO, "BUYING THE RIGHT DRESS"

The quinceañera is a rite of passage ritual celebrating a young girl as she enters adulthood on her fifteenth birthday. The term *quinceañera* (literally "fifteen-year-old") is used by participants to designate both the event and the young woman being celebrated. Historically practiced in Latin America—in particular, Mexico—the tradition has since spread to many parts of the world, including the United States. Since its earliest modest, religious origins, the American Latino quinceañera has evolved into a lavishly celebrated extravaganza with all the trimmings, including an elaborately crafted dress.

Over a three-year period I attended fashion expositions across California organized by *Quinceañera Magazine*, where I interviewed vendors and customers alike. I found that el vestido (the dress) is indeed a primary protagonist in the American Latino rite of passage. While reviewing the latest targeted quinceañera advertising on Facebook, I read the most recent posts from the network of regional *Quinceañera Magazine* franchises. In early 2014, new posts began to appear that exceeded the usual advertisements for expos. What continues to manifest is another way for young Latinas to engage with a specialized social and consumer network facilitated by social media. The hashtag #showoffyourdress is only the latest evidence of how quinceañera celebrations are interpreted as fashion-focused events. Each post, dozens appearing daily, features a photograph of a quinceañera girl in her formal gown, her name, and the date and location of her celebration. Collectively, these posts produce a fashion map covering the

United States and extending into Latin America, including recent posts from girls in Mexico, Guatemala, Colombia, and Peru.

These posts, which are as likely to appear in English as in Spanish, feature young women in a diverse range of spectacular dresses in numerous colors, shapes, and textures, doubling as free advertising for the attendant quinceañera professionals who contribute to these individual celebrations. They simultaneously foreground young Latina consumers as protagonists in the growing narrative of a US Hispanic consumer market that is not clearly divided by assumptions of ethnic-national identity. Instead, the #showoffyourdress hashtag serves as a reminder of how quinceañera consumer networks are viewed collectively as Latina Americans rather than being divided into ethnic and national categories.

Offering young women free promotional space to show off their dresses did not begin online. The practice began by promoting local quinceañeras in regional, group-photo magazine spreads. However, these latest iterations of self-promotion are posted on social media sites such as Facebook, where girls submit their portraits to share with online communities of diverse quinceañera professionals and young Latina fans who follow the latest fashions. This trend in visual self-promotion facilitates the investigation of consumer impact on the performance of current quinceañera celebrations—particularly the choices in fashion—as growing consumer industries integrate the traditional practices of intimate family gatherings into national marketing trends aimed at a general body of US Latina and Latino consumers.

Since 2007, I have conducted ethnographic fieldwork in California, traveling the state and observing how quinceañera family celebrations have become linked to major commercial industries. I have observed hundreds of vendors selling their wares at regional quinceañera expositions, each vying for the ideal quinceañera consumers—the ones who are culturally aware enough to desire a quinceañera, but distant enough from the tradition to need the intervention of industry professionals to organize their events. The consumers need not be wealthy; instead, they generally have access to networks of padrinos, or godparents, willing to invest in the preparation of the celebration. Once financial resources are secured, these large-scale expositions provide families access to all the major industries linked to planning and celebrating a quinceañera in one location. This shift from examining the event from the vantage point of religious ritual toward a consumer model allows the observer to recognize significant changes in the celebration as a whole.

While quinceañera celebrations are significant to families and local communities, as consumer entities they reach far beyond individual families and neighborhoods, creating a public face for a growing Latino populace in the United States. Since the 2000 census, which confirmed the rapid expansion of Latino citizens in the United States, marketing agencies devoted to the Hispanic market have expanded, making their presence known on billboards, magazine covers, and television commercials (Dávila 2). Because of its familiar imagery, which is relatable to both weddings and modern North American prom celebrations, quinceañera imagery has been used to draw Latino consumers to multiple industries. Companies like Verizon Wireless, Dr. Pepper, and even Disney use the quinceañera tradition to appeal to Latino consumers, raising not only the profile of the event but also the profile of the larger community as a desirable and lucrative marketing demographic on a national scale. With the use of quinceañera celebrations to sell phone service, beverages, and even dream vacations, one sees a greater community acknowledgement of the tradition itself, as it is increasingly more visible within mainstream public discourse. These promotions, often featuring a young woman in a floor-length quinceañera gown, promise dream fulfillment through consumer participation and appeal to a body of young Latina consumers and their families who are in the process of shopping for the ideal quinceañera dress. These advertisements contribute to a mythology of dress shared by a new generation of quinceañera celebrants who seek personal fulfillment in the process of finding the "perfect" gown. While no two quinceañeras are exactly the same, the stories that young women shared with me over the course of this study were strikingly similar and included a narrative motif of the "dream dress." As they narrated their stories of the search for the ideal dress on boutique racks, expo floors, and internet sites, they began to reveal their search for their ideal selves. With this understanding of the primacy of ideologies of dress in current quinceañera celebrations, examining the events must also become an examination of connections between the commodification of ritual elements and the developing functions of quinceañera celebrations among new generations of Latina youth.

The Quinceañera Dress: Ritual Object or Commodity?

As rituals of social incorporation, quinceañera celebrations are practiced by Latin American and Latino communities across the hemispheric Americas. Ritual events are those defined by regularity and familiarity over time. In her interpretations of how ritual life affects everyday reality, Deborah

Kapchan notes that through their familiar form and repetition, rituals "transmit the core values of society, implanting ideologies such as religion, patriarchy, and social hierarchy in the very bones of children, in their flesh and breath" (130). Within formal ritual contexts, meaning is derived from the associations of material objects that hold symbolic meaning, retained long after the immersive ritual moment has passed, and participants have transitioned back into the banality of everyday life. Within quinceañera celebrations, one such prominent material object is the quinceañera's formal gown. The understanding of such "aesthetic phenomena" as ritual garb, notes Kapchan, "brings a deeper comprehension of what constitutes self and society" (130). Ritual therefore helps individuals and communities design and refigure experiences of a shared selfhood in which an understanding of a singular "I" and communal "we" becomes overlaid in mutually constitutive interpretations of aesthetic practices, such as the donning of the quinceañera dress.

The folklorist Norma E. Cantú, in "La Quinceañera: Towards an Ethnographic Analysis of a Life-Cycle Ritual," notes that the practice of quinceañera celebrations, including its fashion, is rooted in the colonial histories of Spanish, French, and Indigenous cultural blending (74). The tradition is often understood as a hybridized event, one that draws on the ritual coming-of-age practices of pre-Columbian communities and also captures the pageantry of European court rituals (Erevia 28). The celebration has been embraced among US Latinas/os as part of their Latin American cultural patrimony, particularly on the US–Mexico border, where the celebratory practices of Chicana participants may straddle national as well as ideological borderlands (Cantú, "La Quinceañera," 15).

While a focus on Mexican-origin and Chicana communities has been most common when contextualizing the quinceañera tradition in the United States, as in Norma E. Cantú's work on "Chicana Life-Cycle Rituals" (16; see also Davalos 104), entering the tradition from a material focus allows one to see that within US traditions, ethnic national identity, while present, is not always a distinguishing factor. The ethnic national factors that might affect dress choice are becoming subsumed in a national marketplace that seeks to draw a collective "Latina/o" or "Hispanic" community in broad swaths. However, the character of US-based celebrations, when viewed through a lens of consumerism, can be seen in marketing strategies that are not confined to US Latinas, as indicated by elements such as dress fashions that travel seamlessly across the Americas through international advertising campaigns. Couture Mexican design house BellaSerá markets through *Quinceañera Magazine* using powerful images of models adorned in spectacular gowns with minimal text. This practice allows the dress, rather than the young woman, to be the protagonist. Transcending the limitations of Spanish-language fluency, this type of visually engaging, fashion-forward dress marketing simultaneously promotes and subsumes individual identities while serving Latin American, transnational, and US Latina quinceañera audiences, creating diasporic communities through dress. As an element of US Latina folklore, this celebration serves as an entry into the changing landscape of Latina identity expression across various immigrant communities of the US Latina/o diaspora. The following points focus on quinceañera dress traditions of US Latina youths and the ways in which participants in the quinceañera ritual engage with consumer industries to create new communities in dress that transcend geographic boundaries and ethnic identities, and highlight an empowering process of ritual self-adornment among Latina women.

The quinceañera ritual is divided into two distinct segments: a religious event, which usually includes a Catholic mass (referred to as a misa de gracias), and a reception, often taking the form of a dinner dance. The organization of these two segments affects how dress is incorporated into the celebration as a whole.

In Sanger, California, in April 2010, I watched Jazmin Alcazar walk down the aisle of St. Mary's Catholic Church not with a groom but with a chambelán de honor—that is, her escort for the evening. Jazmin had turned fifteen a month earlier, but her event had been delayed due to the church's busy Lenten season. This variation in date is not uncommon in contemporary celebrations. Interviews with young women in the Bay Area revealed that celebrating a quinceañera at the age of sixteen offers a compromise for families who want to celebrate their Latino heritage and honor their daughters' desire to celebrate the "sweet sixteen" milestone at the same time.

The Catholic mass represents one of the most recognizable ritual elements of the quinceañera tradition among US Latinas/os. While non-Catholic quinceañera religious blessings are gaining popularity among different US Latino diasporas, the Catholic mass is still considered a necessary feature of a complete quinceañera celebration among Mexican-descent communities. The mass is an affirmation of the life of the quinceañera girl and a reaffirmation of her baptismal vow to follow the teachings of the Catholic Church as she grows into womanhood (Ranjith 2). Her personal presentation is also an acknowledgment of her new identity as an adult. Jazmin, a petite young woman, was awash in a sea of pink tulle during the course of the quinceañera mass. Her dress style blended the traditional fitted bodice and ball gown shape with more modern details such as sequins and embroidery. Her shoulders were covered by a shawl of matching pink tulle, a last-minute addition necessary to comply with the rules of modesty outlined by the youth ministries director at St. Mary's Catholic Church. The shawl was discarded almost immediately as Jazmin and her court of honor (her chosen group of male and female attendants) processed outside after the service was over.

After the formal religious segment of the celebration, whether a full Catholic mass or a less formal Protestant blessing, the quinceañera, her court of honor, and a myriad of family members and guests move into the second phase of the celebration. The reception is the secular portion of the event, often drawing greater numbers of attendees than the religious service, which may be attended by only close family and the young woman's godparents. The reception, the focal point of many of the contemporary quinceañeras that I have attended, offers a different venue from which to view quinceañera fashion. The commercialization of the receptions makes them sites of competition among community members, converting what were previously intimate family celebrations into spectacles: dresses have become larger, venues grander, and audiences more demanding. In "Quinceañera Debutante: Rites and Regalia of American Debdom," Karal Ann Marling notes that dress rituals "can be folded into the reception or party organized along the lines of a debut grafted into a Broadway musical, a senior prom, and a dream wedding" (4). While young women might encounter limitations in religious contexts where strict rules of modesty are part of a ritual orientation, the reception is a space where creativity is valued by audiences eager to see something "new." Thus the boundaries of "traditional" femininity are at odds with new trends in quinceañera fashion, creating tensions between multiple generations of participants.

One explicit internal dress ritual executed during the reception is the exchanging of flat shoes for heels. Scholars have noted that the inclusion of this ritual is one way in which womanhood is made material during the event (Cantú, "Chicana Life-Cycle Rituals" 25; Marling 4). What has not been examined is how this symbolic gesture is connected to other sartorial choices prioritized by the quinceañera girl as "fashionable," which becomes a driving force in staging the celebrations and styling quinceañera girls. The exchange of flats for heels is indeed a symbolic gesture wherein fathers acknowledge their daughters' transition to young womanhood. However, in current celebrations, especially those in which planning and performance are heavily influenced by modern quinceañera professionals, young women must often change out of heels before the shoe ritual ever takes place. For young women with whom I worked, high heels were already part of their nonritual sartorial repertoire, but they unanimously agreed to forgo heels to create a more attractive silhouette in their dresses by wearing flats. In similar acts of sartorial defiance, some young women are opting to reject heels altogether, instead having custom-made flats as their signature quinceañera accessory. In 2010, the Los Angeles–based online retailer 15 Kicks dedicated itself to making custom-designed quinceañera sneakers to match any dress. This stylistic shift, in part facilitated by the presence of custom retailers, allows young women to mobilize symbolic systems that bypass the need for parental approval. In fact, as a network of padrinos is likely contributing financially to the quinceañera, mothers and fathers are no longer completely able to control how the money is spent. Excising the exchange of flats for heels from the event renders the public acknowledgment of parental approval of a particular kind of femininity symbolized by high heels moot. It temporarily transfers the source of power to define personal womanhood from father to daughter. Although a seemingly trivial addition to the possible repertoire of quinceañera dress and accessories established by commercial outlets, shopping for shoes creates an opportunity for girls to assert themselves into a narrative of womanhood in transition. Tías, abuelas, and madrinas are now watching events that once were guided by intimate networks of knowledgeable family and friends be *produced* by professional party planners and dress designers who are remaking the qualities of the event, one dress, and pair of shoes, at a time.

Quinceañera fashion is not simply the formal gown donned by the quinceañera girl, but a system of symbolic meanings readable through sartorial choices. It is organized in a circular frame, with the girl at the center. Her choices in form and style set the tone for the entire event, with radiating circles of participants surrounding her—those closest being the most intimately connected. The court of honor, the young woman's chosen attendants, most resemble her in dress and style formality. The court is composed of up to fourteen participants. In 2010, at the *Quinceañera Magazine* expo in San Diego, a Tijuana-based dance troupe advertised a package deal for the rental of male escorts, who were also professional dancers, for the evening. Rather than drawing on traditional sources for the court, such as family members and close friends, professional chambelanes can ensure that the coordinated group waltz will be perfectly executed, impressing the audience and further creating a dream event. Substituting professional performers for friends and family illustrates how the court of honor is a representation of the quinceañera girl and therefore is made distinct as performers, not guests, through conventions in dress. Chambelanes often wear full tuxedos or some version of matching formal wear. In 2010, during my visits to regional quinceañera expos in Watsonville, Sacramento, and San José, California, vendors promoted matching colored suspenders and bow ties as possible variations on formal vests and suit coats. The damas, the quinceañera's female attendants, wear dresses carefully chosen to accent but not detract from the quinceañera's dress. Jazmin wore light pink, and her attendants wore dresses in bright magenta with light pink accents in their bouquets. While Jazmin's dress had a full skirt that extended to the floor, her attendants' dresses were knee-length and lacked the dramatic volume of Jazmin's gown. Together, the male and female escorts serve as matching pairs, promoting a vision of hetero-normative romantic pairing.

The only male participant whose dress stands apart is the chambelán de honor. Unlike the general group of male escorts, who may be professional performers, the chambelán de honor often takes a prominent ceremonial role and is frequently chosen from the inner circle of the celebrant's family. His attire is often characteristically different from that of the other male attendants; as the quinceañera's escort, he must stand apart from all other males in the room, including the quinceañera's father. Jazmin's chambelán de honor wore a white zoot suit, while the other escorts wore similarly styled black suits accented with white suspenders. The choice of zoot suits for the chambelanes reflects the retail options in Jazmin's home area. Christina, Jazmin's mother, notes that her daughter wanted the young men to look interesting in "not just the same old suits"; the only local option that took a dramatic turn was zoot suit–inspired formal wear. However, the zoot suits were chosen entirely for their dramatic statement; Jazmin and her parents had no knowledge of the style's contentious past as signifier of political dissent and cultural resistance among Mexican Americans in the United States (L. Alvarez). This uninformed selection of zoot suits illustrates how the extensive commodification of elements of this celebration potentially alienates participants from deeper cultural meanings that may have been present in the celebrations of earlier generations. Contemporary dress choices highlight the way in which current quinceañera events focus on the quinceañera as an individual. Her attendants, both male and female, are dressed to contribute as accessories to the event and are temporarily stripped of their individualism as they serve to highlight the quinceañera in her moment of social transition.

One way to view the event is as a performance piece, with the quinceañera as a lead performer and the host of friends and families who come to witness this embodied coming-of-age process as an audience. Conceptualizing the event as a performance highlights the ways in which meaning is made through the process of donning a gown, striding down the church aisles, and enacting a series of smaller, internal rituals that create a recognizable quinceañera event. The quinceañera understood as a performance allows audiences to evaluate the event as a form of self-portraiture in which a young woman and her family craft not just *a* quinceañera, but *their* quinceañera. Gown choices play an integral role in helping Latina teens create an intimate celebration through public sartorial display.

Quinceañera gowns can be categorized in multiple ways that illuminate how they function within the larger coming-of-age event. To consider the influences of consumer culture on the quinceañera tradition, one must conceptualize the dress as simultaneously a ritual object and a commodity. Scholars of folklore have often examined the connection between cultural production and consumerism as a question of authenticity (Bendix 4). Can folklore continue to be "authentic" cultural production if it has been recontextualized in a commercial context? Unlike other studies of consumerism and folklore that examine how consumerism often decontextualizes traditional artistry from its home community (Lau vii), quinceañera celebrations have never been completely removed from consumer contexts. Rather than using a bolt of fabric and spools of thread, women have moved toward purchasing complete dresses. What is being traded from one generation to the next is artistic control. The dress now represents not only family values and the individual tastes of teenage daughters, but also the artistic drive of professional designers and the marketing vision of local and national corporations. The question of authenticity will continue to haunt celebrations where dresses draw more criticism than praise, and families must justify how their money is spent and their labor reserved. The collective discussion inevitably returns to the gown as the questionable protagonist in the quinceañera story.

As a ritual object, the gown serves as a symbol of femininity that is worn within the context of the religious and reception portions of the celebration to signal social transformation. "The dress marks a change in the wearer's status in the community," states Cantú ("Chicana" 19). In this context, she is referring to the new responsibilities of adult womanhood in the community of Mexican and Mexican Americans in Laredo, Texas, and Nuevo Laredo, Tamaulipas, Mexico. When speaking of the quinceañera dresses of her generation, Cantú notes, "In 1962 we paid no more than $30 for my dress," whereas dresses purchased in the 1990s could cost upward of $1,000 ("La Quinceañera" 86). My research has shown that quinceañera dresses bought in the 2000s, especially those that claim a couture or international pedigree, begin at $450 and run into the thousands, not unlike modern wedding dresses. And, similar to modern wedding attire, these prices rarely include the potentially elaborate alterations required to make the dress a perfect fit. One can observe that quinceañera fashion has continually been discussed in terms of comparative consumerism, one generation to the next; however, in contemporary celebrations, more than the cost of material and labor, the quinceañera dress is viewed as an investment in affluence. In this case, the new status being ushered in through material expression may not simply be individual interpretations of young adulthood, but the elevation of a family's collective narrative of personal financial success in the United States—a capitalistic coming-of-age. In this context, dresses are reframed as commodities as well as ritual objects and become sites for contestations of the larger tradition's *cost* as well as *worth*. Rethinking the relationship between cost and worth requires one to understand the way in which a young woman's worth within her community has been judged using interpretations invested in the traditional quinceañera dress.

Tradition

Unfortunately, there is no archive of US quinceañera traditions. As expressive traditions, they are subject to the changes of communities in transition and are therefore always in transition themselves. Quinceañera gowns have often been described with respect to wedding gowns. "Often she [the quinceañera] comes to the church dressed as a bride, in a long white gown. The bell shaped skirts favored for the occasion are thought to reflect Spanish court dress of the imperial past" (Marling 3). Yet even this connection is met with tension because young women are expected to distance themselves from wedding-based interpretations of the event that might imply that a quinceañera has the same social rights and sexual freedom with her chambelán de honor as a bride with her groom. These connections to other coming-of-age moments signify the solemnity often brought to the planning and performance of quinceañeras as ritual moments. Collective interpretations often connect the dress's floor-length style, white color, ball gown silhouette, and overall simple form with the demure behavior and high moral values of the quinceañera. In "Performances of Race, Culture, Class, and Religion in the Somerville Community," Sara Arcaya discusses working with Brazilian, Haitian, and Salvadorian quinceañeras, noting that "Somerville girls wear conservative dresses—they do not tend to be very extravagant, though they do try to look like princesses" (96). Here she alludes to the fact that ideal femininity in this community creates a preference for dress styles that maintain control over the female body and do not extend the body too far into public space. Notions of traditionality have also been linked to nationality and ethnicity: "the traditional Colombian color is yellow," while "the traditional Salvadorian girl selects pink" (96). However, these interpretations of traditions are fluid, particularly in the blended American Latino consumer contexts of the United States. Participants in online visual exchanges (#showoffyourdress) reinforce the way in which dress types are rarely categorized as "Mexican," "Colombian," or "Salvadorian"; instead, the question asked is "What kind of quinceañera dress defines *you*?" The question is directed at a contemporary generation of diverse US Latinas who are grouped through their participation in the ritual, not by their specific ethnic heritage. Dress designers and retail outlets, eager to draw in young Latina consumers, respond to this new drive toward individualism by promoting variety and customizability as the hallmarks of their dress collections.

The enormous variety in style, color, and texture—now made possible by the preponderance of mass-produced gowns and the efforts of industrious seamstresses and designers—is helping to replace earlier messages that linked purity and innocence to conservative color palettes. Now vibrant color palettes, once thought to be inappropriate for a quinceañera, are being featured in magazines and on websites boasting the newest lines in quinceañera fashion. In this context, color choice and dress shape are access points to conversations about how young women are refiguring their role as authors in the stories of womanhood woven into narratives of dress in quinceañera celebrations. The changing standards by which quinceañeras choose to adorn their bodies in the ritual moment represent a change in the protagonism in the event. Critiques of color become critiques of individualism. It is in this intimate space, where fabric meets body, that quinceañera gowns become the locus of criticism in contemporary celebrations.

A primary criticism expressed by the older generations of Mexicanas and Chicanas whom I have spoken with during my research was the way in which current quinceañera celebrations—in particular, the choices in dress—appear misguided and at times offensive. Not only was the dress of the quinceañera but also that of her attending audience subject to scrutiny due to the priority given to sartorial choices in this ritual event. Rosario López, who spent her youth in South Texas before moving to California to work in the fields of the Central Valley with her family, explained her distaste for contemporary quinceañera celebrations through a critique of the dress:

> I remember them growing up in Texas. I would get invited to all sorts of quinceañera parties because all my friends were part of the CYO [Catholic Youth Organization] and were daughters of people who had money. I only went to one. They were too expensive, and we did not have the extra money to spend. I did not have a fancy enough dress, but I borrowed one; it was dark green and long, to the floor. I wore a fur stole. But they aren't like that anymore; people just go wearing anything, like they are going to the store or something.

For those growing up in largely Latino areas of the Southwest, quinceañera celebrations may seem like old news, the talk of aunts and grandmothers. For older audience members with a perspective dating from the mid-twentieth century, quinceañera celebrations functioned differently than they do now. The influx of non-traditional dresses, in both shape and color, is viewed by older generations as offsetting the solemnity of the event, which undermines the need for guests to don formal attire. At the same time, a lack of solemnity may also be interpreted as a class-specific interpretation of events, now seen as devoid of efficacy, as the impulses that open the event to shifts in dress also open it to participants outside the upper classes. The commoditization of dress in the United States has led to greater variability in style, but also to variability in cost. In particular, those with little disposable income for whom extravagant gowns were once out of reach can now purchase a mass-produced dress for a fraction of the price. The shifts in dress style, color, and affordability therefore signal a cultural shift in attitudes about the event as a whole, creating a sense of egalitarianism, even as some elders find the free-market quinceañera puzzling, if not downright vulgar. Older participants often cringe at the sight of the newest iterations in form and fashion, even going so far as to wish the celebration away entirely.

Rita Torres of San José, California, shared an anecdote that shows how much quinceañera dress has changed and how that change impacts new audiences. Sitting in her kitchen, drinking a cup of abuelita, she shared with me her insights from watching her step-niece come of age: "I couldn't believe it. She was in that dress, lying on the floor, practically falling out of her dress. I thought, 'Who took those pictures? And why were they on our plates?'" Rita explained that during the reception the party favors at each table setting were miniature portraits of the quinceañera girl posing seductively in her gown. "The worst part was that on the other side of the picture was a business card for the photographer! It was disgusting. She was an advertisement. The only thing we thought was that we could have forgiven her if she had worn white!"

Dress in the context of the quinceañera performance plays a key role in setting the quinceañera apart from the rest of her cohort and guests. Her elaborate gown becomes the event's focal point, drawing in the gaze of audience members as the young woman embodies womanhood by donning the ornate and often expensive dress in the context of dance and public performance. With this performance comes risk, particularly the risk of criticism that may degrade the virtue of the quinceañera on display. However, what is often overlooked in these performative moments of religious and social display is how the quinceañera chooses her gown.

The research that I have conducted expressly focuses on the way dresses are chosen, what influences the style and choice, and the meaning of the dresses to the young women who don them. I assert that there is a third phase of the quinceañera ritual that is just as meaningful as the two public performances enacted in church and at the reception. This additional phase is the preliminary phase of planning and shopping, where value and identities are negotiated through aesthetic choices in dress and adornment. The consumer context, rather than the intimate process of engaging with knowledgeable family members to plan the event and design the formal gown, is a shared process of consumption. The process can include the decision to celebrate the event, the engagement with planning materials such as themed magazines, the participation in online communities of quinceañeras, and the hands-on engagement with regional quinceañera-themed expositions.

Evaluating the Role of Consumer Networks

As a ritual performance the quinceañera is an organized process of united symbolism in two distinct contexts: first, a religious celebration that most commonly takes the form of a Catholic mass; and second, a public presentation highlighting the quinceañera's transition into young adulthood within her wider community. The third context, which I am proposing and which presupposes the more commonly accepted phases of the quinceañera ritual, is the consumer context.

In previous generations, the adornment of young quinceañeras-to-be was chosen by networks of female family members with knowledge of the tradition and its attendant practices (Cantú, "Chicana" 25). A grand-mother or mother, rather than supplying funds for the event, would offer her time and employ her skills to make a gown by hand. The nights spent fitting a dress were more than an investment of hours; they were also a time to share stories of their own coming-of-age moment. In the past, dresses were a catalyst for gaining adult knowledge and learning what it meant to be a woman in one's own family. However, this vision of inter-generational communication is romanticized, as it presupposes nuclear and extended families living in close proximity and with cultural experi-ences that make this ritual familiar, while it alienates participants whose gender identification falls outside rigid hetero-normative qualifications. Patricia Zavella writes that for some reluctant quinceañeras, the highly feminizing experience of a quinceañera was the epitome of everything young queer women wanted to escape from within their Latino families, everything that stifled their ability to be truly themselves, even though the event was meant to withdraw certain restrictions on maturing girls. "The body," she states, "was seen as a map . . . read by others regarding a woman's transgressions" (238). Coded within the clothing styles and colors was sexual abstinence, an obedient temperament, and most impor-tant, adherence to heterosexuality. However, current traditions include a consumer network of quinceañera professionals whose aesthetic inspi-ration is being prioritized over the opinions of family. Not surprisingly, these commercial networks, which include various quinceañera-focused businesses, are changing the culture of the ritual event, featuring dress as a tool for both creating amazing spectacles and creatively (re)imagining community interpretations of ideal womanhood—that is, materializing different levels of the quinceañera ritual itself.

No two quinceañeras are exactly alike. Similarly, no two quinceañera dresses are exactly alike. While the presence of national retailers that carry quinceañera dresses makes duplicate dresses a reality—such as Mary's Bridal, which provides mass-produced gowns made in China to retailers around the country—it is the performance of the dress in situ that creates a holistic vision of the quinceañera as a personalized ritual performance. Although the images of quinceañera celebrations have shifted over time, the presence of the dress has always been a mainstay of the celebration (Davalos 104). However, the form of the quinceañera dress has changed as the labor producing the ubiquitous dress, and indeed the larger cele-bration, has shifted from private homes to a range of public options, from couture ateliers to overseas sweatshops.

In 2013, the quinceañera ritual was reframed as a $680 billon industry in the United States (Lima 2013). Despite its lucrative status, critics lament the current role of consumerism within the quinceañera rite, claiming that it marks the end of the "tradition." However, tradition is nothing if not malleable. In addition to its historic roots, it reflects the values of the time and resonates with contemporary communities. Folklorist Henry Glassie notes that "tradition is the creation of the future out of the past" (395). We pull tradition through time and remake it as we engage with it, creating something new out of something old. Latino consumers are being touted by national marketing agencies as "fast becoming the preeminent driver of growth and likely trend setters in the [US] marketplace" (Neilson 15). Therefore, it is only fitting that the massive influence of neoliberal identity politics be felt at the level of this coming-of-age tradition. Twenty-first-century US Latino/a quinceañeras are a consumer enterprise. Professional quinceañera industries, including dress designers, dress boutiques, and expositions, have raised the public profile of the event. The intense visibility of the celebration makes it newly accessible to families without personal histories linked to the tradition and provides guidance to those who want to claim a distinctly Latino American identity within the United States. The primary shift in the conceptualization of quinceañera dresses in recent decades is the inception of a rhetoric of *choice*.

Although they cannot speak, quinceañera dresses tell a story. In previous generations, the stories they told were family narratives, grouped around female networks and shared visions of feminine virtue coded on the body. Currently, trends in dress tell different stories that prioritize individual aspirations, personal aesthetics, and self-portraiture. While the subtext of this narrative remains collective—an effort beyond the imaginings of a single teenage girl—the primary discourse remains a personal narrative in which the quinceañera girl is the protagonist. Young women now aspire to coordinate events that tell a story about themselves—an idealized narrative that stitches together a glamorous future. The process of choosing a gown and the complex decisions that accompany it encompass its own coming-of-age moment. Examining the dress as a commodity, it becomes a surrogate for shopping for one's self. Young women swirl around expos and dress shops trying to find their selves hanging on the racks, and when they cannot find them, they can elect to imagine a new dress and a new self yet to be constructed. The newest and growing networks of quinceañera professionals around the country have made customization and innovation possible and accessible to anyone who can pay for it. A key location for understanding the power of the shopping process is on the fashion show runways of the quinceañera exposition.

Despite cultural, economic, and geographic diversity, quinceañera events across the country share a common thread: that of a distinct consumer process that illustrates how young Latinas and the events they celebrate are coming of age at the same time. Consumer spaces such as large-scale quinceañera expos become ideological spaces for shared experiences keenly focused on speaking to peer networks. In *Once Upon a Quinceañera: Coming of Age in the U.S.A.*, Julia Alvarez ruminates on the spectacle of quinceañera marketing, stating, "I feel as if I've wandered into the backroom where femaleness of the next generation of Latinas is being manufactured, displayed, and sold" (47). While Alvarez describes an aloof and even alarmed response to the alienating environment she encounters, the process she is observing is actually being coordinated and commercialized by Latino communities and, in many instances, Latina entrepreneurs. While she draws attention to the "manufacturing" of femaleness, she also implicitly acknowledges that said "femaleness" is open to interpretation, criticism, and even change. Although one might interpret these consumer outlets as exploiting traditional knowledge for profit, they remain creative outlets for those whose lives in the United States are decontextualized from idealized outlets of so-called traditional knowledge and are in need of new networks of influence to engage in creative cultural practices. The exposition environment is more than a space to negotiate purchases; it is also a place to explore values and ideologies, those that past generations took as fact, and new generations have the luxury of questioning.

Elena Ocampo says, "It all starts with the dress and everything else falls into place after that." Owner of Dreams of the Queen event planning in San José, California, Ocampo believes she is offering girls a chance to express their individuality through her custom-made couture quinceañera gowns. On the expo runway, she presents gowns that diverge from the styles of more recognizable quinceañera fashions that use soft colors and delicate textures to index accepted notions of mild feminine virtue (Cantú, "Chicana" 19). Instead, she designs dresses in bright colors: teal, hot pink with black and gold accents, orange with black fringe. In 2010 Ocampo featured a miniature ball gown in bright tangerine trimmed in black with a matching pair of tangerine and black leg warmers. The design was risqué, being both physically revealing and nonconforming to traditionally accepted quinceañera styles. In the past such non-conformity might subject a quinceañera to accusations of lurid behavior and temperament; however, today Ocampo's styles help frame quinceañera celebrations as a space to play with as much as to accept norms of female behavior. Her highly changeable designs evoke a sense of rugged individualism, where feminine virtue is changeable, not stagnant. Her styles illustrate how through creative risks and choices that fall outside the standard dress of previous generations, young women can question their public presentation of a gendered and sexualized self. While her color combinations are somewhat jarring, they appeal to young Latinas looking to don a custom work of art.

Ocampo's stylistic divergence from other designers is evident through her disuse of accessories that are often conceptualized as hallmarks of ladylike behavior. Her models often stride down the runway shoeless and braless, with characteristic fearless expressions, more sanguine than subdued. She styles her models in defiance of what is ordinary and expected, embracing a lack of traditionalism. And yet her dresses encapsulate a shared essence of a twenty-first-century quinceañera spirit, one that places young women at the forefront of their event as active, creative agents in their own lives, benefitting from the talents of professional material artists. A focus on Elena's work highlights that there is a space between the monolithic corporate machine that opportunistically draws on cultural traditions for the sake of increasing profit and the wholly private quinceañera event managed only by family and friends. Elena and designers across the country like her who are challenging stereotypical images of the coming-of-age dress are reinventing this seemingly antiquated rite of passage for new generations of young Latinas. As artist-entrepreneurs like Elena collaborate with young women and families, helping them mark their inner desires on their outer selves, the outer self becomes a way to visually inscribe a narrative of the body, readable to select audiences of family and friends. This new narrative represents a kind of visual code-switching from the past.

As John Gumperz explains, shifting from one language or register to another in mid-conversation is termed "code-switching" (59). Within quinceañera celebrations, where girls are more often seen than heard, young women inscribe their stories on their bodies for new audiences. There are three main themes to this visual storyboard: sexuality, personality, and visibility. While young woman have their own stories to tell, these three themes are emergent topics that allow diverse audiences to rethink the purpose and usefulness of modern quinceañera celebrations.

The first theme, sexuality, is observed in the traditional influences on quinceañera dresses, which maintained an air of chastity and a young woman's public honor through choices in the gown's cut and color. Current fashion trends offering brightly colored and multihued gowns alongside soft pastel and white versions offer young women a voice in how they want to publicly claim their sexuality. Similarly, versatility in length, such as a minidress or a multi-part dress (which has increased in popularity since being introduced on quinceañera fashion runways in 2007), allows a young woman to feature and accept her body in ways she finds most comfortable. Through creative innovations in dress colors, textures, and silhouettes, young women can choose to accentuate their bodies on their own terms. Choosing to wear a signature deep purple dress for her quinceañera, a young Chicana I interviewed simply stated, "I didn't want to wear white; I wasn't a bride. I don't care what people say. I know who I am" (Hernandez 2008). This broadening of dress choices acknowledges the capacity for quinceañeras to control and define their own sexuality, especially as heterosexual cultural pressures to marry and be a mother are often at the forefront of the most socially conservative quinceañera rhetoric.

The second theme, personality, draws on the first by highlighting that within the parameters of current quinceañera style there is room for more than one kind of gendered woman. Rather than young women feeling they need to conform to a particular ideal form of femininity, they have the opportunity to customize their vision of womanhood, even if for only one day. The rite need not be determinative, but instead, with the variety of choice and the desire to draw in as diverse a consumer clientele as possible, Latina gender identity can be celebrated and staged in a myriad of ways. Recent years have even seen the growth of quinceañeros, the honoring of young men. These trends open discussions of the future inclusivity of quinceañera celebrations for the range of queer and questioning Latino youths who continue to find themselves outside a tradition they cannot yet choose to call their own.

The final theme that emerges in these narratives of dress is visibility. In "Writing on the Social Body: Dresses and Body Adornment in Contemporary Chicana Art," Laura E. Pérez explores the artistry of Yolanda López, among other Chicana artists. In her interpretation of gender and class identity within works of installation art, she examines a work titled *The Nanny*. Here Pérez interprets López's constructed image of a domestic uniform juxtaposed with markers of upper-class privilege to highlight the social reality of the United States, which renders the diverse labor of Latina women "socially and economically invisible" (31). While there continue to be discrepancies in participation along lines of socioeconomic class, especially with the prominence of quinceañera celebrations as consumer enterprises, we are seeing the idea of the invisible Latina morphing into a new form of social inclusion, one in which quinceañera dresses prove to be anything but invisible. They are brightly colored and audacious. They demand notice, recognition, even critique.

This visibility, a seemingly indulgent result of one's desire for "fifteen minutes of fame," also exposes quinceañera events and individuals to harsh criticism. Performances that challenge accepted community notions of womanhood involve risk. While some view the choice in dress as trivial, for those who invest emotionally and financially in the process, this coming-out celebration exposes more than midriffs and décolletés. The coming-out process and the public acknowledgement of cultural norms in transition means that young women's aesthetic choices incur social criticism that, purposefully or not, critiques a larger process of Latino Americanization in which the loss of cultural values is seen as a result of mainstream success. While families wish their daughters' choices would speak directly to their family's values, in reality this code-switching moment is geared toward peers—those physically present, but also those virtually present, who are able to read about and evaluate events for a shared generational perspective that understands experiences of race, ethnicity, and gender differently than their parents and grandparents. Through these innovative exchanges between peers, Latino youths are reconciling the past with the present and redefining Latino American identity for future generations. In this context of the visual self, the story through dress is only one part of the larger narrative of a collaborative coming-of-age process.

Ritual and Change

The commoditization of the ritual dress of the quinceañera celebration has changed how one can interpret the social significance of this coming-of-age ritual. Cantú writes of the quinceañera as a "living tradition" and an ever-changing organic performance ("La Quinceañera" 73). From white veils to rainbow-colored ball gowns, young Latinas are increasingly finding ways to come of age on their own terms by materially incorporating mainstream consumer values into their dress choices to signal hybridized ritual events that are neither wholly new nor wholly traditional. Ritual dress within the quinceañera celebration has changed to accommodate a new sense of personal and communal aesthetics. While for some these transitions serve as harbingers of the end of an ideal set of shared cultural values, for others it allows marginal discourses of age and identity to begin to speak freely and for themselves. Although there is no pure "choice," twenty-first-century quinceañera celebrants are finding themselves inundated by new networks offering them a chance to assert their own creativity within traditional rituals, allowing young people to formulate identity beyond their family nexus and reorienting assumptions of ownership and power within these shared traditions.

The growth of a recognizable quinceañera consumer niche has set the rite on a new path and a transitional road of its own. Broadening market appeal and the subsequent appearance of television and corporate promotions that take on quinceañera themes mark the ubiquitous presence and power of the Latino consumer in the United States. This celebration has become an industry and as such is being modified by forces beyond the control of family and religious networks. Quinceañeras as embodied public performances are powerful tools, creating a customizable space for the production of an ephemeral visual narrative of the self while also highlighting a new brand of consumer citizenship accessible to a new generation of Latino consumers. Dress and adornment—whether simple or elaborate, contrary or conformist—speak for and through young women on display and resonate with a new generation of Latino youth anxious to find their own way in a changing American cultural context. The question for a new generation of Latino families is not "Will we let our daughters speak?" but rather "Will we like what they choose to say?"

Works Cited

Aguayo, Rafael. "Buying the Right Dress." *Quinceañera Magazine*, 1 Jan. 2010, p. 17.

Alvarez, Julia. *Once Upon a Quinceañera: Coming of Age in the U.S.A.* Viking, 2007.

Alvarez, Luis. *The Power of the Zoot: Youth Culture and Resistance in WWII.* U of California P, 2009.

Arcaya, Sara. "Performances of Race, Culture, Class and Religion in the Somerville Community." *Quinceañera*, edited by Ilan Stavans, Greenwood, 2010, pp. 83–108.

Bendix, Regina. *In Search of Authenticity: The Formation of Folklore Studies.* U of Wisconsin P, 1997.

Cantú, Norma E. "Chicana Life-Cycle Rituals." *Chicana Traditions: Continuity and Change*, edited by Norma E. Cantú and Olga Nájera-Ramírez, U of Illinois P, 2002, pp. 15–34.

———. "La Quinceañera: Towards an Ethnographic Analysis of a Life-Cycle Ritual." *Southern Folklore*, vol. 56, no. 1, 1999, pp. 73–101.

Davalos, Karen Mary. "La Quinceañera: Making Gender and Ethnic Identities." *Frontiers: A Journal of Women's Studies*, vol. 16, nos. 2–3, 1996, pp. 107–127.

Dávila, Arlene. *Latinos Inc.: The Marketing and Making of a People.* U of California P, 2001.

Erevia, Angela. "Quince Años, Celebrating a Tradition: A Handbook for Parish Teams." *San Antonio: Missionary Catechists of Divine Providence*, 1992, pp. 1–42.

Glassie, Henry. "Tradition." *Journal of American Folklore*, vol. 108, no. 430, 1995, pp. 395–412.

Gumperz, John J. *Discourse Strategies*. Cambridge UP, 1982.

Hernandez, Rebeca. Personal interview. 9 Nov. 2008.

Kapchan, Deborah. "Performance." *Eight Words for the Study of Expressive Culture*, edited by Burt Feintuch, U of Illinois P, 2003, pp. 121–145.

Lau, Kimberly J. "Ideology Incorporated: The Politics of Commodified Bodily Practice." U of Pennsylvania, PhD diss., Jan. 1998. Available from ProQuest, paper AAI9829933, 1 Aug. 2014.

Lima, Elva. "Quinceañera Tradition Continues to Grow and Expand." "My Fabulous Quince News Center," *Verizon Wireless*, 15 May 2013, www.verizonwireless.com /news/. Accessed 9 July 2013.

López, Rosario. Personal interview. 10 June 2009.

Marling, Karal Ann. "Quinceañera Debutante: Rites and Regalia of American Debdom." *Quinceañera*, edited by Ilan Stavans, Greenwood, 2010, p. 4.

Neilsen. "The State of Hispanic Consumer: Hispanic Market Imperative Report." *Nielsen*, July 2012, pp. 1–15, www.neilsen.com/us/en/insights/reports/2012 /state-of-the-hispanic-consumer-the-hispanic-market-imperative.html. Accessed 1 Aug. 2013.

Ocampo, Elena. Personal interview. 24 Jan. 2010.

Pérez, Laura E. "Writing on the Social Body: Dresses and Body Ornamentation in Contemporary Chicana Art." *Decolonial Voices: Chicana and Chicano Studies in the 21st Century*, edited by Arturo Aldama and Naomi H. Quiñonez, Indiana UP, 2002, pp. 30–63.

Ranjith, Rev. Malcolm. *Bendición al Cumplir Quince Años, Order for the Blessing on the Fifteenth Birthday*. US Conference of Catholic Bishops, 2008.

Torres, Rita. Personal interview. 5 Sept. 2009.

Zavella, Patricia. "Talkin' Sex: Chicanas and Mexicanas Theorize about Silences and Sexual Pleasures." *Chicana Feminisms: A Critical Reader*, edited by Gabriela F. Arredondo et al., Duke UP, 2003, pp. 228–253.

CHAPTER 7

Visuality, Corporality, and Power

AÍDA HURTADO

The visual and corporeal are primary sites from which to examine unequal
social relations and the ways women across the globe negotiate and challenge them. Using quantitative and qualitative methods, I focus on the
violent processes used to conscript women's bodies to produce and police
nationalisms, whiteness, unequal class relations, and normative genders
and sexualities (Hurtado). By using transnational and transhistorical perspectives, this chapter aims to illuminate the complex and contradictory
ways women across the globe consume and reject these processes.

The social constructions of sexualities in media depend on the relational positioning of racialized groups, creating a hierarchy of desirability.
This research examines transnational media focusing on the consistent
representation of whiteness as constituted through its relationship to
the dark Other (Morrison). Transnational social signifiers create a meta
scale of desirability that reinscribes white superiority across transnational
boundaries. The use of gendered dark Others functions in multiple ways:
as a background to highlight the desirability of whiteness, as servants
attending whiteness, and as sexual deviants to further purify whiteness
(Morrison). Ultimately, these technologies of representation reinscribe
the white womb as the only desirable mechanism to perpetuate the transmission of white patriarchal privilege (Hurtado).

Qualitative and Quantitative Methods in
the Study of Visual Representations

In the research behind this chapter,[1] I use both quantitative and qualitative methods to dissect visual representations of various sexualities/femi-

ninities. The sites of study are the image-filled pages of women's fashion magazines. The analysis is based on a sample of international issues of *Vogue* magazine. *Vogue* was selected as the primary source for study because of its wide reader-/viewership in the United States (over 1,245,420 copies in circulation) and globally. Founded in 1892, *Vogue* is the longest-running fashion magazine in the United States (Weber). Currently there are many international editions as well, in Australia, Brazil, China, France, Germany, Greece, India, Italy, Japan, Korea, Mexico, Portugal, Russia, Spain, Switzerland, Taiwan, and the United Kingdom. The sheer availability through its circulation and historical presence makes this particular women's magazine an important venue for exploring the depiction of sexualities.

The quantitative aspect of the project focuses on the number representation of non-white sexualities as an indicator of marginalization. A second technology of representation is garnered from the qualitative examination of the juxtaposition of raced and ethnicized sexualities *in relation to* white femininities (excluding explicitly gay and lesbian sexualities, which are largely absent in mainstream fashion magazines). In other words, when raced and ethnicized sexualities are present, what is the context that frames the representation, and how does this framing contribute to the persistent exoticizing and darkening of the Other?

Cannibalizing the Dark Other

The dark Other is subject to visual, written, and verbal dissection for the enjoyment of hegemonic forces. The concept of the dark Other as a foil to whiteness, particularly as it is used in white American fiction, was first described by writer and scholar Toni Morrison in 1992. She sees the dark Other as a fabricated Black persona that is "reflexive," a means for whites to contemplate their own terror and desire without having to acknowledge these feelings as their own (Steiner). Power and statuses are secondary to the "availability" of dark Others to indirectly (and inadvertently) enhance the value of whiteness. A case in point is the scrutiny the former first lady Michelle Obama has been subjected to. Since her appearance during the Obamas' first presidential campaign, her hair, body (including arms), speech style, and even eyebrows have been the subject of extensive public comment. In the article "The Evolution of Michelle Obama's Brows," posted on the liberal internet news website the *Huffington Post*, author Karin Tanabe writes:

> I love the first lady, I really do. But lately she looks like Cruella de Vil's aes-
> thetician has gotten her hands on her. What's with her eyebrows? When she
> kicked off her campaign to fight childhood obesity on Tuesday they looked
> almost like stick-ons.

Tanabe continues:

> When Barack Obama was in it to win it, journalists wrote that Michelle
> Obama's brows were going to lose the election for him. Too harsh, too
> severe they said. Well that seemed a tad harsh, but they did look almost tri-
> angular. Americans were screaming that they were more angled than Jack
> Nicholson's; Bill O'Reilly said her intense look was too angry, etc. etc. and
> Michelle Obama's makeup artist Ingrid Grimes-Miles finally listened. They
> came down a few millimeters and were filled in a tad too.

Notably, Michelle Obama is compared here to aging white men rather
than to other women. Her body fails to meet the hegemonic standards of
(white) femininity, and the failure is perceived as indicative of an underlying personality trait — anger. The dark body is scrutinized to find vestiges
of the "essential" characteristics of the Other.

When Michelle Obama's arms are described as too "muscular" or that
her over-arched eyebrows indicate her potential "essential" self as an
"angry black woman," the excavation comes full circle and closes the cognitive gap between what is perceived visually and what is believed to be
her primal nature. The hunt for clues to assuage the cognitive need for con-
sistency between the visual and the primal is complete when the former
first lady is depicted as an ape (at one time, the first image to appear when
"Michelle Obama" was entered in the search engine Google). The dominant
is reassured that it was a wise move to search Michelle Obama's body for
clues of her non-humanness (Goff et al.)

The dark Other, however, is not passive in this dialectical process of de-
tection/representation/affirmation. The self is constructed relationally,
and all that we are is inscribed in the visual strategically. As Fred Davis
writes, "We know that through clothing people communicate some things
about their persons, and at the collective level this results typically in
locating them symbolically in some structural universe of status claims and
life-style attachments" (4). Although capable of individual style, different
social formations have a repertoire of fashion vocabularies that emanate
from histories, social existences, and aesthetics derived from their cultures.
This does not imply that there is one uniform code attached to a specific
social formation, but rather, as Davis indicates, visual self-presentation is

an incipient or quasi-code, which, although it must necessarily draw on the conventional visual and tactile symbols of culture, does so allusively, ambiguously and inchoately, so that the meanings evoked by the combinations and permutations of the code's key terms (fabric, texture, pattern, volume, silhouette, and occasion) are forever shifting or "in process." (5)

Visual Representations and Construction of Self

Individuals are aware of being constructed visually from the outside, be it by the state, by preconceptions of physical completeness and ableness, or by expectations of "normalcy" in intimate interactions, each condition underscoring the significance of visual representations in the construction of self. If certain social formations are not visually available in the public sphere, the sense of invisibility increases, and individuals as well as groups become dependent on constructing the self from what is available, thus further alienating the body as a tool for self-construction. Certainly the visual exclusion results in potentially warping one's self-perceptions and invokes attempts at compliance with impossible standards. At times the attempts may border on the ridiculous and carnivalesque, as when dark-skinned individuals with deep brown eyes wear blue contacts to approximate the hegemonic standard of attractiveness.

Another potential adaptation is using the politicized sense of self for resistance and radicalization. The work of feminists of Color becomes especially relevant in exploring the social-psychological dynamics used by individuals to resist dominant constructions of sexualities, femininities, and masculinities. For example, Chela Sandoval outlines a differential consciousness defined as

the zero degree of meaning, counternarrative, utopia/no-place, the abyss, *amor in Aztlán*, soul. It is accessed through various passages that can include the differential form of social movement, the methodology of the oppressed, poetry, the transitive proverb, oppositional pastiche, *coatlicue*, the middle voice. These puncta release consciousness from its grounding in dominant language and narrative to experience the meanings that lie in the zero degree of power — of differential consciousness. (146)

Individuals who have experienced different social systems by traversing different cultures, languages, and nation-states (among other border crossings [Anzaldúa]) may in fact learn to actively and creatively subvert the pigeon-holing inherent in the limited range of visual representations in mainstream media such as fashion magazines. Sandoval, building on Gloria Anzaldúa's work on border crossings, calls these maneuvers "movidas," translated as moves, shiftings, motions (including jumps, dances, turnings, travels, journeys—anything indicating movement). Movidas are used to subvert the potentially devastating effects of inscribing the body through race, class, ethnicity, ableness, and sexuality using humor, irony, visual display, political action, cleverness, wisdom, and small acts of resistance.

Supreme Court Justice Sonia Sotomayor employed a movida in the case of her personal appearance. As part of the White House strategy to obtain nomination approval, Judge Sotomayor was asked to avoid certain colors, to wear small earrings, and to remove all bracelets during her confirmation hearings (in addition to undergoing elaborate rehearsal on answering questions and "managing" emotional display). Prior to her swearing-in, the White House management team requested that she keep her manicure color "neutral" for the ceremony. She complied. There were a couple of hours between the swearing-in and the White House reception in her honor. Justice Sotomayor entered the reception hall with a new manicure, her fingernails painted in fire engine red. In greeting the president, she showed him her nails. The incident is described in *Latina* magazine:

> Sotomayor's charm and confidence surprised very few people who know her, including the man who nominated her. While President Obama's staff was preparing Sotomayor for the confirmation hearings in a White House office called the War Room, the team covered all the potentially explosive questions and briefed her on every minute detail, including how to dress for the cameras. They even advised her to keep her nails a neutral shade, which she did. But on the day of the White House receptions celebrating her appointment, Sotomayor asked the president to look at her freshly manicured nails, holding up her hands to show off her favorite fire engine–red hue. The president chuckled, saying that she had been warned against that color. She sure had, but Sotomayor was not finished. She then pulled her hair back behind her ears, exposing her red and black semi-hoop earrings, a beloved accessory among Latinas across America—from the South Bronx to Houston to East Los Angeles.
>
> Obama joked that she had been briefed on the size of the earrings as well. Without skipping a beat, Sotomayor replied, "Mr. President, you have no idea what you've unleashed." He responded, "Justice, I know and remember it's a lifetime appointment. And I and no one can take it back." And that, as they say, is the final verdict.

This movida on the part of Sotomayor simultaneously allowed her to observe the demands of the hegemonic visual requirements established for Supreme Court justices and to restore her visual code with highly symbolic meaning for her self-construction as a Latina woman. Such is the thin (color) line between acceptability and igniting the signifiers that lead to essentialized understandings of the Other.

The Role of Pseudo-Movidas in Maintaining the Status Quo

Hegemonic structures are also capable of providing pseudo-movidas to raise our consciousness about our own and the media's oversights and capability to make entire groups invisible. Consider, for instance, an extensive campaign sponsored by the American designer Kenneth Cole that used striking images of individuals who are not usually portrayed in advertising. This campaign focused on models in wheelchairs, models with prosthetic legs, and a lesbian family with a young child. From Sandoval's perspective, movidas are designed to subvert power arrangements; pseudo-movidas can be visual sleights of hand designed to disrupt to some degree, but ultimately to reinscribe the existing technologies of domination. As such, displaying models with physical challenges and diverse families does not necessarily subvert the limitations inherent in these representations; because of the extreme glamorization of these representations, the full range of diversity within the category is not presented. These images may raise consciousness but also lull viewers into capitalistic buying that does not address core structural issues of disadvantage and poverty, promoting instead the seduction of acceptance with no radical structural change. The inclusiveness of such representations may in fact be regressive rather than progressive in terms of social justice outcomes. Such is the ambivalent positioning of advocating for inclusiveness at the risk of co-optation.

Given the expanding importance of visual media in print, television, film, computer games, and the internet, the interconnections between what we see and what we feel to be will only increase. Visual representations hold both the potential for liberation and the policing of boundaries of self-constructions, thus limiting liberal avenues for building the self-agency necessary to join the fight for social justice.

Transnational Media Images in the Creation of Relational White Sexualities through the Consumption of Women of Color

In *Playing in the Dark*, Morrison explores the complexities in the gendered constructions of whiteness that are used to reinforce the interlocking definitions of patriarchy and white womanhoods. The presence of non-whites creates a "humanity" scale in which white men represent the pinnacle of human development: rational, logical, unemotional, industrious, adventurous, in control, and creative (Harris)—privileged characteristics that are then contrasted with the dark Other. The intricate dance of intimacy between heterosexual whites is judged as more "human" because of the presence of the dark Other. Morrison explores these intimate dynamics in Hemingway's novel *To Have and Have Not*. In the novel Harry and his wife, Marie, are making love. Marie asks her husband, "Listen, did you ever do it with the nigger wench?" "Sure." "What's it like?" "Like a nurse shark." Morrison remarks that for Hemingway the Black woman is the furthest thing from human, so distant as to be not even mammal but fish. The Black figure evokes a

> predatory, devouring eroticism and signals the antithesis of femininity, to nurturing, to nursing, to replenishment. In short, Harry's words mark something so brutal, contrary, and alien in its figuration that it does not belong to its own species and cannot be spoken of in language, in metaphor or metonym, evocative of anything resembling the woman to whom Harry is speaking—his wife Marie. The kindness he has done Marie is palpable. His projection of black female sexuality has provided her with solace, for which she is properly grateful. She responds to the kindness and giggles, "You're funny." (84–85)

Morrison argues that our habitual use of racialized language makes us immune to fully grasping how the process of speaking and writing in itself is the methodology by which race is produced. Furthermore, the intrinsic racism in our language is not completely conscious, and therefore it requires our watching what we read while simultaneously being engaged. The use of language, which by its very nature racializes, is not the only thing that limits our imaginations in conceiving non-racist worlds; images are another register of discourse, one that is as powerful as language and one that normalizes racial hierarchies and makes gender hierarchies palatable within systems of white patriarchal privilege.

The Image and Constructions of Self

Mass media is often cited as a major socializing agent in creating, sustaining, distributing, and recycling conceptions of self that are congruent with normative power arrangements. Although mass media may also have emancipatory effects, corporate media are rarely invested in creating alternative views that subvert existing voter disparities. As such, corporate media are geared to making profits by reassuring the populace that what exists is what should be. Simultaneously, old arrangements are reconstituted in innovative and visually stunning ways to engage audiences and to subvert boredom and satiation.

One such medium that has been extremely successful in appearing "new" and "fresh" while changing little is the domain of women's magazines. From a social-psychological point of view, women's magazines create, reinforce, and maintain social schemas. According to Sandra Bem,

> a schema is a cognitive structure, a network of associations that organizes and guides individual perceptions. A schema functions as an anticipatory structure, a readiness to search for and to assimilate incoming information in schema-relevant terms. Schematic processing is thus highly selective and enables the individual to impose structure and meaning onto the vast array of incoming stimuli. (355)

The automatic nature of processing relevant information through social schemas further scaffolds existing non-conscious ideologies—that is, "we remain unaware of it [non-conscious ideologies] because alternative beliefs and attitudes about women [and other groups] go unimagined" (Bem and Bem 42). Social schemas, however, are not merely cognitive tools at the service of organizing social information more efficiently. They are directly related to the creation and maintenance of power differentials in societies and nation-states. In women's magazines, social schemas are proactively nurtured to mobilize desires and longings in the service of heterosexual patriarchal technologies. However, not all womanhoods are constituted with the same content or through the same avenues. Racialized and ethnicized women are constituted to highlight the superiority of hegemonic white, heterosexual womanhoods and the reification of white femininities. In particular, the social constructions of sexualities in media depend on the relational positioning of racialized groups creating a hierarchy of desirability.

In the study described in the following pages, I examined transnational fashion magazines focusing on the presentation of whiteness as constituted in relationship to dark Others. As mentioned earlier, these transnational social signifiers are created through visual representations of gendered dark Others to center the importance of whiteness. These technologies of racialized visual representation reinscribe white hetero-normativity as the most desirable mechanism to perpetuate the transmission of white patriarchal privilege through biological offspring.

The Study

I examined seventeen issues of international *Vogue* magazines published in ten countries (table 7.1). *Vogue* is described by book critic Caroline Weber in the *New York Times* as

> "the world's most influential fashion magazine" in that *Vogue* is to our era what the idea was, in Voltaire's famous parlance, to his: if it didn't exist, we would have to invent it. Revered for its editorial excellence and its visual panache, the magazine has long functioned as a bible for anyone worshiping at the altar of luxury, celebrity and style. And while we perhaps take for granted the extent to which this trinity dominates consumer culture today, *Vogue*'s role in catalyzing its rise to preeminence cannot be underestimated.

Arthur Baldwin Turnure founded *Vogue* in 1892 (and after his death in 1909, it was taken over by Condé Nast). The widespread availability of *Vogue* through circulation and historical presence makes this particular women's magazine an important venue for the exploration of the different depictions of sexualities. Furthermore, a cursory examination of US *Vogue* indicates that, indeed, racialized sexualities are a primary mechanism for reinscribing hierarchies of desirability based on racialization and, to a lesser extent, ethnicization.

"Buscando a Frida": Technologies of Representation

The creation and maintenance of social schemas reinforcing existing power arrangements can be accomplished through visual representations in multiple ways. In this particular study, I focused on two technologies: the quantitative and qualitative. First, the total number of representations of non-white sexualities in the seventeen *Vogue* issues I analyzed is an indicator of which sexualities are marginalized. A qualitative analysis

Table 7.1 . Seventeen international *Vogue* magazines

Country	Issue
1. *Vogue Australia*	August 2007
2. *British Vogue*	October 2007
3. *British Vogue*	January 2008
4. *British Vogue*	February 2008
5. *Vogue España*	August 2007
6. *Vogue España*	October 2007
7. *Vogue España*	November 2007
8. *Vogue España*	December 2007
9. *Vogue Germany*	August 2007
10. *Vogue Greece*	August 2007
11. *Vogue Italia*	September 2007
12. *Vogue Italia*	December 2007
13. *Vogue Japan*	September 2007
14. *Vogue Latinoamérica*	August 2007
15. *Vogue Latinoamérica*	November 2007
16. *Vogue Paris*	October 2007
17. *Vogue Russia*	September 2007

provides a nuanced examination of the context under which racialized and ethnicized sexualities *frame* and *exalt* white femininities. Fashion magazines like *Vogue* depend on a display of the gender binary for most of the visuals. Made invisible are the range of sexualities that are explicitly gay, lesbian, transsexual, and queer. The gender binary extends to a race binary where there are only two raced and ethnicized sexualities constituted by whiteness and dark Others with no specific ethnic or racial origins. The question this study addresses is "How does the context frame the representations that contribute to the continuing exoticizing and endarkening of the Other for the exaltation of whiteness?"

The Salience of Whiteness and the Exclusion of Darkness

Morrison writes that the importance of whiteness is accomplished in literary texts through the strategic marginalization of dark Others, thereby exalting the status of what is present. In discussing the introduction of slavery in the New World, Morrison theorizes that white men's manhood was transformed because "whatever his social status in London, in the

**Table 7.2. Photographic representation in issues
of *Vogue* by gender, race, and ethnicity**

Total images	13,199
Total women	9,534
White women	8,729
Women of Color	631
Black	242
Asian	208
Latina	181
US Native American	0
Other women	174
Phenotype not discernable (e.g., wearing gloves)	99
Women of mixed phenotype	75
Total men	3,179
White men	2,601
Men of Color	408
Phenotype not discernable	166
Men of mixed phenotype	4
Total Children	486
Children of Color	315
White children	167
Children of mixed phenotype	4

New World he is a gentleman. More gentle, more man. The site of his transformation is within rawness: he is backgrounded by savagery" (44). *Vogue*, then, is a space created to reinscribe white patriarchy through the centering of white, heterosexual femininities. As such, it is not surprising to find that in the seventeen international issues of *Vogue* I examined, in which a total of 9,534 images of women were counted (table 7.2), 8,729 were white women, and only 631 were women of Color (in all sections of the magazines).

Vogue, as well as other fashion magazines, is not necessarily interested in portraying specifics of ethnicity or nationality. Fashion magazines are a visual medium that relies heavily on phenotype, physiognomy, and other physical markers of the body to dichotomize representations into white and non-white. When non-white models are present on the magazine pages, there is an expressed preference for a generic "ethnic look" that is not visually identified with one ethnicity or nation-state. The Other, then, is rendered unidentifiable — no history, language, or culture — and the lack of specificity further homogenizes the visual representation of difference.

**Table 7.3. Representation on seventeen *Vogue*
covers by race, ethnicity, and gender**

Models	Number of covers
Total women	16
One white woman	15
Two or more white women	1
Women of Color	0
Other: White women and white men	1
Total covers	17

Another mechanism used to center whiteness is the composition of the photo image placed on the magazine cover. Covers are the most immediately visible component of the magazine, seen even by non-readers who encounter women's magazines in their day-to-day life and who process the cover image without exposure to the inner content. Also, it is the issue's cover that is archived, posted on the internet, and generally discussed in much of the research (table 7.3). On the covers of the seventeen issues under review, not a single one contained a person of Color. The covers exalt and reinforce the privileged (and desirable) position of white, visually heterosexual femininities (with one exception, in which the cover space is shared with white men).

**Framing Difference: Cultural Appropriation
to Center Whiteness**

In August 2007, *Vogue España* created an extensive multipage layout entitled "Buscando a Frida," with the following caption:

Volantes, estampados y plataformas se dan cita con el foclore y el colorido mexicanos. La moda rinde tributo a Frida Kahlo en el año de su centenario y Vogue lo recuerda a ritmo de ranchera. Fotos: Anne Menecke.

[Frills, prints and platforms are brought together with the colorfulness in Mexican folklore. Fashion pays tribute to Frida Kahlo on the occasion of the 100th year of her birth and Vogue remembers her to the rhythm of Mexican ranchera (folk music).]

The feature spread runs over sixteen pages (112–127), the most extensive depiction of an explicitly ethnicized female figure in the seventeen issues reviewed. The model who portrays Frida has dark hair but otherwise displays European facial features, including green eyes; she was reliably judged as white by three coders. The "Frida" model is shown in various settings located in an unidentified, possibly Mexican beachfront pueblo (although it could be in any country). The model wears updated, very expensive versions of the Frida aesthetic, characterized by large ethnic jewelry, bright colors usually associated with a Mexican peasant aesthetic, skirts and blouses with large ruffles, and other elements of Indigenous clothing. Several of the photographs include "locals" within the display. In one depiction, Frida plays lotería with an elderly man dressed in a straw hat and an Indigenous shirt, sporting a disheveled beard. In several other depictions, Frida is captured in various group shots: she is the center of attention and is surrounded by "savagery." In one instance, the display is entitled "Viva Zapata," with no further explanation of the historical and political significance of this Mexican revolutionary figure. Encircling the model are children carrying fake rifles and wearing "costumes" of Indigenous peasantry and painted-on mustaches and goatees. While the Frida model is wearing an outfit that costs 2,668 euros, the children wear straw sombreros, wave small Mexican flags, and stand before a beat-up Volkswagen on a dirt road. In another instance, Frida is at an outdoor fiesta (dressed in an Oscar de La Renta priced at 4,610 euros, not counting accessories, which add up to an additional 2,435 euros) dancing with a young girl in peasant clothing. The depiction is entitled "Fiesta Mariachi." In another display, entitled "Noche de la Iguana," Frida holds a huge iguana while sporting an outfit that costs almost 3,000 euros. There is no commentary, visual or otherwise, addressing the extreme poverty of the surroundings, remarking on the exorbitant cost of Frida's outfits, or acknowledging the glaring contrast between the setting and the adornment. Indeed, the price of each garment and accessory is detailed in each display.

These depictions exalt the exotic nature of mexicanidad. A visual space is created for the whiteness of the model to be temporarily ethnicized through the setting: the updated but nonetheless Mexican-ized (albeit expensive) wardrobe, the inclusion of poor peasant-like Mexicans, the Mexican folkloric artifacts usually found in rural markets, and the punctuation of each visual tableau with a verse from a Mexican folkloric song. The temporary escape from whiteness is further reinforced as Frida sits alone under a palapa on a deserted beach, surrounded by the simplicity of "the uncivilized." She is taking a vacation from "civilization." According to Norma Klahn, historically the (temporary) crossings of the border by whites into Mexico were "voyages" in quests for self-definition, self-indulgence, or self-affirmation. Some of these excursions were evasions, flights from the law or from unspoken societal codes—that is, searches for spaces where rules can be broken. For others, the displacements become rites of initiation and crossings of thresholds toward the unexplored (35).

These temporary transgressions almost always conclude with the traveler crossing back to the United States (and therefore to whiteness), the site of normality. The traveler "returns to the safety of his [or her] home, initiated and transformed, but secure in his [or her] identity and place in the world" (Klahn 38). Indeed, this is the case in "Buscando a Frida." The last tableau shows Frida crossing the cobblestoned street of a dusty old pueblo. She is wearing a casual suit with high heels, a purse, and a scarf, and her hair in a bun. Frida is returning to civilization. To emphasize the point on the following page, an article on the late Princess Diana ("el imborrable estilo Diana") begins with a large photograph of her in black and white. She is sporting a short and tailored haircut, no jewelry, and a simple black dress. The contrast between the two sexualities/femininities—"Frida's" versus the princess's—is visually stunning. For sixteen vibrantly colored pages, the reader is treated to extreme costuming, isolated pueblos, exotic folkloric practices, Chihuahuas sporting sombreros, and cheap Mexican trinkets, including a vintage postcard from the 1950s with bawdy letters stating "Greetings from Tijuana, Mexico" (otherwise known as a "sin city" among US-Mexico border residents). Following this unruly, fictionalized display, the eye rests on a cool and elegant depiction of Princess Diana. This visual subterfuge is readily accessible to most readers, who have come to expect the reinscription of whiteness after a temporary lapse into the world of the dark Other. In fact, in these mainstream fashion magazines there is rarely an extensive depiction of endarkened sexualities without an immediate return to an exaggerated whiteness that erases, recovers, submerges, and reinscribes existing racializing and ethnicizing social schemas for sexualities.

Encontrando a Frida: Conclusions

James Baldwin wrote that he became conscious of the "world's intentions for me and mine" when on a Saturday afternoon he attended the "movies, but which was actually my entrance into the cinema of my mind" (10). Baldwin aptly captures what Oishi theorizes as the double-edged sword experienced in identifying/dis-identifying with visual displays—that is, individuals experience a "perverse" pleasure in seeing one's culture displayed in large public places while simultaneously experiencing ambivalence that is "both objectifying and liberating" (Hurtado 334–335). One can argue that finding "Frida" in the pages of an international issue of *Vogue* elicits an exhale of recognition and simultaneously a sense of revulsion at the appropriation of Mexican culture. Particularly disturbing in the Frida layout is the lack of historical context or cultural analysis of the visual displays without which the culture is rendered characterless, insignificant, and subjugated to whiteness. As I conclude in my previous work, "It is the creation of this multi-layered set of emotions unleashed in the Other that allows whiteness to still be at the center, dominating the multivalent, gyrational gaze of power" (Hurtado 335). In flipping through the pages of *Vogue* and seeing these fashion representations repeated in "television ads and billboards across the globe, the Other learns her or his place in the visual/political/social hierarchies that give and take away life's chances" (335). The challenge remains to create visual geographies in all media that challenge the dominant (white) eye that limits our visualization of a reality without inequalities.

Note

1. Preliminary results of this study appeared in the conference proceedings of the 10th Congreso Internacional Interdisciplinar Sobre Las Mujeres, Mundos De Mujeres / Women's Worlds, 2008, held at the Universidad Complutense de Madrid, Spain.

Works Cited

Anzaldúa, Gloria. *Borderlands/La Frontera: The New Mestiza*. Aunt Lute Books, 1987.
Baldwin, James. *The Devil Finds Work*. Dell, 1976.
Bem, Sandra L. "Gender Schema Theory: A Cognitive Account of Sex Typings." *Psychological Review*, vol. 88, no. 4, 1981, pp. 354–364.
Bem, Sandra L., and Daryl J. Bem. "Training the Woman to Know Her Place: The Power of a Nonconscious Ideology." *The Lanahan Readings in the Psychology of Women*, Lanahan, 1997, pp. 419–428.
Davis, Fred. *Fashion, Culture, and Identity*. U of Chicago P, 1992.
Goff, Phillip A., et al. "Not Yet Human: Implicit Knowledge, Historical Dehumanization, and Contemporary Consequences." *Journal of Personality and Social Psychology*, vol. 97, no. 2, 2008, pp. 291–306.
Harris, Cheryl I. "Whiteness as Property." *Harvard Law Review*, vol. 106, no. 8, 1993, pp. 1709–1791.

Hurtado, Aída. "Sex, Service, and Scenery: Latina Sexualities in the Pages of Vogue." In The Routledge Companion to Latina/o Media, edited by Maria Elena Cepeda and Dolores Ines Casillas, Routledge, 2017, pp. 320–337.

Klahn, Norma. "Writing the Border: The Languages and Limits of Representation." *Journal of Latin American Cultural Studies*, vol. 3, nos. 1–2, 1994, pp. 29–55.

Morrison, Toni. *Playing in the Dark: Whiteness and the Literary Imagination.* Harvard UP, 1992.

Oishi, E. "Visual Perversions: Race, Sex, and Cinematic Pleasures." *Signs*, vol. 31, 2006, pp. 641–674.

Sandoval, Chela. *Methodology of the Oppressed.* U of Minnesota P, 2000.

Steiner, Wendy. "The Clearest Eye." *New York Times*, 5 Apr. 1992, www.nytimes.com /1992/04/05/books/the-clearesteye.html?pagewanted=all&mcubz=0&page wanted=print. Accessed 30 Oct. 2018.

Tanabe, Karen. "The Evolution of Michelle Obama's Brows." *Huffington Post*, 13 Feb. 2010. www.huffpost.com/entry/the-evolution-of-michelle_b_457532. Accessed 30 Oct. 2018.

Weber, Caroline. "Review of 'IN VOGUE: The Illustrated History of the World's Most Famous Fashion Magazine (Rizzoli).'" *New York Times*, 3 Dec. 2006.

CHAPTER 8

Black, Brown, and Fa(t)shionable: The Role of Fat Women of Color in the Rise of Body Positivity

JADE D. PETERMON

Hyper(in)visibility was born in my body. As a fat Black woman and a graduate student in Santa Barbara, California, walking along the beach, sitting in my favorite coffee shop, relaxing in a downtown restaurant with my friends, I did not exist. Despite my fat and Black, no matter where I went, I was invisible. I found solace in a small but rapidly growing group of women online who dubbed themselves "fatshionistas." These women loved fashion above all, as I had for as long as I could remember. They were also on a journey to love their bodies as much as they loved fashion, but this journey was always secondary to the act of self-fashioning (see the introduction to this volume). They supported each other fiercely. And while the group was distinctly diverse, at the helm were a few very young, very ambitious women of Color, including several Latinas.

The vilification of fat in American society has caused fat people, women especially, to suffer from hyper(in)visibility (Petermon). I use this term to describe the paradox that while fat bodies are more visible than others because they take up more physical space, they are also invisible because of the widely held discriminatory beliefs about fat bodies in Western and especially American culture. Simply put, people are unwilling to see them. To be hyper(in)visible is dehumanizing. It is the knowledge that your humanity could be in question at any moment of any day, by strangers on the street, in a boardroom, in the classroom, and in visual media.

While Western culture has upheld a standard of beauty that excludes women of size, traditionally communities of Color, particularly Black and Brown communities, have accepted and celebrated women with more voluptuous body types; to some extent, the fashion industry has followed. Aída Hurtado argues,

The fact that women of color, as exemplified by [Jennifer] Lopez and African-American pop singer Beyoncé Knowles among others, have prominent derrières has been liberating for fashion. . . . [D]esigners have recognized and embraced the fact that Latinas are "voluptuous," and they have reconsidered the mainstream aesthetic of extreme thinness, an aesthetic many writers have questioned, suggesting it may not apply to any significant group of women. (150)

Both Beyoncé and Jennifer Lopez have donned the cover of *Vogue*'s annual Shape Issue in recent years.[1] Unfortunately, this embrace of "nonnormative" body types has not been extended to women of Color who are fat. Despite this, fat women in online fashion communities have decided to make their own rules and free themselves of traditional beauty constructs both inside and outside of their communities. As Gloria Anzaldúa argues,

We perceive the version of reality that our culture communicates. Like others having or living in more than one culture, we get multiple, often opposing messages. The coming together of two self-consistent but habitually incompatible frames of reference causes *un choque*, a cultural collision. (100)

These women receive multiple messages about their bodies; the messages from mainstream culture often contradict the messages they receive in their homes and within their communities. Consequently, as women who are both fat and of Color, Internet Fat Fashion Community (IFFC) bloggers made a decision to "refuse to accept their assigned status as the quintessential 'other'" (Collins, "Learning" 18).

Now, ten years after I first discovered the IFFC, body positivity is a cash cow. Major players in the plus-size industry, like Lane Bryant, have capitalized with their #plusisequal campaign. Additionally, there has been an increase in body-positive products in music, publishing, and television, including but not limited to TLC's *My Big Fat Fabulous Life* (2015), Jess Baker's book *Things No One Will Tell Fat Girls*, and Mary Lambert's album *Welcome to the Age of My Body*. As a result of the mainstreaming of images of fat bodies, body positivity, which is different from fat positivity/acceptance/liberation, has also blossomed. Lena Dunham, Jennifer Lawrence, and Amy Schumer are a few people who have chosen to take up the mantle of body positivity. As a result, frameworks like body positivity and health at every size are becoming more and more popular.

The history of fat acceptance activism is long and well documented (Schoenfielder and Wieser). Additionally, the fashion-focused movement that I took part in while in grad school existed alongside corollary movements in health (for example, Health at Every Size [HAES]), fat sexuality/dating, and body love, among others.[2] However, the mainstream adoption and commercialization of body positivity were made possible in large part through the emotional, physical, and intellectual labor of Black and Brown women in and on fat fashion blogs. Further, the erasure of these women, in both academic and popular spaces, can be attributed to the same white supremacist, capitalist, patriarchal systems that inspired them to create change in the fashion industry and, as a result, popular culture at large. In this chapter, I document the foundations and growth of the IFFC, demonstrating how many of its early leaders, despite the hyper(in)visibility they faced, motivated the fashion industry to view fat women as viable consumers.

Where It All Began

In 2008, when I started this research, I used the term "Internet Fat Fashion Community" to describe a rapidly growing group of women who met on *LiveJournal* (and other early social networks) in online communities such as *Fatshionista* and *What I Wore Today*, and eventually created their own blogs modeled after the posts in these communities. It is no longer possible to talk about a singular IFFC. Not only are there now innumerable individual blogs, fat fashion has spilled over into many different social media platforms, particularly *Tumblr* and *Instagram*. While research has been done about fat fashion communities in these spaces, especially *Tumblr*, these sites often reproduce mainstream erasure of the bodies and ideas of women of Color or reduce the absence of women of Color to questions of access (Connell). Here I give an overview of how the IFFC was born, paying particular attention to the women of Color who helped body positivity become so popular.

The *LiveJournal* community *Fatshionista* dates back to December 2004. Inactive since 2016, it was a vibrant, open community, meaning any *LiveJournal* member could join and post to the blog. Visitors were greeted as follows:

> Welcome, fatshionistas! We are a diverse fat-positive, anti-racist, disabled-friendly, trans-inclusive, queer-flavored, non-gender-specific community,

open to everyone. Here we will discuss the ins and outs of fat fashions, seriously and stupidly—but above all—standing tall, and with panache. We fatshionistas are self-accepting despite The Man's Saipan-made boot at our chubby, elegant throats. We are silly, and serious, and want shit to fit.

Various types of posts were uploaded to *Fatshionista* daily. The most frequent were "Outfit of the Day" (OOTD) posts, in which members of the community posted pictures of themselves in an ensemble they styled. They usually included information about the stores where they were purchased or designers of component parts of the outfit, and newly purchased items were reviewed for the group. "Sale posts" involved individual members selling and trading personal items. Some posts alerted the community to plus-size fashion sales. Additionally, because of the scarcity of on-trend styles and fashion brands for the IFFC, *Fatshionista* was a valuable resource for women who were looking for advice about where to locate a certain item of clothing, including trend pieces and novelty items such as patterned tights or lingerie, which can be very hard for fat women to find.

Miscellaneous posts on *Fatshionista* included questions for the community about the quality or fit of certain items from specific stores or designers, odes to favorite items of clothing and designers, and posts on political topics outside of fashion that were usually related to the fat liberation movement. Interestingly, the plus-size retail establishment has always been very much aware of the existence of the IFFC, and many retailers communicated with the moderators of the community and the more popular individual bloggers in order to alert this fashion-conscious community of upcoming sales so that bloggers could inform their readers. Additionally, the rise of social media platforms in the early days of *Fatshionista* resulted in partnerships between retailers and bloggers, including promotional giveaways and sweepstake-like contests.

A small group of IFFC members acted as moderators and presided over the posts and comments, and also filtered spam and hate speech. Hate speech has always been very common on these blogs, and bloggers deal with these posts differently, all in surprisingly jovial and good-natured ways. For example, some blogs offer "Hate Speech of the Week" posts just for fun. This feature can also be viewed as a means to gain control and empowerment. Hate speech also comes up as a topic on Twitter in a more personal way. In that space, I have witnessed bloggers express pain and seek group support and approval in response to hate speech.

From the very beginning, there were countless individual blogs. However, a hierarchy existed, and some blogs have continued to be significantly more popular than others and, as a result, have greater influence in the industry. The most famous fat fashion blogger is Gabi Gregg. She started her blog *Young, Fat and Fabulous* (now *Gabifresh*) in October 2008. Writing about the same topic, Gabi and several of her friends, including Jay Miranda of the blog *JayMiranda* (formerly *Fatshionable*) and Gabby of *Tumblr's CorazonesRojos*, who are both Latinas. In the early days, individual bloggers often promoted each other on their blogs and on *Twitter*. Their posts were initially similar to the posts at *Fatshionista* but have evolved quite a bit over time. These blogs also featured interviews with famous fat fashion icons, such as models and designers of fat fashions, as well as editorial posts about fashion in general. While these bloggers are not as explicitly political as the *Fatshionista* community, and in many cases state that their goal is to showcase fashions and not get involved in fat politics, it is clear from their conversations with each other on *Twitter* and in the activity of fat fashion blogging itself that they desire to have an impact on how fat women are viewed in the fashion world and in the world at large. Blogger Karen Ward of *Curvy Canadian* says:

> The act of dressing well as a fat woman is a **politically radical act** [boldface in original]. These women have made themselves visible in the most beautiful ways and demanded that they not be overlooked. They have shifted the politics of representation of fat people by using the democratizing force of social media to include their own true and real representation as a part of the dialogue. They have subverted the staid and stale tropes that exist that say that fat women are lazy and/or ill-disciplined slobs who are ashamed of their bodies. They have proclaimed loudly that they are beautiful, strong, fashionable, and unwilling to be ignored by society and the fashion industry.

By blogging, these women are not only doing the work of making themselves visible but also fostering community and providing an example for all fat women who feel ostracized. It is clear that young women are not just reading these blogs but are becoming empowered to act and are desiring to be identified with this movement.

Many of the more popular bloggers fill different niches within the IFFC. For example, Jay is on the small side of the plus-size spectrum (sizes 12–14, figs. 8.1 and 8.2). Therefore, she mixes "straight-sized"[3] clothes (sizes 0–10) with plus-size clothes. She also includes more high-end designers in her wardrobe. Her style is very feminine; she utilizes classic silhouettes that complement her body. On the other hand, Gabi is more representa-

8.1. Jay Miranda. Photographer unknown; courtesy of Jay Miranda.

tive of the norm in plus sizes (16–20), and she tends to be very trendy, with a style that is constantly evolving. Finally, Gabby of *CorazonesRojos* is an active thrift shopper, and almost all the clothes that she showcases on her blog were purchased in thrift stores. Individual style is very important to members of the IFFC and to this community; it is an essential component of what it means to be fashionable.

What gets classified as fat is a contested point within the community. However, as Marilyn Wann points out, "In a fat-hating society everyone is fat. Fat functions as a floating signifier, attaching to individuals based

8.2. Jay Miranda. Photographer unknown; courtesy of Jay Miranda.

on a power relationship, not a physical measurement. People all along the weight spectrum may experience fat oppression" (xv). The last part of this statement largely echoes the logic by which the IFFC proceeds. As such, bloggers in the fat community range in size from 12–32. Intriguingly, in the early days the most popular bloggers were at the lower end of this range. Today there are countless bloggers at the high end, and these women are very vocal in the community through comments and tweets.

Finally, the IFFC is very diverse: women of all races and ethnicities and all over the globe participate. As previously mentioned, women of Color have been instrumental in building this community and using it to leverage opportunities for fat women in the form of increased fashion choices. Additionally, it is remarkable that such a wealth of images of fat women of Color exists online, especially in light of the hyper(in)visibility that women of Color face within mainstream visual culture in general and within fashion in particular. These bloggers have succeeded in producing alternative representations of fat bodies. The fact that women of Color are at the helm of this movement is a welcome change in representational politics.

The Power of Community

As previously mentioned, individual members of the community post pictures of themselves in "Outfits of the Day." The OOTD is the cornerstone of the IFFC and is key in the move away from hyper(in)visibility. I understand this practice as serving two purposes. First, it allows community members to dialogue with each other and get social approval in ways they are often denied in mainstream culture. Second, in posting images of themselves, the bloggers are adding to the wealth of representation of fat bodies within the larger media culture. More explicitly, they are actively making themselves visible on their own terms. In taking pictures of themselves in an outfit and sharing it with the wider community, bloggers work against the hyper(in)visibility that is imposed on them within the larger society. For example, Xtina, the African American blogger of the now-defunct *Musings of a Fashionista*, in the "About Me" section of her blog, claims:

> Just like tons of others, every month I excitedly flip through the month's latest fashion mags. . . . 95% of everything featured on those glossy pages are not made for women like myself who are not sized 10 and under. For women like us, we're often only able to peek into the party from behind the red ropes. Although for me [this] makes getting dressed that much more fun . . . the fun in fashion is in the experimentation. . . . Every morning getting dressed is another chance to try something new out and become someone different.

These sentiments continue to be expressed throughout the fat fashion community. The women of this community feel empowered when they are able to express themselves through clothes because of the element of play involved, as well as the ways in which they are able to subvert the social norms and expectations that are often placed on fat bodies. This aspect of identity formation is critical for the community and the ways in which they have changed the culture at large. It is because of the lack of representation of fat women that these blogs function as a site for the construction of subjectivities. Leslie Rabine claims, "Fashion communicates primarily cultural messages about the feminine or feminized body as the bearer of social meaning" (59). While the structure of the fashion industry often reproduces mainstream ideologies about fat bodies through fat invisibility, and also through the production and distribution of drab clothes for fat women, the IFFC creates representations of fat women as fashionable. The cultural messages produced by these bloggers work to resist the invisibility imposed by the hegemonic fashion industry and thereby provide alternative modes of self-fashioning for members of the IFFC.

Further, the fact that many of the visible bloggers are women of Color turns traditional hierarchies of beauty embraced by the fashion industry on its head. Race and class are topics that are rarely addressed in the fashion industry. This has not been the case in the IFFC. For example, Gabby, the meXicana blogger behind *CorazonesRojos*, says,

> I realize there aren't many Latin@ bloggers (I'm sure there are a lot now, but I can probably count five at most), and that's something I always wanted to showcase as well—that my culture and socio-economic status frame my style and shopping. Fuck, I have shopped everywhere from the swap meet to dollar stores to thrift shops to the mall, but to this day, I will never spend more than $20 on any one item. This is important to me to uphold because, fuck, I do not make a lot of money and I refuse to use my credit card.

Here Gabby affirms her intersectional identity and explains how these vectors of identity impact her ability to self-fashion and her goals as a blogger.

In addition to conversations about race and class, there are many other conversations that have come up in the community, including but not limited to: how being fat impacts dating and relationships, whether fatshionistas could or should wear sky-high heels, the size of plus-size models and what qualifies as fat, what language is preferred in reference to fat bodies, and, arising over and over again in several blogs, the question of style.

In a post entitled "Meaty Topic of the Week: Let's Talk Idolatry and Bias," Nik of the now inactive blog *MezzoFashionisto* questions the basis for judging what is (and what is not) fashionable within the community. She questions the ways in which the IFFC rallies behind certain celebrities as icons and shuns others. For example, indie rock singer/songwriter Beth Ditto is widely regarded in the fat fashion community as a fashion icon. She has relationships with major designers and has appeared in numerous magazines, including *Out*, *Love*, and *V*. She is known for her outrageous fashion choices. However, other famous plus-size women, such as Mo'Nique and Queen Latifah, are not considered fashionable and are rarely mentioned in fat fashion blogs. Nik asks the IFFC in the post:

> How much is YOUR view of what is fashionable dependent on size. . . . As plus-size fashion bloggers, are we sometimes scared to go outside of the box for fear of being ridiculed? Can a plus-size fashion blogger wear the same thing as one of her straight-size counterparts and be given the same praise/rejection? Are our standards higher or lower?

The conversation that followed was quite revealing and very diverse. Some readers, like Stephanie, who is also the author of a fat fashion blog called *StephanieDJL* (formerly *Buttons, Bows and Brogues*), expressed the importance of confidence when attempting to establish style as a fatshionista because of the lack of choices. She claims:

> It does not take much effort to dress well, but it takes confidence to dress amazing. . . . I love how due to the lack of resources and options when it comes to clothing, seeing plus-size girls rock clothes and look amazing is always good to see regardless of how exciting the outfit is because it's so much harder to do.

However, other women expressed disappointment with how their style is received both inside and outside of the IFFC. Tiffany of the blog *Fat Shopaholic* commented on this same post, claiming:

> I think when it comes to being a fatshion blogger I'm never afraid to get out of the box. I post pictures on my blog of things I would absolutely wear outside. When I wear things like bow patterned leggings on my blog I don't get a ton of comments but, when I wear a more casual look I get more comments and I have no idea why that is. But, in a way that mimics people's reaction on the street. I take public transit in Chicago and when I wear certain things most people point and stare but there are a few people that admire me for being bold. I have no idea why this is. Sometimes I think that if I were a size 6 and wore patterned leggings and sequin dresses no one would care but, because I'm a size 24/26 people care more.

This comment points toward the hierarchies that exist within the fat fashion community in regard to size. As previously stated, most of the popular fat fashion bloggers fall within the lower size ranges, between sizes 12 and 16. But, more importantly, Tiffany's statement demonstrates that she is comfortable being vulnerable within the community about her desire to explore more dramatic styles. These types of blog posts and the dialogue that follows display the significance and value of the IFFC in working through these ideas and issues. These conversations affirm individuals within the group as well as help establish and maintain the community.

Conversations such as these are truly egalitarian in nature and demonstrate the power of representation to create and sustain spaces of resistance. Because of the nature of social inequalities in the current era, marginalized communities tend to be more vulnerable, not only within the society itself but also in the public sphere. The internet allows for fractioning of the public sphere in which members of a small community have a public forum but also understand they exist within the larger public and have a desire to enact both individual and public change. This is the value of the IFFC: the blog space is not simply about fashion or fat; it engages questions about democracy and identity in the current political and technological age. In the medical discourse around fat, there is a lack of attention to the actual experience of being fat. This is part of the dehumanization process. In her masterwork, *Black Feminist Thought*, Patricia Hill Collins claims,

> Maintaining the invisibility of Black women and our ideas . . . in the United States . . . and other places where Black women now live . . . has been critical in maintaining social inequalities. Black women engaged in reclaiming and constructing Black women's knowledges often point to the politics of suppression that affect their projects. (5)

Collins is making a connection between experience and consciousness. Representations of fat people bypass the experiential knowledge that comes with living in a fat body. This is subjugated knowledge, or the knowledge, according to Foucault, that

> derives power solely from the fact that it is different from all the knowledges that surround it. . . . [I]t is the reappearance of what people know at a local level . . . singular, local knowledges, the noncommonsensical knowledges that people have, and which have in a way been left to lie fallow, or even kept in the margins. (8)

The blog space provides a mirror into alternative ways of being.

In an interview with *Darling*, Tanesha Awasthi of the blog *Girl With Curves* says,

When I received the first note from a reader saying that seeing me made her feel better about herself because she could relate to having curves, I had the feeling I was on to something. Being able to help women feel good about themselves is an amazing feeling, and I'm beyond fulfilled just in knowing I'm helping at least one person in the world.

The blog posts themselves are testimony, the undeniable proof that we exist. In blogging, these women are not only producing media objects, they are resisting the institutional invisibility that is imposed on fat women in our culture. I speak of invisibility not simply in terms of representation, but also the weight of the connotations that accompany taking up space as a fat woman. These blog posts exist as testimony in that they provide a space for fat women to be unapologetic about their bodies, a space to be proud, to move toward radical self-love. According to Vivian Mayer,

> As women liberate knowledge about fat from the medical monopoly, fat women will come out of the closets of our minds and realize that there is nothing wrong with us. It is time to struggle to realize that there is nothing wrong with us. It is time to struggle with the implications of thin privilege and fat punishment the same way as we struggle with other social injustices that we've recognized for years. (12)

It is clear that while there have been strides made in changing the way women understand fat, especially in feminist circles, negative ideas about fat women are still hegemonic. The IFFC is a place where fat women come for practical reasons but eventually find their place and learn to love and accept themselves. Now that I have given an overview of the community and demonstrated how it functions, I would like to explore how the community has impacted the larger culture.

Moving and Shaking

There are a few moments in fat fashion that I outline here to help illustrate the relationship between the early IFFC and the fashion industry writ large. Using these examples, I demonstrate how early bloggers of the IFFC pursued and developed relationships with movers and shakers in the fashion industry, with the sole purpose of increasing the quality and quantity of fashionable options for fat women.

In June 2009 Gabi Gregg, along with a handful of other bloggers, was invited to attend Full Figured Fashion Week in Los Angeles. After the show, Gabi posted on her blog about her disappointment with the fashions presented. In a post called "The Runway" she asks, "Would these designs be good enough for Fashion Week at Bryant Park? Am I lowering my standards just because this fashion is for fat women?"

Her disappointment is echoed in the comments. Xtina from *Musings of a Fashionista* says,

> i think it was cool for what it was but i wasn't impressed. at all. i just feel like sometimes plus size fashion always equates to flowy floral prints and jersey knits AND I HATE IT. so i was looking forward to this being our coming out party and it was in a way, just not the way i'd hoped.

The organizer of FFF Week, Gwen DeVoe, then responded in the comments section, chastising Gabi for not being more appreciative. She says,

> Not every plus woman calls herself a fatshionista. There are some that just want quality, well-fitting clothing that she can afford. If you read our press release, the hype was about the union of lesser-known designers, sponsors, and producers who united to bring a quality fashion event to plus size consumers. I think to say that you were underwhelmed by the clothing is a bit harsh, but again, that's my opinion and you are certainly entitled to yours.

After a lengthy back and forth, Gabi responds:

> i think as fat women, we are too often told "just be happy that you have clothes" . . . and i refuse to do that. i want us to have the SAME stylish, quality clothing that straight sized women have, period. i think to lower our expectations and simply celebrate that we have designers at all is a bit insulting. i will continue to critique plus size designers in the same way that i critique any others, because i think it's the only way fat fashion will progress.

In her reading of Black celebrity gossip bloggers, Catherine Knight Steele argues that they resist oppression at the level of the personal, the communal, and the institutional. The example above demonstrates these three levels of resistance. Also, this conversation is an origin point for open and honest conversations between industry professionals and the IFFC, who were not willing to settle for anything less than complete and total parity on the fashion stage.

Then, in July 2010, Gregg organized a conference that brought bloggers to brands and brands to bloggers. In speaking about her goals for the conference on her blog, Gabi says:

> Between curvy models making front page news and magazines dedicating complete issues to size diversity, it's clear that plus-size women are finally beginning to receive the recognition they deserve in the fashion industry. With this transition, 2010 has become the year of the fat fashion bloggers. Media outlets and fashion houses worldwide have realized our impact, seeking us out for advice, input and clothing reviews. . . . Eleven of fatshion's best have been invited to spend a weekend in New York City to discuss the issues surrounding our community, preview fall lines, meet our readers, and, of course, shop!

Herman Gray asks us "to consider some of the ways that new communication technologies get inscribed and articulated by social relations that produce greater exploitation, domination, and inequality—represented through narratives of freedom, choice, and progress" (134). This is a crucial moment because as the bloggers are blind in their pursuit of "freedom, choice and progress" via better/more fashion choices, the institutions they are engaging were created for the sole purpose of exploitation, domination, and inequality.

Finally, in October 2011, The Limited clothing company teamed up with Gabi to launch a new plus-size brand based on the needs and desires of the IFFC. Kim, writing for *The Curvy Fashionista*, says of the launch:

> I'm kinda beyond stoked that the Limited is FINALLY hearing us. . . .
> I thank fellow plus size blogger Gabi from GabiFresh.com for her voice and collaboration with Eloquii by The Limited for the launch. Bloggers seem to be the new models and certainly the retail world is benefiting from it.

This is concrete institutional change as a result of the bloggers' labor.

These three examples demonstrate the way the IFFC forced their own recognition outside the community itself. The fashion landscape for fat women and girls is drastically different today. For many plus-size millennials and future generations of fat women for whom fashion is a huge part of their already mediated experience, trend-driven shopping, whether online or in stores, will be a much easier experience than it was for me as a fat Black graduate student in Santa Barbara years ago. Not only this, they will witness fat women in music, on television, in film, and in magazines and books.

This success has its limits. How do we quantify the positives and negative gains in the fashion industry in relation to late capitalism? Gray argues, "Consumer sovereignty, choice and the availability of commodities are the economic expression and political realization of this neoliberal vision of democratic possibility and economic freedom" (134). To be sure, the increase in choice and visibility is a direct result of retailers and media moguls who view this community as a market opportunity. This is positive insofar as the community gets what it wants: more options. Unfortunately, the power that this community has to change the plus-size fashion industry only goes so far as its capital. Indeed, the system has not undergone change; we have simply had our tastes commodified. Fat fashion bloggers have become implicated by paying into a system that further oppresses fat women at large. The paradox here is that this mainstream recognition leads to a wider movement toward body positivity.

In 2015 *Time* magazine published an article entitled "Why I'm Over the Size Acceptance Movement." The author, Cary Webb, identifies herself as "a Black woman who weighs about 355 lbs, has chronic conditions, is educated but is lower middle class [rather] than upper." She asks, "What has the size acceptance movement done for me lately?" She argues that alongside mainstream adoption of body positivity, there has also been a streamlining of the message to fat people within the community itself: for example, "eat healthy, exercise regularly, don't gain/lose weight, don't have/stop struggling with an eating disorder, love your body, resist stigma and shame, wear what you want, date who you like, and only flaunt your sexuality if you are under a size 20." She also says:

> I'm particularly disheartened by the way straight white women's needs seem to be prioritized over POC, LGBTQ, men or people who are masculine of center, and people who are visibly not able bodied even though I think we probably do the most subtle everyday activism around the subject just from being so visibly othered. There just aren't any women who look like me who can speak for me in this movement.

The author is searching for a size acceptance movement, or even a conversation, that goes beyond the simple ideas listed above. And while these questions about who fits go back to the early days of the IFFC, because of the mechanisms of Western market capitalism and neoliberal democracy, the fat bodies doing the "everyday activism" are left behind, unknowable and hyper(in)visible, in favor of the bodies who learned how to capitalize on the conversations, alliances, and identifications of the early IFFC.

Indeed, I learned at TheCurvyCon in 2016 that the most successful fat fashion bloggers earn well over six figures annually. While *Gabifresh* enjoys widespread name recognition, the many women of Color with whom I had conversations that ranged from where to find thigh-highs to the artistry of Oscar De La Renta, women whom I witnessed as they took selfies in crop tops and bodycon dresses, exposing their bulge long before Hannah Horvath did[4] — these women remain largely unknown, unacknowledged, and invisible.

Patricia Hill Collins says, "Maintaining the invisibility of Black women and our ideas . . . has been critical in maintaining social inequalities" (*Black Feminist Thought* 3). If our bodies remain invisible, so does our struggle. When we make ourselves visible, as I hope to do through my work, we are engaging that struggle and resisting hyper(in)visibility.

Notes

1. Beyoncé appeared on the cover in April 2009, March 2013, September 2015, and September 2018, and Jennifer Lopez was on the cover in April 2012.
2. See Bacon, *Health at Every Size*; and Tovar, *Hot & Heavy*.
3. This is the language that is used in the IFFC, so I retain it here.
4. Hannah Horvath is the main character in Lena Dunham's *Girls* (HBO, 2012–2017), played by Dunham herself.

Works Cited

Anzaldúa, Gloria. *Borderlands/La Frontera: The New Mestiza*, Aunt Lute Books, 1999.

Bacon, Linda. *Health at Every Size: The Surprising Truth about Your Weight*. BenBella, 2010.

Baker, Jess. *Things No One Will Tell Fat Girls: A Handbook for Unapologetic Living*. Seal, 2015.

Borton, Natalie. "The Stylist Embodied: Tanesha Awasthi." *Darling Magazine*, 30 Nov. 2012, darlingmagazine.org/the-stylist-embodied-tanesha-awasthi/. Accessed 25 Sept. 2018.

Collins, Patricia Hill. *Black Feminist Thought: Knowledge, Consciousness, and the Politics of Empowerment*. 10th ed., Routledge, 2000.

———. "Learning from the Outsider Within: The Sociological Significance of Black Feminist Thought." *Social Problems*, vol. 33, no. 6, 1986, pp. s14–32, academic.oup .com, doi:10.2307/800672.

Connell, Catherine. "Fashionable Resistance: Queer 'fa(T) Shion' Blogging as Counterdiscourse." *Women's Studies Quarterly*, vol. 41, no. 1/2, (Spring/Summer) 2012, pp. 209–224.

"Eloquii by the Limited Launches October 26th." *The Curvy Fashionista*, 3 Oct. 2011, thecurvyfashionista.com/eloquii-by-the-limited-launches-october-2011/. Accessed 1 Aug. 2018.

Fatshionista—Profile. fatshionista.livejournal.com/profile/. Accessed 28 Aug. 2018.

Foucault, Michel. *"Society Must Be Defended": Lectures at the Collège de France, 1975–1976.* Translated by David Macey, Macmillan, 2003.

Gabby. "Thoughts." *Corazones Rojos*, 15 Mar. 2018, corazonesrojos.tumblr.com/post /45432530264/thoughts. Accessed 25 Aug. 2018.

Gray, Herman. *Cultural Moves: African Americans and the Politics of Representation.* U of California P, 2005.

Gregg, Gabi. "About." *YFF Blogger Conference*, yffconference.tumblr.com/post/5312 21135/about. Accessed 28 Aug. 2018.

———. "The Runway." *Gabifresh*, 1 July 2009, gabifresh.com/2009/07/the-runway/. Accessed 28 Aug. 2018.

Hurtado, Aída. "Much More Than a Butt: Jennifer Lopez's Influence in Fashion." *Spectator*, vol. 26, no. 1, Jan. 2008, pp. 147–153.

Lewis, Christina. Introduction. *Musings of a Fatshionista*, 22 Mar. 2009, blog.musings ofafatshionista.com/post/88823825/001-the%09introduction#disqusthread. Accessed 8 Nov. 2013.

Mayer, Vivian. "The Fat Illusion." *Shadow on a Tightrope: Writings by Women on Fat Oppression*, edited by Lisa Schoenfielder and Barb Wieser, Aunt Lute Books, 1983, pp. 3–14.

Petermon, Jade. "Race (Lost and Found) in Shondaland: The Rise of Multiculturalism in Primetime Network Television." *Adventures in Shondaland: Identity Politics and the Power of Representation*, edited by Rachel Alicia Griffin and Michaela D. E. Meyer, Rutgers UP, 2018, pp. 101–119.

Rabine, Leslie W. "A Woman's Two Bodies: Fashion Magazines, Consumerism, and Feminism." *On Fashion*, edited by Suzanne Ferriss and Shari Benstock, Rutgers UP, 1994, pp. 59–75.

Schoenfielder, Lisa, and Barb Wieser, editors. *Shadow on a Tightrope: Writings by Women on Fat Oppression*, Aunt Lute Books, 1983.

Steele, Catherine Knight. "Signifyin', Bitching, and Blogging: Black Women and Resistance Discourse Online." *The Intersectional Internet: Race, Sex, Class, and Culture Online*, Peter Lang, 2016, pp. 73–93.

Tovar, Virgie, editor. *Hot & Heavy: Fierce Fat Girls on Life, Love & Fashion.* Seal, 2012.

Wann, Marilyn. "Fat Studies: An Invitation to Revolution." *The Fat Studies Reader*, edited by Esther Rothblum and Sondra Solovay, New York UP, 2009, pp. xi–xxvi.

Ward, Karen. "The Ultimate #ThrowbackThursday." *Curvy Canadian*, 29 Aug. 2012, networkedblogs.com/OyXUe. Accessed 8 Nov. 2013.

Webb, Cary. "Why I'm Over the Size Acceptance Movement." *Time*, 5 Jan. 2015, time .com/3654669/size-acceptance-movement/. Accessed 28 Aug. 2018.

CHAPTER 9

Fashioning Decolonial Optics: Days of the Dead Walking Altars and Calavera Fashion Shows in Latina/o Los Angeles

LAURA PÉREZ

From 2003 to 2006, and again from 2008 to 2010, Tropico de Nopal Gallery Art-Space, in Los Angeles, produced a yearly Calavera Fashion Show, featuring what by 2006 were called Walking Altars, as part of its month-long Days of the Dead art exhibition and events.[1] The Calavera Fashion Shows and Walking Altars formed a new chapter of Days of the Dead celebrations in Los Angeles and the United States. They are vibrant new art forms that draw on mixed-media altar installation, performance art, and a unique contribution to the Los Angeles phenomenon of dress-based installation and performance art, alongside the "paper fashions" pioneered there.[2] By coining the "walking altar" concept in their 2006 artists' call, Tropico refocused the production of this hybrid performance installation art form, beyond literal fashion shows and Halloween costumes. This new media performing altar-installation-as-dress became for many artists a device for exploring the core idea that on Days of the Dead, November 1 and 2, the living visit with their dead, according to Mesoamerican Indigenous worldviews.[3]

Like other Days of the Dead artwork, Walking Altars commemorate deceased family members and friends, cultural hero/ines, and the unknown whose deaths trouble the living. At Tropico, Walking Altars have honored and made socially visible the "disappeared" young women of Juárez, casualties of the US-Iraq war, the homeless, and victims of domestic abuse and rape. They also remember undocumented migrants who have died crossing the border, and the lethal toll on the environment due to the methods of the Immigration Naturalization Service (INS). Walking Altars have paid homage to artists, singers, dancers, and poets, both the well known and the lesser known, and to inspiring figures such as Sor Juana Inés de la Cruz and John Waters's transvestite star, Divine.[4] But above all, the Walk-

9.1. Rigo Maldonado, *Callas* (walking altar), detail. © Rigo Maldonado.

ing Altars have provided a communal space for the artists to mourn for relatives and friends, and to lovingly remember them during this season.

Some of the Walking Altars broached death philosophically, in particular the Mesoamerican Indigenous concept of the duality of life and death, a worldview seeing the continuity of life in the beyond, and thus the presence in our own lives of our ancestral dead. Many of the Walking Altars worked against erasure caused by racism and marginalization of the historical contributions of Latin American female, US Latina/o, and queer artists. As live events, the Calavera Fashion Shows and Walking Altars created a space for communal, interactive celebration of the life of the dead, and a public space for acknowledging and mourning both physical deaths and social losses. In creating such a space through community art, Calavera Fashion Shows and Walking Altars worked toward restoring an individually and socially healthier way of dealing with physical death, social marginalization, and psychological or emotional losses.[5] In this, Calavera Fashion Shows and Walking Altars, like other Days of the Dead art and religious practices, enact a social critique of the denial and repression of death in dominant cultures. They speak to recognizing death in its many guises (trauma, violence, loss, extinction) and the human necessity of survivors to do something about it, both for themselves and for the dead.[6] In effect, the Walking Altars of the Calavera Fashion Shows worked to transform discourses of life and death in the mainstream of US culture, circulating ancient and persistent ideas about the coexistence of the living and the dead, and the necessity of mourning and commemoration, for both the living and those who have passed on.

To the extent that they articulate themselves through respectful reclamation of Mesoamerican worldviews about the spiritual nature of being and reality, recirculating and reinterpreting aspects of these philosophies for the betterment of our communities in the here and now, the Calavera Fashion Shows and Walking Altars operated in ideologically decolonizing ways. Even where not culturally intact, and given that they are not religious ritual but rather spiritual art practices to some degree, such engagements form part of five hundred years of resistance against the historical repression of Mesoamerican Indigenous spiritual practices and their folklorization in the service of Eurocentric, Latin American elite nation-building.[7] Such Chicana/o and Latina/o Days of the Dead practices consciously self-authorize themselves against (neo)colonizing censure and prohibitions that charge that non-Anglo, Hispanic "mixed-bloods" have no right to claim Indigeneity; or that the Indigenous is irrecuperable, and therefore, that attempts to identify with Indigenous identities and practices are expressions of intellectually and spiritually naïve nostalgia, politically ineffectual, ostensibly idealizing the past rather than addressing the present and future.[8]

As performance events, the Calavera Fashion Shows produced a way of seeing and understanding that consciously fashions an optics beyond the blinders of centuries of widely popularized pseudoscientific racializing mythologies claiming that non-Europeans are biologically, intellectually, and culturally inferior; that is, that they are somehow less fully human, and therefore less deserving of respect, rights, and services, and in short, unworthy of full social existence. The colonial, and its persistence in contemporary neocolonial logic, consigns the Indigenous, the Indigenous-identified "mixed," and even at times the completely "deracinated" to socially liminal presence, to de facto segregation, to ghettoization in underserved yet tax-paying neighborhoods, to stereotyped, projected criminalization and disproportionate incarceration, that is, to various forms of social death-in-life.[9] In the face of this, the Calavera Fashion Shows and Walking Altars are also a performance of the survival and the vitality of the supposedly better-left-as-dead. They point the way to philosophies of how to live and social visions of successful communal life that do not depend on the domination-unto-death of others.

The first decade of the new millennium was a time, as continues to be, of the historic concentration of wealth into the hands of a different kind of minority: the numerically tiny, extremely wealthy, disproportionately "white" and male. Correspondingly, the number of poor has grown, with the majority of the impoverished in many parts of the world, including the United States, continuing to be women of color, female-headed households, and their children. A callous, extreme profit-driven logic continues to rationalize and sharpen economic and social inequities. Regardless of claims that the United States is now "postracial" and "postfeminist," the most "modern" economic policies and the radically materialist values they spawn and circulate through mass media re-marginalize, re-gender, and re-racialize the Indigenous and Third World poor and impoverish the lower middle classes.[10] Within this context, the production of art performance "fashion shows" might seem frivolous, and in any case, an ineffectual ideological response to the powerful advances of domination in this phase of postmodern "phantom capital" globalization, as economist David Korten has called it. I am arguing, however, that communal Days of the Dead practices in the United States "revivify" still negatively racialized Chicana/o and other Latina/o artists and their communities precisely against the forms of psychological, social, political, economic, and physical deaths that such marginalization, exploitation, and criminalization bring. Days of the Dead practices, even those that are artistic rather than religious ritual proper, allow for greater individual and communal integration with the community of our dead, as well as with personal, intra-psychic losses or "deaths."[11] The Calavera Fashion Shows and Walking Altars are particularly apt and new expressions of integrative bridge building to the disincarnate within the self, to each other, and to the physically deceased that somehow also function as our larger community, according to the living traditions of ancient beliefs in the Americas.

Articulated conceptually and formally through Mesoamerican philosophies of humanity's responsibility to maintain harmonious relationships within one's body (which includes "mind" and "spirit"), with each other, and with the rest of the natural world, including the world beyond physical life, the Calavera Fashion Shows as a whole, and certain Walking Altars in particular, also shed light on what is life- and death-giving in terms of the economic, the social, the political, the cultural, the psychological, and the spiritual, as well as the physical. Building on four decades of community-based Days of the Dead celebrations and events in the Chicana/o-Latina/o United States, by performing as the dead the Walking Altars "tell it like it is," from the socially and materially disinterested perspective of death as the place where "you can't take it with you."

The Calavera Fashion Shows gather Walking Altars that are witty, humorous, satiric, joyful, educational, sad, religious, predictable, or completely unexpected. As a whole, they are beautiful and startlingly creative, so many evidently crafted with great care as part of the homage, akin in this way to religious art. In ranging across a wide spectrum of figures and themes, they are like Mexican popular folk craft figurines that humorously depict the worlds of the living and the dead as mirror images of each other come to life, with calavera (skull face and exposed body part) mariachi bands, skeletons in curlers at the beauty salon, and newlyweds in coffins. In some respects, they are like José Guadalupe Posada's "calaveras," satiric skeleton drawings lambasting political corruption and social folly of the late eighteenth and early nineteenth centuries. But in making use of performance, in mobilizing the altar installation via the body, Walking Altars and the Calavera Fashion Shows go one step further in literally animating the ideas that the dead are alive and that the living are dead. The "models" perform the body as altar. The "dress" is the installation of various objects. And while all the dress installations are exquisite, complex, or wonderfully creative, mastery of media is not the central point, nor is exploration of this new media. Performance and commemoration is what takes center stage: the play of the living and the dead celebrating coexistence.

Renewal with a Little Help from Our Dead

Marialice Jacob and Reyes Rodriguez opened Tropico de Nopal in 2000 with a Days of the Dead exhibition of altar installations. Following artist Yreina D. Cervántez's suggestion, they called these installations "ofrendas" in order to center the ancestral, Indigenous spiritual tradition of remembering, honoring, and caring for one's dead on November 1 and 2 through rituals, offerings of food and flowers, and other memorial acts. This foundational emphasis on the spiritual also served to interrupt the tendency to appropriate Days of the Dead in culturally decontextualizing ways as nothing more than a Mexican-style Halloween party.[12] Tropico, that is, Jacob and Rodriguez, in dialogue with a circle of friends and seasoned artists, thereby chose to continue a tradition within Chicana/o art and cultural politics of recentering Indigenous worldviews. As it is so often misread, it must be said that this conscious effort to reincorporate or reanimate the Indigenous within Chicana/o and US Latina/o cultures, a cultural and spiritual politics dating to the 1960s, is a path markedly different from that of Mexico's and Latin America's Eurocentric "mestizo" discourses that "celebrate" the achievements of the Indigenous civilizations of the Aztec, Maya, and Inca but are contemptuous of living Indigenous peoples and their supposedly degraded cultures.[13] Pioneering Los Angeles–based Chicana art historian Sybil Venegas, creator of a Walking Altar herself, observed of the Indigenous relationship for Chicana/os that

> it is the return to the ceremonies, practices, and ways of their ancestors and the revival of these practices in complex, oppositional contexts that give Chicanos strength, healing, direction and empowerment. This can be seen as a central and key element in the evolution of Chicano political struggle and artistic development in the past twenty years. The Day of the Dead in Aztlán is one of the most significant contemporary expressions of this sacred act of self preservation and empowerment. (53)

Venegas thoughtfully theorizes "the overwhelming community-based response" to Days of the Dead in the United States as

> a reflection of the postmodern condition of demographic change, uncertainty, and an absence of meaning, spirituality, and spontaneous creativity in contemporary, established social ritual. It is also a phenomenon rooted in Mexican/Chicano history and grounded in . . . the conquest of the Americas by European colonizers. For it is only against a backdrop of crisis, trauma, dramatic loss of life and economic exploitation that we encounter the tremendous human capacity for survival, adaption, and reinvention, which can be identified as "sacred acts of self-preservation." (53)

Four decades of the enthusiastic popularization inside and outside the Chicana/o-Latina/o communities of Days of the Dead spiritual and religious practices speak to their usefulness in creatively and meaningfully

engaging social, economic, political, and cultural realities while functioning as vehicles of spiritual expression and connection, of a healing and empowering perspective about death, whether physical, social, or cultural.[14]

Making Altars Walk

The Calavera Fashion Shows would seem to have drawn on the post-1970
Chicana/o art tradition of calavera makeup for Days of the Dead and on
the Los Angeles phenomenon of "paper fashions" that Patssi Valdez and
Diane Gamboa came to develop as signature art forms. But if this is so, it
appears only indirectly. Gamboa, in particular, would deploy paper fashions as worn, sculptural, and mobile "hit and run" performance art pieces
that escape and exceed the limits of curatorial acknowledgment and in-
clusion/exclusion by essentially crashing exhibitions that the artist was
excluded from, oftentimes stealing the show.[15] In response to my queries
about the possible influence of early Asco-circle and other paper fashion
shows, and in particular of Diane Gamboa's paper fashion work with Asco
and after,[16] Rodriguez clarified that though he had never been to a paper
fashion show, he had seen Diane Gamboa's "hit and run" pieces over the
years. He conceived the idea of a calavera fashion show as a Tropico Days
of the Dead event and discussed it with Gamboa, who, with Marialice
Jacob, Yreina D. Cervántez, and Consuelo Norte (who were influential in
the development of the Calavera Fashion Show's spiritual component),
influenced its signature Chicana/o–Latina/o urban aesthetic. Rodriguez
captured the influence of Gamboa's punk aesthetic in an anecdote, recalling Self-Help Graphic's Days of the Dead procession to Evergreen Cemetery, where Diane Gamboa showed up dressed as a cowgirl with calavera
makeup. "Who does that?!" he asked, laughing. "The whole city is her
stage, her 'calavera walk.' It's that spirit that underlies the whole thing
[the Calavera Fashion Show]."[17]

   As Rodriguez observed in the opening text of the video he made of the
Calavera Fashion Show in 2005, "Friends and fellow artists have all inspired Tropico de Nopal's Calavera Fashion Show. For over twenty-five
years the Chicano art community has refined and celebrated the calavera
look in Los Angeles. The event is a natural evolution of the process."[18] Indeed, the walking part of the Calavera Fashion Shows and the Walking
Altars can also be seen as natural outgrowths of Self-Help Graphics' artist-
led Days of the Dead processions from 1972 to 1979 in East Los Angeles,
and of the Galería de la Raza's San Francisco Mission District neighbor-

hood Days of the Dead processions from 1981 to 1986, and subsequent Days of the Dead processions that continued under the direction of different organizations.[19]

As to the roots of Days of the Dead altar making and altar installation in the Bay Area, Tere Romo, curator and historian of some of the earliest Chicana/o art exhibitions, recounted that artist Yolanda Garfias Woo taught altar-making for Days of the Dead, which she learned from her Oaxacan father, in the early 1960s. An artist herself, Garfias Woo introduced other Chicana/o and Latina/o Bay Area artists to altar-making, including Amalia Mesa-Bains, whose powerful installations have brought the medium the most attention in the dominant cultural art world. Garfias Woo also introduced altar-making to the collective of artists that cofounded the Galería de la Raza.

The success of Days of the Dead in both California epicenters of Chicana/o and Latina/o arts, Los Angeles and San Francisco, would lead to annual events that eventually attracted thousands of people, including the media and outsiders in Halloween costumes looking for "the parade" (Romo 34–37).[20] Lourdes Portillo's and Susana Muñoz's film *La Ofrenda: The Days of the Dead* (1988) sheds light on the popularity of Days of the Dead among both Latina/os and non-Latina/os, particularly during the 1980s. Using interviews, the film suggests that Days of the Dead provided a necessary language for people to begin to honor their dead against not only homophobic repression of the HIV and AIDS crisis but also more generally in mainstream culture where death may be repressed as embarrassing, as something that is best forgotten and thus becomes doubly wounding.

More Calavera Fashion Show Bones

The Calavera Fashion Shows and Walking Altars in Los Angeles also emerge from the sensibilities, aesthetics, and politics of Chicana/o 1970s underground rock and urban punk culture, infused with intergenerational after-effects of 1940s and 1950s pachuca/o culture.[21] They are immersed in Hollywood film and popular media culture. But these cultures in turn have been influenced by Chicana/o and East Los Angeles artistic and street cultures, as Tim Burton's *The Night Before Christmas* and Disney/Pixar's unsuccessful 2013 bid to copyright the words "Día de los Muertos" show.[22] While many of the Walking Altars share the wit and raw talents of a Tim Burton film production, the occult world of the spirits is not domesticated as the unreal. Like the religious altars they pay homage to and elaborate on as art, the Calavera Fashion Shows and many, perhaps most, Walking Altars seem to take the life-death, human-spirits liminal threshold seriously.

On one level, the space of the Calavera Fashion Show has real elements of the memorial and of Days of the Dead religious rituals: of recalling the dead, grieving their loss, celebrating their lives, and dwelling with them through the creation of altars holding favorite foods, beverages, candies, and other objects. In Juana Flores's *Pachuca Educada*, this is seen in how the artist's mother, a stylish young pachuca in her youth who later became a teacher, is recalled.[23] The "model" performs her in skull body makeup, fine pachuca clothing, hairstyle, stylishly matching baby stroller carrying baby and books, dancing her way up and down the calavera catwalk to the music of the "Pachuco Boogie."[24] In Walking Altars such as this one, the dead really are being lovingly remembered, their presence somehow felt in their re-creation through the human-as-medium that embodies the spirit of the honored.

For other Walking Altar artists, the reality factor behind their performance of the body-as-art-installation may involve more direct identification with religious Native American, "folk Catholic," or other beliefs that the dead continue to live, but differently. Orquidia Violeta's *Angel*, for example, suggests this. Her "Artist Dedication" states: "The boundaries which divide Life from Death are at best shadowy and vague. Who shall say where the one ends and the other begins? The Premature Burial. 1844. To all the Poets and Writers whom [sic] affected our lives" (Calavera Fashion Show 2008, program). This dedication points to a "real" something that survives in artwork itself, and that survives in us, shapes us, and in some literal way does dwell in us, sometimes feeling more real and affecting than many of those living around us. There are many Walking Altars dedicated to artists that suggest such feeling. In the 2008 Calavera Fashion Show, these included *Homage to J. G. Posada* by Guadalupe Rodriguez and Sandy Rodriguez, *Viva la Vida* to Diego Rivera and Frida Kahlo by Rosanna Ahrens, *Homenaje a Nahui Olin: A Woman of Eternal Cosmic Movement* by Lara Medina, and *Homenaje a Rosa Covarrubias: The Chicana as Tehuana* by Sybil Venegas. In all but the Posada piece, where the Mexican printer's iconic image of Death as an elegant lady in a hot pink slinky dress is courted by one of his frolicking signature devils, these Walking Altars pay homage to the artist by performing her or him. Thus, though Walking Altars are an art form that fictionalizes embodiment of a dead or fleshless other (e.g., a spirit, deity, or archetype), the human performer is a "carrier," a "channel" of the invoked spirit. In Spiritism, and in the temporary ritual spirit possession of individuals in Santería, for example, what is plain is that living bodies are the places, the altars, where divine and human, living and dead cross.[25] Walking Altar performances of the dead as the living enact this logic.

Undead Still Lives

In the Calavera Fashion Shows, Walking Altars are living bodies performing memory. They are altar installations in motion, performing the reanimation of the dead and the reality of spirits and deities. They perform the dead as part of a living spirit world, and the living, as the dead. Walking Altars also enact or activate the crossing of various "languages" through the performance of body as altar, dress as altar installation, and fashion show as the world, the stage of life and death, human and spirit worlds. They operate through synesthesia, addressing multiple senses simultaneously through the choreography of discourses of dress, movement, and music, and crossing performance and multimedia installation such that the performing body is both stage and protagonist. In being set to music, with dance, swaying, or synchronized movement, Walking Altars literalize the idea of the dance of life and death.[26]

The performers give body to what memory returns through its various "archives": music, style, objects, a feeling or a mood. Walking Altars embody the idea of memory as a persistence, a paradoxical *pervivencia*, a kind of living, within the mind and feelings of the undeceased, or in museums, books, and other forms recording social memory more generally. In the altar dresses, memory of loss is a kind of hologram, a three-dimensional reconstitution of the apparently invisible, momentarily garbed in the flesh of the actor and model, a stand-in for the living. This symbolic coexistence of living and dead, of the tangible and the intangible, a literal coexistence in the religious altar, signifies the identification of the living and the dead, the fleshed and the disincarnate, not just in terms of the spirits of the dead but also in the unseen dimensions of corporality or the body: thoughts, emotions, desires, fantasies, and visions.

In skeletal makeup covering exposed body parts, what such performances of the dead-as-living and the living-as-dead materialize is, of course, that not all is as it appears, and that being is not simply appearance, easily accessible through visuality. The body as skeleton is the body inside out. It externalizes the internal, makes visible that which is invisible, because it is shrouded behind flesh and the tissues of muscles and organs. What is contained is released, dissolved even, to the bare bone, symbolizing the imbrication of life and death, and the cyclic nature of this embrace.

Larger Than Life

It is hard to describe the great energy, the enthusiasm and appreciation for the Calavera Fashion Shows' wonderfully creative takes on the idea of the Walking Altar or the centrality of the communal in their production and reception. Walking Altars became a venue for exploring a new, performance- and installation-based hybrid medium. Few of the mainly visual artists had experience with performance.[27] According to Rodriguez, Cervántez, and Rigo Maldonado, the collaborative nature of creating Walking Altar pieces and of producing the Calavera Fashion Shows was particularly welcome given the typically solitary nature of making artwork.[28] That the exploration of this new hybrid medium offered fresh, genuinely original possibilities for rethinking the meaning of Days of the Dead and memorials more generally is strikingly evident, even in documentary photos and films. Perhaps the stimulating new possibilities offered by Walking Altars and the warm support and festive spirit of Calavera Fashion Show events explain why many of the artists have participated in the Calavera Fashion Shows more than once: Consuelo Flores, Rigo Maldonado, Orquid Velazquez (aka Orquidia Violeta), Araceli Silva, Sandy Rodriguez, Guadalupe Rodriguez, Robert Quijada, Margaret Guzman, Zoe Aguirre, Poli Marichal, CiCi Segura, Carolyn Castaño, Ofelia Esparza, Abel Alejandre, Rosanna Ahrens, Maria Elena Castro, Daniel Gonzalez, Katiria Gomez, Juana Flores, and Edith Abeyta.

While it is difficult to single out a few from the dozens of Walking Altars that have appeared since 2003, I will briefly describe some in order to give a sense of the range of these works and, where possible, their reception. Poli Marichal is a Puerto Rican printer and painter, now a part of the Chicana/o-Latina/o arts community of Los Angeles. In 2008 she performed a moving tribute to her deceased father, silently narrating her parents' love story, *The Dance of Love and Death* (fig. 9.2) to operatic music, "Felice," by Nicola Piovani.

El [altar ambulante] del 2008 es el que dediqué a mi padre, el artista canario, Carlos Marichal. Mis padres vivieron un gran amor que mi madre, Flavia Lugo, ha mantenido vivo a través de los años. Yo quise honrarlo con

9.2. Poli Marichal, *The Dance of Love and Death* (walking altar), detail. © Poli Marichal.

este altar ambulante. En él, mi madre va a visitar [*sic*] la tumba de mi padre
y él se le aparece. Ella se sobrecoge asustada pero, cuando se da cuenta
que es él, le toca la cara y después lo abraza. Juntos en ese abrazo, los dos
amantes bailan y, luego crean un corazón con las mitades que cada [*sic*] uno
tiene en su mano al unirlas.[29]

The character of "Death," both puppet master and stage, was dressed in
a long, silver-gray skirt and matching overalls-style bib that, with a large

cross on it, had the effect of a tombstone. The face of the model (as Death, the Puppet Master, and Stage) was covered in a silver mask, the Moon, with a circular perimeter extending some six inches or so all around the face, and a long gray veil trailing from it to the floor. From the arms of the figure's black, close-fitting sweater, two hand puppets emerged, representing the artist's father and mother, and worn like gloves but projecting about a foot and a half beyond the hands. The impression of the Walking Altar, performed by the artist, was of death as the looming stage against which the dance of courtship and life occurred, a dance of stage and puppets paced to complex and dramatic operatic music. Marichal also created *Tanta Vanidad: So Much Vanity* . . . (2006), dedicated to her grandmother, and in 2009 performed as La Muerte / Blue Death with a puppet, Los Ojos, "un niño indigente," in *La Muerte de los Niños de la Calle / The Death of Homeless Children.* Her 2010 Walking Altar, *Soul Catcher,* was based on Remedios Varo's "Star Catcher," she explained, "a sort of merciful death" (program notes), and dedicated to her recently deceased aunt (fig. 9.3).

Rigo Maldonado created three Walking Altars in 2005 whose construction details are useful to understanding the significance of Walking Altars to some of the artists. He explained that he had never sewn before the Calavera Fashion Shows but had grown up watching his mother construct wedding and *quinceañera* (sweet fifteen) dresses, though he did remember drawing dresses as a child.[30] *La Divina . . . A Tribute to Gia* (2004) was constructed of drawings and other things that the artist found when helping to clean out the apartment of his friend, a young female fashion illustrator and designer who committed suicide. Maldonado later installed this dress in Tropico de Nopal's gallery with other, longer-term *Ofrenda* installations. *Callas* (2005), used on the Calavera Fashion Show invitation for 2006, featured a beautiful diva in a copper wire mesh skirt cage decorated with flowers and photos of the opera singer (see fig. 9.1). Other materials beside textile included pearls, silk, feathers, and birds. The artist's statement explained, "The guilded birdcage skirt is left open, offering an alternative to life in the public eye amidst powerful men and morally flexible jet-setters. Through it all the fighting spirit of Callas lives on . . . Vine [sic], Vidi, Vici!" In Tropico's video documentation of this piece, the performer stepped delicately and slowly to one of Maria Callas's tragic arias. *Basquiat* (2005) honored Haitian Puerto Rican New York painter Jean-Michel Basquiat and incorporated his New York City tag, "SAMO" (same ol' shit), into the design. *Chávez, Cruz, and Warhol* (2005) played upon a Kellogg's Corn Flakes promotion that strangely lumped together the Cuban salsa chanteuse and a very serious-looking César Chávez, head of the United Farm Workers. Maldonado created a dress and matching purse made of Corn Flakes boxes.

9.3. Poli Marichal, *Soul Catcher* (walking altar). © Poli Marichal.

Maldonado's *Too Much Is Never Enough* (figs. 9.4–9.6) celebrated John Waters's transvestite film star, Divine, and the actor and drag queen Harris Glenn Milstead (1945–1988) who performed her. The artist described the music, the name of the piece, and the spirit of its design in his artist's statement:

Fashion Name: Too much is never enough. Music: Little Richard—Girl Can't
help it. Model Name: Shakina Nayfack. *Statement*—In celebration of one
of the most important figures in too-wrong fashion, glamour and glitz,
this walking altar is dedicated to "the most beautiful woman in the world,"
Divine! Even today we can still look to her, the originator and reigning
queen of camp, trash and sass, for the inspiration and courage to be shame-
lessly excessive, ruthlessly indulgent and in all ways larger than life![31]

In an interview with me, Maldonado further explained that the dress was
inspired by the tradition of quinceañeras. The bustier was composed of the
traditional Days of the Dead flower, marigolds, and the skirt from a vintage green lace tablecloth. The corsage and the headdress were made from
flowers and images of Divine from Waters's films, framed in little hearts.

In Sandy Rodriguez and Guadalupe Rodriguez's *Una Ofrenda a los Santos
Inocentes* (Calavera Fashion Show 2006), death-masked Frida Kahlo and
Diego Rivera danced around a buxom Death dressed in a white bustier-
topped, wide-skirt diaphanous dress and shawl, imploring her to deliver
the three baby *calaveritas* crawling at her feet, barely visible beneath the
long hem of her skirt. Death is the last to exit, triumphantly holding up

9.4. Rigo Maldonado, *Too Much Is Never Enough* (walking altar). © Rigo Maldonado.

one of the skeleton babies. The effect is not gruesome, however. Based on Kahlo's biographical miscarriages and medically mandated abortion, the scene appears philosophical: memorializing the Mexican artists' lost children and their grief as a couple.

Maldonado's and Sandy and Guadalupe Rodriguez's pieces also convey two other elements central to many Walking Altars, whether through the

9.5. Rigo Maldonado, *Too Much Is Never Enough* (walking altar), detail. © Rigo Maldonado.

9.6. Rigo Maldonado, *Too Much Is Never Enough* (walking altar), detail.
© Rigo Maldonado.

"dress," the music, or the movement of the models: the manifestations of
desire and of humor. Death is often represented as sexy, a desirable seduc-
tress or seductor, draped in the US flag while dancing with a soldier, for
example, or slow dancing while surrounded by daggers, or as an updated
Catrina (following Diego Rivera's *Dream of a Sunday Afternoon in Alameda
Park* [1947–1948]), serenaded by a lascivious leaping red devil that mugs
to the audience. Whether dancing seductively to salsa or rock music, or
cavorting humorously, the audience sways, claps, or laughs appreciatively
and is often engaged directly, through eye contact by the performers. This
is as close to a Latin American holy day procession and festival, with its
mixture of serious spiritual ritual and earthy human feasting, as some will
ever get north of the US-Mexico border.[32]

Fashioning a Decolonizing Optics

According to specialists in trauma and nonviolence, enacting and surviving violence requires psychologically distancing mechanisms.[33] This ob-
servation can be applied to visuality as well. When violent, our gaze can
be penetrating, hostile, and objectifying, and yet we typically do not let

our vision dwell on what we are violencing or what has been violenced by others. Discourses of dehumanization function similarly. We consign to the margins of social visibility and ethical accountability (i.e., intellectual or spiritual awareness) what is ideologically minimized as inferior, uninteresting, dispensable, or despicable. Similarly, what we oppress culturally is what we endeavor not just to refute or to minimize but to obliterate from the shared worldview, the cultural imaginary, social perception, and psychological awareness. This shuttered view produces erasures within the social imaginary, a "narrowmindedness" that reproduces the violence of colonialism and neocolonialism, of patriarchy, homophobia, and classism, on the cognitive level and the visual, as hardly visible, if not unreal or nonexistent. Violence then becomes masked as something other than what it is, something normalized within dominant cultural logics, a nonissue to all but the survivors of such dismissals, reductions, denials, oppressions, erasures.

The uncolonized or the less colonized, however, exist apart from the narratives that dominant culture fabricates, which labor to limit our capacity to perceive more fully, more universally, rather than in very culturally and ideologically bound ways. Thus, while dominant cultures do not wish to see what they consign to the shadows, this does not mean that these other spheres do not exist, and with optics of their own, obeying different logics. And while colonial domination involved physical and cultural genocide of millions of Native Americans throughout the Americas and the Caribbean islands, they have not exterminated their core philosophies based on spiritual and scientific knowledge about the natural world in its human and nonhuman dimensions. Human beings are not the masters of the natural or spiritual worlds, nor of each other. And those who resort to violence to uphold such fantasies are not even masters of themselves, according to spiritual adepts cross-culturally.

Chicana/o and, more broadly, Latina/o art practices around Days of the Dead such as the Calavera Fashion Shows and Walking Altars are one set of practices among many that people "of color" in the United States and Indigenous peoples of the Americas have discovered, re-created, or received and by which they survive and strengthen themselves in the face of centuries of violence. In the Calavera Fashion Shows and Walking Altars, racist, classist, sexist, and homophobic dehumanizations are counteracted, reminding us of the profoundly political, democratizing, and ecological view from which Days of the Dead celebrations arise: that life and death exist in a continuum, and are part of the interdependence of all being, the visible and the invisible, the human and the nonhuman.

The Calavera Fashion Shows and the Walking Altars create a crossroads where dominant culture meets supposedly dead cultures, dead people, and dead ideas. As Marjorie Garber observes in her book *Vested Interests* (1997), crossing is crisis-inducing when the space of crossing is revealed as such, as a space beyond, as a borderlands (to invoke Gloria Anzaldúa), a third space outside binary logic, a zone operating by multiple codes, and not just those of dominant cultures. In the Calavera Fashion Shows and Walking Altars, the twilight citizenships and undocumented lives of the negatively racialized Chicana/o and Latina/o communities of Los Angeles are brought into view. But the objectified are now subjects with stories to tell, insights to share, pictures to show, energies to transmit.

Ideologically, intellectually, spiritually, and visually, the Calavera Fashion Shows operate from a different dimension, a culturally real way station of hybrids, righteous misfits, inevitable rebels, and brainiacs. The audience claps enthusiastically at the beauty, the imagination, the creative brilliance, the loveliness of the affection, the beauty of the respect, the incomprehensible rightness of remembering our dead, our losses. What has gone missing in our hearts, our heads, and our lives is collectively found in these sold-out gatherings of initiates and sympathizers, of Chicana/o and Latina/o artists, family, friends, and fans. A Calavera Fashion Show is an event to fill the eye and feed the soul. Neither a marketplace for the selling of fashion or art nor a museum or pretentious gallery event, the Calavera Fashion Shows are a display of an unruly cultural logic. Taking Death as advisor, they parade for inspection that which gives life, nourishes, ministers to the losses of our loved ones, showing us that they can and must be incorporated into our lives, as must the many other forms of death we suffer while in the flesh. Calling for a little help from our dead, as my mother says, things will get better, you will see. Ya verás.

Notes

I would like to thank Marialice Jacob and Reyes Rodriguez for inviting me to see some of the preparation and staging of the Calavera Fashion Show in 2008, and for providing me with documents at that time. For speaking extensively with me about the Calavera Fashion Shows, I would like to thank Reyes Rodriguez, Marialice Jacob, Yreina D. Cervántez, and Rigo Maldonado. The gallery was in transition during the time of my research and writing, and many materials were no longer on the website or accessible. I appreciate Rodriguez for providing some documentary photos, videos, and an art video of the Calavera Fashion Show through Vimeo, Jacob for accessing and sending Calavera Fashion Show programs to me, and Maldonado for sharing his PowerPoint presentation on Days of the Dead and jpegs of his Walking

Altars. Thanks to Aída Hurtado and Norma Cantú for thoughtful suggestions. A note on the usage "Chicana/o-Latina/o": the Los Angeles and San Francisco "Chicana/o" art communities, like the neighborhood communities they arise from, have historically been predominantly Mexican American, but they have also included Central Americans, Puerto Ricans, Cubans, and populations of other Latin American artists, including those from the Southern Cone.

This chapter originally appeared as "Fashioning Decolonial Optics: Days of the Dead Walking Altars and Calavera Fashion Shows in Latina/o Los Angeles" in Laura E. Perez, *Eros Ideologies: Writings on Art, Spirituality, and the Decolonial* (Duke University Press, 2019); used by permission.

1. Reyes Rodriguez initiated a new version of the Calavera Fashion Shows on the streets of East Los Angeles in 2014 that I will not address here.

2. See my chapter "Body, Dress" in *Chicana Art* for more about paper fashions and Diane Gamboa's paper fashion work.

3. Detailed information regarding the gallery, the Calavera Fashion Show, and the Walking Altars is drawn from telephone interviews I had with artist, gallery cofounder, and originator of the Calavera Fashion Show idea Reyes Rodriguez on July 9 and 12, 2013, and with artist and cofounder Marialice Jacob on December 13, 2014. My usage of *Mesoamerican* follows that of the late Guillermo Bonfil Batalla, who notes that over millennia the different peoples of the vast region of "middle" America created a common, core culture theologically and philosophically, which includes the "Aztecs" or Mexica, the Maya, and numerous other peoples with their own local and specific cultural variations. I am indebted to the artist Celia Herrera Rodríguez, a colleague and friend, for first bringing this work to my attention. For more continental generalizations about common and core traditional Indigenous beliefs, see *Native Science*, by Tewa education and science scholar Gregory Cajete.

4. See, for example, Consuelo Flores's *Pictures of Juarez* (Calavera Fashion Show [cfs] 2008) and José Lozano's *Las Meseras de Juarez* (cfs 2008). On the undocumented, see Rosanna Ahrens, *El Camino Norte: Dedicated to the Mexican Immigrant* (cfs 2006). On the US-Iraq war, see Consuelo Flores, *Sacrificed Truth* (cfs 2006). On the homeless, see Edith Abeyta, *Street Wear* (cfs 2008). On powerful female figures, see Araceli Silva, *Recuerdos-Reminders—Honoring Mama Lola and All That Is Sacred* (cfs 2005); Victoria Delgadillo, *Ay Mami! Honoring Celia Cruz* (cfs 2005); Maria Elena Castro and Sara Arias, *Azucar! Para Celia Cruz* (cfs 2006); Carolyn Caştaño, *Homenaje a Sor Juana Inés de la Cruz* (cfs 2006); Aida Landeros, *Farewell to Selena* (cfs 2006); Cici Segura Gonzalez, *Circus Poetry: Homenaje to Maria Izquierdo, a Mexican Artist* (cfs 2006); Lara Medina, *Fashion Homenaje a Nahui Ollin: A Woman of Eternal Cosmic Movement* (cfs 2008); Sybil Venegas, *Fashion Homenaje a Rosa Covarrubias* (cfs 2008); Miguel J. Barragan, *Baile Sorpresa . . . A Tribute to Selena* (cfs 2010); Joe Bravo, *La Reina de las Gitanas*, in honor of Carmen Amaya (cfs 2010); and Guadalupe Rodriguez and Sandy Rodriguez, *Ofrenda to Gloria Anzaldúa* (cfs 2010). Other well-known artists who were memorialized were J. G. Posada, Pablo Picasso, Frida Kahlo and Diego Rivera, David Alfaro Siqueiros, Keith Haring, Jean-Michel Basquiat, and Andy Warhol.

5. West African traditional healers Sobunfu Somé and Malidoma Patrice Somé (also a PhD) have written about the human importance of grief rituals and have spent a great deal of time teaching people in the United States how to create griev-

ing rituals. In personal communications years ago, they expressed the need for our tears as the canoes that enable the spirits of our dead to travel to appropriate realms. When our dead are not sufficiently grieved, they explained, they are trapped here, in the realm of the living, inadvertently causing havoc. In a book distinguishing mourning from melancholia, *The New Black*, psychoanalyst Darian Leader writes, "The public display of grief allows each individual to access their own losses. . . . Public mourning is there in order to allow private mourning to express itself" (76). Furthermore, "This is a basic function of public mourning rituals. The public facilitates the private" (77). I have found this book particularly useful for understanding the idea of melancholia as a kind of psychological and social death:

> This is exactly the melancholic problem: the symbolic Other is not there to situate him, and so all he is left with is his own image unanchored and unchained, left at the mercy of not the symbolic but the very real Other. With no stable anchoring point, no fixity in the way he situates himself in relation to the other, how can any ideal point be established from which the person can see themselves as lovable? And so, perhaps, comes the certainty of being worthless, unwanted or condemned. And, perhaps, the very identification with the dead which we have seen to be at the heart of melancholia. (186)

Also extremely useful in understanding death and psychological experiences of loss for Indigenous and other non-Western traditions is the work of Latina Jungian psychologist Clarissa Pinkola Estés. On the relationship between melancholia and racialization, see Cheng; and Viego. Nicole M. Guidotti-Hernández's *Unspeakable Violence* is particularly useful for thinking about the repression of the violence of US-Mexico borderlands histories of racialization.

6. On the importance of acknowledging trauma, violence, and loss, as well as death, see the work of Judith Herman; Estés; and Leader.

7. On the uses by dominant elites of discourses of Indigeneity and mestizaje, including the image of "the Indian," see Earle.

8. Reclamation of culturally Indigenous cultural practices such as Days of the Dead celebrations are misread as nostalgic because ostensibly they express the wish for an impossible return to a decisively broken cultural wholeness; as falsely Indigenous because supposedly Hispanic mestiza/os are not allowed to recognize the Indigeneity of our living cultures nor to lay claim to our ancestry, unlike non-Hispanic US and Canadian mixed-bloods; as spiritually naive in that Indigenous religions are supposedly a throwback to a primitive era in the history of religions; and as intellectually inferior because we are to believe that the highly educated and most intelligent people have evolved into atheism.

9. The language of "deracination" is highly problematic, given that "race" is a pseudoscientific concept created by imperialist science and rationalized by imperialist and Eurocentric philosophy, social sciences, and humanities to justify Eurocentric colonial invasion, occupation, cultural oppression, and Native American and African enslaved extreme exploitation and consequent death. See Dussel; Maldonado-Torres, who partly focuses on Dussel's work; and Mignolo for further elaboration of the construction of Eurocentric knowledges and decolonizing critique of same.

10. For statistics on the global economics of extreme wealth and poverty of these times, see Korten.

11. There is a large body of work in psychology on the healing role of the arts in their various forms. To quote again from Leader's *The New Black*:

> The arts exist to allow us to access grief, and they do this by showing publicly how creation can emerge from the turbulence of a human life. . . . (87)
>
> We are encouraged so often to "get over" a loss, yet bereaved people and those who have experienced tragic losses know full well that it is less a question of getting over a loss and on with life, than finding a way to make that loss a part of one's life. Life with loss is what matters, and writers and artists show us the many different ways in which this can be done. (99)

Note also that Estés's phenomenally successful *Women Who Run with the Wolves* is structured as storytelling. Indeed, this Jungian psychologist, whose practice includes trauma, privileges the retelling of ancient and cross-cultural wisdom tales as medicinal in the rethinking of them for the conditions of our times.

12. Telephone interview with Reyes Rodriguez, 12 July 2013. This tendency was also reported in Tere Romo's account of Days of the Dead at the Galería de la Raza in San Francisco and by Sybil Venegas with respect to Self Help Graphics, located in Los Angeles and responsible for both art and cultural centers ceasing to organize Days of the Dead processions. See their essays in the exhibition catalog edited by curator Tere Romo. For Disney/Pixar's community-thwarted attempt to trademark the phrase "Día de los Muertos" see "Pixar's 'Day' Is Dead."

> It doesn't come as a surprise that both Mexicans and even other peoples of different cultures didn't take the action so nicely citing that Dia de los Muertos was a part of one's culture, not something that should be a money-maker. Long story short, Disney eventually took back their application [for US trademark of "Día de los Muertos"].

The article explains that Disney/Pixar foresaw using the phrase in the title of one of their films then in production (released as *Coco* in November 2017, without the words in its title). See also Ellison. Learning from this fiasco, the *Coco* team at Pixar assembled a team of Chicana/o writers, museum directors, and scholars, which included myself, to advise throughout development. Leadership of Pixar's creative team also included Chicana/os, including the film's writer, Adrian Molina, who was promoted to codirector in 2016.

13. The late anthropologist Guillermo Bonfil Batalla wrote incisively about this point, arguing that twenty-five centuries of Indigenous cultural knowledge did not disappear over the past five hundred years. He further argues that even popular, rural, non-Indigenous culture is saturated with the core beliefs and practices of a pan-Mesoamerican culture that developed over millennia and that unifies countless Indigenous peoples who are otherwise different in distinct, locally specific ways.

14. On the development of Days of the Dead in California, see Romo; and Venegas. See also Marchi; and Medina. For Days of the Dead museum exhibits, see Davalos.

15. I owe the last point to Gamboa herself, who in conversation throughout the years has remarked on the function of the uncurated or uncommissioned paper fashions, sometimes worn by herself and sometimes by others.

16. It has become customary to limit Asco, the Los Angeles conceptual and performance art group, to the four founding members: Harry Gamboa Jr., Glugio "Gronk" Nicandro, Pattsi Valdez, and Willie Herrón. However, Asco artwork and performance involved collaboration with other artists, including regular collaboration with Gamboa's younger sibling, Diane Gamboa, as well as other artists, as pointed out to me on several occasions by Gamboa herself. Documenting Asco's history from this perspective of fluid "membership" or collaborations remains an ongoing task.

17. Telephone interview with Rodriguez, 12 July 2013. Diane Gamboa was very active in the early years of the gallery's history, curating an *Ofrendas* altar installation exhibition, creating puppets for the first Calavera Fashion Show in 2003, and showing her own work in her *Bruhaha* exhibition.

18. The four-minute clip by Reyes Rodriguez was available at Tropico de Nopal's website, from which I downloaded it and the 2008 Calavera Fashion Show video, which includes footage from the end of the 2006 Calavera Fashion Show (57:23). Tropico uploaded "Tropico de Nopal's Calavera Fashion Show © 2006" (8:57), featuring fifteen Walking Altars, on *YouTube*, 21 Sept. 2012. The gallery has uploaded some Calavera Fashion Show videos on *Vimeo*, and *YouTube* has shorts of particular pieces uploaded by audience members and artists from the 2009 shows. Tropico also had a *Facebook* page with images and announcements.

19. See Romo; Benítez; and Venegas.

20. Romo also emphasizes the influence of pre-Columbian art and of Posada's satiric broadside calavera (skull) imagery circulated by Manuel Hernández among fellow artists who would go on to cofound the Galería de la Raza (e.g., René Yáñez, Ralph Maradiaga, Rolando Castellón, Francisco Camplis, Rupert García, and Peter Rodriguez).

21. For a fine feminist analysis of the unruly, gender-bending, and defiant aesthetic of pachucha/o youth, see Ramírez.

22. Disney/Pixar's bid was shut down successfully by the Chicana/o-Latina/o community's protest. See note 12.

23. The "Artist Dedication" appearing on the program of the 2008 Calavera Fashion Show reads: "To my mother, Juanita T. Flores, a pachuca from East Los Angeles who married and had her first child at the age of 15. At 52, the pachuca became a teacher. This is a celebration of her courage and fierce determination."

24. Monet Soto is credited as the "model." The music was a recording by Cuarteto Don Ramon Sr. and Don Tosti's Pachucho Boogie Boys.

25. See artist, professor, and Santería priestess Marta Moreno Vega's *The Altar of My Soul*.

26. The Calavera Fashion Show has invited local radio personality Rick Nunhes and the political satire cartoonist, author, and founding, one-time member of Chicano Secret Service Lalo Alcaraz to serve as master of ceremonies. Fellow visual artist and DJ Jose Ruiz has coordinated the music. According to Rodriguez, about 95 percent of the music for particular Walking Altars was selected by the artists. Telephone interview with Rodriguez, 12 July 2013.

27. Telephone interview with Rodriguez, 12 July 2013.

28. Telephone interview with Rodriguez, 12 July 2013; telephone interview with Rigo Maldonado, 25 Aug. 2014; telephone interview with Yreina D. Cervántez, 29 Aug. 2014.

29. Poli Marichal, email to author, 24 Nov. 2014.

The walking altar of 2008 is the one I dedicated to my father, the Canary Islands artist, Carlos Marichal. My parents lived a great love that my mother, Flavia Lugo, has maintained alive through the years. I wanted to honor him with this walking altar. In it, my mother goes to visit my father's tomb and he appears to her. She is frightened, but then when she realizes it is him, she touches his face and then embraces him. Together in that embrace, the two lovers dance and then they create a heart with the halves that each of them has in their hands when they unite them.

30. Telephone interview with Maldonado, 25 Aug. 2014.
31. *Tropico de Nopal* website, archives, Calavera Fashion Show 2004.
32. I thank David Walker for a question about the relationship of the Evergreen Cemetery procession and US Days of the Dead parades to religious processions in Mexico, and Theresa Delgadillo for asking about the humor in Walking Altars, both of which helped to expand the essay.
33. I have made reference to other works that focus on the effects of loss, trauma, violence, and death. Here I will add the work of nonviolence scholar Rachel M. MacNair, who, drawing on extensive research, notes in *The Psychology of Peace*, "The third mechanism of moral disengagement, discounting the effects, is similar to the concept of distancing. To continue violence one can create mental distance from the reality of what is happening—isolation from the horror, a mental barrier" (3–4).

Works Cited

Benítez, Tomás. "Sister Karen Boccalero Remembered." *Chicanos en Mictlán: Día de los Muertos en California*, exhibition catalog, curated by Tere Romo, Mexican Museum (San Francisco), 2000, pp. 12–18.
Bonfil Batalla, Guillermo. *México Profundo: Reclaiming a Civilization*, 1987, translated by Philip A. Dennis, U of Texas P, 1996.
Cajete, Gregory. *Native Science: Natural Laws of Interdependence*. Clear Light, 2000.
Cheng, Anne. *The Melancholy of Race: Psychoanalysis, Assimilation and Hidden Grief.* Oxford UP, 2001.
Davalos, Karen Mary. *Exhibiting Mestizaje: Mexican (American) Museums in the Diaspora*. U of New Mexico P, 2001.
Dussel, Enrique. *Ética de la liberación en la edad de la globalización y de la exclusión*. Editorial Trotta, 2009.
———. "Europe, Modernity, and Eurocentrism." *Nepantla: Views from the South*, vol. 1, no. 3, 2000, pp. 465–478.
Earle, Rebecca. *The Return of the Native: Indians and Myth-Making in Spanish America, 1810–1930*. Duke UP, 2007.
Ellison, Chappell. "Digging into Disney's 'Day of the Dead' Problem." *Cartoon Brew*, 18 May 2013, www.cartoonbrew.com/disney/digging-into-disneys-day-of-the-dead-problem-82956.html.
Estés, Clarissa Pinkola. *Women Who Run with the Wolves: Myths and Stories of the Wild Woman Archetype*. Ballantine, 1992.

Garber, Marjorie. *Vested Interests: Cross-Dressing and Cultural Anxiety*. Routledge, 1997.

Guidotti-Hernández, Nicole M. *Unspeakable Violence: Remapping U.S. and Mexican National Imaginaries*. Duke UP, 2011.

Herman, Judith. *Trauma and Recovery: The Aftermath of Violence—From Domestic Abuse to Political Terror*, Basic Books, 1992.

Korten, David C. *Agenda for a New Economy: From Phantom Wealth to Real Wealth*. Berrett-Koehler, 2010.

Leader, Darian. *The New Black: Mourning, Melancholia, and Depression*. Graywolf, 2009.

MacNair, Rachel M. *The Psychology of Peace: An Introduction*. Praeger, 2003.

Maldonado-Torres, Nelsón. *Against War: Views from the Underside of Modernity*. Duke UP, 2008.

Marchi, Regina. *Day of the Dead in the USA: The Migration and Transformation of a Cultural Phenomenon*. Rutgers UP, 2009.

Medina, Lara. "Communing with the Dead: Spiritual and Cultural Healing in Chicano/a Communities." *Religion and Healing in America*, edited by Linda L. Barnes and Susan Starr Sered, Oxford UP, 2004, pp. 205–215.

Mignolo, Walter D. *The Darker Side of Western Modernity: Global Futures, Decolonial Options*. Duke UP, 2011.

Moreno Vega, Marta. *The Altar of My Soul: The Living Traditions of Santería*, Ballantine, 2000.

Pérez, Laura E. *Chicana Art: The Politics of Spiritual and Aesthetic Altarities*. Duke UP, 2007.

"Pixar's 'Day' Is Dead." *Disney Examiner*, 28 May 2013, disneyexaminer.com/2013/05/28/pixars-day-is-dead-dia-de-los-muertos-title-controversy.

Portillo, Lourdes, and Susana Muñoz, directors. *La Ofrenda: The Days of the Dead*, Xochitl Productions, VHS, 1988.

Ramírez, Catherine S. *The Woman in the Zoot Suit: Gender, Nationalism, and the Cultural Politics of Memory*. Duke UP, 2009.

Rodriguez, Reyes / Tropico Productions. "Calavera Fashion Show 2005." Downloaded from Tropico de Nopal Gallery–Art Space, 3 July 2013.

———. "Calavera Fashio[n] Show & Walking Altars 2008." Downloaded from Tropico de Nopal Gallery–Art Space, 3 July 2013.

———. "2006 Calavera Fashion Show. Tropico de Nopal Gallery Art-Space." *YouTube*, 21 Sept. 2012, www.youtube.com/watch?v=xbmqBzXoAaA.

Romo, Tere. "Curatorial Perspective." *Chicanos en Mictlán: Día de los Muertos en California*, exhibition catalog, Mexican Museum (San Francisco), 2000, pp. 6–8.

———. "A Spirituality of Resistance: Día de los Muertos and the Galería de la Raza." In *Chicanos en Mictlán: Día de los Muertos en California*, exhibition catalog, curated by Tere Romo, Mexican Museum (San Francisco), 2000, pp. 30–41.

Somé, Malidoma Patrice. *Ritual, Power, Healing and Community*. Penguin, 1997.

Venegas, Sybil. "The Day of the Dead in Aztlán: Chicano Variations on the Theme of Life, Death, and Self-Preservation." In *Chicanos en Mictlán: Día de los Muertos en California*, exhibition catalog, curated by Tere Romo, Mexican Museum (San Francisco), 2000, pp. 42–54.

Viego, Antonio. *Dead Subjects: Toward a Politics of Latino Loss*. Duke UP, 2007.

CHAPTER 10

"Fierce and Fearless": Dress and Identity in Rigoberto González's *The Mariposa Club*

SONIA ALEJANDRA RODRÍGUEZ

In 2002, Gwen Araujo was brutally murdered in Newark, California, by three male friends, two of whom she had been sexually intimate with, after they discovered that she was transgender. Although her family supported her, public spaces, including her school, were unsafe for Araujo. The seventeen-year-old transgender Latina also had previous encounters with bullying and harassment for wearing makeup and women's clothing to school.[1] In "Learning from the Death of Gwen Araujo?," Linda Heidenreich examines the intersectionalities of race, sex, and gender in relationship to Araujo's murder and the trial of the three perpetrators. She claims that "much of the violence that transgender and transsexual women of color experience is due to hetero-patriarchal violence asserted by white and Chicano men seeking to protect their masculine privilege" (57). She further argues that violence against transgender people is rationalized and rendered invisible in certain aspects of society, the media, and the law. In other words, violence is used to preserve the supremacy of hetero-patriarchal masculinity and becomes a medium through which to control gender and sexuality; furthermore, this becomes codified when, for example, these violent acts are not recognized as hate crimes by legal and/ or public institutions.[2]

The tragic murder of Gwen Araujo and other transgender and transsexual Latinas[3] prompted my investigation of dress (clothing, makeup, accessories) and its relationship to the identity construction of young queer Latinxs. I explain the power—which I later elaborate on and refer to as presence—of dresses and makeup on bodies read by society as cis-male to demonstrate how dress serves to articulate the construction of particular identities. Through an examination of Rigoberto González's *The Mariposa Club*, I argue that certain types of dress—as employed, for example, by the character Trinidad Ramos, a queer Latina teen who often dresses in drag[4]—serve to disrupt hetero-patriarchal structures and can also function as a way through which the novel's characters create and assert their queer identity.

The Mariposa Club tells the story of "the Fierce Foursome"—Maui, Isaac, Lib, and Trini—and their attempt to create the first GLBT club at Caliente High School in Southern California. Through Mauricio "Maui" Gutierrez, the reader gets insight into the lives of each member of the group and the various forms of homophobia and discrimination they face at school, the local mall, and their homes. As high school graduation approaches, the Fierce Foursome share a strong desire to be remembered. Their fear of being forgotten or erased from Caliente High history motivates them to organize the GLBT club; however, the task proves to be more difficult than anticipated when they encounter little support from the high school principal and a great deal of discrimination from their peers and other community members. The Mariposa Club becomes a catalyst through which the Fierce Foursome begin to examine not only their individual histories but also their very near futures as adults. González has created a unique character in Trinidad Ramos, who speaks to the complex coming out / coming-of-age experiences of young queer transgender Latinxs. *The Mariposa Club* is one of the few texts aimed at Latinx young adult audiences that breaks the silence around issues of queerness in Latinx homes and communities.[5] Trini is described as wearing loud, walking louder, and talking loudest (56). Her character straddles a thin line between visibility and invisibility. Because of her use of makeup and women's clothes, she is the character that poses the most threat to the hetero-patriarchal masculinity in her high school and predominantly Mexican community.[6] Ultimately, her dress makes her visible; that is, her community and peers have to look at her and have to recognize her existence because she challenges white hetero-normativity. However, this visibility also poses a potential danger to her life as those around her attempt to make her invisible through the use of violence in order to preserve the dominant structure. I examine the complexity that Trini's dress presents and further discuss how she constructs and claims a Latina queer identity.

Dress and Ornamentation: Using Style for Identity Construction

In *Accessorizing the Body*, Cristina Giorcelli and Paula Rabinowitz define dress "not only as clothing but also as mental and behavioral attitudes and rhetorical and linguistic modes [and] can be used as a mask to deceive others as well as a way to protect one's inner freedom" (2). Dress is no doubt connected to attitudes and expression, mainly as it relates to identity, but even though dress "can be used as a mask," it can also be used to reveal what may hide behind the mask and demand public freedoms. Catherine S. Ramírez offers a similar understanding of dress through her articulation of "style politics." In *The Woman in the Zoot Suit* she notes that "'style' refers to a signifying practice, in this case, the display of the zoot subculture's codes via clothing, hair, and cosmetics. And . . . 'style politics' refers to an expression of difference via style" (56). Ramírez's theorization of style and style politics explains the cultural and gendered significance of dress, which can provide insight into why Trini's use of women's clothes and makeup challenges gender normativity in her high school and community. Ramírez suggests that clothing, hair, and makeup, for the most part, have very specific cultural and gender codes. Pants, for example, signal masculinity, while a dress points to femininity. Via style politics, clothing, hair, and makeup can be a way to assert difference and ultimately identity. For example, the Pachuco draped pants and the pompadour hair, which Ramírez examines in her book, indicate a very specific type of Mexican American masculinity and femininity that stood outside of dominant white society (68). When such difference became visible, Ramírez says, the Pachuco style stopped being merely about fashion and became politicized. Therefore, Mexican Americans wearing Pachuco dress were othered and criminalized for not conforming to the dominant power. The Pachuco style is just one example of how dress can signal difference and how the ways those differences are read can lead to unjust attitudes such as criminalization and unjust behaviors such as violence to assert dominance.

Recognizing the important rhetorical differences between *decoration* and *ornamentation* is useful for understanding how dress can challenge hetero-patriarchal structures of oppression and how it can then be understood as a means through which to express an identity. In his book *Keepin' It Hushed*, Vorris Nunley says,

> Decoration in a simplistic sense could be thought of as adornment that is self-referential or object referential in that it seems to function in, of, and for its own sake, disconnected from an ordering, framing, or epistemic function desutured from social hierarchy or social distinction. Ornament then can be considered more thoughtfully as scriptings, motifs, patterns, visual tropes, and other verbal commonplaces and visual images that order, frame, distinguish and enhance the meaning of an entity. (90)

In other words, decoration calls attention only to itself and does not disrupt or change normative or dominant structures of power, whereas ornamentation serves as a way to challenge such structures by also calling attention to that outside of what is being ornamented. In *Chicana Art*, Laura Pérez provides an example of the potential of ornamentation. She notes that the domestic or nanny dress used in *The Nanny*, an installation piece by Chicana artist Yolanda López, brings "into view the power differentials among women of different classes and ethnicities" (52). She explains that the dress brings up a particular image of a woman of Color, suggesting that the domestic dress is not only gendered but also raced. López's display of the nanny dress as art transforms the dress into ornamentation because it is no longer referring to itself but instead makes visible the class and ethnic differences among women by disrupting its original significance. While Pérez does not necessarily articulate López's work as ornamentation, it nonetheless serves that purpose.

Reading dress as ornamentation proves beneficial when grappling with Gwen Araujo's death and Trinidad Ramos's dress as a means of constructing a queer Latina identity. The makeup and women's clothing that Araujo wore to school were not mere decoration: they not only called attention to themselves but also disrupted the assumed hetero-normativity of their high school and community, whether she wanted them to or not. In other words, her dress rendered her visible and also reflected the homophobia and discrimination present in the school, which became explicit through the students' reactions of bullying and harassment. Similarly, in *The Mariposa Club*, Trini helps demonstrate how reading her dress as ornamentation is a useful way to discuss the construction of her identity.

Ornamentation requires an examination of what is being ornamented and that which it stands in opposition to. For Cherríe L. Moraga,

> There is no critique of the "normal" without the queer. The beauty of the queer is that s/he requires society to question itself, its assumptions about desire, about masculinity and femininity, about power. Of course, the majority culture turns away en masse from the real depth of such inquiries; but the inquiry exists, nagging nagging until it one day erupts into revolt. (188)

In this way, Trini's ornamentation calls out the "normal" by standing in contrast to it. Her dress forces society "to question itself." She is a "nagging" force that challenges hetero-patriarchal powers in her community.

Dress and Passing: Challenging Gender Codes

At the beginning of *The Mariposa Club*, Maui reveals that Trini was forced to transfer to a different school because she was brutally attacked for attending the Homecoming dance dressed in drag (22). He later explains that

> Trini, fierce and fearless, decided to run for Homecoming court, and no one caught that the gender-neutral name, Trinidad, was not a girl but that queer kid who walked around the school in eyeliner and dressed in girl's sweaters, until it was too late to do anything about it. (23)

Trini's gender-neutral name allows her to momentarily pass for a young woman because her classmates do not read her name as a threat to the gender norms their Homecoming court upholds. It is only once the school jocks, the quintessential representations of masculinity in the novel, see Trini in her Homecoming dress that she is no longer able to pass and is subjected to violent consequences at the hands of her peers. Passing practices are mentioned throughout the novel, which suggests that such practices can be strategies for resistance and survival in a hetero-normative society. In the introduction to *Passing*, Maria C. Sanchez and Linda Schlossberg explain passing as a contradictory notion because while it seeks to provide visibility to an individual, it can also keep "larger social hierarchies in place"; they note that "passing can be experienced as a source of radical pleasure or intense danger; it can function as a badge of shame or a source of pride" (3). Although Trini is not attempting to pass for a cis-woman, that is precisely why she poses a threat to gender normativity and is therefore subjected to violence. In other words, the strict gender binary upheld by Trini's peers leaves little room for her to exist, but plenty of space for her to be attacked. Maui, on the other hand, tries to pass for straight to avoid the harassment and bullying normalized in their high school. It is this form of passing in order to survive that often causes Maui to lash out at Trini for being so "fierce and fearless." For the majority of the novel, Maui is uncomfortable with Trini's inability to fit in to the prescribed gender binary because it threatens his own survival and forces him to question his own queer identity.

Trini's eyeliner and girls' sweaters disrupt the hetero-normative paradigms of her high school, and those disruptions reveal the prevalent homophobia and transphobia. Her Homecoming dress serves as ornamentation that makes clear what is inside and outside of hetero-normativity.

Trini's ornamentation through drag highlights her high school's hetero-normative expectations, but in wearing the dress to Homecoming, she stands in opposition to these gender constructions. Trini's dress and style politics not only disrupt the structure of her high school but also signal their importance in her queer identity construction. However, this construction has consequences.

Maui recalls the harassment that Trini faced when she ran for Homecoming queen:

> It became a joke that all the other outsider and popularity rejects enabled as an affront to the jocks and school princesses. Everything had been engineered all the way up to the announcement of the king and queen, when Trini would walk up to the stage in an evening gown. But as soon as the jocks got wind of it, they cut her catwalk short by rushing her behind the stage and breaking her arm and two ribs. (23)

Trini is further marginalized by the high school's outcasts when she becomes the joke meant to challenge "the jocks and school princesses." The outsiders are those who "nag" or disrupt the hetero-patriarchal masculinity preserved by the jocks and princesses; however, it is important to point out that even within this community of "rejects" Trini represents excess and is therefore more vulnerable to bullying by those within hetero-normative society and those rejected by it. Because Trini seems to stand outside of both groups, she seems the most threatening. Wearing an evening gown appears to be the ultimate threat to hetero-normativity because the jocks violently attack Trini when they discover she will be their Homecoming queen. Trini disrupts the dominant power structure by being elected queen, a position traditionally meant to represent hyper-femininity and usually held by the most popular cis-girl. The "school princess" is the one who sets the standard for feminine gender performativity, so allowing Trini to be Homecoming queen would suggest that she is an accepted representation of the school princess and that her challenge of gender is also acceptable. The jocks, however, make it clear that this is not the case. Maui does not indicate that the jocks faced any consequences for their violent attack; instead, Trini is forced to leave the school, and the gender structure resumes its status quo.

Throughout the novel, Trini's dress is a site of tension, and the situation becomes far more complicated when she also encounters cultural resistance from some people in her community. When the Fierce Foursome are asked by Mr. Gutierrez to wear traditional male folklórico outfits and serve food at a Latino Caucus banquet, Trini chooses to wear one of the Jalisco female dresses and is confronted by one of the banquet's male guests.

> The grey-haired gentleman dressed in a conservative three-piece suit is pissed that Trini's in drag and Lib's wearing makeup. Trini, wearing a pair of thick braids with orange ribbons, is pissed that the shoulders on her colorful Jalisco dress are a bit too wide for her frame and she looks like she's wearing shoulder pads. (102)

Even though Las Cazuelas, the restaurant that Mr. Gutierrez manages, "is a stereotype of a restaurant—garish red and green colors, piñatas and wagon wheels, mariachi music, and lovely señoritas in white skirts and embroidered blouses" (95), Trini's dress stands out and creates anxiety for the Latino Caucus. Her dress is ironically excessive in a space that depends on excessive Mexican decorations to establish its authenticity. The juxtaposition of Trini's Jalisco dress with the gentleman's three-piece suit also points to the power dynamics at play. In "Men's Clothing and the Construction of Masculine Identities," Diana Crane explains that the business suit has been a staple "uniform" for indicating social class and a sign of success and power (173). The confrontation between the man in the suit and Trini and Lib (who is wearing Goth makeup)[7] suggests that class is also a factor in asserting hetero-normative Latino masculinity. And because the man is paying for the banquet, and Trini is just a server, he feels entitled to remove her. Mr. Gutierrez, who does not seem to understand Trini's identity but nonetheless respects her choices and the friendship she has with his son, would not have asked Trini to leave if the man had not insisted. His class privilege, represented by the three-piece business suit, establishes his dominance over Trini and Mr. Gutierrez. And while he does not resort to physical violence to preserve gender codes and structures of power, his actions are another example of the microaggressions that Trini and the rest of the Fierce Foursome have to confront.[8]

Dress and Presence: "Making Face" to Affirm Identity

A conversation about Trini's dress must also include a discussion about the effect that her style politics creates, which cannot be solely understood through cultural meanings. In *Production of Presence: What Meaning Cannot Convey*, Hans Gumbrecht defines *presence* as "the point of convergence between different contemporary reflections that try to go beyond a metaphysical epistemology and an exclusively meaning-based relationship to the world" (77). In other words, presence moves beyond an understanding of the world that depends mainly on meanings and abstract ways of knowing. In this sense, presence is the recognition of what cannot be captured by meaning. Gumbrecht says there is a tension between presence and meaning, but one cannot be without the other (77). Trini's ornamentation, then, creates a presence that commands attention. An evening gown on Trini disrupts the hetero-normative meaning of the dress. Thus, the dress alone, which serves as decoration, and the dress on Trini have different presences. The dress as decoration has a presence that is commodified, meaning that it elicits an acceptable reaction. The dress as ornamentation has a more productive presence because it challenges common meanings of the dress.

A productive presence can create discomfort, anger, and confusion — among other affective forms — that make clear the various structures of oppression in a given space. Trini's presence produces such great discomfort for the jocks and the gentleman that they must exercise violence in order to restore the normalcy of their respective spaces. It is important to reiterate that the violence inflicted on Trini goes unpunished; instead, Trini must adapt to the attacks by transferring to a different school and leaving the restaurant. Violence in the novel seems to be symptomatic of the transphobic gender constructions and the ideologies practiced at Caliente High School and within the community; more broadly though, the violence in the novel is representative of a longer history of state violence against transgender people of Color. In "Unmasking the State: Racial/Gender Terror and Hate Crimes," Andrea Smith provides a rhetorical analysis of hate crimes as recognized by the law and asks, "How do we address racial and gender terror if we simultaneously recognize that the state also hates us and has no interest in protecting us from hate?" (56). And while Smith does not speak of hate crimes against trans people directly, her question is more than applicable here, considering that there has only been one case in the nation that has been recognized as a hate crime against a transgender person: in 2009 Angie Zapata's murderer was charged with committing a bias-motivated crime.[9] In this way, it is easier to understand how the violence that Trini's presence elicits and which she endures demonstrates how institutions such as public schools can perpetuate hate against difference.

Trini's dress further demonstrates that ornamentation and presence have a connection to the construction of identity. Giorcelli and Rabinowitz explain that dress can function as a medium through which to express one's identity: "there are various reasons for making such alterations in one's dress: for necessity (to save one's life), as a joke (to make a fool of somebody), to overcome bans and barriers or the limitations of social class and gender" (1). The reasons most relevant in this case are those of necessity and for overcoming boundaries of class and gender. Trini makes clear that wearing women's clothes and using makeup are part of her queer identity and serve as a site of embodied knowledge production by her refusal to dress any other way. Maui confronts Trini several times throughout the novel about her exaggerated style because the consequences of her ornamentation also impact those around her. Maui reads Trini as performing outside of an acceptable form of queerness; however, through dress, Trini creates what Gloria Anzaldúa describes as conocimiento,[10] or "subversive knowledges"; for Anzaldúa, "these conocimientos challenge official and conventional ways of looking at the world, ways set up by those benefitting from such constructions" ("now let us shift" 542). She further describes how conocimiento "is reached via creative acts—writing, art-making, dancing, healing, teaching, meditation, and spiritual activism—both mental and somatic (the body too, is a form as well as a site of creativity)" (542). Anzaldúa's explication of the body as a site of knowledge production is crucial for reading Trini's body and use of ornamentation as a way of creating epistemologies that challenge hetero-normative ways of thinking. These subversive knowledges allow Trini to assert a queer identity through style and style politics.

Anzaldúa's concept of "making face" is key for assessing dress as ornamentation in light of queer identity formation for Latinx youth in *The Mariposa Club*. In her introduction to *Making Face, Making Soul*, she says "'making faces' is [her] metaphor for constructing one's identity" (xvi).

> Among Chicanas/Mexicanas, haciendo caras, "making faces," means to put on a face, express feelings by distorting the face—frowning, grimacing, looking sad, glum or disapproving. For me, *hacienda caras* has added the connotation of making *gestos subversivos*, political subversive gestures.... "Face" is the surface of the body that is most noticeably inscribed by social structures, marked with instructions on how to be a *mujer, macho*, working class, Chicana. (xv)

"Haciendo caras / making faces" suggests vulnerability because one's feelings are expressed on one's face, but it may also serve as a mask to hide one's true feelings. A theorization of the term includes gestos subversivos, which can disrupt or transform larger structures of oppression through the strategic use of one's face. In a similar vein, scholar LuMing Mao argues this in respect to Chinese Americans and Chinese American rhetoric:

> As border residents, we look different and we may choose to act differently, too — so that we can better claim allegiance to our face and to what our face represents (that is, to our ancestral home and culture). Our face becomes both a liability — we get "recognized" because of it — and an asset — we are a "model minority" in spite of it. (37)

For Anzaldúa and Mao, "face" becomes an indicator of difference and can also serve as a form of empowerment. Both explanations suggest that it is a method through which to create an identity or form an "allegiance . . . to what our face represents" (Mao 37). Both authors also signal the presence that faces can have because of the particular responses they produce. Anzaldúa's and Mao's theories about face are applicable for how bodies in general are visible and how such visibility can create a meaning and a presence through which identity is articulated. For example, Trini's face and body are read as that of a Latino man because of her body structure and facial features, which further suggests that there are specific gender codes that she must follow; however, she disrupts the socially constructed meaning when she ornaments herself with makeup, accessories, and women's clothing to assert her queer and transgender identity. Her use of ornamentation also shifts her presence in a given space because people do not know how to read her or what to make of the discomfort she produces in others. For Trini, "making face" is a subversive act because she is challenging white and Chicano hetero-normative expectations. Understanding "face" as both an asset and a liability helps further elaborate the construction of identity. The Fierce Foursome's desire to make faces at Caliente High by starting the school's GLBT club is an example of how the legibility of faces and bodies construct identities.

Throughout the novel, the Fierce Foursome reveal that they do not have many places where they feel safe to ask questions or discuss their queer identity. They also lack an adult mentor who could be a resource and ally, and their coming-out experiences and family support vary within the group. Maui explains, "Of all our families, it is Lib's religious parents who are the most accepting, it seems. They don't reject him like Trini's folks, they don't abuse him like Isaac's, and they don't pretend or avoid talking about it like my father" (42). Because of their family situations and the discrimination they deal with at school, their main source of support is each other. Maui believes there is safety in numbers, and that is why their friendship is so important to him (46). The group makes clear that a sense of invisibility and isolation surround the construction of a queer Latinx identity within Caliente High and their community. Because the Fierce Foursome's faces and bodies are read to be outside of Caliente High's acceptable gender codes, they are therefore othered and marginalized. Visibility is an important aspect of identity formation because it provides those feeling invisible with an opportunity to resist erasure, silencing, and other forms of oppression. In young adult literature, visibility is a common theme that expresses the conflict of wanting to belong but being unable to do so. Roberta Trites Seelinger suggests that school is the institution where adolescents learn to accept their role in society (32–33). The Fierce Foursome recognize that if they are invisible at Caliente High—they do not have a voice and access to power—they will probably remain invisible when they graduate and become part of the larger society. The invisibility that they feel is very much tied to their queer identities and demonstrates that queerness is an identity that is still devalued and contested. To combat these feelings, they decide to start the Mariposa Club, which will serve as a representation of their presence at Caliente High. Maui says,

[Q]ueers, well, we don't need much except visibility—a nice full-colored photograph for the yearbook that we can all look back a decade from now and say, *There we were, we existed. And we still do.* . . . High school might want to keep us invisible, but here we are, ticking away. (42)

Maui signals the important relationship between identity and political representation: starting the first GLBT club at Caliente High is a political and subversive act considering they receive very little support from their peers and teachers. It is a statement about who they are and what they stand for. They demand visibility and a space where they can learn about themselves. The Fierce Foursome tried looking for knowledge in other venues, but as Maui puts it, "We couldn't rely on film or television to tell us the truth. The media lied to us about everything: about what it was like to be gay and what it was like to be Latino" (40). He speaks to the significance of having a space where he and his friends can learn about themselves because the popular images of queer people, Latinxs, and queer Latinxs do not speak to the reality they have experienced. Maui is also pointing to the intersectionalities of race, gender, and sexuality by identifying as a queer Latinx.[11] The Fierce Foursome are "making faces" by giving their bodies visibility and creating their club. The Mariposa Club's goal, however, is complicated by Trini's own construction of a queer identity through her dress.

Trini and Tony: Dress as Survival and Dress as Resistance

There is a connection between "making face" and Giorcelli and Rabino-witz's definitions of dress that is helpful in understanding how Trini and other characters in the novel construct identity. Ornamentation can be seen as a politically subversive act. Trini deploys dress as a way to challenge the hetero-patriarchal structures in her community and high school; her dress is part of who she is. She is well aware of the consequences, but she continues to express the part of her identity that cannot be understood by reading her body as male. Throughout the novel, Trini reveals that she has been subjected to violence because of her identity:

> Trini stands in front of me in the nude, but covering her privates. A large burn, long since healed, lies splashed across her chest, the nipple has been left discolored and misshapen. Satisfied that I have seen the front, Trini turns around to show me her back side, where a cigarette burn has been nailed in at the middle of her spine. (31)

As a child, Trini was physically abused by her father and grandfather because of who she is; their violence was an attempt to preserve a hetero-patriarchal masculinity in their family. Trini says she has shown Maui her scars because she is grateful to finally be with people who do not want to hurt her (31). After being attacked at Homecoming, Trini is sent to live with her Aunt Carmen under the pretext it is for her own protection. But Trini is part of a larger structure of violence that does not permit her to fully embrace her queer and transgender identity. The novel shows that Trini's dress and presence elicit negative feelings from those she threatens the most. The straight cis-men around her have inflicted the most pain, showing how hate and gender terror are deeply engraved in hetero-patriarchal societies (Smith 56). As the four friends prepare for life after graduation, they learn that Trini's poor grades will keep her trapped at Caliente. While the others talk about moving to L.A. or going to college, Trini plans to work her way up in management at a nearby gay club. This is similar to what happened to Gwen Araujo; according to Heidenrich, she did not drop out of school but was pushed out by the vehement homophobia and transphobia she experienced (50). The same could be said for Trini; the violence she confronts at home and the violence she deals with at school ultimately impact her education and her future. The various forms of violence in Trini's life suggest that dress and presence alone cannot completely change larger structures of oppression, but they can serve as ways to begin creating change. Unfortunately, there is no indication in the narrative that there are other trans people at Trini's high school or in the community who are as visible. And while she benefits from the support of her small queer community, the different types of violence that each of the friends encounter cannot be conflated as being the same.

While Trini uses her dress and presence to express her identity despite the violence she experiences, Tony Sánchez, who has not come out, uses his dress to pass for straight as a means of survival. Tony is a member of Los Calis, Caliente's local gang, and wears "the tell-tale baggy pants and over-sized jacket of our Caliente Valley gang members" (125). Maui says, "Tony's trying very hard to pass himself off as a tough guy among Los Calis, and as a straight boy in front of me. It must be hard to pretend to be who he wants people to believe he is" (127). According to Maui, Tony uses gang dress as a way to hide his identity and perform a hetero-patriarchal masculinity to deceive those around him. Even though Tony does not say much through-out the novel, he does share some intimate moments with Maui, which Maui uses to provide his own reading of Tony. And while it is problematic to impose a queer identity on someone who does not yet identify as such, Maui's reading points to how dress and identity can fluctuate. As Giorcelli and Rabinowitz note, dress can also function as a mask to protect one's "inner freedoms" (2). Because the novel does not reveal much about Tony's life, his dress is the main signifier for how he constructs his identity. In contrast to Trini's choice of dress, Tony's Los Calis dress does not func-tion as ornamentation because it does not challenge existing structures of power. That is not to say that baggy pants and a hooded sweatshirt can never be ornamentation,[12] but in the space of Caliente Valley and Caliente High, where this dress is typical of a particular group, Tony's dress does not challenge prescribed gender codes in the same way that Trini's does. Instead, as a closeted gay man, his dress offers him a mask that allows him to remain invisible and, to a certain extent, safe from homophobic violence. However, this tension between his identity and dress escalates when Los Calis demand Tony put a stop to the Fierce Foursome's attempts to recruit members for the Mariposa Club. While marketing the club at the mall, the Fierce Foursome are accosted by several shoppers, as well as members of Los Calis, who misunderstand the group's efforts and react in a homophobic manner. This moment is significant because Tony is forced to choose between a group that represents his true identity and a group that has offered him protection. The relationship between dress and iden-tity is made clearer to Tony when he is expected to behave a certain way be-cause he wears the Los Calis "uniform." As a result of the conflict he feels in the chaos at the mall, Tony pulls out a gun and, instead of inflicting more violence on the Fierce Foursome, he takes his own life.

Tony's suicide shows how the various structures of violence and oppression make it difficult for youth of Color to come out. His use of dress as a means of survival can be understood as a way of making face. Tony "distorted" his identity to stay alive (Anzaldúa xv). Toward the end of the novel, Maui describes Tony's multiple ways of "making face." He says, "Tony Sanchez will live in my memory having three faces: the hateful one he wore to survive among Los Calis, the sad one looking at me from the corner of the library, and the defeated one I saw when I lifted the white sheet at the mall" (212). In this way, Maui reveals the complexity of Tony's identity. The juxtaposition of Tony and the Fierce Foursome indicates a tension between dress and identity. Maui later notes that Tony's suicide was "reduced to a headline, another cautionary tale of youth gone astray" because of his alliance to the Los Calis gang (211). Popular media erased Tony's sexuality and identity by focusing on his dress as a "gang member" and his legibility as a Brown man. Heidenreich says of Gwen Araujo's murder, "[D]eath sent a message to all of us who are queer, but especially to those of us who are queer and Latina, queer and raced, queer and mixed race—we are not safe—even when loved and embraced by our families" (52). Tony's suicide and Trini's abuse are a reminder of those lived experiences. Queer Chicana playwright and performer Adelina Anthony added to the conversation by writing an open letter in response to media coverage of the multiple queer teen suicides within the last few years. She writes, "It's dangerous to come out. And, if some of our youth continue to stay in the closet because of the very real and historically grounded fears of taunting and persecution, I am just as proud of them for surviving as best as they can" (41). Both Heidenreich and Anthony explain how the inherent violence in mainstream society against queer youth of Color, in particular, can make death a consequence of affirming their identity. In other words, given the violence against Trini and the Fierce Foursome, it is not coincidental that Tony committed suicide. The Caliente Valley community and high school demonstrate there are no safe spaces for queer youth of Color. As Smith points out, hate can be perpetuated through the same institutions that seek to challenge it. Schools are one of the institutions that teach young people their expected roles in society and reaffirm existing ideologies. It is arguable that Tony learned to hate himself enough to commit suicide because of the displacement he experienced and witnessed. His suicide demonstrates there is still a great need for spaces that empower queer youth, and highlights the significance of Trini's resistance through dress and presence to the dominant structures that seek to erase her.

Fierce and Fearless: Creating a Political Identity

The Fierce Foursome's efforts to create a GLBT club at their high school articulate how dress and presence can be a catalyst for social change. *The Mariposa Club* details the dangers and complexities of coming out as seen through the violence against Trini, Tony's suicide, and the discrimination experienced by the Fierce Foursome. Although families and other adults can be a supportive space, as they are for Lib and Maui, homophobia is very much present in their communities, so they are always in danger. The novel also shows the importance of a collective political identity, one that can demand change. The Mariposa Club represents that identity and power for the Fierce Foursome. When Trini and Maui petition the principal for the club, Maui declares,

> We feel it's time our beloved high school address the reality of the times, that gays and lesbians are everywhere, including in our halls, and that we need to have an organization in place for future generations of queer teens to meet, socialize, feel safe, and advocate for their right to be who they are without fear or resistance. (51)

Maui points out the need for a safe space for gay and lesbian students at Caliente High to let other GLBT students know they have a place to turn. A strong enough presence of GLBT students can indeed counter the heteropatriarchal ideologies that dominate many schools. As Maui makes clear, at Caliente fear has a stronger presence, so students and teachers alike do not feel comfortable coming out. Although I am not suggesting that the club would have saved Tony's life, changing the discourse of homophobia at their school could have potentially had an impact on him and other students. Gwen Araujo's high school should have intervened when she was being bullied for her dress. When institutions of higher learning stand up and directly challenge the structures that oppress their students, those institutions are declaring that these students' lives matter. The impact that can have on a community can be significant.

It is not only important for the Fierce Foursome to establish a GLBT club on campus; they also make a political decision by including the Spanish word *mariposa* in the club's name, broadly invoking Latino culture and history.[13] Trini warns Maui,

> If you're going to be a fag of the twenty-first century, your frame of reference needs to expand to include all knowledge of fag culture from the

ancient twentieth century. Otherwise you're without history, context or queer lineage. Furthermore, you have twice the responsibility because you're a brown fag—a *queena*—so your sissy savvy needs to encompass the entirety of the Americas. (118)

Trini's words are powerful as they convey an understanding of a "history, context or queer lineage" that crosses the Americas and calls for a transnational grounding in queer Latinx identity and community. Trini also speaks to the intersectionalities of race, gender, and sexuality by pointing to the difficulties of being queer and Latinx. Her articulation of the responsibilities of being a "Brown fag" also suggests that they will continue to be oppressed by the dominant society and their Latinx culture. While the establishment of the Mariposa Club at Caliente High would have created a productive presence, it is ultimately Trini's dress and own presence that frighten the principal, who reads Trini as excessive and therefore too much for the school to handle. He argues that forming the club might bring them more harm than good, and it might be better for everyone not to. Nevertheless, the novel ends with the group informally establishing their club. They dedicate their first meeting to their honorary member, Tony.

Gathering at Trini's home empowers the friends to remain "fierce and fearless" despite the discrimination they each face (222). But it is important to note that the novel does not end with a resolution of the Fierce Foursome's problems; instead, it leaves hope that change is possible. Trini's abuse and Tony's death complicate the notion that queer youth merely need to navigate adolescence to find acceptance as adults. However, the discrimination and fatal violence that transgender and transsexual people of Color continue to experience are proof that transphobia is not a high school phase, but state-sanctioned violence that transcends age.

González's novel presents the realities of constructing a queer Latinx identity through Trini's character. She is one of the few, if not the only, transgender characters in Latinx children's and young adult literature, and her character continues to be pivotal since many stories like hers remain marginalized, silenced, or unacknowledged.[14] Her presence transcends the page in a profound manner that has a lasting impact on readers and, more broadly, adds to the archive of queer Latinx youth cultural productions. Trini is unapologetic and fierce; she wears it loud and is proud. At the end of the novel, it is Trini who seems to be the most confident about her identity. Her dress, ornamentation, and presence allow her to construct an identity that challenges her hetero-normative community while also creating a political identity that can speak to future generations of GLBT youth of color.

Notes

The author wishes to thank the following people: Traise Yamamoto, Phillip Serrato, and Erica Edwards, for believing in this project since its inception; the author's cohort at the 2017–2018 Faculty Fellowship Publication Program at City University of New York, for providing feedback for revision; and Vorris Nunley and Richard T. Rodríguez, for reading first drafts of this project.

1. For more analysis on Araujo's life, see Franklin and Lyons, "'I Have a Family.'"
2. In the case of Araujo, Heidenreich explains that the high school was notified that she was being harassed and bullied. Her mother even requested special bathroom accommodations, but the school did not comply. I would argue that the school administrators' investment in preserving a hetero-patriarchal structure prevented them from recognizing her bullying as a hate crime, and therefore they did not take the appropriate measures to protect her.
3. See the Human Rights Campaign website for records of how many transgender people in the United States are murdered each year.
4. Throughout the novel, Trini dresses in drag and is referred to as "she," but she is not identified as transgender by the narrator or the characters.
5. A few other books for children and young adults that center on the experiences of Latinx queer youth and/or the experiences of having a queer family member are Velasquez's *Tommy Stands Alone*; González's illustrated children's book, *Antonio's Card / La tarjeta de Antonio*; McLemore's *When the Moon Was Ours*; and Saenz's *Aristotle and Dante*. For more on Latinx gay young adult literature see www.gayya.org /2016/06/latinx-gay-ya/.
6. The terminology to capture LGBTQ experiences in *The Mariposa Club* stems from the time period when the novel was written and subsequently published. The violence and oppression Trini experiences are due to the gender binary of her world. Being gender queer, gender nonconforming, or gender nonbinary are not discussions in this novel. In a 2013 interview with *Lambda Literary*, González identifies Trini as a trans character. For the full interview, see Lumpkin.
7. In this case, the Goth makeup and clothes are ornamentation because they are disrupting the "normalcy" of the Latino banquet. In *Goth*, Lauren Goodlad and Michael Bibby demonstrate how the Goth subculture challenges hetero-normativity through dress, makeup, and gestures.
8. Tara Joy Yosso defines microaggressions as

> subtle, stunning verbal and non-verbal put-downs of People of Color, often done automatically or unconsciously. Microaggressions are layered insults, based on notions of race, gender, class, sexuality, culture, language, immigration status, phenotype, accent, and surname. Microaggressions are cumulative and cause undue stress to People of Color privileging Whites. (44)

However, people of Color can also inflict microaggressions on other people of Color, thus privileging dominant ideology.

9. Eighteen-year-old Angie Zapata was brutally murdered in rural Colorado in 2008 after her boyfriend learned she was transgender. See Cram, "'Angie was Our Sister.'"

10. For more on conocimiento and Latinx children's and young adult literature, see Rodríguez.

11. Patricia Hill Collins defines intersectionality as "an analysis claiming that systems of race, economic class, gender, sexuality, ethnicity, nation, and age form mutually constructing features of social organization" (278).

12. In the case of Trayvon Martin, the wearing of a hooded sweatshirt can be analyzed as ornamentation and presence. After his murder in 2012 and during the trial, the hooded sweatshirt was used in popular culture as a way to point out the inherent racism of George Zimmerman's actions and, more broadly, in US society. During the trial, the hoodie was racialized, gendered, and classed.

13. For more on use of the word *mariposa*, see Enrique Pérez.

14. There is a large volume concerning queer children's and young adult literature (Abate and Kidd), but very little that focuses on the experiences of Latinx youth.

Works Cited

Abate, Michelle Ann, and Kenneth Kidd, editors. *Over the Rainbow: Queer Children's and Young Adult Literature.* U of Michigan P, 2011.

Anthony, Adelina. "Activist Notebook: An Open Letter on Media Coverage of Teen Suicides." *Chicana/Latina Studies: The Journal of Mujeres Activas en Letras y Cambio Social,* vol. 10, no. 1, 2011, pp. 40–42.

Anzaldúa, Gloria. Introduction. *Making Face, Making Soul / Haciendo Caras: Creative and Critical Perspectives by Feminists of Color,* Aunt Lute Books, 1990.

———. "now let us shift . . . the path of conocimiento . . . inner work, public acts." *This Bridge We Call Home: Radical Visions for Transformation,* edited by Gloria E. Anzaldúa and Analouise Keating, Routledge, 2002, pp. 540–576.

Cram, Emily. "'Angie Was Our Sister'; Witnessing the Trans-Formation of Disgust in the Citizenry of Photography." *Quarterly Journal of Speech,* vol. 98, no. 4, 2012, pp. 411–438.

Crane, Diana. "Men's Clothing and the Construction of Masculine Identities: Class, Lifestyle, and Popular Culture." *Fashion and Its Social Agendas: Class, Gender, and Identity in Clothing,* U of Chicago P, 2000, pp. 171–201.

Franklin, Cynthia G., and Laura E. Lyons. "'I Have a Family': Relational Witnessing and the Evidentiary Power of Grief in the Gwen Araujo Case." *Journal of Gay and Lesbian Studies,* vol. 22, no. 3, 2016, pp. 437–466.

Giorcelli, Christina, and Paula Rabinowitz, editors. *Accessorizing the Body: Habits of Being I.* U of Minnesota P, 2011.

González, Rigoberto. *Antonio's Card / La tarjeta de Antonio.* Lee and Low, 2016.

———. *The Mariposa Club.* Alyson, 2009.

Goodlad, Lauren, and Michael Bibby. *Goth: Undead Subculture.* Duke UP, 2007.

Gumbrecht, Hans. *The Production of Presence: What Meaning Cannot Convey.* Stanford UP, 2004.

Heidenreich, Linda. "Learning from the Death of Gwen Araujo? — Transphobic Racial Subordination and Queer Latina Survival in the Twenty-First Century." *Chicana/Latina Studies: The Journal of Mujeres Activas en Letras y Cambio Social*, vol. 6, no. 1, 2006, pp. 50–86.

Hill, Patricia Collins. *Fighting Words: Black Women and the Search for Justice.* U of Minnesota P, 1998.

Lumpkin, Bernard. "Rigoberto González: Populating the Bookshelves." *Lambda Literary*, 4 May 2013, www.lambdaliterary.org/interviews/05/04/rigoberto-gonzalez-populating-the-bookshelves/. Accessed 23 Sept. 2018.

Mao, LuMing. *Reading Chinese Fortune Cookies: The Making of Chinese American Rhetoric.* Utah State UP, 2006.

McLemore, Anna-Marie. *When the Moon Was Ours.* A Thomas Dunne Book for St. Martin's Griffin, 2016.

Moraga, Cherríe L. *A Xicana Codex of Changing Consciousness: Writings, 2000–2010.* Duke UP, 2011.

Nunley, Vorris. *Keepin' It Hushed: The Barbershop and African American Hush Harbor Rhetoric.* Wayne State UP, 2011.

Pérez, Daniel Enrique. "Toward a Mariposa Consciousness: Reimagining Queer Chicano and Latino Identities." *Aztlán: A Journal of Chicano Studies*, vol. 39, no. 2, 2014, pp. 95–127.

Perez, Laura E. *Chicana Art: The Politics of Spiritual and Aesthetic Altarities.* Duke UP, 2007.

Ramírez, Catherine S. *The Woman in the Zoot Suit: Gender, Nationalism, and the Cultural Politics of Memory.* Duke UP, 2009.

Rodríguez, Sonia Alejandra. *Conocimineto Narratives: Challenging Oppressive Epistemologies through Healing in Latina/o Children's and Young Adult Literature.* University of California, Riverside, PhD diss., 2015.

Sáenz, Benjamin Alire. *Aristotle and Dante Discover the Secrets of the Universe.* Simon and Schuster Books for Young Readers, 2012.

Schlossberg, Linda, and Maria C. Sanchez, editors. *Passing: Identity and Interpretation in Sexuality, Race, and Religion.* New York UP, 2001.

Smith, Andrea. "Unmasking the State: Racial/Gender Terror and Hate Crimes." *Australian Feminist Law Journal*, vol. 26, 2007, pp. 47–57.

Trites Sellinger, Roberta. *Disturbing the Universe: Power and Repression in Adolescent Literature.* U of Iowa P, 2000.

Yosso, Tara Joy. *A Critical Race and LatCrit Approach to Media Literacy: Chicano Resistance to Visual Microaggressions.* U of California, Los Angeles, PhD diss., 2000.

Velasquez, Gloria. *Tommy Stands Alone.* Arte Público, 1995.

THE POLITICS OF ENTREPRENEURSHIP: MAKING (IT)/SELLING (IT)

CHAPTER 11

Lydia Mendoza, "Reina de la Música Tejana": Self-Stylizing Mexicanidad through China Poblana in the US-Mexico Borderlands

MARCI R. MCMAHON

I sew my own costumes for my performance work. I make the flowers, and then I make the dresses, my housedresses, everything. . . .

My sisters often tell me, "Ay, Lydia, you have so much spirit. Where do you get the energy to be fixing yourself up, doing your hair, makeup, dressing up, going to the radio station and television stations, and . . . well, not me." They say they couldn't bear to do it anymore. "Well, I can," I tell them.

LYDIA MENDOZA, QTD. IN BROYLES-GONZÁLEZ, *LYDIA*

In 1950, Tejana singer Lydia Mendoza was asked by the mayor of Chihuahua City, Mexico, to perform in two concerts for which he would pay her five thousand dollars. At that point in her career, she had already established her popularity among working-class mexicano audiences in the United States and Mexico. She was hailed by fans with the nicknames La Alondra de la Frontera (the Meadowlark of the Border) and La Cancionera de los Pobres (the Singer of the Poor), and later honored as Reina de la Música Tejana (Queen of Tejano Music), titles that would follow Mendoza throughout her long career—from the early 1930s to the late 1980s—as a singer and guitarist performing canciones rancheras and norteño. Mendoza's childhood and performance life indicate a cross-regional and crossnational existence: she was born in Houston, Texas, in 1916; lived in Monterrey, Mexico; and then moved to San Antonio, Texas, before she began traveling throughout the United States, Mexico, and Latin America as a performer.

Mendoza first began performing in the late 1920s and early 1930s with her family in San Antonio's Plaza del Zacate (Haymarket Plaza, now Milam Plaza), singing and playing the mandolin. She then began to sing canciones rancheras and play a twelve-string guitar with her family's musical group, which included her mother, brothers, and sisters. They performed in variedades (variety shows), carpas (tent shows), and teatros (Spanish-language theatre) throughout the Southwest, including New Mexico and California, entertaining primarily working-class mexicano audiences. She also performed with her family in the Midwest in the 1930s and in New York in the 1940s. While Mendoza was playing in the Mendoza Family Variety Show, from the 1930s to the 1950s, she simultaneously established her popularity and celebrity as a performer of the ranchera genre in her own right; during this time she recorded several solo records, many for major American labels, including RCA Victor.

Acknowledging Mendoza's popularity, the family frequently made her the headline act in their variety show. When she began to perform solo in the 1950s, including a performance at the Chihuahua City show, Mendoza's fame increased among audiences throughout Mexico and Latin America.[1] From the 1960s to the 1980s, Mendoza propelled herself into the US national spotlight as she toured folklife festivals and universities (Broyles-González, *Lydia* xi-xv; Strachwitz and Nicolopulos).

The Chihuahua City concert invitation in 1950 was the first time Mendoza was asked to perform solo, and the five thousand dollars she was paid was a considerable amount by the day's standards; it was also the largest sum of money Mendoza had ever been offered to perform her music (Strachwitz and Nicolopulos 274). With this in mind, both Mendoza and her promoter, Ramiro Cortés, agreed to do the two night concerts and headed to Chihuahua in Cortés's car (274). Cortés recalls that when they approached the city, they were met by what he first believed to be immigration officials standing alongside a makeshift tent on the side of the highway (275). When the residents discovered that the much-anticipated Lydia Mendoza was in the car, she and Cortés were greeted by the mayor of Chihuahua, the chief of police, and two other politicians, who told Cortés, "We have a parade going, we have a parade fixed for Lydia, and we want her to get dressed in that little tent—put on her costume, you know, for the parade" (275). As her promoter, Cortés explained to Mendoza what was expected:

> so I told Lydia what it was all about, and she got dressed in that little tent. She changed into one of her costumes and everything. Then they put her in an open car, a brand-new Oldsmobile convertible, which was followed by a truck, a big, beautiful truck, all with ribbons and flowers, a full mariachi band and a big arch that says, "Lydia Mendoza" riding on the flatbed. (qtd. in Strachwitz and Nicolopulos 275)

The costume Mendoza changed into was one of the many hand-sewn and sequin-embroidered versions of the china poblana dress that had already become an iconic feature of her public performance persona both on- and offstage. The china poblana outfit typically consists of an embroidered white blouse, sequined skirt, and petticoat, and a rebozo in the colors of the Mexican flag (green, white, and red).[2] This type of costume for female singers of canciones rancheras—a genre that emerged in post-revolutionary Mexico and is considered by many to be "an ideal expression of lo mexicano" (Nájera-Ramírez 186)—has functioned generally as a symbol of Mexican nationalist identity and culture. Female ranchera singers such as Mendoza who chose to don china poblana costumes in the mostly male-dominated music industry and performance spaces in both the United States and Mexico in the early and mid-twentieth century confronted and negotiated the multiple and contradictory racialized and gendered meanings of this iconic attire. This style of dress (the loose-fitting blouse, colorful rebozo, and sequined skirt) was first worn by Indigenous and mulatto women in the region of Puebla, Mexico. By the late eighteenth century and early nineteenth century, the term *china poblana* came to designate "a well-dressed mestiza woman" in Mexico (Randall 72).[3]

Due to its fusion of European and Indigenous elements, china poblana attire was appropriated in post-revolutionary Mexico as a nationalist symbol of modern Mexican identity. This identity was defined through mestizaje, which signifies the mixture of Spanish and Indigenous cultures in Mexican nationalist discourse, even though Mexican cultural identity encompasses multiple racial and cultural influences in the Americas, including African, Native American, European, and Asian (Pérez-Torres xi). The term *mestizaje* was used by nationalists to depict a "teleology of progress" (Pérez-Torres 14), thereby subsuming Indigenous identity and other racialized identities in the Mexican nation into the "more formulaically more progressive mestizo" (Saldaña-Portillo 407).[4] As a symbol of Mexican modernity from the 1920s to the 1940s, the china poblana style was adopted by Mexican intellectuals and elites, and became fashionable attire for celebrities and society ladies (Hershfield 106; Randall 133). While some popular figures, such as the Mexican actress Lupe Vélez, wore china poblana dresses as the latest fashion trend, thereby romanticizing Indigenous cultures, others, such as the painter Frida Kahlo, wore china poblana outfits to demonstrate solidarity with Indigenous women.[5]

By the time of Mendoza's Chihuahua City concerts in 1950, the china poblana costume was everywhere as an image of lo mexicano (or Mexican-ness) in Mexican and US films, advertisements, calendars, tourist bro-

11.1. Lydia Mendoza (*center*) is honored in Chihuahua City, Mexico, with a parade, June 27, 1950. MSS 00123-0021. Houston Public Library, Houston Metropolitan Research Center.

chures, and public cultural events. For the Chihuahua City officials and the public, the costume was such a signature piece of Mendoza's performance persona that they expected her to don this outfit for their parade, even setting up a tent for changing into this costume.

In a photo of the singer in the parade, Mendoza is propped up on the back seat of the Oldsmobile convertible between two smiling women not wearing the costume (fig. 11.1). She wears a white embroidered blouse with an image of herself in china poblana sewn on the front (a unique feature), her hair in ponytails with colorful ribbons, along with long earrings and necklaces. By sporting two ponytails, Mendoza self-stylized the costume. Even though there are variations in the hairdos of women who perform in china poblana outfits, the style constructed by nationalist imagery is two long braids tied with red, green, and white ribbons. But in the many photos of Mendoza throughout the 1940s and 1950s, she has two side ponytails (pigtails), a typical feature of her hairstyle during this period. The 1950s parade photo also shows Mendoza's sequined skirt, which she wore in all performance and publicity photos during this time. The outfit included a petticoat, which she fashioned to the fullest extent toward the end of her career.[6]

In this chapter, I argue that Mendoza's self-stylizations of the china poblana costume, including her exaggerated and unique fashioning of this well-established symbol of Mexican national identity both on- and off-stage, provided a spectacle by which to produce mexicanidad on both sides of the border. The concept of lo mexicano, what Laura Gutiérrez defines as "all things Mexican," connotes a fixed understanding of Mexican identity and culture, even as the concept cautions against equating Mexican-ness with the commercialization of Mexican culture or as an entertainment novelty (Gutiérrez 21; Vargas, *Dissonant Divas* 39). Mexicanidad, on the other hand, functions as a malleable concept, and when deployed by artists and performers, as Gutiérrez explains, it becomes a "performance/performative strateg[y] to challenge general and fixed understandings of 'lo mexicano'" (21). Significantly, even while deploying mexicanidad, artists do not "completely distance themselves from this dominant narrative of national and cultural belonging" (Gutiérrez 21). With this understanding of mexicanidad, I suggest that Mendoza's self-stylizations of the costumes were consumed as a pleasurable spectacle by transnational mexicano audiences that embraced the china poblana as a symbol of Mexican identity and culture, even as the iconic attire risked corresponding with the commercialization and exoticization of the outfit as a stereotypical symbol of Mexican culture and identity. As Deborah Vargas points out in regard to Rosita Fernández, a contemporary of Mendoza who also wore the china poblana costume as part of her performance persona, it is crucial to situate "how, where, by whom, and for whom 'lo mexicano' is produced and how it is engaged" (*Dissonant Divas* 39).

The ranchera musical genre and mexicano performance venues, including las carpas and los teatros, were critical spaces in which Mendoza began to perform china poblana as a symbol of mexicanidad. Her choice of the china poblana did not come from an outsider, such as a promoter directing her what to wear; rather, she donned and self-stylized the dress from a confluence of factors derived from her personal history and the transnational mexicano audiences for which she performed. Significantly, Mendoza's mother, Leonor, first began to hand-sew the costumes for the family's variety act in the early 1930s (Broyles-González, *Lydia* 50; Strachwitz and Nicolopulos 120). In addition to the china poblana outfits for her daughters, the mother sewed accompanying charro attire for her sons, an outfit characterized by tight, ornamented pants, boots, a broad hat, and an equestrian jacket (Broyles-González, *Lydia* 50).[7] Leonor sewed the costumes herself because the family could not initially afford to buy them, and they were unavailable in San Antonio. Mendoza recalled,

> We had no money; there were no means with which to go to Laredo and buy a *charro* outfit. Well, my mother used her imagination. She went and bought black pants and stitched them on the inside in order to taper them like a *charro* outfit. Then she sewed a zipper on the side seams. . . . She went and bought a few dozen very pretty buttons that looked just like silver, just like on those *charro* pants. . . . Same thing for my sister Juanita: she fixed up her Mexican dress. . . . After time passed and we began to make some money, we did go to Monterrey and she bought my brother his real *charro* outfit. (qtd. in Broyles-González, *Lydia* 50)

Mendoza's brother said that when their mother first began to sew these costumes, she envisioned "herself as wearing a typical Mexican costume, one of those fancy ones like the famous Mexican ranchera singers wear" (qtd. in Strachwitz and Nicolopulos 120). Fully aware that the china poblana and male charro figures were already staples of Mexican popular media, the mother made a savvy choice to create the costumes for their performances in las carpas and los teatros, entertainment spaces influenced by Mexican popular culture. Following her mother's example, Mendoza continued to hand-sew her china poblana costumes even after she became popular and had the money to buy them. By sewing her own costumes, Mendoza was able to self-stylize the outfits in a variety of ways, and the act of sewing her own dresses, in some respects, contributed to audiences' perception and embrace of Mendoza as a working-class figure. Furthermore, as evidenced by the epigraph to this chapter, Mendoza derived great pleasure from the artistic endeavor of sewing and designing.

Scholars who have analyzed Mendoza as a musical figure have paid scant attention to her costuming as integral to the cultural, emotional, and spiritual dimensions of her performances for transnational mexicano audiences. Yolanda Broyles-González's scholarship and published oral history of Mendoza have provided scholars with path-breaking work on this legendary figure. She analyzes the roles of Mendoza's music, voice, and aurality in the "formation and sustenance of mexicana/o working-class identity," which she suggests provided a "shared affirmation of a common experience" for Latina/o audiences (*Lydia* xiii). She also centers a crucial gendered history of Mendoza's life and performance career, spotlighting how the women of the Mendoza clan were the backbone of the family, arguing that Mendoza's oral history provides an important "womanist and woman-centered document" (xi). Broyles-González's oral history with Mendoza and Chris Strachwitz and James Nicolopulos's biography of the iconic singer and her family provide rich, detailed histories of Mendoza's musical and performance career, her encounters with racial discrimination as she and her family sought to play in segregated performance spaces in the US Southwest, and her profound influence on working-class mexicano audiences who were racialized and deemed "foreigners" within the literal and figurative boundaries of the United States. For Broyles-González, Mendoza's costuming, along with her music, was central to her claiming space and belonging for mexicanos in the United States. She explains, "Her flamboyant performance attire as well as song style and repertoire loudly proclaimed a *mexicana* politics of place and of belonging for native people officially deemed as not belonging to the United States — and targeted for deportation and 'repatriation'" (*Lydia* 188).

This chapter explores Mendozas's self-stylizations of the china poblana outfit as a central component of what Nájera-Ramírez refers to as the "dynamics of performance," which for Mendoza included a variety of elements, including her singing style, costuming, gestures, and other theatrical devices (199). With her music and china poblana costuming, Mendoza presented an overall integrated performance that moved audiences on both sides of the border; her artistry and constructed costuming created a form of unity despite differences in history, language, citizenship, and temporal circumstances. Through her fashioning of the china poblana costume in ways that made it integrated and central to her sonic performances, Mendoza as a performer bridged two nations and two peoples that have deep historical and cultural connections; such transcultural connections became embodied and expressed in Mendoza's attire as part of her performance of mexicanidad throughout her career.

Performing China Poblana in Canciones Rancheras in las Carpas and los Teatros

Ranchera music, as a transnational genre, connects two interconnected geographies and nations of a migratory people with deep historical roots. The canción ranchera first developed and emerged in post-revolutionary Mexico as the nation experienced an increase in urban migration. Within the space of Mexico itself, the genre therefore first expressed a longing for lo mexicano, conceived as a romanticized way of life on the hacienda before the emergence of modernization and industrialization (Peña 11). As

Nájera-Ramírez explains, "[E]voking a rural sensibility, the ranchera expressed nostalgia for a provincial lifestyle and projected a romanticized idyllic vision of the past" (185). In Mexico, the ranchera became widely popular through comedias rancheras (western musical comedies, both filmed and on the radio). They rose to popularity in the 1930s using aspects of comedy, tragedy, popular music, and folklore, and incorporated nationalistic themes and songs typical of the ranchera genre (Hershfield 106; Nájera-Ramírez 186). Joy Elizabeth Hayes explains how the comedias rancheras throughout the 1920s and 1930s "engaged listeners in a unifying national discourse" (245–246). For mexicano migrants in the US Southwest (a population that grew from the 1920s to the 1940s due to the aftermath of the Mexican Revolution, agricultural labor demands, and the implementation of the bracero program, among other structural factors) the ranchera helped listeners "remember what displaced peoples are supposed to forget," particularly "the heart-felt longing for a return to the beloved homeland — the return that immigrant populations often yearn for and rarely achieve" (Broyles-González, "Ranchera Music(s)" 357).[8]

The transnational circulation of lo mexicano through ranchera music and the comedias rancheras, and the centrality of this genre as a form of entertainment in las carpas and los teatros in the US Southwest, inspired the Mendoza family to don china poblana and charro costumes in the late 1930s. When Mendoza first began performing at a very young age with her family in Plaza del Zacate in San Antonio and other spaces (mostly cantinas and restaurants) throughout Texas and the Midwest during the late 1920s and early 1930s, the family did not wear costumes. As Mendoza explains, "We have never worn costumes when we were singing down there in the Plaza del Zacate. We would just be there singing in whatever clothes we had. But when we started to put on a real show, to do salons, halls and theaters and all that, we realized that we needed costumes" (qtd. in Strachwitz and Nicolopulos 119). Mendoza and her family also did not wear costumes when they performed as El Cuarteto Carta Blanca in community halls throughout the Rio Grande Valley and elsewhere in Texas during this period. Nor did they wear costumes when they traveled north to Michigan, where they followed the migrant farm work circuit with the intention to perform and earn money entertaining. They traveled to Michigan with contracts to work in the beet fields, but after a week they got a job performing in the only Mexican restaurant in the area (Broyles-González, *Lydia* 6–7).

The china poblana attire became central to Mendoza's performance in the Mendoza Family Variety Show in carpas from approximately 1933 to

1935, and in Spanish-language teatros throughout the US Southwest from about 1935 to 1941. The family stopped touring in 1941 due to the escalation of World War II (Broyles-González, *Lydia* 50; Strachwitz and Nicolopulos 120).[9] The Mendoza Family Variety Act resumed six years later and performed in both teatros and carpas from about 1947 to 1954.

Mendoza's mother developed not only the costumes for their shows but also the routines. Mendoza's brother Manuel and sister Juanita did comedy skits and performed Mexican dances (including the jarabe tapatío, a popular dance that dates back to the colonial era in Jalisco, and which by the 1920s was associated with both the charro and china poblana). Juanita also performed duets and danced with her sister María, and as the closing act, Mendoza sang and played her guitar. She never performed in the comedy skits (Strachwitz and Nicolopulos 161).

During these decades, las carpas and los teatros were infused with entertainment that deployed images of mexicanidad reflecting the transnational Mexican audiences that frequented these venues. Carpas offered Spanish-language shows and circus-like entertainment, and initially were sites for showing Spanish-language Mexican movies, many of which featured Mexican actresses in china poblana attire (Vargas, "Rita's Pants" 5, "Rosita Fernández" 170). Mendoza described the atmosphere and entertainment of the most well-known carpas in Texas (where she and her family performed)—including Carpa Cubana, Carpa García Mendoza, Carpa Monsivais, and El Teatro Carpa—as including several carnivalesque elements, including trapeze artists, jugglers, dancers, clowns, tightrope walkers, pantomimes, chorus dancers, and comedy skits (Strachwitz and Nicolopulos 77). These tent shows differed from those in teatros or Mexican-operated theaters in San Antonio, including Teatro Nacional, which catered mostly to middle-class mexicano audiences and offered other forms of live entertainment (Vargas, "Rita's Pants" 5). As Vargas explains, in the early decades of the twentieth century, carpas provided alternatives to segregated performance venues such as dance halls and public theaters, which specifically prohibited non-Anglo performers and audiences (*Dissonant Divas* 23).[10] As they began to enter los teatros, Mendoza and her family were often the opening, intermediary, or closing act for popular and celebrated Mexican films from the late 1930s, which featured famous Mexican actresses wearing china poblana costumes, as well as English-language Hollywood films. Mendoza described how at the California Theater in Los Angeles in 1939, she and her family performed between the showing of a "very popular Mexican film and another, English-language movie" (qtd. in Strachwitz and Nicolopulos 143).

A poster announcing the Mendoza Family Variety Act at Teatro Azteca in Calexico, California, on March 3, circa 1940s, illustrates the close associations between the costumes worn by the Mendoza family in their variety act and the clothing worn by Mexican film stars in the ranchera movies. In this performance, Mendoza and her family opened for the Mexican film *Bajo el Cielo de México* (1937), directed by Fernando de Fuentes, who also directed the comedia ranchera *Allá en el Rancho Grande*, which established the genre and featured Mexican film actor Esther Fernández wearing china poblana costumes in both the film and publicity stills.[11] The film *Bajo el Cielo de México*, similar to the other Mexican comedias rancheras, romanticizes rural life on the hacienda. The movie focuses on a rancherita named La China (played by the popular Mexican actor María Luisa Zea) who falls in love with the foreman, Juan Manuel (played by Argentinean actor Rafael Falcón). Zea, who appeared in many ranchera films, played another china poblana character in the popular Mexican film *La India Bonita* (1938).[12] The china poblana archetype in Mexican films continued throughout the 1940s, with popular Mexican actor María Félix playing one in the popular film *La China Poblana* (1944), directed by Fernando Palacios. The narrative follows her character, Señora de la Barca, the wife of Spain's first Mexican ambassador, who comes across a china poblana dress that is cursed and known to bring disaster upon anyone who wears it; she chooses to defy superstition by wearing the forbidden gown.

As evidenced by publicity posters of the period, Mendoza fashioned a modest look in her performances in las carpas and los teatros, rarely donning the off-the-shoulder and low-cut blouses worn by other performers during this period. Even though carpas offered, as Vargas explains, "a financially accessible and 'respectable' performance space for young women, as carpas were often a family venue and young women singers were often chaperoned by elder family or members in the troupe" ("Rita's Pants" 5), women who performed in these public venues confronted sexist views that deemed their presence a violation of hegemonic gender roles. As Nájera-Ramírez suggests, "For women to sing outside of domestic spaces is already a transgression of traditional gender roles, but to sing in adult-oriented sites is especially challenging" (201). Mendoza directly confronted such sexist views when she played in nightclubs and bars later in her career when her first husband publicly—and even at one venue, angrily—disapproved of her performances (Nájera-Ramírez 201). With self-costuming, therefore, female performers could stylize the china poblana costume to negotiate or mitigate the view of their chasteness and sexuality as suspect.[13] Mendoza certainly donned modest china poblana costumes early in her career, even if she did not do so consciously, perhaps in response to the dominant cultural view of women as sexually transgressive when they stepped out as performers in public.

Self-Stylizing the China Poblana as a Tejana and Ranchera Singer On- and Offstage

As Mexican nationalist symbols, ranchera music and the accompanying china poblana costume construct idealized womanhood shaped by hetero-normative constructions of the nation (Vargas, "Rita's Pants" 3–4; Nájera-Ramírez 186). As a representative of mestizaje, the china poblana has been rendered symbolically as the nation and, as part of nationalism, has been considered the ideal woman. Mexican poet Amado Nervo's 1938 poem "Guadalupe La Chinaca," for instance, elevates la china poblana to the status of another iconic Mexican nationalist and gendered figure, La Virgen de Guadalupe (Gillespie 32–34). The poem portrays both la china poblana and La Virgen as chaste, proper women who represent the Mexican nation; in the poem, both figures are recognized for their adornment in the colors of the Mexican flag. Many have also highlighted china poblana dress as emphasizing the wearer's demureness but also sexual availability; for example, travel writers in Mexico in the nineteenth century depicted women who danced the jarabe tapatío in china poblana costumes as faithful to their dancing partners yet sexually available.[14] The sexualized connotation of the outfit itself, along with the dominant view of peasant women as loose and sexually available, led many during this period to associate women who wore china poblana dress as having loose morals (Earle 73).[15] European travel writers in Mexico during this period also frequently emphasized the lower necklines of the blouses (Randall 57). This style of attire, worn by working women who were visible in the public sphere, contrasted starkly, as Randall explains, "with the more cloistered lives of Mexican elite women for their movements were often limited to a morning walk to mass dressed in traditional Spanish black with mantilla" (45).

Just as female singers of rancheras self-stylize the musical genre to employ feminist interventions, specifically in their performance of gendered lyrics that transpose gender roles, female ranchera singers have employed costume choices, as Nájera-Ramírez explains, to manipulate and expand male/female gendered binaries (192, 200). For example, Rita Vidaurri, a contemporary of Mendoza, alternated between the china poblana and charro outfits worn by women, and she self-stylized them depending on the genre of music and the spaces in which she performed (Vargas, "Rita's Pants" 6–9). As Vargas explains, Vidaurri "dressed in long, elegant dresses when she sang boleros and with big orquestas, and wore charro attire when she sang rancheras with her guitar" ("Rita's Pants" 6). As a singer in Mexico in the 1940s, Vidaurri wore full charro attire with pants instead of a skirt, and, as Vargas explains, she "dislodge[d] femininity from the colonial project of a disempowered hetero-masculinity" ("Rita's Pants" 9).[16] Lucha Reyes, a Mexican mariachi and ranchera singer who was popular on both sides of the border throughout the 1930s and 1940s, wore traditional china poblana costumes in her performances, yet with her low vocal range and singing voice, similar to Mexican singer Chavela Vargas's in the twentieth century, she was "consistently coded as performatively incongruous with gender normative femininity" (Vargas, "Rita's Pants" 11). In Reyes's case, her choice of the hyper-feminine china poblana costume combined with her low voice and masculinized public presence queered the heteronormative attire. Rosita Fernández, who mostly sang canciones románticas and boleros, and who was frequently accompanied by large Mexican orquestas, wore china poblana costumes that looked more like ball gowns and included off-the-shoulder and low necklines; such self-fashioning of the china poblana outfit suggests how she stylized the dress to underscore her femininity (Vargas, "Rosita Fernández" 170; Peña 64).

Mendoza's donning of china poblana attire, as evidenced by publicity photos, advertisement photos, and album covers, indicates a self-stylization that both conformed to the hyper-feminine associations of the costume and deemphasized focus on her female body. Her use of designs and materials in her modifications of the dress focuses the viewer's attention on the elaborate designs of her costumes as powerful spectacles of mexicanidad. Mendoza's unique self-stylizations included her addition of colorful sequin appliqués, embroidery, and ribbons to the top; a fuller petticoat; and use of a variety of colors, including pink and black. Later in her career she also sported high heels, a unique characteristic of her self-fashioning of the dress. Mendoza also self-stylized the costume by incorporating elements from other regional Mexican musical traditions, as well as US country music. Photos show Mendoza wearing full blouses, not low-cut ones, that covered her arms, with some images showing her in long-sleeved, high-necked blouses fully covering her chest, more in the style of ballet folklórico costumes. Other photos show her in ruffled, embroidered blouses and full petticoats that share similarities with the costumes of Anglo-American country western singers of the time, such as Kitty Wells.

A unique element of Mendoza's performance aesthetic is her powerful

11.2. Mendoza recording at home, 1938. © *San Antonio Express-News*/Zuma Press. Courtesy of Zuma Press.

embrace of her twelve-string guitar in a classical guitarist position (figs. 11.2 and 11.3). In most photos she is shown with the guitar raised in front of her body in a playing position, by her side, or in front of her (a traditional pose for US country western female guitarists of the period). When Mendoza held her guitar prominently in front of her body, attention shifted away from her frame, deemphasizing her sexuality and redirecting

11.3. Mendoza during a recording session for RCA Victor, 1936. © *San Antonio Express-News*/Zuma Press. Courtesy of Zuma Press.

the focus instead on her artistry as a singer and guitar player. The prominent display of her guitar in front of her body or lower torso, as Castro explains, "minimize[s] the gaze on her female body and force[s] it to focus on her guitar and strong expression on her face." In publicity photos, Mendoza also rarely looks directly at the camera (a pose common among Mexican female performers), instead focusing attention on her guitar. In these photos the instrument is not only an element of her musical artistry but also an integral part of her self-styling. In many images, it appears her guitar flows into her costume and is therefore an essential part of her physical presence and performance persona.

Unlike that of other female singers working in the ranchera musical tradition during the early twentieth century, Mendoza's costuming was not only an integral feature of her performance persona but also a crucial aspect of her public appearance. As shown in archival photos, the china poblana costume became a defining feature of her image from about 1938, when she began to wear the costume in all public appearances, until the end of her singing career in the late 1980s. Indeed, it is rare to find any photos of Mendoza taken after 1938—either onstage or off—not wearing some version of the china poblana costume (see fig. 11.2). From 1938 to the end of her career, images of Mendoza wearing a china poblana costume and holding her twelve-string guitar were used as publicity photos, performance advertisements, and music compilation covers.

Even though the china poblana costume became a defining feature of her onstage performances in the Mendoza Family Variety Act in the early and mid-1930s, Mendoza still wore everyday clothing in publicity photos. In a photo from October 21, 1936, of her recording for RCA Victor in San Antonio (fig. 11.3)—three years after she had started donning china poblana dress for the Mendoza Family Variety Act—Mendoza wears contemporary clothing, including a long-sleeved, button-down paisley shirt, long black skirt, and short-heeled shoes. Two years later, however, in a photo of Mendoza recording in her home in San Antonio (see fig. 11.2), she is shown wearing her characteristic china poblana attire. In describing the 1938 photo, which was taken after she returned from touring in California, Mendoza recalled,

> When we got back to San Antonio, well, I guess that my name had spread from my recordings, the family show, and, especially, from our highly publicized tour to California, so then the local press began to come to my house to do interviews. I was even interviewed by the *San Antonio Light*. . . . One time, they even took a picture of me and my two little girls. It was probably around 1938. It was a photograph of me seated with my two little girls at my side. (Strachwitz and Nicolopulos 139)

In a circa-1940s photo of Mendoza and her two oldest daughters, Yolanda and Lydia, at her San Antonio home she is also wearing china poblana dress, suggesting she consciously chose to wear this attire when the press visited to take photos. Mendoza likely derived great confidence and pleasure from donning the attire for public appearances: it was the costume by which audiences began to recognize her, and by which she began to recognize herself as a performer. Mendoza's choice to wear china poblana in all public appearances also enabled her to project and construct her performance persona as an embodiment of mexicanidad. As evidenced by the 1938 photo (fig. 11.2) and all photos thereafter, the china poblana costume became the defining feature of *all* of Mendoza's public appearances, including documentaries and photos taken of her at home and in recording sessions. The documentary *Chulas Fronteras* (directed by Les Blank, 1976), for example, shows Mendoza making tamales with her sisters and other relatives, but she is the only one in traditional Mexican dress. In this sense, the china poblana costume became the frame by which she was constructed as a domesticated woman in the documentary, illustrating the risk that Mendoza took by wearing the costume in all aspects of her life. In her senior years Mendoza was still wearing china poblana and traditional Mexican costumes in photo shoots and public appearances. Even after she suffered a stroke in the 1980s, public photos show her wearing house-dresses that she had sewn in the china poblana style. And for an audio interview conducted by Deborah Vargas for the Smithsonian Institute's Latino Music Oral History Project in the 1990s, Mendoza also donned a china poblana dress.[17]

China Poblana as Performance of Mexicanidad in the National Spotlight

From the 1960s to the 1980s, Lydia Mendoza's popularity increased as she toured folklife festivals and universities, which propelled her into the national spotlight. She performed at the Smithsonian Festival of American Folklife in Montreal in 1961 and was a guest speaker at universities, including California State University, Fresno in 1982, where she was interviewed by Professors Gene Bluestein and Manuel Peña. Mendoza also performed at the inauguration of President Jimmy Carter in 1977, and she became one of the first recipients of the National Heritage Fellowship Award from the National Endowment for the Arts in 1982. After she stopped performing, in the late 1980s, she was honored by both mexicano and US national institutions, inducted into the Conjunto Hall of Fame in San Antonio, and awarded the highest national honor for artists in the United States, the National Medal of the Arts, from President Bill Clinton at the White House in 1999 (Broyles-González, *Lydia* xi–xv).

In all these performances, as evidenced by photos and performance footage, Mendoza continued to wear—both on- and offstage—distinctive and elaborately detailed hand-sewn costumes in the china poblana style. Yet, distinct from her earlier costumes, these consistently combined several styles of Mexican dress, including china poblana and ballet folklórico, and unlike earlier color palettes, these costumes were in the traditional colors, those of the Mexican flag. In one photo from a 1970s performance, for instance, Mendoza wears a red, white, and green china poblana costume with a backdrop of woven Mexican serapes and a stereotypical Mexican sombrero, a costume signaling a generalized Mexican identity common in US popular culture and media. Public photos from the 1970s suggest the ways in which Mendoza's dress came to characterize typical or generalized Mexican dress during this period to non-Latina/o audiences, deploying mexicanidad and risking aligning itself with stereotypical signifiers of Mexican identity and culture, such as the serape and Mexican sombrero, prevalent in US Hollywood film and popular culture.

But during this same period Mendoza also deployed mexicanidad to self-stylize lo mexicano in an innovative way, wearing fuller petticoats and high heels, and sporting black china poblana gowns with elaborately detailed sequin appliqués on her blouses and skirts. She also continued to wear her hair pulled back with colorful ribbons, adding more ribbons and paper flowers. As in photos of her earlier performance years, the later photos of Mendoza wearing these costumes reveal her pride and self-confidence, signaling a politics of claiming Mexican identity in front of audiences in both the United States and Mexico. Just as Deborah Paredez views Selena Quintanilla's self-fashioning in Tejana music, I suggest that Mendoza's performance attire signaled the "bold assertion of a working-class racialized style without apology" (160).

It would be remiss, however, to not consider the function of china poblana costuming for Mexican female performers in the United States as revealing the "demand of authenticity placed on minoritarian communities and, in particular, on racialized female bodies" (Paredez 3). As Mendoza's audience base grew beyond a working-class mexicano audience from the 1960s to the 1980s, her costuming choices risked fulfilling a stereotype for mainstream US audiences desiring a familiar, feminized, and domesticated "other." At the Smithsonian American Folklife Festival in Montreal in the 1960s, Mendoza's performance stood in for and represented "Mexican folk music" among other multicultural forms of folk music; at Jimmy Carter's inauguration, Mendoza represented "authentic" Mexican identity amid other multicultural performers at the event. Donning her self-stylized traditional Mexican dress costumes in these performances, Mendoza offered a stereotype of Mexican female identity prevalent in US popular culture and Hollywood film. Her long career therefore suggests how she carefully negotiated "between [an] exquisitely crafted self-image and an embodiment of authenticity" (Paredez 160).

Mendoza's Legacy: Archives and Representation in Chicana/o Visual Art

Today Mendoza's china poblana dresses are held by national museums and university archives, including the Smithsonian Folklore Museum Collection, the Ester Hernández Papers at Stanford University, and the Yolanda Broyles-González Papers at Texas A&M University.[18] In 2005 the Smithsonian acquired one of Mendoza's china poblana costumes for its permanent collection (along with Rosita Fernández's and Selena's costumes); the costume was included in the Smithsonian traveling exhibit *Corridos*, which was on display throughout 2002 (Vargas, *Dissonant Divas* 243n93). Her costume was also featured, along with those of other famous Tejana singers, in the exhibit *Mexican Treasures of the Smithsonian*, which was shown from September 5, 2007, through January 27, 2008. In the context of the Smithsonian, Mendoza's costumes are referred to as "objects" of Mexican culture, signaling the risk of fetishizing her costumes as artifacts of authentic Mexican identity, whereas Mendoza's costumes in the university archives are included within a large body of work and scholarship by Hernández and Broyles-González, who have situated and contextualized Mendoza's voice and perspective in their art and scholarship, respectively.

Mendoza's self-stylizations of the china poblana dress are so central to the memory of the singer that her elaborately sewn dresses and fashion are also included in Chicana public muralism and visual art, particularly by Chicana artist Ester Hernández. Hernández's visual depictions of Mendoza's performance aesthetics suggest the artist's own deployment of mexicanidad through her focus on the figure. Specifically, she deploys a Chicana feminist framing of Mendoza as a powerful female role model, underscoring Mendoza's "style politics" (Ramírez) and emphasizing how, through her artistry, which was both sonic and visual, Mendoza claimed space and belonging for mexicanas. Hernández's artistic depictions of the figure claim Mendoza's dress as central to her legacy for mexicanas and Chicanas. By focusing on individual elements of Mendoza's self-stylizations — her hair, makeup, and high heels — Hernandez elevates the sites of costume and fashion, arenas traditionally deemed as passive and of gendered femininity, as active and central aspects of Mendoza's legacy as a performer. Throughout the late 1990s, Hernández created many visual art pieces that pay homage to Mendoza, whom she describes as her artistic madrina:

> Lydia Mendoza is one of my favorite people in the world. I consider her my madrina, my godmother. There were times in my life when I didn't know what I was doing and I was really struggling. I was at a real turning point when I met her. She gave me advice about how hard life is, but if you find something you really want, then do it. (qtd. in Harlan)[19]

In this way, Hernández fashioned Mendoza as a powerful role model for Chicanas. For example, her 1998 serigraph *Con Cariño Lydia Mendoza* (fig.

11.4. Ester Hernández, *Con Cariño Lydia Mendoza (With affection . . .)*, 1998. Serigraph, 30″ × 22″). Self Help Graphics Collection, California Ethnic and Multicultural Archives, University of California, Santa Barbara.

11.4), depicts Mendoza as a feminist icon of mexicanidad by including pre-Columbian imagery that deconstructs binary gender roles. The serigraph recontextualizes a popular photo of Mendoza wearing a china poblana costume in the Mexican color palette of red, white, and green while resting her guitar in front of her. Hernández's rendering of this classic photo includes a background element that fuses Indigenous and Mexican imagery: the medallion behind Mendoza simultaneously invokes the syncretic form of the pre-Columbian Coyolxauhqui, as well as the Aztec symbology of an eagle eating a serpent. Many of Mendoza's china poblana outfits often included sequined images of the eagle and serpent, particularly on the flowing black capes she wore later in her career (Broyles-González, *Lydia* 187). For Chicana artists, Coyolxauhqui represents "not only an incredibly violent dismembering of a warrior woman but also the need to re-member and heal not only ourselves but also our histories and cultures from this violent and misogynistic past. . . . [W]e have a long history of goddess warriors to guide and protect us" (A. López 272). By invoking Coyolxauhqui through the image of the eagle, Hernández uses Chicana feminist reconfigurations of Aztec symbology to portray Mendoza as a powerful feminist icon.

Many Chicana/o artists have also depicted Mendoza in public murals in Latina/o neighborhoods and art centers in Texas. While these murals signal the role of art in educating the community about Mendoza's life and career, they also — by spotlighting her costuming — show Mendoza's physical presence and self-stylizations as part of her claiming of public space. Broyles-González's view of Mendoza's deployment of mexicanidad in her dress throughout her performance career is useful here: "Her body, a billboard of Mexicanness, bravely flaunted those boldly sequined, flowered, brightly colored dresses even through historical periods in which public displays of Mexicanness targeted you for governmental harassment and/or deportation" (*Lydia* 187–188). Mendoza is featured in Judy Baca's mural *Danza de la Tierra* (2009), commissioned by the Dallas Latino Cultural Center, which graces the lobby of the cultural center's performance hall; the mural focuses on two dancers in motion, with the female dancer wearing a colorful folklórico skirt featuring iconic Latino performers and artists, including Mendoza.[20] Theresa A. Ybáñez also depicts Mendoza's image in the mural *Corazones de la Comunidad* (1999), along with three other local female heroes, as part of her mural series *Mujeres de San Antonio*, which covers the walls of buildings on San Antonio's South Side. The mural *La Música de San Anto* (2009), located in the Westside, was coordinated by the San Anto Cultural Arts Community Mural Program and painted by lead artist David Blancas. It features Mendoza among other images of female Tejana singers and performers from the 1930s and 1940s, including Rosita Fernández and Eva Garza. Blancas comments that "these women were huge and I think it's essential that we center these women here because we knew they never played at most of the venues the other artists played in, so we want to be able to create their own space within the mural since they were so significant and continue to be so" (qtd. in Romero 4). These public murals featuring Mendoza's powerful physical and artistic presence, depictions that emphasize her beautiful and elaborate china poblana costumes, function as sites of mexicanidad that necessarily claim space and belonging for various mexicana/o communities in the United States.

In published interviews, Mendoza did not explicitly comment on her costume as a crucial aspect of her public persona, but her contemporary Rosita Fernández did: "Para nosostros [mujeres] era el vestuario. Quiero decir la mitad de tu actuación / For us [women] it was the costume. What I meant to say is that, it was half of the performance" (qtd. in Vargas, "Rosita Fernández" 179). As this chapter illustrates, Mendoza's self-stylizations of the china poblana costume were not only half of the performance, but an integral and powerful aspect of her unique working-class aesthetic that, like her music, appealed to mexicano audiences in both the United States and Mexico.

Notes

1. When Mendoza's mother, Leonor, passed away in 1954, the family variety act disbanded, and Mendoza began to perform consistently as a solo artist from 1954 to the end of her career in the 1980s.

2. The colors of the Mexican flag and the eagle imagery, which are now associated with la china poblana, first developed in a 1910 centennial celebration when Spanish performer Maria Conesa wore a skirt with an eagle on it for President Porfirio Díaz (Velázquez and Vaughan 99).

3. The term *china poblana* also refers to an Indian (South Asian) slave named Mirra who was kidnapped and christened Catarina de San Juan, and who lived in Puebla, Mexico; the term *china* meant "slave" or "servant" in seventeenth-century Mexico (Gillespie).

4. As Pérez-Torres explains, "Mestizaje implies a doubleness experienced through the mixed-race bodies of the mestiza and mestizo, one in which a sense of belonging coexists within an awareness of exclusion" (12).

5. As Rick López explains,

Before the *china poblana* and *tehuana* vogue reached new heights in the 1920s, they already were ubiquitous in festivals, revue theater, film, and public cultural events.

Mexico's elite also adopted these outfits to celebrate national holidays, and by 1921 these styles had become so generalized that even members of the United States diplomatic and business colony, with a reputation for being insulated from Mexican culture, donned *china poblana* outfits for their celebrations of the Fourth of July. There was nothing particularly novel or revolutionary about the *china poblana* and the *tehuana*, which largely had been emptied of racial and social class implications. (36)

6. Images of Mendoza self-styling the china poblana outfit can be found in the Lydia Mendoza Collection of the Houston Area Digital Archives. This extensive online digital photo archive of Mendoza is held by the Houston Metropolitan Research Center of the Houston Public Library and includes publicity stills, photos of her public performances, and photos of recording sessions at her home and in the studio. See digital.houstonlibrary.org/cdm/search/collection/images/searchterm/mss0123 /order/nosort/.

7. The charros orginated in the haciendas of eighteenth-century Mexico, serving as part of private militias known for equestrian skills and expert marksmanship that protected ranch estates. In post-revolutionary Mexico, the charro emerged as a symbol of Mexican nationalism, particularly as a masculine symbol of home, family, and nation (Nájera-Ramírez; Vargas, "Rita's Pants"). By the 1930s, the charro costume had become linked with mariachi music because the Mexican government required mariachi musicians to wear the outfits (Nájera-Ramírez 7). Today the charro is still most often associated with mariachi music and continues to be a powerful symbol of Mexican nationalism and stereotyped masculinity. As Nájera-Ramírez explains, "Ideals of patriotism (nation) and manhood (gender) become fused together so that the *charro* continues to be a powerful symbol through which to foster a sense of Mexicanness even, perhaps especially, for those mexicanos living in the U.S." (11). While men mostly sport charro costumes in the ranchera genre, some women, notably Rita Vidaurri, wear charro pants, which Vargas argues produces a "trans-sensuality of mexicanidad" that "initiates differently configured constructions of femininity— ranging from effemininity to counter-hegemonic femininity—that will not allow its reduction simply to a place of disempowerment" (9).

8. The bracero program was a contract labor agreement intended to bring Mexican laborers to the United States as temporary legal migrants who would not adversely affect the wages and working conditions of domestic farm workers. Instead the program led to an influx of thousands of undocumented Mexican migrants who began to work and live in the United States; many of them entered without documentation because only one out of ten applicants ever received a contract under the bracero program. Racial discrimination directed at this new wave of Mexican immigrants led to Operation Wetback, a series of Border Patrol operations that swept across the agricultural regions of the Southwest. These threats of mass deportation were intended to pressure undocumented Mexican immigrants to leave voluntarily, but led to the direct deportation of Mexican immigrants and US citizens of Mexican descent (García 169–182).

9. From 1941 to 1947, Mendoza and her sister María would sing and appear occasionally around San Antonio at fiestas or other special family and political events (Strachwitz and Nicolopulos 147).

10. Mendoza and her family found it very difficult at first to get invitations to

perform at Anglo-owned theaters due to racial segregation. Even those theaters that were owned by Anglos but catered to mexicano audiences did not invite her at first because they had not heard of Mendoza's music. After they performed at the Colon Theater in El Paso, Texas, in 1936 to sold-out houses, the owner of the theater, Mr. Calderón, phoned other theater owners, including Anglo Americans, who operated theaters across the US Southwest, on Mendoza and her family's behalf. This phone call led to the family receiving invitations to perform, and Mendoza noted that her family's 1937 performance at the Mason Theater in Los Angeles was an extremely successful sold-out show (Strachwitz and Nicolopulos 131–133).

11. La china poblana was popular in many state-sponsored Mexican films, including *Redes* (directed by F. Zinnemann and E. Gomez Muriel, 1934) and *Vámonos con Pancho Villa* (directed by F. de Fuentes, 1935) (Randall 133). Mexican films of the 1920s that preceded the comedias rancheras—such as *El Caporal, En la Hacienda,* and *La Raza Azteca*—also included Mexican actresses wearing china poblana costumes in idealized hacienda contexts. La china poblana also appeared in *La historieta de Aventuras Rancheras* (comic book serials that idealized life on the Mexican hacienda), including *Los Bandidos de Río Frío, Los Plateados, Los Charros del Bajio,* and *Juan Gallardo* (Hershfield 132).

12. María Luisa Zea was so well known for her performance in the film that she was referred to as La India Bonita throughout her career (Aviña 24).

13. Both Broyles-González (*El Teatro Campesino*) and Hurtado describe how Chicanas in El Teatro Campesino during the 1960s and 1970s confronted the sexist view of female performers in the public sphere as transgressing normative femininity. As Hurtado explains, "Even though participation in El Teatro was to bring political consciousness to Chicano communities, many of the women actors were criticized in their families for what they perceived as inappropriate behavior for women" (81).

14. German-born Mexican photographer Hugo Brehme's photographs of Mexican women and men dancing the jarabe tapatío while wearing china poblana and charro costumes exemplify this characteristic of the china poblana as loyal yet sexually available (Hershfield 136).

15. Lithographs of women donning la china poblana attire from 1836, for instance, frequently show them smoking and talking unchaperoned (Gillespie 31). Fanny Calderon de la Barca, the wife of a Spanish minister, wanted to wear a china poblana outfit while on a visit to Mexico during this period but was discouraged from doing so because china poblanas were considered "unsavory women" (Gillespie 31–32); this point highlights the loose moral character associated with the figure.

16. Vidaurri explains that she felt more freedom to break gendered fashion binaries in Mexico:

> I was the only woman to wear pants. . . . I liked them. I could never do that here [in Texas] but I loved wearing them and I became known for that. At that time in Mexico, las mujeres no usaban pantalones [the women didn't wear pants]. I used to come out with real high heels and my tight black *charro* pants [and they yelled] "Esa. Jorge Negreta!" I wanted to wear pants like a *charro*. (qtd. in Vargas, "Rita's Pants" 10)

17. Lydia Mendoza, interview with Deborah Vargas, 15 July 2000, Smithsonian Latino Music Oral History Project.

18. Mendoza's costumes have also been acquired by academic archives, specifically as part of Chicana artist Ester Hernández's papers (costumes that Mendoza donated to Hernández) in the Special Collections and University Archives at Stanford University, and in Chicana scholar Yolanda Broyles-González's papers at the Cushing Library Special Collections at Texas A&M University (which holds two costumes donated by Mendoza to Broyles-González).

19. Hernández's visual representations of Mendoza include: *Con Cariño, Lydia Mendoza* (1987); *Con Cariño Lydia Mendoza (With affection . . .)* (1998 and 1999), produced as both a serigraph and graphite drawing; *Lydia Mendoza, La Reina Tejana (Lydia Mendoza, Texas Queen)* (1987 and 2005), both a pastel portrait and acrylic on canvas; *Portrait of Lydia Mendoza 1983* (1999); *Portrait of Lydia Mendoza 1985* (n.d.); *Los Tacónes de Lydia Mendoza (Lydia Mendoza's High Heels)* (1999), a pastel portrait; and other works. This work was part of the *Cantos del Pueblo: Tejano Musical Landscapes* (2007) exhibit at the Museo Alameda in San Antonio and the *Sounds Latino* exhibition (2008) at the University of California, Santa Barbara.

20. Judy Baca produced the mural in the UCLA Social Art and Public Art Resource Center (SPARC) Cesar Chávez Digital Mural Lab.

Works Cited

Aviña, Rafael. *David Silva: Un Campeón de Mil Rostros*. Universidad Nacional Autónoma de México, 2007.

Broyles-González, Yolanda. *Lydia in Music / La Historia de Lydia Mendoza*. Oxford UP, 2001.

———. "Ranchera Music(s) and the Legendary Lydia Mendoza: Performing Social Location and Relations." *Chicana/o Cultural Studies Reader*, edited by Angie Chabram-Dernersesian, Routledge, 2006, pp. 352–360.

———. *El Teatro Campesino: Theater in the Chicano Movement*. U of Texas P, 1994.

Castro, Kelley Merriam. "Partial Deaths, Femininity, and (ahem) Mendozidad?" Blog post, *Folklore Studies, Ideology, and Authenticity*, 22 Nov. 2011.

Earle, Rebecca. "Nationalism and National Dress in Spanish America." *The Politics of Dress in Asia and the Americas*, edited by Mina Roces and Louise Edwards, Sussex Academic, 2007.

García, Juan Ramon. *Operation Wetback: The Mass Deportation of Mexican Undocumented Workers in 1954*. Greenwood, 1980.

Gillespie, Jeanne L. "Gender, Ethnicity, and Piety: The Case of the *China Poblana*." *Imagination Beyond Nation: Latin American Popular Culture*, edited by Eva P. Bueno and Terry Caesar, U of Pittsburgh P, 1998, pp. 19–40.

Gutiérrez, Laura G. *Performing Mexicanidad: Vendidas y Cabareteras on the Transnational Stage*. U of Texas P, 2010.

Harlan, Teresa. "A Conversation with Ester Hernández." *The Art of Provocation: Ester Hernández*, C. N. Gorman Museum, 1995.

Hayes, Joy Elizabeth. "National Imaginings on the Air: Radio in Mexico, 1920–1950." *The Eagle and the Virgin: Nation and Cultural Revolutions in Mexico, 1920–1940*, edited by Mary Kay Vaughan and Stephen E. Lewis, Duke UP, 2006, pp. 243–258.

Hershfield, Joanne. *Imagining La Chica Moderna: Women, Nation, and Visual Culture in Mexico, 1917–1936*. Duke UP, 2008.

Hurtado, Aída. *The Color of Privilege: Three Blasphemies of Race and Feminism*. U of Michigan P, 1996.

López, Alma. "It's Not about the Santa in My *Fe*, but the Santa Fe in My *Santa*." *Our Lady of Controversy: Alma López's Irreverent Apparition*, edited by Alicia Gaspar de Alba and Alma López, U of Texas P, 2011, pp. 249–292.

López, Rick A. *Crafting Mexico: Intellectuals, Artisans, and the State after the Revolution*. Duke UP, 2010.

Nájera-Ramírez, Olga. "Unruly Passions: Poetics, Performance, and Gender in the Ranchera Song." *Chicana Feminism: A Critical Reader*, edited by Gabriela F. Arredondo et al., Duke UP, 2003, pp. 184–210.

Paredez, Deborah. *Selenidad: Selena, Latinos, and the Performance of Memory*. Duke UP, 2009.

Peña, Manuel. *Música Tejana: The Cultural Economy of Artistic Transformation*. Texas A&M UP, 1999.

Pérez-Torres, Rafael. *Mestizaje: Critical Uses of Race in Chicano Culture*. U of Minnesota P, 2005.

Ramírez, Catherine. *The Woman in the Zoot Suit: Gender, Nationalism, and the Cultural Politics of Memory*. Duke UP, 2009.

Randall, Kimberly. "The Traveler's Eye: *Chinas Poblanas* and European-inspired Costume in Postcolonial Mexico." *Latin American Fashion Reader*, edited by Regina A. Root, Berg, 2005, pp. 44–65.

Romero, Cynthia. "Mural to Honor Notable Musicians: Blancas Takes Lead on Artwork." *Conexión*, 24 July 2008, p. 4.

Saldaña-Portillo, Josefina. *Who's the Indian in Aztlán? Re-Writing Mestizaje, Indianism, and Chicanismo from the Lacandón*. Duke UP, 2001.

Strachwitz, Chris, and James Nicolopulos, editors. *Lydia Mendoza: A Family Autobiography*. Arte Público, 1993.

Vargas, Deborah R. *Dissonant Divas in Chicana Music: The Limits of La Onda*. U of Minnesota P, 2012.

———. "Rita's Pants: The *Charro-Traje* and Trans-Sensuality." *Women & Performance: A Journal of Feminist Theory*, vol. 20, no. 1, 2010, pp. 3–14.

———. "Rosita Fernández: La Rosa de San Antonio." *Gender on the Borderlands: The Frontiers Reader*, edited by Antonia Castañeda et al., U of Nebraska P, 2007.

Velázquez, Marco, and Mary Kay Vaughan. "*Mestizaje* and Musical Nationalism in Mexico." *The Eagle and the Virgin: Nation and Cultural Revolutions in Mexico, 1920–1940*, edited by Mary Kay Vaughan and Stephen E. Lewis, Duke UP, 2006, pp. 95–118.

CHAPTER 12

(Ad)Dressing Chicana/Latina Femininities: Consumption, Labor, and the Cultural Politics of Style in Latina Fashion

STACY I. MACÍAS

Many people on the margins in one way or another know from experiences,
the world of representation and of aesthetics is a site of struggle where
identities are created, where subjects are interpellated, where hegemonies can
be challenged. And taking seriously that pleasure, that life-giving capacity
of aesthetics, performance, bodies, and the sensuous is, within our regime of
power and truth, an indisputably political act.
DORINNE KONDO, *ABOUT FACE*

In this chapter, I engage Chicana/Latina cultural practices of femininity and their contradictory relationship to neoliberalism[1] by examining the politics of a Latina-themed fashion line. I argue that besides capturing neoliberal capital's dangerous ability to benefit from any historically and structurally disenfranchised group, including Chicanas/Latinas, a Latina-themed fashion line also enables and avows alternative femininities. Such alternative femininities are transmitted through Chicana/Latina self-styling and fashion practices, which I call "racialized rasquache raunch aesthetics." Racialized rasquache raunch resists normative white femininity and disembodied subjectivity; in effect, it constitutes an aesthetic system that holds significant epistemological value.[2] In particular, I explore how Chicanas/Latinas produce and channel racialized rasquache raunch aesthetics by dressing, making up, embellishing, and encoding the body as explicitly non-white and as unbound by contemporary trends and time.

I turn to three examples that capture some of the excessive, sullied, and otherwise "ugly"—or non-normative and thus queerly racialized feminini-ties—that are deemed "inauthentic" or "deviant" in hegemonic Chicana/o studies frameworks and mainstream popular culture. I begin with a brief mother-daughter fashion tale, recounting the ways in which my mother's practices of a non-white racialized, working-class femininity shed light on Chicana/Latina aesthetic knowledges, which I also find paralleled in the character of Hilda Suarez of *Ugly Betty* fame.[3] I next examine the consumer contexts and aesthetic qualities of the fashion line Latina Life, commenting on the cultural legibility and theoretical relevance of femininity and style in the vision of a mainstream global corporation. Finally, I consider an "alternative to the alternative" of mainstreaming racialized rasquache raunch aesthetics by exploring the paper fashion work of the prolific artist Diane Gamboa, who reimagines Chicana/Latina style and aesthetic knowledges.[4]

Embodying and Representing Racialized Rasquache Raunch Aesthetics

The year 1987 marked a rite of passage in my young adult womanhood. That is when I shifted from being my mother's juvenile, under-opinionated, and shy shopping bystander to becoming a co-conspiring, creatively contributing, and fully involved player in my mother's purchasing practices, transitioning into a flourishing young consumer. At my mother's side, I made discount clothing shopping trips, frequented the local mini-malls, and participated in other mundane consumptive practices of pleasure and survival in South El Monte, California, our working-class neighborhood. Within walking distance was the apartment complex where in 1995 one of the most egregious examples of sweatshop labor exploitation occurred, involving young undocumented Thai women.[5]

As a Catholic school student, my body was assigned daily to a drab plaid uniform, with little occasion to veer from such an unadventurous dress routine. Luckily, "free dress days" allowed my mother the opportunity to hurl my body into an imaginative universe of endless color, shape, material, and style options. She looked forward to my free dress days, with only our family's modest income and my father's cautious spending habits standing between her otherworldly fashionista desires—under which I would be subsumed—and her object of focus: me. Our excursions to satiate her fashion appetite usually landed us in one of the novel mini-malls dominated by non-English-speaking Asian immigrant owners and working-class Latina customers. In these stores, buyers could find the best low-priced, low-end stylish items. Whether it was at the 5-7-9 or Susie's Deals, my mother was always able to locate the most expensive-looking item, the latest avant-garde runway copy, or a conversation-inciting accessory. She reveled in the process of coordinating colors, matching fabrics and details, and assembling the most fashion-forward creation with only a fifteen-dollar budget.

One of the main reasons I dreaded free dress days was my mother's unpredictable, unrivaled sense of taste. Bordering on outlandish and irreverent on the one hand, and fresh and modern on the other, my mother managed to create one-of-a-kind ensembles that garnered curious attention from my schoolmates and neighbors alike. The knack that my mother possessed, though, was truly an underrecognized talent, at least before professional costumers and celebrity stylists became lucrative, legitimate professions. Unfortunately, my mother's employment as a cashier at Pic 'N Save and later as a girl's PE locker-room attendant at a local high school would be the closest she would formally get to becoming a costuming practitioner. While the lowest-priced objects at the already discounted stores were not challenging to find, the art of refining a trend-worthy, let alone wearable, outfit from a seemingly random assortment of items offered a high-stakes challenge. Somehow—surely by a supernatural force, I thought—my mother was always able to devise and deliver a chic outfit directly off the racks of low-end retail stores selling mass-produced clothing.

While I never personally encountered my mother as a young consumer who worked in and made studied purchases throughout the urban centers of Los Angeles, I came to know the tangible manifestations of that young woman embodied in my mother's femininity: it was an amalgamation of a discount-driven, ostentatiously imagined, sensually embodied Mexican American rasquache style,[6] what I call a racialized rasquache raunch aesthetic. In examining this aesthetic, I am indexing how Chicanas/Latinas like my mother evoke a non-white racial femininity that cannot be disembodied or congruent with universality, unmarkedness, and social privilege. Racialized rasquache raunch does not merely reference but claims the specific hyper-embodied modes through which Latinas inhabit and display their non-white femininities while also attenuating the politics of respectability that dictate much of the aspirational discourses of Latinidad. My mother's styling choices represent such a world in which unapologetic desires, fleshy imperfections, sexual excesses, and the downright "ugly" veer far from the images of adoring wife, saintly mother, or dutiful activist associated with the ideal and dominant categories of Mexican American and Chicana womanhood circulating from the 1960s onward. A second-generation Mexican American, my mother's rightful place has always seemed to be alongside the figures commensurate with inadequately socialized feminine genders best epitomized, for example, in the image of the working-class, street-smart, publicly scorned pachucas and cholas or the flashy, saucy *Ugly Betty* character Hilda Suarez as opposed to her saintly, homely sister Betty.[7]

Through its on-screen styling practices, *Ugly Betty* rehearses the ways in which the femininity of Latinas, and Mexican American women in particular, is mobilized through racial, ethnic, and class-based discourses. Coproduced by Mexican national Salma Hayek—a Hollywood actress, director, and producer—*Ugly Betty* starred Honduran American America Ferrera in the lead role of Betty Suarez. The comedy-drama series garnered critical attention for its nuanced portrayal of a young Mexican American woman's earnest and often humorous plight while working in the cutthroat industry of *Mode*, a fictitious high-end fashion magazine akin to *Vogue*.[8] In addition to spotlighting Betty's scrupulous nature, motherless family, and humble socioeconomic class roots, the series prominently features Betty's eccentric, off-trend, and indecorous self-styling choices. Her style is consciously depicted to stand in contradistinction to her coworkers' beautiful designer outfits and the air of entitlement with which each character wears her or his fashionable head-to-toe look. As the title of the series conveys, the audience was to perceive Betty as "ugly" because of her poor styling sensibilities. By costuming Ferrera's character in nonmatching prints, uncoordinated color combinations, ethnic flourishes, and unflattering shapes, the series ensures that Betty's short bangs, red-rimmed glasses, and silver braces are anything but pretty or contemporary.[9]

As a naive Latina who is thrust into the unfamiliar world of elite fashion, Betty's awkward, outdated, and ill-fitting style choices not only emphasize her appearance in contrast to the series' sophisticated, modern, and well-groomed characters, but also ascribe Betty's unglamorous nature to her racial, ethnic, and class differences. The series sets the tone for how the audience should read Betty's style in the opening episode, her first day at work, in which she infamously wears a bright red poncho with "Guadalajara" scrolled in yellow cursive letters across her chest.[10] By dressing her in a traditional Mexican article of clothing like a poncho, the series codes Latinas as sartorially "behind the times." While Betty—as the show's titular character—commands the most attention for her unappealing self-fashioning aesthetic, Betty's sister, Hilda, often materializes at the other end of the style spectrum, rivaling her sister's unconventional fashion concoctions, but to an entirely different effect. Played by actor Ana Ortiz, Hilda is the Latina bombshell and modern spitfire who excels in her non-white racialized fashion world where tight-fitting clothes, loud colors, gaudy prints, and risqué designs dominate. As Paul Hagen described in a

2010 issue of *Metro Source*, "In 2006, Ana Ortiz exploded onto our television screens—all oversized ruffles and loud prints and sass—playing *Ugly Betty*'s Hilda Suarez: Big sister of Betty and single mother of on-the-way-to-gay-teenager Justin."

In a dual move, the series managed to produce Latina femininity as provincial on the one hand and provocative on the other. Whereas Betty signifies a desexualized and maternal Latina archetype, Hilda represents an overly stylized, ill-mannered, and prurient Latina archetype. I thus describe Hilda's fashion sense as racialized rasquache raunch, a working-class style of graphic colors, excessive details, inexpensive fabrics and constructions, and sensual allure. Commenting on rasquachismo as a Chicana cultural form, scholar Amalia Mesa-Bains states that it materializes out of "an imposed Anglo-American cultural identity and the defiance of a restrictive gender identity within Chicano culture" (160). I gesture here to Hilda because as an arbiter of racialized rasquache raunch style, she is situated neither in sisterly accompaniment with Betty nor in the ultramodern, fresh, contemporary couture world of *Mode*. If I had to imagine where Hilda shops, as well as the source of her fashion sense, I could see her clicking her cha-cha heels, invoking an alternative multicolored fashion-scape and leading us off the beaten path into a working-class universe of global corporate giants like Sears, Kmart, and Kohl's, and their Latina-themed fashion lines of racialized rasquache raunch styles.[11]

It is no coincidence that not long before the premiere of *Ugly Betty* and the nationwide expansion of the cheap-chic chain store Forever 21, self-described Latina fashion lines entered the US consumer market.[12] Primarily produced by non-white racialized women in garment factories inside and outside the United States and sold at nationwide department stores, these fashion lines reconfigure contemporary Latina femininity and the contemporary Latina body politic. In her book *Latino Spin*, Latina/o cultural studies scholar Arlene Dávila astutely reveals the contemporary contradictions of this reconfiguration:

> In the contemporary neoliberal context, contests over the "values" people are given as constituencies are more than ever exacerbated by the spin created by marketers and political pundits. And in these realms, Latinos are more than ever recognized to be the one group that will provide institutions and marketers with the most consumers and constituents. (164)

Dávila's insights about the roles that media and political institutions play in constructing the specialized consumer market–worthiness of Latinos in general instructively applies to the ways in which department stores, magazines, and Hollywood celebrities form a powerful nexus to mediate racialized, gendered ideologies of Latina femininity. In this sense, I extend Dávila's analysis to consider the value that Latinas have acquired through a product line specifically catering to their marked style sensibilities, the aesthetic I call racialized rasquache raunch. In other words, the cultural by-products that neoliberal modes contradictorily produce as an effect of their proliferation are significant to consider given that economic globalization is not a homogeneous process with purely predictable outcomes. In this way, I draw upon Néstor García Canclini, who describes how the participation of minoritized subjects in the exchange of goods and services indexes a process that may also mark oppositional rationalities and creative tactics. I identify these oppositional rationalities and creative tactics as alternative practices that constitute cultural sites in which femininity functions as a vector for processes of racialization and queerness, while also laying claim to epistemological significance.

The Latina Fashion Matrix: Cotton Incorporated, Latina Life, and Constructing the Exceptional Latina Consumer

In October 2005, the global research and marketing company Cotton Incorporated issued a press release entitled "Latina Fashion: From Vogue to K-Mart," which corresponded with national Hispanic Heritage Month. In describing Latina style, the press release states:

> If the retailers are benefiting from the Latina surge, general consumers are also benefiting from the Hispanic woman's special style. Today, colors and embellishments traditionally favored by Latina women, such as reds, lace, and beading, are finding a place in the closets of stylish women everywhere. (Cotton Incorporated)

These discursive statements of Latina style are historically linked to the interlocking systems of gender, race, class, and sexuality. The press release's vivid description of the style "traditionally favored by Latina women" correlates with historically dominant tropes and archetypes of representation. In particular, the stylized costume-like aesthetic that emphasizes non-white racialized sexuality and unruly, working-class Latina femininity corresponds to the insidious ways in which the media historically has treated Latinas. Whether in painting and photography, film and literature, or other popular mediums of representation such as television, media advertising, and an assortment of consumer products, the representation of Latinas falls within a set of taxonomies that many media, feminist, and Latina/Chicana studies scholars have outlined.[13]

In the introduction to a collection of essays she edited, *From Bananas to Buttocks*, Myra Mendible delineates the Latina archetypes on which mass media and other social institutions have ubiquitously depended (1). She describes how, all too predictably, Latina representation historically follows a discursive arc that oscillates among a few popular tropes: the saucy, aberrant, and hypersexual Latina embodied in the Spitfire; the palatable yet still exotically coy and highly feminine Latina epitomized in la Señorita; and finally, the maternal, desexualized, working-poor yet criminalized illegal immigrant Latina figured in la Doméstica (3). Thus, the historical tropification of Latinas as alternately sexually exotic and criminally pathological is what forms the arc of predominating Latina popular representations.

While Cotton Incorporated's dependence on and reproduction of a historical Latina archetype is clear, the press release's discourse contains contradictorily legitimizing racialized rasquache raunch aesthetics. The press release is in direct contest with the interests of Latina politicians, ethnic studies scholars, and immigrant rights activists who wish to move Latina femininity away from non-white racialized embodiments and into "appropriate" gendered territory. In this way, the corporate valorization of Latinas' "special style" concomitantly validates racialized rasquache raunch aesthetics and queerly racialized techniques of femininity. Latina aesthetics that include excessive embellishments, sensual accents, and vibrant colors resist the call to subscribe to historically dominant models of white femininity and also validate the relationship of Latina consumers to a historically racist fashion industry. As the press release indicates, non-Latinas have begun to benefit from the aesthetics that Latinas have long exhibited and prized.

Another interesting highlight from the Cotton Incorporated press release compares the remarkable position of Latina consumers in relation to other female consumers to "explain why the Latina consumer spends significantly more time shopping than her Caucasian and African-American counterparts" (Cotton Incorporated). It quotes Kim Kitchings, the company's director of research and strategic planning: "We know from our research that the female Hispanic consumer is highly cognizant of trends and styles and likes to shop for fashion.... This customer likes to jump on a trend as it's happening, rather than catching it when it's reached the mainstream" (Cotton Incorporated). Additionally, the press release shows the statistical differences that Cotton Incorporated's *Lifestyle Monitor* tracked:

> Hispanic females spend an average of 135.1 minutes in stores shopping for apparel whereas Caucasian and African-American female respondents recorded an average of 89.4 and 109.27 minutes, respectively. Latina women are also more fastidious about their appearance than women of other ethnicities. A significant 57% of Hispanic females told the Monitor that they preferred clothing that looked better on them, over clothing that was comfortable for an evening of dinner and dancing. This was considerably higher than Caucasians (45%) and African-Americans (46%).

The above data not only reflects the fact that fashion in general is deeply enmeshed in the idioms of temporality but also reveals the significance of time in relation to racialization strategies. In particular, the media represents Latinas (and Latinidad in general) in provincial and outmoded ways, associating Latinas with the past and old traditions rather than with present contexts or future possibilities. For example, the Suarez family of *Ugly Betty* lives in New York, a fashion capital, but both Betty and Hilda are outdated aesthetically compared to their on-screen fashion-forward white female counterparts. According to the press release, however, Latina consumers surpass other consumer groups because of their style perspicacity and forecasting of fashion trends. To support this statement, it quantifies in minutes the exceptional devotion of Latinas to shopping. Through its research and report, Cotton Incorporated constructs the unlikely model consumer: a modern Latina who perpetually shops ahead of the crowd and wears clothing regardless of the cost to her body and, presumably, her bank account.

While Cotton Incorporated was creating media buzz around the female "Hispanic" consumer, Sears strategically premiered its Latina Life fashion line. However, this was not the first attempt by Sears to market and design a fashion line for "Hispanic" women. In 2003, Sears collaborated with Lucy Pereda—a Cuban-born television host, anchor, and cookbook author who was popularly dubbed the "Hispanic Martha Stewart"—to launch the first-ever Latina fashion line in the United States (Yerak). After two years of low sales and no loyal customer base, Sears dropped the apparel line and formally cut ties with Pereda. The company's executive vice president and general merchandise manager, Gwen Manto, explained the company's decision: "Lucy [Pereda] had a limited appeal. It was barer, more sexy, more clubby-type looks. . . . [The new apparel line] is very body-conscious with a lot of detail and print but not 'cha-cha-cha'" (Anderson). While Sears attributed the apparel line's lackluster success to design elements that seemingly relied too heavily on youth-driven trends and sexual appeal, Manto's use of the expression "cha-cha-cha" reveals that Sears could embrace racial, ethnic, and class diversity only to an acceptable limit. In other words, the Latina aesthetic moved from acceptable to sullied when the design elements were as identifiably ethnic as the hip-centered dance and music beats of the Cuban cha-cha-cha. In place of the Pereda line, Sears pursued *Latina* magazine, and together they debuted Latina Life to reignite its appeal to a broader Hispanic female clientele.

The aesthetics and consumers of Latina Life originally caught my attention as I wondered how someone like my mother, who initially informed me that there was a "really cute Latina fashion line at 'the Sears,'" would manage to wear these clothes. It is plausible to argue that my mother—in her late sixties; a former janitorial worker; and, by Western medical standards, considered overweight—would not be the targeted consumer of Latina Life. Yet on various visits to Sears department stores throughout greater Los Angeles County, I noted that women in a range of ages, from adolescents to women older than my mother, were buying and wearing similarly designed clothes. Middle-aged women with ample body types were the primary Latina customers adopting that look, which obscures any attempt to prescribe an ideal wearer. It is clear that Sears had researched and thus was catering to the Latina demographic that would embrace its Latina Life fashion line.

In their joint marketing campaign, Sears and *Latina* magazine describe what they imagine is a Latina style aesthetic:

> Key Latina Life™ wardrobe separates include animal print faux fur jackets, embellished camis, shrug sets with velvet piping, sheer mesh tops, ruched paisley skirts and fitted pants with contoured yokes, rich colors in lux suede, metallic, faux fur, croc leather and animal print, along with studs, beading and rhinestone embellishment . . . a little more colorful, always a little spice, a little flavor, and something flirty. ("Sears and Latina Team Up")

Presumably, Sears, in its revamping effort to appeal to a larger Latina constituency, would have eschewed design elements like those mentioned above, all of which accentuate rather than deemphasize sexual, racialized allure, as well as the dominant "cha-cha-cha" look of Pereda's line, from which they sought to distance themselves. While Sears claimed it was redirecting its Latina-themed fashion line toward a more sedate, professional look, the Latina Life clothing and accessory products actually *re-inscribed* the racializing tropes of Latina femininity. In other words, the company's desire to overcome the archetype of a *too* sexy señorita was undermined by its discursive articulations—"colorful," "spice," "flirty"—in conjunction with the products, which posited it once again as a working-class, sexually titillating racialized rasquache raunch aesthetic. Latina Life, touted as the corrective apparel line to its edgier precursor, not so subtly succumbed to the same terms of representation from which it sought to distance itself.

Despite the fact that Latina fashion lines—much like Cotton Incorporated's research and press release—may consciously uphold and reproduce historical tropes of racialized representations of femininity, they also unwittingly, ironically, and contradictorily provide Latina consumers the means to display their racialized rasquache raunch sensibilities. Chicana feminist scholar and visual art historian Laura E. Pérez provides a productive point of entry for extracting alternative meanings of self-styling and consumer identities. She proposes that this style of dress and body ornamentation can be viewed as social garments, or "writings on and about the body." In Pérez's theoretical estimation, such social texts contain the ability to mark and produce gender and racial identities, "whether these be normative or historically newer forms of constructing and representing femaleness, femininity, or the undecidability of gender" (51).

Although Latina Life can be read as harkening back to tropes of hypersexuality, unabashed embodiment, and excessive pleasure, it contradictorily reorients femininity away from modern disembodied and assimilating styles, and instead references the power nestled within alternative practices and representations. Here I find it useful to consider a Foucauldian notion of power to highlight the complex, uninducted, horizontal, and proleptic forms of power that subjects may negotiate between individual agency and social structures. Rather than relying on a model that only legitimizes a hierarchical system of power between oppressors and the oppressed—in this case, between neoliberal capitalism/corporations and Latina consumer subjects—I draw upon Foucault to emphasize that power constantly circulates through a variety of contextually based networks. Within this frame, I view Latina femininities as sites of noncentralized power. Inversely, I understand that power can be reimagined through self-styling and consumption, practices that historically often functioned to invoke contempt of femininity. The range of bodies and sizes engaged in the artful act of wearing and consuming Latina Life symbolizes the contradictions of consumer capital that proliferate through Sears's commodification of Latina femininity, yet not without Latinas inventing, negotiating, and subjectivizing their styles and selves to their own desires and effects.

For all of its desire to overhaul and thus upgrade Latina Life in the direction of a normativizing, digestible, yet still explicit Latina femininity, Sears also provides the means to legitimize Latina consumers who shop and style their clothes in ways that exceed normativizing systems of gender. The racialized rasquache raunch aesthetic of Latina Life invests femininity with a sense of power that is opaque to both the mainstream fashion world and the universe of respectable Latina style.

While shopping as a leisurely activity is usually not considered serious, remunerative labor, the Latina consumers patronizing Sears—a department store known for serving hardworking, average-earning, all-American citizens—are not simply a sign that Sears, like other large retail corporations, knows how to remain culturally relevant and profitable. As with other types of nonremunerative labor, I understand Latina consumers to be queerly exhibiting their racialized, working-class femininity and subsequently engaging in the real labor required "to work" such a stylized outfit. Wearing clothing items such as fitted miniskirts, leopard print faux fur shrugs, and glittery accessories does not necessarily amount to a critically resistant practice of femininity; however, the fact that the subjects engaging in this practice are diversely shaped Spanish-speaking immigrant and non-immigrant Latinas who don clothing during the day to participate in a mundane activity (like shopping in department stores in working-class barrios) signifies a different relationship to racialized femininity, consumptive behavior, neoliberal capital, and self-styling practices.

Some may interpret this relationship as a catastrophic symbol of how neoliberalism, through transnational capital, has managed to, as Angela Davis states, "create new structures of feeling and insinuate itself into our intimacies and intimate lives" (19). In this frame, shopping is just another normativizing technique for aspiring populations, including Latinas, who clumsily attempt to mimic their white feminine counterparts by spending their time and (likely scarcer) expendable income on trivial commodity buying. On the other hand, one can view such Latina self-styling measures as resistant practices of a marginalized group proactively opposing hegemonic structures that dictate normative ideologies of femininity and consumer identity. Yet another way to view this relationship is to search beyond the design of the garment, the identity of its wearer, and the place of its purchase and instead look behind the garment's label to examine its politics of production. In this real-life scenario, often the exploitation of women of Color in the United States and the Global South working in sweatshop-like conditions is rampant, enabling companies such as Sears to mass produce medium-quality goods at low prices and pass on these "savings" so that working-class, non-white racialized, and immigrant Latinas can increase their store-brand purchasing power.

The operations of capital that in the United States invent, manage, and discipline the non-white racialized femininity of Latinas also serve as a raw material worth reconsidering given how, in the contemporary moment, neoliberalism tethers Latina femininity to concepts of labor, sexuality, and nation. However, to draw attention only to Marx's "murderous, meaningless caprices of fashion" is to participate directly in a form of misogyny, with charges of frivolous consumption, autocommodification, and near-complete capitulation to neoliberal global capitalism (525). In all of these understandings, assimilation/capitulation and resistance/counterhegemony are set up in an unproductive binary that releases from this relationship its rhizomatic features of contradiction, negotiation, and heterogeneity. And because nothing can completely escape commodification, it is essential to acknowledge, explore, and continue to ask what Latina self-styling practices and Latina-themed fashion lines have to offer to an analysis of consumption and labor within the frame of neoliberal global capitalism.

While examining Latina Life through a complex optic can indeed highlight disidentificatory cultures and practices of femininity, there is another way to imagine Latina consumption, fashion lines, and self-styling efforts. As an example, artist Diane Gamboa turned to creating paper fashion alternatives to the items and lines that corporate stores offer.

Re-Dressing Racialized Latina Femininity in Diane Gamboa's Paper Fashions

Style is a big question in our communities. We are not a superficial people.
We are beautiful and stylish beyond poverty.
DIANE GAMBOA, FROM A PANEL DISCUSSION ON THE ART EXHIBIT
DEADLY STYLISH AT SELF-HELP GRAPHICS, EAST LOS ANGELES

Diane Gamboa, who has been creating art, including paper fashions, since the early 1980s, has produced more than seventy-five pieces of paper fashion that touch directly on the politics of fashion, femininity, consumption, and society. Created out of paper and requiring a labor-intensive process, Gamboa's paper fashions blur the line between high-end haute couture commodity culture and low-brow do-it-yourself invention. In this concluding section, I explore how Gamboa's paper fashions illuminate anthropologist Dorinne Kondo's keen reminder that for historically marginalized groups, the world of fashion and aesthetics comprises representational sites of intervention and strategies of survival just as valuable as other conventional political processes and tactics (4). And as she attests in the above epigraph, regardless of economic status and financial resources, style is a high-stakes concept—one that can steer our understanding toward valuing desire, affect, and ephemerality as political modalities that historically underwrite practices of femininity.

In her paper fashion *Guard Yourself Against Gardasil*,[14] Gamboa spotlights the biomedical violence that young female bodies of Color may experience under the guise of state-based protection. The piece expresses a critique of contemporary social ills in a culture where, for Gamboa, "it is still dangerous to be female."[15] In particular, Gamboa references the vaccine that the health care industry overwhelmingly favors administering to young girls before the onset of menstruation (and, increasingly, young boys) to prevent the human papillomavirus, which can lead to female reproductive system cancers and sexually transmitted diseases such as genital warts. The vaccination program recalls the historical disregard for women of Color in the United States and the Global South in self-determining their health and well-being, subjecting them, without their knowledge, to violent and invasive medical procedures that ruined or debilitated their sexual reproductive systems. Through GYAG, Gamboa creatively gestures to normative regimes of power that cohere in the health care industry, which calls into question the terms by which such a vaccine has become a seductive technology.

In July 2010, Gamboa created GYAG for display at an exhibition at the third annual street and graffiti art fair Peel Here 5, Brace Yourself, held at East LA's community cultural arts center, Self-Help Graphics. As the only featured female artist in the Chicano male-dominated artistic form of street graffiti, Gamboa doubly exposes the violence of erasure that Chicana artists experience in historic Chicana/o art scenes and the quotidian violence that non-white racialized female bodies experience vis-à-vis regulatory regimes of power such as the biomedical industry. Modeled by a young Chicana who self-identifies as a punk, the whimsical three-piece paper construction includes a black pleated skirt, a papier-mâché bustier plastered with the event's stickers, and a miniature top hat featuring a bouquet of pretty pink petals and pastel green leaves bursting from its base (fig. 12.1).

12.1. Diane Gamboa, *Guard Yourself Against Gardasil*, July 2010.

From the use of unremarkable art supplies—including cellophane, markers, crayons, ribbon, and stickers—to the fleeting temporality of paper fashion constructions, Gamboa literally re-dresses Chicana/Latina femininity. The series of inexpensive yet extravagantly detailed paper artwork that Gamboa has created for nonprofessional models to "work" in live art runway shows, for mannequins in public art galleries, and for her own body to display in Chicana/o art scenes wryly thematizes a politics of disposability. Valuing disposability within the confines of the fashion world is not a unique concept; the tempestuous nature of fashion trends excites customers for fall and spring designer collections months prior to either calendar season arriving.[16] Purchases become a timed, patterned consumer activity in which each fashion item is construed as replaceable due to its lost currency from one season to the next. It is improbable, however, for a business to turn a profit within an accelerated time frame without cutting the cost of production by employing the cheap materials and low-wage labor available in many urban centers and third world countries.

It is also nearly impossible in this contemporary moment to consider fashion products and purchases without conjuring up images of sweatshop fabrication and racialized women's labor. To regard notions of dispensability and fashion unequivocally means to confront the thorny operations of the garment industry and the ways in which neoliberal capitalism colludes with historical discourses of femininity to make non-white racialized women more fit for threading, sewing, and sweating. Like the leftover scraps scattered on a sweatshop factory's floor, third world women constitute material equally as cheap, replaceable, and ultimately disposable. This is nowhere more apparent and harrowing than along the international border between the United States and Mexico, where the maquiladora industry, in particular, has rendered Mexican women disposable.[17] Thus, concurrent with the appearance of Latina-themed fashion over the last twenty years has been the violent disappearance of countless young Mexican women employed in garment factories in the US-Mexico border region. In this context, Gamboa summons a politics of disposability through sourcing her own costs of production and making paper her primary fabric. For unlike the spaces where fashion lines are produced, displayed, and sold, Gamboa's wearable paper fashions come to life, exist, and perish in sites of Latina/o and Chicana/o cultural exchanges.

The model wearing Gamboa's paper fashion in figure 12.1 suggests that biological tactics of warfare favor the bodies of women of Color as sites of experimentation. However, she wears a striking juxtaposition of colors—black and white, pink and green—and a flirty design that signifies more than a prostrate body ready for a vaccination. The playful hat exploding with vibrant pink flowers calls attention to the site of the female brain from which logic, decision-making, and self-determination emanate—a site traditionally divested of femininity and thus social, cultural, and intellectual power. In all, Gamboa revels in endowing the concepts of style and consumption with new meaning as she fiercely, courageously, and brilliantly reimages and reimagines power. Through her paper fashion art, Gamboa carves out a counter politics of style that departs from patriarchal valences that have historically equated femininity with powerlessness and disposability.

At the nexus of Latina style, transnational labor, and border brutality lay significant contradictions about Latina bodies and subjectivities. The cultural and corporate landscapes of the United States produce both the consummate US Latina shopper and the mechanisms for the erasure of not only her lived realities but also, crucially, for those of the women who produce the garments on both sides of the border. Methodologically, Gamboa creates ensembles that jettison racialized female labor—not to diminish the facts of neoliberal capitalism and the transnational garment industrial complex, but to denounce their high costs. By constructing alternative fashion lines that revel in a form of racialized feminine extravagance, allure, and beauty, Gamboa is able to queerly style her way out of a normativizing regime of power that makes style, consumption, and femininity incommensurable with any transformative political desires. Accordingly, I understand that Gamboa's paper fashion provides a set of sartorial resources that, without thwarting pleasure or desire, help us reimagine consumption and self-styling while making plain the gruesome costs of global capitalism and the fashion industry. Gamboa's work generates another type of queerly racialized femininity, one that does not stop at the wardrobe closet's door but signals our collective queer desires to open the door to radical materialisms, unfashionable femininities, and imaginative sensibilities.

Conclusion: Customizing Style, Claiming Politics

When we galvanize claims for social justice and argue for inclusion by relying on properly gendered Chicana figures, what becomes evident is that the project of Chicana/o/x studies must acknowledge the violent exclusion of "bad" feminine subjects; as Catherine S. Ramírez states in regard to women zoot suiters, "Pachucas' absence in narratives of Mexican American history, cultural identity, and community constitutes epistemic violence" (xiv). I also reflect back to a moment with my mom when she put on a black-and-white leopard-print, stretchy fabric blouse and asked me to help her adjust its unflattering neckline. She assumed that the blouse was marked down to $4.99 because the elongated keyhole crossing her chest had been sewn incorrectly, as there was too much loose fabric that covered up rather than exposed her décolletage. Rather than toss out the inexpensive top, she asked her neighbor to reconstruct the neckline so that her vision of it could be brought to life. With a deeper plunge and tauter fit, my mother achieved the aesthetic outcome she had hoped to show-case when she originally made the purchase. As my mom and her neighbor spent several minutes discussing the fit and design options, finally settling on attaching a button to hold the neckline's structure together, I realized how that moment animated the politics of style, consumption, labor, and non-white racialized femininity among Chicanas/Latinas. Not only did the blouse and its redesign capture my mother's racialized ras-quache raunch aesthetic, but her decision to ask a neighbor to rework the neckline crystallized the fact that styling and consumptive practices are as much collaborative endeavors as they are attempts to construct indi-vidual subjectivities of desire. When the blouse recently reappeared—this time worn by my mom's older sister, my Aunt Alice, on the occasion of her seventy-fourth birthday brunch—I realized another value of rasquache raunch racialized practice: it is not only a technique of self-styling but also a negotiated process of underground commodity exchange and the rule of the informal economy.

This moment also encapsulated an alternative temporality, with the women talking about, considering, and reconstructing an article of cloth-ing that some may believe is not worth its cost. Rather than avow that femininity is a nonconsequential, oppressive gender technology full of frivolous desires of a disposable nature, Latina-themed fashion lines, Diane Gamboa's paper fashions, and my mom's styling practices challenge how femininity is relegated to the repository for what is debased and dis-posable. The fact that a Chicana like my mother can achieve recognition of her unique social and cultural position under neoliberalism reveals the value of self-styling practices that can denaturalize normative aesthetics of femininity and consumer identity.

Notes

1. Under late capitalism, neoliberalism (or market globalization) is a political phi-losophy and economic policy that has established a new regime of order, power, and politics. Cultural geographer and Marxist economist David Harvey argues that under neoliberalism, capital is the primary motor that fuels all political, structural, and cultural shifts. Within this purview, there is little space for individuals and commu-nities to meaningfully resist the omnipotent regime that is neoliberal global market capitalism.

2. I acknowledge the critical feminists of Color who have laid the foundations for

my analysis of the epistemic value of femininity, most notably: Patricia Hill Collins, *Black Feminist Thought*; Angela Davis, *Women, Race, and Class*; bell hooks, *Ain't I a Woman*; and Aída Hurtado, *The Color of Privilege*.

3. I use the term *non-white racialized* to modify objects such as "femininity" and subjects such as "Latinas" to denote that whiteness also is racialized. See, for example, Omi and Winant, *Racial Formation in the United States*.

4. I am grateful to Diane Gamboa for her candor, sheer talent, and enduring creative presence. While I comment on only one piece of Gamboa's extensive paper fashion designs, elsewhere I write about her print work series *Alien Invasion*. See also the works of Karen Mary Davalos, Laura E. Pérez, and Yvonne Yarbro-Bejarano.

5. For further details on the experience of the more than seventy workers who endured months of slave-like conditions sewing garments for nearly no compensation, and what happened in its aftermath, see Hair.

6. Rasquache is "a working-class style with vivid colors, vernacular forms, and recycled materials." *CARA*, an exhibition at the Wight Gallery, UCLA, 30 Apr. 2010.

7. The series *Ugly Betty* was created by Silvio Horta and debuted on US network television in 2006. It is based on the original Spanish telenovela *Yo soy Betty, la fea*, filmed in Colombia.

8. For a thorough and excellent analysis of *Ugly Betty* in relation to comedy and camp studies, see González and Rodriguez y Gibson, in particular, chap. 4, "Bringing Sexy Back: The Complexities of Latina Sexuality in *Ugly Betty*."

9. Bill Keveney additionally notes, "'Bettification' is an act of reverse glamorization. To create Betty Suarez, whose smart sensibility doesn't extend to her appearance, stylists had to twist Ferrera fashion-backward."

10. The *Ugly Betty* poncho moved from the screen to the retail world of Halloween costumes. Along with the poncho, Halloween stores and online sites sell *Ugly Betty* accessories, including red-framed glasses, fake braces, and a dark-colored wig of long hair and bangs.

11. Sears has manufactured two Latina-themed fashion lines since 2003: the Lucy Pereda Collection and, in conjunction with *Latina Magazine*, Latina Life. Kmart produces Latina-themed "lifestyle" clothing, accessories, and home collection lines in conjunction with Mexican singer and actress Thalia Sodi. In collaboration with the Colombian-born Sofia Vergara, star of the ABC sitcom *Modern Family*, in September 2011 Kmart debuted the Sofia Vergara Signature Collection, "a new line of miniskirts, jeggings, leopard bustiers, tight dresses and sultry tunics" (Moin). Additionally, in May 2013 Kmart announced the Sofia by Sofia Vergara shapewear collection. The retail store Kohl's collaborates with Daisy Fuentes on her eponymous fashion line, which launched in 2004, and with Jennifer Lopez, whose fashion and home furnishing lines launched in 2011.

12. I studied the Latina fashion line that was sold exclusively at Sears from August 2005 to approximately June 2007. As of June 2011, Sears was advertising its Latina Life products for purchase online in its sale section. Although production of the line was reportedly (and quietly) halted not much later than its fall 2005 debut, products remained in its stores through 2007. Sears, which merged with Kmart in 2006, never issued a formal press release on its decision to discontinue the line. I speculate that Sears likely halted production of Latina Life because there was no "hot Latina" Hollywood star with whom to connect the line. Interesting to note is that in September

2011 the infamous Kardashian sisters launched their Kardashian Kollection at Sears. Despite its significantly higher price range, I would characterize the aesthetic of the Kardashian Kollection as racialized raunch, minus the rasquache factor. Additionally, through social media sites such as *Instagram*, *YouTube*, and *Facebook*, Latina fashion and style have democratized rapidly, enabling the rise of new and multiple style icons, noncommercial and do-it-yourself Latina fashion lines, community-organized runway shows, and other subterranean cultural producers and products.

13. For scholarship on popular Latina stereotypes, see, for example, Aparicio and Chávez-Silverman; Beltran; Bost; Fregoso; Habell-Pallán; Molina-Gúzman; Rodríguez; and Valdivia.

14. I will refer to *Gamboa's Guard Yourself Against Gardasil* paper fashion piece as GYAG.

15. In conjunction with the annual celebration of Day of the Dead held at Self-Help Graphics in East Los Angeles, Gamboa curated an art show she titled *Deadly Stylish*, which ran 1–28 Nov. 2009. Gamboa, along with thirteen other exhibiting artists, participated in a panel discussion that explored ideas of style, tradition, ritual, and death. The following quotes from Gamboa are from the discussion held 21 Nov. 2009, at Self-Help Graphics.

16. For a history of the shift in the fashion industry from one that focused on exclusivity, individual craftsmanship, and couture clothing to mass production and seasonably trendy items, see, for example, Breward; and Cumming.

17. For further elaboration on the politics of the garment industry, transnational labor, and what has become known as the "maquiladora murders"—most of which have occurred without recourse for victims' families since 1993—see Fragoso; Fregoso; Guzman and Gaspar de Alba; and Wright.

Works Cited

Anderson, George. "Sears Looks for Broader Appeal With Latinas." *Retail Wire*, 20 Apr. 2005, retailwire.com/discussion/sears-looks-for-broader-appeal-with-latinas/. Accessed 21 Feb. 2011.

Aparicio, Frances R., and Susana Chávez-Silverman, editors. *Tropicalizations: Transcultural Representations of Latinidad*. UP of New England, 1997.

Beltran, Mary. *Latina/o Stars in U.S. Eyes: The Making and Meanings of Film and TV Stardom*. U of Illinois P, 2009.

Bost, Suzanne. *Mulattas and Mestizas: Representing Mixed Identities in the Americas, 1850–2000*. U of Georgia P, 2003.

Breward, Christopher. *The Culture of Fashion: A New History of Fashionable Dress*. U of Manchester P, 1995.

Canclini, Néstor García. *Consumers and Citizens: Globalization and Multicultural Conflict*. U of Minnesota P, 2001.

Cotton Incorporated. "Latina Fashion: From Vogue to K-Mart." *The Lifestyle Monitor*, cottoninc.com/pressreleases/?articleID=354. Accessed 3 July 2009.

Cumming, Valerie. *Understanding Fashion History*. U of Michigan P, 2004.

Dávila, Arlene. *Latino Spin: Public Image and the Whitewashing of a Race*. New York UP, 2008.

Davis, Angela. *Abolition Democracy: Beyond Empire, Prisons, and Torture.* Seven Stories, 2005.

———. *Women, Race, and Class.* Vintage, 1981.

Foucault, Michel. *Abnormal: Lectures at the Collège de France, 1974–1975.* Edited by Valerio Marchetti and Antonella Salomoni, translated by Graham Burchell, Picador, 2004.

———. *Discipline and Punish.* 2nd ed., translated by Alan Sheridan, Vintage, 1995.

Fragoso, Julia Monárrez. "Serial Sexual Femicide in Juárez, 1993–2001." *Aztlán,* vol. 28, no. 2, 2003, pp. 153–178.

Fregoso, Rosa Linda. *meXicana Encounters: The Making of Social Identities on the Borderlands.* Minnesota UP, 2003.

Gamboa, Diane. *Deadly Stylish.* Exhibition at Self-Help Graphics, East Los Angeles, 21 Nov. 2009.

González, Tanya, and Eliza Rodriguez y Gibson. *Humor and Latina/o Camp in Ugly Betty: Funny Looking,* Lexington Books, 2015.

Guzman, Georgina, and Alicia Gaspar de Alba, editors. *Making a Killing: Femicide, Free Trade and La Frontera.* U of Texas P, 2010.

Habell-Pallán, Michelle. *Loca Motion: The Travels of Chicana and Latina Popular Culture,* NYU P, 2005.

Hagen, Paul. "Bye Bye Betty." *Metro Source,* vol. 21, no. 2, 2010, p. 49.

Hair, Penda D. "Client-Centered Lawyering: Garment Worker Advocacy in Los Angeles." *Louder Than Words: Lawyers, Communities, and the Struggle for Justice: A Report to the Rockefeller Foundation,* Rockefeller Foundation, 2001.

Harvey, David. "Neoliberalism as Creative Destruction." *Annals of the American Academy of Political and Social Science,* vol. 610, March 2007, pp. 22–44.

Hill Collins, Patricia. *Black Feminist Thought: Knowledge, Consciousness, and the Politics of Empowerment.* 2nd ed., Routledge, 2000.

hooks, bell. *Ain't I a Woman: Black Women and Feminism.* South End, 1999.

Hurtado, Aída. *The Color of Privilege: Three Blasphemies on Race and Feminism.* U of Michigan P, 1997.

Keveney, Bill. "It's a 'Bettification' Project." *USA Today,* 10 Apr. 2006, www.usatoday .com/life/television/news/2006-10-04-betty-transform-main_x.htm. Accessed 21 Feb. 2011.

Kondo, Dorinne. *About Face: Performing Race in Fashion and Theater.* Routledge, 1997.

Marx, Karl. *Capital: A Critique of Political Economy,* vol. 1. *The Process of Capitalist Production,* Cosimo, 2007.

Mendible, Myra, editor. *From Bananas to Buttocks: The Latina Body in Popular Film and Culture.* U of Texas P, 2007.

Mesa-Bains, Amalia. "Domesticana: The Sensibility of Chicana Rasquache." *Distant Relations: Cercanías Distantes / Clann i Céin, Chicano, Irish, Mexican Art and Critical Writing,* edited by Trisha Ziff, Smart Art, 1995.

Moin, David. "Kmart Shows Its Sexy Side." *Women's Wear Daily,* 1 Jan. 2011, www .com/eye/people/kmart-signs-sofia-vergara-3451370/. Accessed 3 July 2011.

Molina-Gúzman, Isabel. *Dangerous Curves: Latina Bodies in the Media,* NYU P, 2010.

Omi, Michael, and Howard Winant. *Racial Formation in the United States from the 1960s to the 1990s.* 2nd ed., Routledge, 1994.

Pérez, Laura E. "Writing on the Social Body: Dresses and Body Ornamentation in Contemporary Chicana Art." *Decolonial Voices: Chicana and Chicano Cultural Studies in the 21st Century*, edited by Arturo J. Aldama and Naomi H. Quiñonez, Indiana UP, 2002, pp. 30–63.

Ramírez, Catherine S. *The Woman in the Zoot Suit*. Duke UP, 2009.

Rodríguez, Clara E., editor. *Latin Looks: Images of Latinas and Latinos in the U.S. Media*, Westview, 1997.

"Sears and Latina Team Up on Apparel Line." *WebProNews*, 20 Apr. 2005, archive .webpronews.com/authors/webpronews. Accessed 21 Feb. 2011.

Valdivia, Angharad N. *A Latina in the Land of Hollywood*. U of Arizona P, 2000.

Wright, Melissa. "A Manifesto Against Femicide." *Antipode*, vol. 33, no. 3, 2001, pp. 550–566.

Yerak, Becky. "Sears Drops Lucy Pereda, Adds Line of Latina Life." *Chicago Tribune*, 20 Apr. 2005, www.chicagotribune.com/news/ct-xpm-2005-04-20-0504200213 -story.html. Accessed 21 Feb. 2011.

CHAPTER 13

Urban Xican/x-Indigenous Fashion Show ARTivism: Experimental Perform-Antics in Three Actos

CHELA SANDOVAL, AMBER ROSE GONZÁLEZ, AND FELICIA MONTES

In the United States today there are approximately 7 to 8 million persons of predominantly Native American descent, of whom about 1 million are "Indians" descended from tribes native to the United States . . . and the balance are . . . "Chicanos" descended from [native] tribes.
JACK FORBES (POWHATAN-RENAPÉ AND LENAPE), *AZTECAS DEL NORTE*

The work of Xicana and Latina feminists . . . points toward new directions in understanding Xicana and Xicano artistic practice from an Indigenous and indigenist perspective.
DYLAN MINER (MÉTIS), *CREATING AZTLÁN*

I will no longer be made to feel ashamed of existing. I will have my voice: Indian, Spanish, white. . . . I will overcome the tradition of silence.
GLORIA ANZALDÚA (INDIAN/SPANISH/WHITE), *BORDERLANDS*

Prologue: Fashioning Xican/x-Indigeneity

What are Xican/x-Indígena aesthetics? To begin addressing this question, we call attention to this book's title, *meXicana Fashions*, where a defiant *X* appears as a twenty-first-century identity marker.[1] During the 1990s a cohort of Chicana feminists began replacing the *Ch* in "Chicana" with a capital X (Xicana)[2] in order to summon the lexical appearance—and sound—of Nahuatl, an ancient but still living Indigenous language.[3] Nahuatl does not deploy the English language sound *ch* [tf] nor its written version, as in *Ch*icana. Rather, the nearest Nahuatl sonic is [SHH], which is indicated lexically with an *X*. Contemporary Xicana feminist sonic, lexical, and political replacements of the *Ch* with an *X* are meant to point to Indigenous uprisings within and throughout Chicana, Chicano, and Chicanx identities. Today, the spoken and written grapheme *X* acts as a mobile signifier that points to identities-in-redefinition.[4]

There is another and different kind of *x* redefinition also taking place in Chicana/o and Latina/o studies. This second change relies upon the cross-cultural meaning variability of the *x* sign. In this case, an *un*capitalized *x* is substituted for colonially gendered *a* and *o* word endings; for example, Chican-x, Latin-x, herman-x, and compañer-x. This end-of-word usage of the *x* does not carry with it the Nahuatl [SHH] pronunciation; instead, it is pronounced as the ['eks] heard in the neologism *Chican-x*. Moreover, theorist Francisco Galarte (229–236) intervenes in this conversation by pointing out how this uncapitalized end-of-word, gender-transforming *x* must undergo yet another transformation to appear as a star on the horizon of possibility: Chican* or Xican*.[5]

We understand all such legible and sonic forms of the *X* [SHH], the *x* ['eks], and the silent * as entry points into the complex notions of meXicanidad self-fashioning, designing, and tailoring that are analyzed in this book. We identify Xican/x-Indigeneity within, alongside, and sometimes apart from Chicana/Latina/meXicana formations; we do so to acknowledge the resurgence of diverse Indigeneities out of all previous, simultaneous, and future permutations, iterations, and definitions.[6]

This chapter draws together the authors' activism and research on US, urban-based Xicana-Indígena fashion art shows that center the contributions of women in the Los Angeles area.[7] At the time of this writing there are at least eight such groups, including Mujeres de Maíz (Women of the Corn), In Lak Ech (You Are My Other Me), Las Ramonas, Entre Mujeres (Between Women), Ovarian Psycos, El Puente Hacia la Esperanza (The Bridge Towards Hope), INCITE!, and Tongues. Each group is a collective of feminists of Color.[8] Members of these groups—whether tribalized, de-tribalized, re-tribalizing, or never tribalized—see themselves as political descendants of Third and Fourth World liberation movements and the women of Color feminisms of the 1970s through the 1990s. Contemporary members, however, emphasize their *Indigenous* heritages as integral to their histories, survival, politics, and aesthetics. We three authors are members of and/or supporters of these groups.[9]

Over the years we have attended, organized, produced, and/or documented Indigenous fashion shows. We have traveled within and outside the United States participating and sharing within Indigenous communities as members or as fashion activists. We have studied the blendings of symbols, rituals, meanings, and ceremonies created at Indigenous fashion shows mounted in major urban areas, including Albuquerque, Phoenix, Vancouver, and Los Angeles. In every situation we found peoples exhibiting apparel, jewelry, makeup, and the movements and attitudes of the body in ways that redraw and alter fashion.[10] Many of these fashion shows deploy perform-antics inspired by the imperatives of (other)worldly demands.

The perform-antics described in this chapter are organized into five sections, which include this prologue; Actos I, II, and III; and the epilogue. Acto I introduces readers to Indigenous aesthetic uprisings, while Acto II, the heart of the chapter, provides a scripted performance of a Xicana-Indígena fashion show. This performance features the real-world creations of internationally renowned Xicana-Indígena designer Felicia "FE" Montes. The show is a collectively produced textual-spectacle introducing readers to three of Montes's best circulated designs. We then move to Acto III, a "Fashion Show Community Speak-Out." Taken together, these three actos demonstrate the links that connect Xican/x-Indígena fashion ARTivism with global twenty-first-century Indigenous aesthetic uprisings.

Our chapter weaves together the voices of feminist urban Indigenous, Xican/x, and Radical Indigenous Mestiz/x organizers, curators, designers, re-fashioners, students, supporters, advisers, audiences, and authors. We stitched their stories, theories, activism, world-art performances, interviews, histories, and fictions together to make the truths we tell.[11] Our method combines what the folklorist and theorist Norma Cantú describes as "autobioethnography" (xi) and what the philosopher/writer Gloria Anzaldúa names "autohistoria-teoria" ("Border Arte")—approaches that creatively combine fiction, documentary, history, theory, and self-reflexive ethnography.[12] The resulting interdisciplinary chapter is an experimental scripted production of counter-representational scholarship—a medium for de-colonizing perform-antics.[13]

Acto I: Indigenous Aesthetic Uprisings

Let's present a new version of the "Indian" in fashion and pop culture. Who has the power to represent us to the world? . . . To be complacent or accommodating when it comes to (mis)representation is one thing. To critique is another. [But a significant alternative to these is] to offer counter-representations for advancing the dialogue.
JESSICA R. METCALFE (TURTLE MOUNTAIN CHIPPEWA),
BEYOND BUCKSKIN LOOKBOOK

*As fast as she sews, the dog unravels her work. And if she should ever finish
her quillwork, the world will end at that instant.*
COLLEEN CUTSCHALL (OGLALA LAKOTA), "DRESSES, DESIGNERS
AND THE DANCE OF LIFE"

The preceding epigraphs speak to the ties that bind Indigenous fashion
to the everyday work of liberation.[14] Cultural theorist and critic Jessica
Metcalf (Chippewa), a leading scholar of Indigenous fashion studies, focuses on the now global Indigenous fashion show phenomenon. Shows
produced between 2005 and 2015 have been launched across Africa, Australia, Korea, Polynesia, the Pacific Islands, and the Americas.[15] Organizers describe them as "Native," "Aboriginal," "Indigenous," "Indian," and
"Xicana-Indígena," and as "art events," "festivals," "powwows," "fashion
shows," and "cultural performances." These shows reflect a transcontinen-
tal phenomenon — an aesthetic resurgence that crosses all geo-historical
borders.[16] Reading Metcalf's work, we have identified four primary aesthetic approaches to contemporary Indigenous fashion design and fabrication: (1) the traditional, ancestral approach, which differs by nation,
clan, territory, or time; (2) the planned innovation of such (traditional)
designs; (3) an aesthetic mode aimed toward countering Western fashion design; and (4) the counter-representational aesthetic form recom-
mended by Metcalf in the preceding epigraph. This differential form draws
from any of the previous three approaches, and in any combination. The
counter-representational approach is accomplished by designers we call
Indigenous re-fashioners.[17] Re-fashioners create counter-representational
aesthetics that challenge the very notion of representation itself.[18]

Lakota artist Colleen Cutschall tells an ancient tribal story that illustrates the spiritual and political ethics of counter-representational aesthetics. Her story describes an Indigenous re-fashioner and her animal
companion engaging in a living process of fabrication/destruction/re-
fabrication — a process where there can be no final or dominant making
because "the world will end in that instant" (65). Rather than finishing,
these re-fashioners engage in a constant process of tangling and disen-
tangling strands of information, signs, and meaning. All of these are in
constant transformation, destruction, and re-generation — the forces of
creation itself.[19]

Navajo re-fashioners Shayne Watson and Tiffany Begay, globally recognized designers, utilize de-colonizing perform-antics to create counter-
representational aesthetics. At the 2013 Arizona Indigenous Fashion
Show, Watson honors his "inspiration for Navajo fashion design," which he

says comes from one Native seamstress in particular, his grandmother.[20] "But we put a twist on it," Begay added. "Our fashions reflect our ancestral traditions while at the same time demonstrating the ways our cultures are evolving." For this reason, they continue, "we do not call ourselves Indigenous fashion 'designers'" but instead "Indigenous re-fashioners" (Melchor). Sometimes Watson and Begay use the normative language of the Western fashion industry to describe what they do (using words such as *runway, catwalk, models, stylists, designers, dressers,* and *audiences*)—but sometimes they do not. In every case the meanings of these words transform when Watson and Begay use them as perform-antics, as storytelling devices for re-fashioning participants on both sides of the runway.

Such were the storytelling perform-antics that gave life to three fashion shows we studied in Santa Barbara, Albuquerque, and Los Angeles. The Good Red Road fashion show in Santa Barbara, for example, began with the Chumash welcome song with MCs walking the aisles, teaching attendees how to repeat sacred vocables.[21] Once the crowd joined in the soundings, the MCs added rattles and drums, and circulated smoke from a burning sage bundle. At that point models began moving down the runway. In Albuquerque, at the Gathering of Nations Powwow Fashion Show, perform-antics included live singing and drumming for models dancing on the runway, while graffiti artists painted the ramps on both sides. In Los Angeles, another popular site for Indigenous fashion shows, one of their primary organizers is ARTivist[22] Felicia "FE" Montes, who describes her shows as Xicana-Indígena expressions. Montes's de-colonizing perform-antics include the invention of new types of MCs and models, with the MC becoming a "mujer en ceremonia," a woman who guides the fashion show journey, and the models being actual community role models. All these are examples of de-colonizing perform-antics that create counter-representational art forms. Their effect is to push against settler colonial meanings.[23] Their purpose is to liberate fashion, perception, language, beauty, race, the human body, and sex and gender identities.[24]

Our final and primary example of fashion show perform-antics is provided below. This counter-representational script textually re-enacts a feminist urban Xicana-Indígena re-fashion show and results from several twists in meaning. One twist is the synchronization of Felicia Montes's voice with a character we name "re-fashioner Corazón de FE." Our script also harmonizes the voices of the coauthors and the many Indigenous, Xicana-Indígena and Radical Indigenous Mestiz/x fashion show participants we interviewed. Our interviewees described themselves as "curander-xs," "healers," "curators," and/or "caretakers" of our cultures.

These identifications reflect their hope for the healing, restoration, and/ or resurgence of our past, present, and future stories. Their voices are represented through the narration of our fashion show MC, whom we call the maestr-x de curación or curatrix.[25] She is a teacher of healing, a keeper of wisdom, and a lover of innovation. Her (collective) voice directs participating fashion show bodies, minds, and narratives. Many more voices crowd this script.[26] All rise and fall, as do our own, in conflict and collaboration.[27]

Acto II: Welcome to a Xicana-Indígena Fashion Show! The Script-Game-Performance

(The maestr/x de curación [MC] appears on the runway.)

MC: Hello, Bienvenidos, Mai, Tsilugi and Be-pu-wa-ve![28] I'm the voice of your collective MC, co-curatrix of today's fashion show. My words are functioning as a runway today; they serve as a narrative bridge that is connecting many territories and witnesses. Our runway crosses to visible and invisible worlds; its suspension has room for every Body!

(The program director [PD] walks quickly onto the runway brandishing a wobbling metal tape measure over her head while speaking to the audience.)

PD: Don't believe it! I'm the program director. The "bridge" our maestr/x describes is a dangerous place made with words that neither calibrate nor synchronize! Where are they headed? This so-called "runway" has become a *run-a-way* story!

MC *(in a low soothing whisper only the PD can hear)*: Yes, PD, our destination is not to any singular location; we head toward countless possibilities! *(The MC looks skyward, lifting her arms, smiling.)* There are so many stories waiting to be told. Even as you speak, PD, I can hear them: the murmurs of subordinated humanity rising up. Querida, our very *bodies* on this run-a-way rewrite colonial narratives of what it means to be "human," to be "beautiful," to be "smart." *(The MC turns toward the audience.)* Friends. The following run-a-way narratives aim to release Indigenous aesthetics from colonial traps of perception. Today we take part in perform-antics aimed to re-fashion colors, contours and affects for every Body!

Let's begin by asking three of our most beloved leaders, elders, and role models to join us on this platform. Help me welcome community role models Wowatsi, Binesi, and La Nepantlera.[29] *(Wowatsi steps onto the platform with loud applause from the audience.)* Wowatsi, please accept our heartfelt appreciation. *(To the audience.)* Wowatsi comes to us from the Hopi-Tewa Hano Pueblo on First Mesa in northern Arizona. She's taken time away from her work as an activist/organizer with the collective In-

13.1. The maestra de curación (MC), played by Yolanda Hernandez Flores, wearing a T-shirt designed by Tewa Women United for their Gathering for Mother Earth: Honoring Her Lifegivingness. Photo by Chela Sandoval.

digenous Women United to be with us today. The IWU works to protect and defend sacred lands and traditional Indigenous lifeways. Today the IWU is challenging New Mexico's Los Alamos Laboratory for its contamination of water, earth and air.[30] (*Wowatsi lifts her arms to the audience in greeting.*) Next, please welcome, from the White Earth Nation Tribal College in Minnesota, Anishinaabe role model Binesi. (*Benesi steps up to the platform.*) Internationally renowned civil rights lawyer Benesi, along with a team of Native American activist lawyers, filed suit against the Washington, DC, R*dskins football team. Their lawsuit seeks to overturn the protected use of this offensive and disparaging racial slur. (*The two role models greet one another at the run-a-way's edge. Applause continues.*) Our third role model is from the local L.A. area. Please welcome La Nepantlera, two-spirit daughter of our beloved elder La Facultad.[31] Many of you know La Nepantlera and her mother very well. For countless years they've been our elders and ceremonial guides during urban Indigenous healing ceremonies. (*The three role models stand at the edge of the run-a-way. Each poses differently.*) Before displaying the fashion designs, could I ask each of you to gift us with your words?

WOWATSI: Hello, friends. I'm pleased to be on the ancestral homelands of the Tongva peoples. I bring you greetings from Hano Pueblo on First Mesa! When I agreed to participate in today's alterNative fashion show, I wondered just how "alter" it could be. Would this fashion show allow audiences and participants to *perceive* differently? (*Moves to the edge of the run-a-way.*) Will this fashion show present my body—its movements, my voice, my thinking and feeling . . . my very being—in a way that disrupts settler-colonial perceptions? Can we together push back against settler-colonial powers, transform them, even as they circulate around us, in us? As I stand before you, do you *see* me, dear friends (*opens her arms wide and lowers her head*) as a being whose presence is a challenge to the very laws of coloniality? (*Looks up.*) No? Then shift what you see . . . now. (*The other two role models begin speaking to Wowatsi, and to one another, in what becomes a public conversation.*)

BINESI: Take heed, Wowatsi. Settler coloniality is blinding our vision. The first step toward changing colonial perception is to recognize ourselves as members of sovereign Indigenous nations. Our peoples signed treaties that provide us complete autonomy and jurisdiction over everything that happens on our lands. Control over our territories brings us control over our political systems, intellectual work, our clothing, dance, music and art, as well our health care, food security, languages, spiritual sustenance, and moral fortitude. To regain sovereignty is the only way that we can gain control over our bodies and how we are perceived.

I warn you, this run-a-way will become just one more colonizing narrative if our Indigenous clothing ends up being sold at Walmart. (*Stops to consider.*) Then again, any Indigenous runway can inadvertently narrativize our traditional clothing and "re-museumize" us. (*Turns toward the audience.*) My hope is that all Indigenous fashion shows will honor our traditional, ancestral forms of dress, even though I am sad to say that everything under capitalism will become co-opted, extracted, mass-produced, and marketed to mainstream retailers and consumers.

WOWATSI: I have a different hope. I want to see Indigenous fashion shows with designs drawn from *many* tribal locations, whether these are traditional, innovative, challenging, or something else. Perhaps doing so will provide me freedom from my own stereotypes of myself. (*Turns to Benisi.*) How do we become free of coloniality? Become something new, something else?

MC (*interrupting*): I don't know, dear role models, if you're expressing reverent or irreverent attitudes toward our fashion show! I'm curious. Are you implying that when we wear Western attire we're supporting colonial aesthetics?

WOWATSI: Most of us living inside US colonial borders wear Western attire. But I believe when *we* wear Western clothing, the *meanings* our Indigenous bodies convey are a provocation to Western perception. I mean our very bodies: their shapes, colors and genders, our eyes, hair, faces, voices, their sounds, lilts and cadences. So, I use fashion very self-consciously in Western spaces. At home I usually wear my own people's traditional clothing. But yesterday I testified at a court hearing on behalf of a tribe fighting for their water rights. I wore high heels, a pencil skirt, a suit jacket and a Xican/x-Indígena T-shirt. I believe the purpose of Indigenous fashion shows is to return our bodies, minds, emotions and spirits to one another. They should return us to our homelands, our cultures, and to our own aesthetics. *That* is the promise of our ongoing survivance. I wear clothing best designed to get us *there*.

LA NEPANTLERA: Get us *where*, sister? Yes, today's run-a-way invites us on a journey. But my homecoming has never been to any single Indigenous site . . . land, culture, language, territory. . . . I no longer know my ancestral tribes, they do not know me. My homecoming returned me to a site of *re*-tribalization, but this restoration has been only to a site of liminality. I borrowed a name for this place, "Nepantla," from the Nahuatl language. Some people describe Nepantla as a bridge. But for me, Nepantla is a dwelling place for a new kind of tribalization.

MC (*intervening*): Thank you for your honesty, role models. Let's find out what the designer thinks. Please help me welcome the internationally renowned Rarámuri (Tarahumara)-Xicana re-fashioner, Corazón de FE![32] (*The audience cheers and applauds. Re-fashioner Corazón steps out from backstage. The applause slowly ends. The audience, role models, MC and the re-fashioner survey one another. There follows a long assertion of presence without words. The silence becomes a non-logocentric reality.*)

AUDIENCE MEMBER/SPECT-ACTOR[33] (*interrupting the silence*): ¿Escucharon? Es el sonido de su mundo derumbándose.[34]

COYOTE (*a loud voice emerging from the crowd*): Can you hear it? It's the sound of the world transforming![35]

WOWATSI AND LA NEPANTLERA (*speaking in unison*): That sound is of an Indigenous aesthetic uprising.[36]

MC (*interrupting*): Let's find out how. Re-fashioner Corazón de FE, this fashion show is organized to honor your work as a leading L.A.-based ARTivist, organizer, and fashion designer. Maestra, would you teach us about your clothing line and introduce us to the worlds of Indigenous Xicana territories, cultures, and fashions?

RE-FASHIONER CORAZÓN DE FE: Of course. (*Stepping to the run-a-way's microphone.*) To begin today's fashion show, I'd like to direct your attention to the dress worn by our esteemed role model Binesi. (*Music comes up. Binesi walks the run-a-way, then leans against the backdrop. Applause.*)

Binesi's dress is the prototypic piece of the FE clothing line. It reflects the foundational principles upon which my entire fashion line is based. But first I want to point out that its fabrication and distribution—indeed, the entire clothing line—would never have been possible without the collective contributions of the L.A. Re-Fashioning ARTivists with whom I work. Our collective is deeply committed to sharing our Indigenous heritages. For example, I named this pivotal dress you see here the meXicana Anahuac to honor a social movement that seeks to connect all Indigenous peoples. This movement imagines the Anahuac heritage as a route to becoming liberated from European occupation by connecting our territories into a hemispheric unity. My fashions are thus a tribute to this hemisphere understood as a beautiful mosaic of Indigenous civilizations and cultures. My meXicana Anahuac dress honors our peoples' shared processes of transculturation and hybridity—processes people like us have undergone because of colonization.

But when most people speak of this garment, they call it "the FE Dress." (*She pauses reflectively, then points to the upper half.*) Please direct your attention to the neckline, where you see the letters *F* and *E*. This reads "FE," a word that means faith, hope, conviction, or belief. I put the word FE at the center of the dress to remind me to have faith in myself and in the Indigenous Xican/x-ARTivists with whom I work. This is the only dress in my collection with written text. I enclosed the lettering inside a diamond shape. The diamond's four points visually represent the four directions: north, south, east, west. Growing up out of the lettering you see a cornstalk rising, which symbolizes our people's constant state of becoming. I then surrounded this entire section with blooming flowers. This upper complex is one of four parts. Look to the middle of the dress to see the second part. (*Gestures again to Benisi.*) It is a maíz, a large corn glyph stylized in shape and meaning to replicate the corn design found in the ancient Mesoamerican Codex Borgia.

The third design-story can be found on the dress's lower half, appearing as an anatomical corazón. But look closely. You'll see that the veins of this heart replicate a map of the entire continent — North *and* South America. The life of the heart is symbolically expressed through three important elements. From the heart's right ventricle flows the energy of fire, and from the left, water and air. I learned about these three elements through my active participation in L.A.–based Xicana-Indígena circles. We share ceremonies and rituals with diverse urban Indigenous participants using song, dance, music, workshops, sweat lodges, and talking circles. Through my participation I learned how the generative and transformative elements of fire, air, and water are connected to the bodies of women. That's why I placed the heart over the anatomical location where the female body reproduces life. Just as our Xican/x-Indigenous ARTivist collective honors the Earth's reproductive capacities, so too do we honor the reproductive capacities of women.

We women live our lives in relation to the variety of creation, so the dress's final and fourth message is about diversity. I surrounded the continental female heart with a cadre of individualized corn kernels in order to protect the beings who carry within them the very possibility of diversity: women. (*Scanning the audience.*) Why? Because all across the Americas Indigenous peoples tell stories about the connections between human existence and corn. Corn is a life form with the ability to morph into multitudes and varieties, to create diverse forms of being — just like women. To honor the possibilities of diversity that women can create, I added a cross pointing to the four sacred directions.

COYOTE (*interrupting*): Cool! But what about the social hazards of gendering? What about the possibilities of the *x*? The star as a utopian horizon of being? Yes, la tierra is a generative mother. But mother energies are everywhere: in the oceans and the moon, in the mind-body-emotions, in the spirits of all human, nonhuman, and other than human beings . . .

13.2. Binesi, played by community role model Joanna "Mixpe" Ley, wearing the MeXicana Anahuac T-dress by Urban Xic. Photo by Felicia Montes. www.urbanxic.com.

13.3. Wowatsi, played by community role model Cristina Serna, wearing the Chiapaneca Heart T-shirt by Urban Xic and jewelry by Ilaments. Photo by Felicia Montes. www.urbanxic.com.

MC (*intervening*): I agree, Coyote. Corazón's dress is an art-y-fact; it combines myth *and* truth. Her design-story reminds me to have the courage FE requires. Let's move on. Corazón de FE, your FE dress is only the first of *three* dresses you brought for us to see. Tell us about your second dress. (*Binesi exits the run-a-way. Wowatsi takes her place. Applause.*)

RE-FASHIONER CORAZÓN (*to the audience*): Join me in welcoming our next role model, Wowatsi. (*Wowatsi walks to the run-a-way's edge and slowly turns around.*) Wowatsi is wearing the Chiapaneca Heart T-shirt. Here again the focus is a heart, but the Chiapaneca Heart design is very different from the one we saw on the FE dress. The intent of the Chiapaneca Heart design is to honor the Zapatista women ARTivists of Chiapas and the EZLN. I've cultivated a close collaboration with Zapatista women over two decades, and I've developed a deep respect, friendship, and love for them and what they do. This design resembles, in a print medium, the predominant weaving and textile aesthetics developed by the women ARTivists of Chiapas.

The Chiapaneca Heart is designed to be very small, stylized, and diamond-shaped. It's an aesthetic *translation* designed to move Chiapanecan women's weaving and textile media into another but connected realm: that of a radical feminist northern Indigenous Xicana style, expressed the way we do it—on a silkscreened T-shirt.

This same heart is tattooed on my arm. (*Lifts the sleeve of her T-shirt, revealing the tattoo. The audience gasps.*) This tattoo is also a Zapatista-style heart, except it's pierced by a cross. This piercing symbolizes the actions of the colonial Catholic Church entering Indigenous hearts, languages, arts, and cultures. My tattoo symbolizes the colonization of the hemispheric Americas and the so-called "discovery" of Indigenous peoples and our lands. I made this tattoo to symbolize colonization, resistance, and the strength of our traditions.

COYOTE (*calling out*): Are we finished? My tattoo appointment is in two hours.

RE-FASHIONER CORAZÓN: Not yet. (*Turns to Wowatsi.*) Look closely *inside* the Chiapaneca liberated heart. Do you see another, very small cross? *This* cross is designed to be a compass, like the cross on the FE dress. I designed both to summon the powers of the four directions.

Step back for a moment, take in the entire design. Doesn't it look like hand-stitched embroidery? I found a way to artistically create the *look* of embroidery using silkscreen print techniques by outlining and repeating shadows around every shape. It is inspired by the small and very densely packed ancient embroidered Mayan weaving style that is still seen on Chiapanecan and Guatemalan huipiles.[37] Of course, this achievement through graphic design is a *re*-invention, my own trans-interpretation.[38] (*The audience applauds.*) I achieved very similar effects on the third and final design I brought today.

MC: Thank you, maestra. Let us welcome our final role model, La Nepantlera. (*Wowatsi moves to one side. La Nepantlera takes her place on the platform.*)

RE-FASHIONER CORAZÓN: La Nepantlera wore this dress last night at the Mujeres de Maíz live art show. Everyone loved it! I named this dress the Tehuana Xicana for several reasons. During the Mexican mural movement of the mid-twentieth century, many artists, such as Frida Kahlo, painted the cultures, traditions, and aesthetics of the Tehuanas—the warrior women from Tehuantepec, Oaxaca.[39] These artists believed that Tehuanas represented our shared Indigenous pasts on this continent, along with our refusal to accept cultural and racial inferiority and dependency. I wanted to design a Tehuana-*Xicana* artwork, so I studied contemporary Tehuana-invented textiles and huipiles before coming up with the final design. I used the same silkscreen approach I developed for the Chiapaneca Heart T-shirt. But this time I surrounded each decorated flower with what appears, from a distance, to be Tehuana-style embroidery. I then placed the majority of this faux-embroidery around the neckline.

13.4. La Nepantlera, played by community role model LeighAnna Hidalgo, wearing the Tehuana Xicana T-shirt by Urban Xic and jewelry by Ilaments. Photo by Felicia Montes. www.urbanxic.com.

Before concluding, let me make one final point about this design and about my entire clothing line. Everything I do, from community organizing to fashion ARTivism, is imagined and brought to life in conjunction with the L.A. Indigenous Xican/x cultural ARTivists with whom I work. It's crucial to our growth as a people, and as an urban L.A. community-in-transformation, that we work collectively to create personally and culturally relevant art.

BINESI (*intervening*): I wear each of FE's designs as T-shirts, dresses, or tunics. I wear them to powwows, yoga, while political organizing—I even wore them when pregnant. Thank you, FE, for making comfortable, affordable, stylish clothing. And I'm grateful that the fabric was provided by a *non-sweatshop* company, American Apparel of Los Angeles.

MC (*intervening*): And I'm grateful to everyone here. (*Applause begins.*) Please join me in thanking our role models Binesi, Wowatsi, and La Nepantlera. (*Applause rises.*) Help me honor re-fashioner Corazón de FE for her creativity, generosity, and political organizing. Our gratitude also goes to the collective of ARTivists and co-curanderxs for their roles in today's story. (*The role models, Corazón de FE, and the MC stand side-by-side on the run-a-way. Applause slows and ends. A silence envelops the room like that which occurred at the beginning of the show.*)

Acto III: The Community Speak-Out

MC (*interrupting*): Our audience has questions and comments.

AUDIENCE SPECT-ACTOR: Corazón, what are your goals as a re-fashioner?

RE-FASHIONER CORAZÓN: My main goal is to encourage people who buy my designs to commit to a politics of Indigeneity and engage in spiritual activism.[40] Another goal is to encourage buyers to enact alterNative relationships to the mainstream garment industry.

MC: Re-fashioner, earlier you said your designs carry what you call a "Xicana-Indígena" spiritual-politics. Are these politics unique? Are they only generated within highly urbanized areas like Los Angeles? Are they feminist politics? Or are they the politics of an ancient historical consciousness that's rising globally today?

RE-FASHIONER CORAZÓN: I use the term *Xicana-Indígena* to refer to Xicanas who recognize their Indigenous heritages. After all, Indigenous peoples express different forms of politics and different approaches to spirituality. Yet, there is an element that connects all our different spiritual-politics. It's our shared love and respect for Mother Earth.

I use the word *Raza* when I refer to the diverse ARTivists involved in the creation of my FE clothing line. For me, the word *Raza* is an inclusive term. I use it to acknowledge that in spite of our geographic, racial, cultural, ethnic, language, gender or sexual differences, my compañer-xs and I are similarly committed to carrying on Indigenous traditions. Of course, people are specific to what they know—and what they know comes from where they live—from our own lands and from our lineages. For me, urban Indigenous peoples are expressing a form of hemispheric Indigeneity that links those of us living in the United States, Mexico, the Caribbean, Canada, Central, North and South America. We are raza-Indígena.

COYOTE (*calling out*): We are all "Idle No More."[41] Korea! Africa! The West Indies! The Philippines! India! Japan! Samoa! Russia! Europe! (*Spect-actors cheer in agreement. Coyote raises a fist.*) East Side San Jose ¡Presente!

WOWATSI: Aho Mitákuye Oyás'iŋ. All our relations, Coyote![42] Thank you, Corazón de FE. I want to add that Indigeneity is a pluriverse, not a single universe of thinking, being, and doing. This continent is composed of many different sovereign nations and clans who live on, understand, and care for the land—and each other—differently. We speak different languages, have different histories, cultures, territories, and understandings of being itself. This is true when I speak of the Hopi, or the Indé (or Apache), Diné (or Navajo), Ute, Tewa, Indo-Hispan-x, or Genízar-x peoples of the US Southwest, where I'm from. It's also true for the Kanaka Maoli of Hawai'i, the Koori of southeast Australia, and for the many distinct sovereign nations all over the world, no matter how small or large, federally recognized or not. Our Native world is made up of many distinct worlds.

LA NEPANTLERA: My *prima* is Lebanese/Laguna. Some of the peoples who live in my barrio are Apache/Hispana, Nez Perce/Tejana, Black Seminole, cross-blood, or just plain Mestizo. I myself am Chilipina, Chicana/Filipina. We are Radical Indigenous mestiz-xs![43]

JEWELRY DESIGNER LISA ROCHA (*calls out from the audience*): I too represent multiple Indigenous heritages. I'm Hopi/Xicana.[44]

LA NEPANTLERA: Indian people today are reframing continental meanings. I use *Turtle Island* to name this hemisphere. For me, *Turtle Island* is used as a pan-Indian concept,[45] though I've heard peoples from other nations using different names, like Pachamama, Abya Yala or Aztlán.[46] Today, the continental Indigenous polyverse is populated with culturally rich and diverse Indigenous—and settler—cultures. The whole planet is in a decolonial time—a reclaiming time for Indigenous peoples everywhere. My goal is to seek joyful cohabitation with this diversity of human and other human life forms.

RE-FASHIONER CORAZÓN: I agree! Everyone who contributes to

the FE fashion collection—designers, silk-screeners, artists, organizers, buyers, and vendors—each is committed to live, learn, practice, and share mixtures from *all* our diverse Indigenous heritages. We then sell our cultura wares in an online web store called UrbanXic—UX for short. These wares include T-shirts, publications, music, and jewelry.[47] UX is a current day trade center developed for peoples who connect to our Xicana-Indígena worldviews. All our art wares are fashioned to summon up spiritual politics. Our collective's aim is to bring peace, dignity, and respect to *all* Indigenous peoples.

MC (*intervening*): So far you've provided us definitions for terms like *Xicana-Indígena* and *Raza* as well as ways to think about the land. Would you say a bit more about the meaning of the term *Xic* in UrbanXic?

RE-FASHIONER CORAZÓN: Our online store UrbanXic uses an *X* instead of a *Ch* as in *Chicana*. *Xic* stands for Xic-an/x peoples. An *X* used in this way signifies our commitment to recognizing, remembering, and practicing our living ancestral Indigenous traditions. Our UX ARTivist collective is thus composed of urban Xican/x-Indígena peoples. Customers sometimes pronounce the word *Xic* like *chic*—as in stylish clothing and fashion. We use the *X* to include those among us who are detribalized or de-Indianized through slavery, genocide, and displacement.

COYOTE (*calling from the audience*): Hey! Many of us *are* tribalized. We live on our lands. We know and live among our relatives. Today, I call on everyone! I name you! I witness you!

RE-FASHIONER CORAZÓN: I feel you. My work supports a growing social movement of urban Xican/x-Indígenas. The UrbanXic webstore is the mercado for this movimiento.

AUDIENCE SPECT-ACTOR (*calling out*): Tell us more about UX's customers.

RE-FASHIONER CORAZÓN: We have a diverse, creative clientele. Our UX collective caters to and is inspired by them. We find each person brings their own style to an outfit, often incorporating their own specific regional and alternative musical flair into the mix. Our customers, for example, wear FE designs blended with a huipil and/or rebozo combined with jeans, a cowboy hat, and tennis shoes or high heels. Most often customers' clothing doesn't represent where their families and ancestors are from. Instead, the mixes we see create an urban Indigenous style that appreciates the diversity of the thousands of living Indigenous nations on the planet. *This* is the basis of UrbanXic. We've found that our customers are mostly college-educated and self-identify as people of Color. Many are activists or educators who work for social justice. UX has received orders from Germany,

Japan, and Mexico, as well as vending invitations and orders from across the United States, including Alaska, and Canada.

MC: Yes, there's a long, rich precolonial history of cross-cultural trade among our peoples. These routes traverse the American continent. Folks should check out Oglala Lakota scholar and curator Emil Her Many Horses's map. It tracks Indigenous trade routes and centers that flourished before 1000 BCE to after colonization.[48] Anthropologist Juan Vicente Palerm reveals that present-day swap meets are a continuation of Tianguis, ancient Mesoamerican open-air marketplaces. So let me ask you, Corazón, do you see your webstore as a continuation of these ancient hemispheric, cross-cultural centers and trade routes?

RE-FASHIONER CORAZÓN: Yes, UrbanXic is part of an expanding number of Indigenous trade routes and centers. I want to give you an example. Laura Palomares and Emma Pintado operate a fair-trade clothing and art import organization that collaborates with recognized Indigenous cooperatives across the Americas.[49] They call it El Puente Hacia la Esperanza. This organization hosts community-based artisan markets in L.A. They are a crucial contemporary trade center. And there are many more!

MC (*interrupting*): Everyone! We have with us today the three coauthors of this chapter. (*A surprised murmur moves through the crowd.*) I want to directly address Felicia "FE" Montes, the tocaya twin of re-fashioner Corazón de FE. Coauthor Montes, have you an alternate summary of your connections to these redeveloping trade centers and routes?

COAUTHOR FELICIA "FE" MONTES (*speaking from the audience*): I do. I'll tell you a story. (*The audience makes space around her as she speaks.*) In 1997 I traveled with fair-trade organizer Laura Palomares to Chiapas. There we became part of the first culture-and-dialogue gatherings of Indígenas, Chicana-o-xs, Xican*s, and Zapatistas. This trip had a profound influence on my generation, so much so that we began to co-identify as Generation Z.

We returned from that trip with an agreement to support, import, and sell the goods made by the Zapatista women's clothing cooperatives. This was an alterNative US/Chiapas trade agreement, and it deeply influenced many aspects of my life, including my politics and organizing, my art and poetry, my personal style, my clothing and fashion designs, my teaching and my spiritual practices. These trade exchanges also deeply influenced an emerging L.A. alterNative music scene in the late 1990s. Many of us began connecting our music with Zapatista solidarity work.[50] I wore the first design you saw today, the FE Dress, as band gear on music stages across the country. Today I continue making affordable, socially responsible, and culturally relevant art and clothing inspired by the Zapatista women, designed to encourage wearers and viewers to take pride in their bodies.

COYOTE (*calling out*): Re-fashioning is decolonial ARTivism!

COAUTHOR MONTES: The FE fashion line is about liberation from colonial racism. UrbanXic is committed to do this work, collectively. I believe that when we work in collaboration, we become stronger, more creative, more relevant to the world. For example, I worked with Xicano artist Joel "RageOne" Garcia as a codesigner for many years, during which time Joel became the main graphic ARTivist-designer for the UX web store and the FE clothing line. Also, today's fashion show was co-curated with the great Hopi-Xicana re-fashioner Lisa Rocha, owner of Ilaments jewelry.[51] Her expertise was critical in styling today's role models. UrbanXic encourages this kind of collaboration between artisans.

JEWELRY DESIGNER LISA ROCHA (*from the audience*): Thank you. (*The audience readjusts their focus to Lisa Rocha.*) I, too, participated in the 1997 Indigenous, Xican/x, Zapatista gathering in Chiapas. My jewelry line, Ilaments, is also linked to expanding Indigenous trade centers and routes. Ilaments is a word that marries different worlds: *Ila* is a Hopi word for "one who takes on challenges." I combined *Ila* with the English word *elements* to create a hybrid word: *Ilaments*. My jewelry line is inspired by the natural world, synced with my own Native American, Hopi, Xicana, and Mexican roots. I keep oral traditions alive by infusing stories from my cultures into each handmade piece of jewelry.

COYOTE (*blurting out*): Radical Indigenous Mestiz/x aesthetics!

MC (*moderating*): Our thanks to Ilaments founder Lisa Rocha, re-fashioner Corazón de FE, and coauthor Felicia "FE" Montes for providing us important information on how Indigenous trade routes are built through supportive collaborations. Coauthor Montes, would you tell us the story of how your life moved between being a fair-trade importer to a performer, to an organizer for Mujeres de Maíz, to a fashion activist?

COAUTHOR MONTES (*from the audience*): My personal involvement as an Indigenous fashion show organizer began in 2009. I was inspired by the annual Por Vida fashion show sponsored by Mi Vida Clothing Boutique in L.A., another Indigenous trade center. Mi Vida caters to women of Color who want to share their politics and heritages through clothing. That year the boutique's co-owners invited me and jewelry designer Lisa Rocha to participate as featured re-fashioners and models.

Two years later, the Harmony Keepers decided to put on a fashion show featuring all Indigenous designers, and they requested my participation. The Harmony Keepers Center is an East L.A. Indigenous organization that hosts classes, workshops, performances, and educational sessions, and coordinates a great deal of Indigenous trade and exchange. That fashion show became a life-changing experience for me.

After that experience I decided to organize my own fashion show to feature the FE clothing line. I was passionate about the idea of inviting community leaders, *real* role models, to wear my designs. Those who agreed were activists, artists, educators, local politicians—you know, people in leadership positions. Western fashion industry models are expected to be a specific weight, height, color, age, gender—their bodies judged by the racist values of the Anglo colonial West; I intentionally switched all that up. In my fashion shows community role models are people whose work inspire everyone to live better lives. Their presence on a run-a-way challenges dominant conceptions about what a model is. My overall goal was, and still is, to communicate noncommercial, non-exploitive, and community-centered messages to audiences, especially to the youth. Today Indigenous Xicana fashion shows in L.A. continue to present community role models who constantly refigure what it means to be human.[52]

MC: Thank you for your response, coauthor Montes. This is a good place to end our Fashion Speak-Out. (*Addressing the audience.*) Please join me in thanking the participants, designers, organizers, re-fashioners, coauthors, and interviewees who have made this show possible. (*The audience applauds.*) Let's conclude our work together by asking our three coauthors to gift us with a few parting words.

COYOTE (*calls out*): Do we have to?

(*A banner on the stage unfurls. It contains two emblazoned quotes, one by Leanne Simpson, the other by Gloria Anzaldúa. The three coauthors emerge from behind the banner.*)

Epilogue: The Coauthors' Post-Fashion Show Re(X)Marks

My creative work is more political than my nonfiction academic and activist work, because in art, you don't, you can't really ask permission. You do. You make. You create. Your responsibility is to smash boxes, not play nicely in their confines.
LEANNE BETASAMOSAKE SIMPSON, "FALLING INTO DECOLONIAL LOVE"

Creative acts are forms of political activism. They employ definite aesthetic strategies for resisting dominant cultural norms and are not merely aesthetic exercises.
GLORIA ANZALDÚA, *MAKING FACE, MAKING SOUL*

Coauthors: This chapter has introduced a different kind of "fashion-ability," which we produced by experimentally weaving ethnographic and counter-representational storytelling designs. The intertextual fashion show presented here interlaces interviews, testimonials, travel notes, fictions, and truths with the aim of providing a run-a-way that trans*forms academic scholarship, history, consciousness, bodies, and beings. The chapter's run-a-way narrative presents a particular kind of urban feminist Indigenous Xicana/o/x/* fashion show. This run-a-way re-codes language, symbols, meanings, ideologies, and bodies in order to interrupt those monovoices-that-silence, re-codings that Chippewa fashion scholar Jessica Metcalf suggests are key to creating "counter-representational" aesthetics.

In this chapter we authors performed as re-fashioners, our designs in creative negotiation between continuity and transformation. We experimented with techniques, visual languages, and complex systems of meaning to re-engage what is written and imag(in)ed. Our intention has been to build a counter-representational production through perform-antics that can release and uncover caches-of-democracy. Our shared commitment to an ethics of equality binds us across our differences as we continue working in collaboration to create fashion art-y-facts. As fashion designers, teachers, organizers, and activists, we value combining elements of elevated meaning with affordable cost. For us, there is no one set approach to creating an urban Indigenous Xicana/o/x/* fashion show or for writing about it—no one set code to follow when one's work is unraveled as quickly as one sews. The fashion shows we surveyed do not enforce current fashion forms, do not return fashion to a pre-contact clothing tradition, do not dictate what Indigenous clothing should look like for the twenty-first century. Instead, the shows we considered were devised with decolonizing perform-antics AIMed[53] to awaken the imagination. Urban Indigenous Xicana/o/x/* fashion shows ride the edges of symbol and meaning. Their presence is another indication of a planetary Indigenous aesthetic uprising.

Notes

Dedicated to our foremothers beautifully dressed in light: Pearl Sandoval, Ruthann "Rudy" Gonzalez, Olivia Montes and Norma Alarcón, Gloria Anzaldúa (Nepantlera), Yolanda Broyles-González (Yoeme), Norma Elia Cantú, Inés Hernández-Avila (Nez Perce), Chrystos (Menominee), Paula Gunn Allen (Laguna Pueblo), Joy Harjo (Mvskoke), Aída Hurtado, Elder Kathy Sanchez (Tewa, San Ildefonso Pueblo), Corinne Sanchez (Tewa, San Ildefonso), Ines Talamantez (Apache), Tías Georgia Serrano and Agueda Martinez (Inda-Hispana/Navajo/Pueblo), Prima Marian Naranjo

(Tewa, Santa Clara Pueblo), Josefina Naranjo Lucero Martin-Serrano (Cañones, Abiquiu, Genízara/Hispana), Beata Tsosie-Peña (Tewa), Pabla Archuleta Lucero-Serrano (Genízara, Abiquiu), Del Archuleta (Española, Hispana), Delcie Lucero (Cañones, Hispana), and Tewa Women United.

1. The designation *meXicana* was proposed by cultural critic Rosa Linda Fregoso in 2003 to call up and name "the historical, material, and discursive effects" of contact zones (xiv). The name works to make evident, she believes, the colonial and decolonial exchanges that mark and make our peoples.

2. Early deployments of the term *Xicana* include Ana Castillo's *Massacre of the Dreamers: Essays on Xicanisma* (1994) and La Red Xicana Indígena, founded in 1997. Members of La Red are "actively involved in political, educational and cultural work that serves to raise Indigenous consciousness among our communities and supports the social justice struggles of people of Indigenous American origins North and South" (La Red website). The name signifies an "alliance with all Red Nations of the Américas, including nations residing in the North." They say,

> We are a pueblo made up of many Indigenous nations in diaspora who through a five hundred year project of colonization, neocolonization and de-indianization, have been forced economically from their place of origin, many ending up in the United States . . . [and] we come together on the belief that, with neither land base nor enrollment card—like so many urban Indians in the North, and so many displaced and undocumented migrants coming from the South, we have the right to "right" ourselves.

Fifteen years after participating in La Red, Cherríe Moraga published *A Xicana Codex of Changing Consciousness*. For the group's members and other similarly identified Xicanas, a capital *X* marks, claims, and reasserts who we are, and thus links us "as Native people in diaspora" (Moraga xxi). See also Davalos et al., who claim Chicano Studies is a form of outlaw studies called "Xican Studies."

3. Nahuatl is a Uto-Aztecan language spoken predominantly in countries from El Salvador through Mexico. It also can be heard in other small localities across the Americas. Anthropologists report that an ancient Uto-Aztecan language similar to Nahuatl is spoken by a group of Hopi in an unceded territory within the southwestern United States. For the history of the Nahuatl language, see Kaufman.

4. More examples of the *X* as an identity marker for redefinition include the book *X-Marks: Native Signatures of Assent* by Scott Richard Lyons (Ojibwe/Dakota), which documents uses of the *X* in US history. The X-mark that Lyons identifies refers to the one North American Indians were asked to make (in lieu of a signature) on British/US property and treaty documents to sign away their rights to ancestral lands. Further, Lyons proposes that the X-mark also signifies an alternative state of being to either normative colonial invitations to be assimilated or alternatively, to an Indigenous politics of violent resistance. Any utopian re-namings with or without an *X* cannot and must not erase the living presence of Inde´ (Apache), Tewa, Tiwa, Keres, Diné (Navajo), Ute, Zia, Zuni, Comanche, Piro, Chumash, Genizar-x, Indo-Hispan-x peoples—the list goes on: peoples who still live on their native lands, who daily live with, visit, and know their Indigenous relatives, territories, and ancestors.

5. The *X* is a visible crossing of two different singularities and can be considered a visual representation of a chiasmus. The political slogan "We didn't cross the border, the border crossed us" is organized as a meaning chiasmus, a metaphoric device based on an X-shaped structure wherein concepts are repeated, but in a modified, cross-wise arrangement. Each side repeats the other—in order to transform it. This rhetorical device balances two or more clauses against each other—but reverses their structure to produce a transformative effect. For more on the chiasmus see Sandoval's discussion of Fanon's "Black Skin/White Masks" (*Methodology*). Also see the Davalos et al. definition of the *X* in the discipline of Chicano studies.

6. Numerous scholars are grappling with these complex relationships (Contreras; Hernandez; Castellanos et al.; Miner; Garcia and Madrid; Blackwell et al.; Trujillo). Their work can be seen as a part of a radical Indigenista turn in the field of Chicana/o studies that deals with Indigeneity, mestizaje, xicanidad, mexicanidad and/or latinidad. According to González, this body of work can be categorized as "Radical Indigenous Mestizaje." These scholars ask similar questions regarding Indigeneity: Who gets counted and who gets left out as a result of mixture? How do we understand the enigma of interconnected transculturalities, hybridities, economic interdependencies, and the cultural exchanges that link borderland peoples?

7. Regarding Los Angeles and all major global urban locations, Turkish political sociologist Luciano Baracco demonstrates that twenty-first-century Indigenous transnational migration has made "indigeneity a more pronounced feature" for colonial cities than ever before (183). The result is that urban Indigenous communities are "assimilating and indigenizing many aspects" of European and US city life (184).

8. Group members use their tribal names, their language or territory names, their nation or clan names (from Zapotec to Tewa to Tamil), or they describe themselves as urban Indians, Indigenous, Native, or Indian. They also self-identify as Indigenous mestizas, Apachicanas, Chicanas, Indo-Hispanas, Afro-Indigenous, Afro-Latinas, Mexipinas, Xicanxs, Xicana Indígenas, cross-bloods, Genizaras, or (laughingly) as Wop'ajos (Italian/Northern Native mixes). For an excellent review of Native women's politics and consciousness see Goeman (Tonawanda Band of Seneca); Goeman and Denetdale; and Blackwell et al. All of their works are mobilized for and by differentially acting, *many-world* decolonial Indigenous feminist liberation activists.

9. Collectively, we three authors descend from Navajo, Tewa, Comanche, Indé, and/or Rarámuri peoples. We also share New Mexican (i.e., Indo-Hispana/Genizara) and/or Mexican heritages. We identify these cross-blood mixes as Xican/x-Indígena and/or Radical Indigenous Mestizaje. Each year we travel to visit our living Native relatives and to support and care for our homelands. We are retribalizing urban-Indigenous-Xican-xs in survivance. The word *survivance*, a cross between the words *survival* and *resistance*, was revived by Anishinaabe writer and scholar Gerald Vizenor. It extends Derrida's definition, which is to live an existence that is neither in life nor death, to instead exist as another kind of presence. In this existence Native stories continue on. In Vizenor's terms, our life work is not "about reaction" or carrying forward "a survivable name." Instead, Vizenor writes, "Native survivance stories are renunciations of dominance, of tragedy, and victimry. Survivance means the right of succession" (32). We coauthors celebrate our succession and inheritances. We continue transforming and are constantly ready to resist colonial fashions of absence, tragedy, powerlessness, and domination.

10. In regard to the altering of fashion, cultural theorist Alicia Gaspar de Alba makes a relevant remark, writing that "'Alter' means to change, to make or become different, as the altering of consciousness or the alteration of an outfit" (15). Gaspar de Alba popularized the term *alter-Native* in Chicana/o studies, writing that to be alter-Native "contests the ethnocentric academic practice of categorizing marginalized indigenous cultures as 'subcultures' or objects of discovery" (10). Also see the journal *AlterNative*. According to the editors, "*AlterNative* publishes scholarly research on Indigenous worldviews and experiences of decolonization from Indigenous perspectives from around the world."

11. Some of the interviews of Indigenous fashion designers, artists, activists, and organizers were drawn from Amber Rose González's dissertation research, published as *Another City Is Possible*. In 2010 González organized The Good Red Road Indigenous fashion show in Santa Barbara.

12. Tara J. Yosso and Daniel Solórzano develop a similar method they call "counter-storytelling." They write,

> Counter-storytelling is different from fictional storytelling. We are not developing imaginary characters that engage in fictional scenarios. Instead, the "composite" characters we develop are grounded in real-life experiences and actual empirical data and are contextualized in social situations that are grounded in real life, not fiction. (23–44)

13. Counter-representational aesthetics are achieved through "perform-antics." According to Aldama et al. "[D]ecolonizing perform-antics" are "manufactured aesthetic components no matter how small or large . . . objects, tools, and techniques necessary for making or transforming material and psychic cultures"; in other words, "[D]ecolonizing perform-antics are interventionist 'actions' designed to intercede on behalf of egalitarianism within any larger (social, cultural, aesthetic or scholarly) performance" (6). Such are the perform-antics that rise out of Indigenous and Xicana-Indígena fashion making with the aim of making the world anew. For more, see Sandoval et al.

14. This chapter develops and extends fashion scholarship produced by five activists: Jessica Metcalf, Roland Barthes, Dick Hebdige, Marjorie Jolles, and Fredric H. Douglas. Each scholar is interested in changing how people think about adorning the body, how humans conceptualize the liberatory elements of fashioning, fashion shows, and the very "perform-antics" of being. Prior to Barthes's groundbreaking work, *The Fashion System*, histories of clothing primarily focused on European aristocratic garments, and scholars did not consider the wider contexts in which these garments were produced. Barthes argues that the "rhetoric"—the way a written text *expresses a code*—"reflects a certain vision of the world, an ideology" (*Fashion System* 99). Barthes proves that dress is a "functional network of norms and forms. The transformation or displacement of any one element can modify the whole, producing a new structure" (*Language of Fashion* 8); Barthes's contributions to the study of fashion allow us to theorize the social function of Indigenous clothing codes expressed within Xicanidad (14). Hebdige explores "how subcultural styles are constructed" and the concept of "style" as "bricolage" (256–257). The argument is that through rasquache "structured improvisations" we become "bricoleurs" who destabilize the

meaning of a dominant object (like fashion) through radical adaptations organized to "erase or subvert" their suffocating and "straight meanings" (259).

In the feminist anthology *Fashion Talks: Undressing the Power of Style*, Shira Tarrant and Marjorie Jolles argue that the meaning of fashion is dependent on "(1) whose interests [fashion] serves, (2) what its audience and practitioners bring to their engagement, and (3) how fashion protects and transforms social divisions" (2). Jolles's "Stylish Contradiction: Mix-and-Match as the Fashion of Feminist Ambivalence" points to the ways young women, through mixing clearly registered styles, express defiance to being defined (239–240). We understand this mixing as a celebration of contradiction with political potential, as long as these aesthetics are linked to a political ethics committed to social change.

Douglas, a curator of the Denver Art Museum in the 1940s and 1950s, intended to advance this liberatory political potential of contradiction. He introduced Indigenous fashion to the mainstream fashion industry, hoping this would challenge racist stereotypes of Indigenous peoples and promote cross-cultural understanding. This tactic did not work. Instead, it bolstered anthropological approaches to Indigeneity that ended up "museumizing" Indigenous clothing. Metcalf extends each of these theoretical positions, while our chapter takes up and extends Metcalf's work.

15. A sampling of Indigenous fashion shows follows: the Nigerian Native and Vogue International Fashion Week; Ghana Fashion and Design Week; the Australian show Indigenous Fashion Unearthed; the Canadian show National Aboriginal Fashion Week; California's Por Vida Day of the Dead fashion show; American Indian student fashion shows; New Mexico's Beyond Buckskin runway fashion show and Rhymes and Runways fashion show; Arizona's In Beauty I Walk fashion show; and Hawai'i's MAMo Wearable Art Show.

16. For more on Indigenous resurgence see Taiaiake (*Wasáse*), Simpson (*Dancing*), and Coulthard. Refer to the *Idle No More* website (www.idlenomore.ca/) for additional references.

17. We utilize the term *re-fashioner* as defined by Navajo designers Shayne Watson and Tiffany Begay in place of *fashion designer* throughout the chapter. See Melchor for their full interview at the Phoenix American Indian Fashion Show.

18. According to the *OED*, *representation* is "the action of speaking or acting on behalf of someone, or the state of being so represented." Thus, all representation is a RE-presentation of something or someone else. In the transition between presentation (of self) and re-presentation (which is a *translation*), there is transformation. Thus, Metcalf's *counter*-representation" refers to something *against* representation itself. What is offered instead is another version that goes against the representation of what "is," the dominant. To re-present means one must re-fashion. If representation is understood as the imitation of something, as a token for something else, then counter-representational aesthetics are self-consciously aware of this kind of imitation. Xican-Indigenous scholar Gerardo Aldana examines Indigenous representation further in "Deciphering Ancient Mesoamerican Foundational Texts."

19. In the *OED*, *fashioning* as a verb refers to the "action or process" of "making," "building" or "shaping." This fashioning is the action of Cutschall's seamstress who designs the world anew.

20. See Melchor.

21. For more information, see González.

22. The first two documented uses of the word *artivism* appeared in 2008. See Asante; and Latorre and Sandoval.

23. Settler colonialism is a specific historical, cultural, ideological, and imperial formation that requires its own analytic framework, which is powerfully provided by scholars of critical Indigenous studies. In this regard the foundational contributions of Australian anthropologist and ethnographer Patrick Wolfe demonstrate that settler colonialism is "a *structure*, not an event" ("Settler Colonialism" 96). Settler-colonialism thus does not end; it is, rather, an ongoing phenomenon. While colonialism is about conquest, the processes of settler colonialism vibrate through and continually transform every layer, material and psychic, of occupied lands. To recognize settler colonialism is to fundamentally extend and transform Michel Foucault's theories of power in a way that re-fashions, once again, history, being, the planet, time, and space.

In studying the structure of settler colonialism, we engaged at different levels in the processes of (re)understanding the politics of knowledge in Chicana-o-x studies; Xicanx Indigeneity; the norms of academic scholarship; and in our own positions in relation to Indigenous world-making. Our thinking is in process with Native American studies scholars who are developing and advancing critical Indigenous studies (CIS); for example, Barker; Coulthard; Moreton-Robinson; A. Simpson. We also engage in divergent conversations within critical Native American studies, Chican-x studies, and Latin-x studies that have given rise to: (1) the challenge to legal "recognition" (Anderson; Barker; Coultard; Lawrence); (2) the paradigm shift that is settler colonialism (Fujikane and Okamura; Rifkin; Wolfe); and (3) powerful resurgence and survivance manifestos (L. Simpson [*Dancing*]; Taiaiake; Vizenor). We also pay attention to new names and terminologies for describing different lifeways, from Xicana-o-x Indigeneity (Castillo; Moraga; Contreras; Hernandez; Saldaña-Portillo, "Who's the Indian") to the Nican Tlaca Anahuac Mexica Movement (www.mexica -movement.org), to Radical Indigenous Mestizaje (González), cross-blood Indigeneity (Miner), and to critical Latinx Indigeneities, an emerging multidisciplinary framework that Saldaña-Portillo calls a "paradigm drift" (see the special issue of *Latino Studies* entitled *Critical Latinx Indigeneities*, edited by Blackwell et al.).

24. For discussions of Indigenous gendering see Driskill et al.; Rifkin.

25. Our MC is a maestra de curación or a curatrix. According to the *OED* a maestra is "a teacher, a mistress of the arts and a builder" and a curatrix is "a female healer or curer"—indeed, "to curate" means "to heal." On the other hand, the word *curator* often signifies one who organizes and traps Indigenous stories and peoples inside Western colonial museums. Our script requires the MC to act as a maestra/o/x de curación and as a curatrix/healer who guides us in an urban-ceremony-of-another-human-kind.

26. The fashion show cast has twelve characters: the MC; the program director (PD); three role model co-curatrixes: Binesi, Wowatsi, and La Nepantlera; refashioner Corazón de FE; jewelry designer Lisa Rocha; audience members/spect-actors; Coyote; and this chapter's three authors.

27. The phrase "Women of Color in Conflict and Collaboration" was first used by a 1983 collective of women of Color at UC, Santa Cruz.

28. The MC says "Welcome" in four languages: Bienvenidos (Spanish), Mai (Maori), Tsilugi (Cherokee), and Be-pu-wa-ve (Tewa, northern New Mexico Pueblos).

29. *Wowatsi* is defined by Tewa Women United (TWU) as "Our breath, our prayer, our commitment to live life with purpose and good intentions" (tewawomenunited.

org/). The nishnaabemwin dictionary of the Anishinaabe language defines *Binesi* as "thunderbird," as cited by Simpson in *Islands of Decolonial Love*. The word *Nepantlera* is a contemporary neologism based upon the Nahuatl word *nepantla*, which means "world between worlds." Among contemporary *Ch*- and *Xi*-canx feminists, and based on Anzaldúa's re-definition, a Nepantlera is a person with the ability to live and move in, and between, realities for the sake of creating loving connections between peoples.

30. The characterization of this organization was inspired by Tewa Women United (TWU), a northern New Mexico multicultural and multiracial organization founded and led by Native women. As a tribal community living downstream from Los Alamos, TWU is concerned with the health of our waters, lands, and peoples. We based the fictional IWU and Wowatsi's activism on the real-life work of TWU. Elder Kathy Sanchez, Gilbert Sanchez (San Ildefonso Pueblo), and TWU filed a lawsuit against the Department of Energy and the Los Alamos Laboratory for violations of the Clean Water Act in 2008. See tewawomenunited.org.

31. *Facultad* is a Spanish word redefined by Anzaldúa to mean the abilities and faculties that oppressed peoples develop in order to survive.

32. Reminder: The character Corazón de FE is the fictional alter, the tocaya, of real-life fashion designer and coauthor Felicia Montes. Much of the following descriptions of the fashion designs are drawn from Montes's written testimonios and her presentations at real-life fashion shows. In this script Montes permits her fictional apprentice, Corazon de FE, to speak for her various histories, identities, and fashion designs. Montes is cofounder of the Xicana-Indígena online store UrbanXic, where her fashion and art are available to people worldwide. She is also cofounder of the Los Angeles-based ARTivist collective Mujeres de Maíz, as well as the performance group In Lak Ech. Montes's fictional alter re-fashioner, Corazón de FE, is a character created and edited by the coauthors of this chapter.

33. Augusto Boal coined the term *spect-actor* to describe members of an audience taking part in a performance. For excellent scholarship on Boalian matters see Schutzman.

34. This question and statement are taken from the Zapatista (EZLN) march that took place December 12, 2012, in San Cristóbal de las Casas, Mexico. The march marked the arrival of a new Baktun (era) on the Mayan calendar. Video available at youtu.be/5K_z_ceSlwE.

35. The character Coyote provides unexpected commentary, challenge, or wisdom. Coyote opens up meanings in any way possible. In this script the character mediates between the roles and personas summoned to create this chapter. In Native American literature the trickster figure is best known as a shapeshifter, creator and destroyer, truth-teller and liar, and sometimes as Coyote. One of the primary characteristics of the trickster is ambiguity. The great Anishinaabe theorist Gerald Vizenor writes that most people (he names academic anthropologists and other social scientists) do not understand the aesthetics of Indigenous oral traditions in which traditional trickster stories have been told. Moreover, Vizenor continues, they don't seem to comprehend the communal aspect of the trickster's narrative event (199). Vizenor teaches us that the trickster is a collective, discursive sign that generates "a communal signification that cannot be separated or understood in isolation" (189). Its signifiers are what both Saussure and Vizenor refer to as "acoustic images," and these are

bound, writes Vizenor, "to four points of view [the author's, narrator's, characters', and readers'] while . . . it's signified as an event, a narrative event—or a translation" (189). The work of the trickster is to accomplish transformation, Vizenor continues. A successful trickster will make listeners and readers themselves "trickster[s], a sign and semiotic being in discourse" (189). Our character Coyote loves this kind of work, as do a couple of the coauthors. It is also worth mentioning the Brazilian teatrista and activist Augusto Boal, who defines a joker as intermediary between audience and performers, and whose actions are not attached to any one party. Boal's Joker functions to ensure the smooth running of any game that is designed to teach attendees how to live life. The rules of the game are taught to participants as they go.

36. For more on Indigenous aesthetic uprisings see Martineau's excellent dissertation. His work examines the transformative and decolonizing potential of Indigenous art-making and creativity. He writes that there is a "colonial injunction to 'represent' indigeneity according to a determinate set of coordinates." Against that injunction, people should see Indigenous art-making and creativity "as the noise to colonialism's signal: a force capable of disrupting colonial legibility" and the "imposition of the normative order" (iii-iv). Martineau thinks we can act self-consciously as "decolonial cyphers," and in that way create "new forms of being elsewhere and otherwise" (iv).

37. A huipil is a pre-Columbian garment still worn by women in Mesoamerica.

38. For more on trans-interpretation see Gaspar de Alba and Lopez's *Codex Nepantla* website.

39. Tehuana style is known for (re)presenting the "unbowed body" standing "assertively" to create an end-of-coloniality culture, according to fashion theorist of Indigeneity Oriana Baddeley (586).

40. Corazón agrees with art historian Janet Catherine Berlo, who asserts that Indigenous fashion "extends into metaphysics; its artistry links human and spiritual realms" (97).

41. The Idle No More movement "calls on all people to join in a peaceful revolution to honour Indigenous sovereignty and to protect the land and water" (see www .idlenomore.ca/). IDM is a protest movement founded in Canada in 2012 by four women: three First Nations women and one non-Native ally. Its slogan is "Self Determination—not Termination."

42. A Lakota phrase that means "all my relations" or "We are all related."

43. For more on this concept see González.

44. Inspiration for Lisa Rocha's words came from an interview with Amber Rose González in 2014. See Rocha's jewelry line at ilaments.net/.

45. We are interested in a politics that does not erase differences, as theorist Gerald Vizenor (Anishinaabe, Chippewa, White Earth) suggests. By "pan-Indigeneity" we refer to a movement participated in by many differing Indigenous nations that is capable of linking multiworlds and cultures, peoples, aims, and goals on behalf of creating "a world in which many worlds can live" (Subcomandante Marcos). Also, the crucial work of Chadwick on trans-Indigeneity provides examples. Moreover, Gloria Anzaldúa speaks of a "new tribalism" composed of country people whose identities cross imperial borders: this is pan-Indigeneity (Anzaldúa and Keating).

Vizenor, however, challenges such terms, especially the term *Indian*, as social science constructions. The problem, he writes, is that our peoples are destructively addressed *en masse* through an occidental "corrupt" Euro-American "humanism" (vii). Western academics have replaced distinction and difference between Native peoples, who instead become "fugitive." Thus, he continues with some irony that academic Indian studies should be renamed "post-Indian Studies" (viii).

46. Indigenous, Xican/x, and Mestiz/x peoples have many names for the American continent that do not revolve around colonially demarcated state borders. The Panamanian Kuna peoples call it Abya Yala, meaning "land in its full maturity" or "land of vital blood." A different name is Turtle Island, the original name for North America used by the Iroquois, Ojibwe (Anishinaabe), Seneca, Lenape, and the northeastern Woodlands peoples. It is interesting to note that new Indigenous, Xican/x-Indígena, or Mestiz/x political constituencies organized during the twentieth and twenty-first centuries are (re)inventing terms for the continent. Nican Tlaca, for example, is used by the México movement to identify all Indigenous peoples of the Western Hemisphere (see www.mexica-movement.org). Their movement names North and South America together as Cemanahuac, while North America considered singly is Anahuac. So too, Aztlán is a name used by Xican/x peoples to refer to pre- and post-conquest locations and mythologies.

47. Spect-actors and audiences can access UrbanXic at urbanxic.com.

48. These trade routes can be seen on the 1590–1800 map provided by Emil Her Many Horses in his book *Identity by Design*. Indigenous scholars Masaquiza and B'alam write, "Long ago, our Indigenous ancestors traded over vast distances. We suggest we build a new infrastructure of political and economic exchange" (7). UrbanXic is deeply involved in building a contemporary Indigenous trade route infrastructure.

49. The organization El Puente Hacia La Esperanza (The Bridge Towards Hope) produces the *Anti-Mall: People Before Profit* website. It is "a space for ARTivists, performers, and conscious consumers to come together and invest their money, time, and energy into putting PEOPLE b4 Profit." This site is a digital example of a contemporary Indigenous marketplace and trade center.

50. Solidarity with the Zapatistas has influenced the artistic and political work of many L.A. collectives, including Mujeres de Maíz and In Lak Ech. For detailed cultural histories see Speed et al. and González. For a detailed history of Xicana/o/x music in L.A. (including Aztlán Underground, Blues Experiment, Ozomatli, Ollin, Quetzal, Quinto Sol, and others) and the influence of Zapatismo on this scene, see Viesca.

51. Ilaments.net.

52. The film *Miss Navajo* (2007), provides one example of this type of role model. Miss Navajo contestants are evaluated on proficiencies in sheep butchering, weaving, and fry-bread making.

53. AIM is the acronym for the American Indian Movement.

Works Cited

Aldama, Arturo J., et al., editors. *Performing the US Latina and Latino Borderlands*. Indiana UP, 2012.

Aldana, Gerardo. "Deciphering Ancient Mesoamerican Foundational Texts: Challenges of a Non-Logos-Based Creation Narrative." *Foundational Texts of World Literature*, edited by Dominique Jullien and Peter Lang, 2011, pp. 47–68.

AlterNative: An International Journal of Indigenous Peoples. 2005–present, journals .sagepub.com/home/aln. Accessed 10 Aug. 2018.

Anderson, Kim. *A Recognition of Being: Reconstructing Native Womanhood.* Second Story, 2000.

Anzaldúa, Gloria. *Borderlands / La Frontera: The New Mestiza.* Aunt Lute Books, 1987.

———. "Border Art." *La Frontera / The Border: Art about the Mexico/United States Border Experience,* San Diego Museum of Contemporary Art, 1993.

———. "Haciendo caras, una entrada." *Making Face, Making Soul / Haciendo Caras: Creative and Critical Perspectives by Women of Color,* edited by Gloria Anzaldúa, Aunt Lute Books, 1990, pp. xv–xxviii.

Anzaldúa, Gloria, and AnaLouise Keating, editors. *This Bridge We Call Home: Radical Visions for Transformation.* Routledge, 2002.

Asante, M. K., Jr. "By Any Medium Necessary." *It's Bigger Than Hip Hop.* St. Martin's, 2008, pp. 53–74.

Baddeley, Oriana. "Engendering New Worlds: Allegories of Rape and Reconciliation." *The Visual Culture Reader,* edited by Nicholas Mirzoeff, Routledge, 2002, pp. 584–590.

Baracco, Luciano. "Review of Comparative Indigeneities of the Américas: Towards a Hemispheric Approach." *AlterNative,* vol. 9, no. 2, 2013, pp. 182–184.

Barker, Joanne. *Native Acts: Law, Recognition, and Cultural Authenticity.* Duke UP, 2011.

Barthes, Roland. *The Fashion System.* U of California P, 1967.

———. *The Language of Fashion.* Translated by Andy Stafford and Michael Carter, Berg, 2006.

Berlo, Janet Catherine. "Creativity and Cosmopolitanism: Women's Enduring Traditions." *Identity By Design: Tradition, Change, and Celebration in Native Women's Dresses,* edited by Emil Her Many Horses, HarperCollins, 2007, pp. 97–148.

Blackwell, Maylei, et al., editors. *Critical Latinx Indigeneities, Latino Studies,* vol. 15, no. 2, 31 July 2017, pp. 126–137.

Boal, Augusto. *Games for Actors and Non-Actors.* Routledge, 1992.

Cantú, Norma E. *Canícula: Snapshots of a Girlhood en La Frontera.* U of New Mexco P, 1995.

Castellanos, Bianet, et al., editors. *Comparative Indigeneities of the Americas: Toward a Hemispheric Approach.* U of Arizona P, 2012.

Castillo, Ana. *Massacre of the Dreamers: Essays on Xicanisma.* Plume, 1994.

Chadwick, Allen. *Trans-Indigenous: Methodologies for Global Native Studies.* U of Minnesota P, 2012.

Contreras, Sheila. *Blood Lines: Myth, Indigenism and Chicana/o Literature.* U of Texas P, 2008.

Coulthard, Glen. *Red Skin, White Masks: Rejecting the Colonial Politics of Recognition.* U of Minnesota P, 2014.

Cutschall, Colleen. "Dresses, Designers and the Dance of Life." *Identity By Design: Tradition, Change, and Celebration in Native Women's Dresses,* edited by Emil Her Many Horses, HarperCollins, 2007, pp. 65–94.

Davalos, Karen Mary, et al.. "Roundtable on the State of Chicano Studies." *Aztlán: A Journal of Chicano Studies,* vol. 27, no. 2, Oct. 2002, pp. 139–152.

Derrida, Jacques. *The Beast and the Sovereign,* vol. 2. Edited by Michel Lisse et al., translated by Geoffrey Bennington, U of Chicago P, 2011.

Dorsey, Kristen. "Decolonizing the Runway: Jessica R. Metcalfe Brings Native American Fashion into the Spotlight." *Cultural Survival Quarterly*, vol. 37, no. 2, 2013.

Douglas, Frederic H. *Material Culture Notes (1939–1969)*. Denver Art Museum, 1969.

Driskill, Qwo-Li, et al., editors. *Queer Indigenous Studies: Critical Interventions in Theory, Politics, and Literature*. U of Arizona P, 2011.

Forbes, Jack. *Aztecas del Norte: The Chicanos of Aztlán*. Fawcett, 1973.

Forbes, Jack, et al. "Selections from the Brief Proposal for Deganawidah-Quetzalcoatl University." U of California P, 1970, p. 46.

Fregoso, Rosa Linda. *meXicana Encounters: The Making of Social Identities on the Borderlands*. U of California P, 2003.

Fujikane, Candice, and Jonathan Y. Okamura, editors. *Asian Settler Colonialism: From Local Governance to the Habits of Everyday Life in Hawai'i*. U of Hawai'i P, 2008.

Galarte, Francisco. "On Trans* Chican@s: Amor, Justicia y Dignidad." *Aztlán: A Journal of Chicano Studies*, vol. 39, no. 1, 2014, pp. 229–236.

Garcia, Peter, and Arturo Madrid. "Performing Indigeneity in the Nuevo Mexicano Homeland." *Comparative Indigeneities of the Américas: Toward a Hemispheric Approach*, edited by María Castellanos et al., U of Arizona P, 2012, pp. 96–110.

Gaspar de Alba, Alicia. *Chicano Art Inside Outside the Master's House*. U of Texas P, 1998.

Gaspar de Alba, Alicia, and Alma Lopez. *Codex Nepantla*. codexnepantala.com, 2006.

Goeman, Mishuana. *Mark My Words: Native Women Mapping our Nations*. U of Minnesota P, 2013.

Goeman, Mishuana, and Jennifer Nez Denetdale. "Native Feminisms: Legacies, Interventions, and Sovereignties." *Wicazo Sa Review*, vol. 24, no. 9, 2009, pp. 169–187.

González, Amber Rose. *Another City Is Possible: Mujeres de Maíz, Radical Indigenous Mestizaje and Activist Scholarship*. U of California P, 2014.

Her Many Horses, Emil, editor. *Identity By Design: Tradition, Change, and Celebration in Native Women's Dresses*. HarperCollins, 2007.

Hebdige, Dick. "Style." *Fashion Theory*, edited by Malcolm Barnard, Routledge, 2007, pp. 256–266.

Hernandez, Roberto. "Running for Peace and Dignity: Traditionally Radical Chicanos/as to Radically Traditional Xicanas/os." *Latin@s in the World System: Decolonization Struggles in the Twenty-first Century U.S. Empire*, edited by Ramon Grosfoguel et al., Paradigm, 2005.

Jolles, Marjorie. "Stylish Contradiction: Mix-and-Match as the Fashion of Feminist Ambivalence." *Fashion Talks: Undressing the Power of Style*, edited by Shira Tarrant and Marjorie Jolles, SUNY P, 2012, pp. 227–244.

Kaufman, Terrence. "The Story of the Nawa Language Group from the Earliest Times to the Sixteenth Century." *The Documentation of the Languages of Mesoamerica*, March 2001, www.albany.edu/pdlma/Nawa.pdf.

Latorre, Guisela, and Chela Sandoval. "Chicana/o Artivism: Judy Baca's Digital Work with Youth of Color." *Learning Race and Ethnicity*, edited by Anna Everett, MIT P, 2008.

Lawrence, Bonita. *"Real" Indians and Others: Mixed-Blood Urban Native Peoples*. U of Nebraska P, 2004.

Lyons, Scott Richard. *X-Marks: Native Signatures of Assent*. U of Minnesota P, 2010.

Marcos, Subcomandante Insurgente. "Fourth Declaration of the Lacandón Jungle."

Indigenous Clandestine Revolutionary Committee General Command of the Zapatista Army of National Liberation Mexico, January 1996.

Martineau, Jarrett. *Creative Combat: Indigenous Art, Resurgence, and Decolonization.* U of Victoria P, 2015.

Masaquiza, Martina, and Pakal B'alam. "A Pan-Indigenous Vision of Indigenous Studies." *Indigenous Nations Studies Journal*, vol. 1, no. 1, 2000, pp. 3–9.

Melchor, Jorge Martin. "Scenes from the 2013 AIGSA Fashion Show at Arizona State." *Indian Country Today Media Network*, May 2013, www.youtube.com/watch?v=IH1pWchMdM8. Accessed 2 July 2013.

Metcalfe, Jessica R. *Beyond Buckskin Lookbook.* Beyond Buckskin, 2013.

———. *Native Designers of High Fashion: Expressing Identity, Creativity, Tradition in Contemporary Customary Clothing Design.* U of Arizona P, 2010.

Miner, Dylan A. T. *Creating Aztlán: Chicano Art, Indigenous Sovereignty, Lowriding Across Turtle Island.* U of Arizona P, 2014.

Miss Navajo. Directed by Billy Luther, World of Wonder Productions, 2007.

Montes, Felicia. *Urban Xic.* UrbanXic.com.

Moraga, Cherríe. *A Xicana Codex of Changing Consciousness: Writings, 2000–2010.* Duke UP, 2011.

Moraga, Cherríe, and Celia Herrera Rodríguez. *La Red Xicana Indígena.* www.freewebs.com/laredxicanaindigena/.

Moreton-Robinson, A. *Critical Indigenous Studies: Engagements in First World Locations.* U of Arizona P, 2016.

Online Nahuatl Dictionary. U of Oregon, whp.uoregon.edu/dictionaries/nahuatl/.

Palerm, Juan Vicente. "Exploring Tianguis Markets in Rural/Agricultural California." Unpublished manuscript.

Palomares, Laura, and Emma Pintado. *Anti-Mall: People Before Profit.* El Puente Hacia La Esperanza, theantimall.weebly.com/.

Rifkin, Mark. *Settler Common Sense: Queerness and Everyday Colonialism in the American Renaissance.* U of Minnesota P, 2014.

Saldaña-Portillo, Josefina. "Critical Latinx Indigeneities: A Paradigm Drift." *Critical Latinx Indigeneities*, special issue of *Latino Studies Special Issue*, vol. 15, no. 2, July 2017, pp. 1–18.

———. "Who's the Indian in Aztlán? Re-writing Mestizaje, Indianism, and Chicanismo from the Lacandon." *Latin American Subaltern Studies Reader*, edited by Ileana Rodriguez, Duke UP, 2001, pp. 402–423.

Sandoval, Chela. "Author's Note." *Metodología de la Emancipación*, U Nacional Autónoma de México P, 2017, pp. 29–34.

———. *Methodology of the Oppressed.* U of Minnesota P, 2000.

———. "Philosophy Uprising: The Feminist Afterword." *Asian and Feminist Philosophies in Dialogue: Liberating Traditions*, edited by Jen McWeeny and Ashby Butnor, Columbia UP, 2014, pp. 271–278.

Sandoval, Chela, et al. "Introduction: Toward a De-Colonial Perform-antics." *Performing the U.S. Latina and Latino Borderlands*, edited by Arturo Aldama, Chela Sandoval, and Peter J. García, Indiana UP, 2012, pp. 1–31.

Sandoval, Chela, and Guisela Latorre. "Chicana/o Artivism: Judy Baca's Digital Work with Youth of Color." *Learning Race and Ethnicity*, edited by Anna Everett, MIT P, 2008, pp. 81–108.

Schutzman, Mady. *A Boal Companion: The Joker Runs Wild.* Taylor and Francis, 2015.

Simpson, Audra. *Mohawk Interruptus: Political Life across the Borders of Settler States.* Duke UP, 2014.

Simpson, Leanne Betasamosake. *Dancing on Our Turtles Back: Stories of Nishnaabeg Re-creation, Resurgence and a New Emergence.* Arbeiter Ring, 2012.

———. *Islands of Decolonial Love.* Arbeiter Ring, 2013.

Speed, Shannon, et al., editors. *Dissident Women: Gender and Cultural Politics in Chiapas.* U of Texas P, 2007.

Taiaiake, Alfred. *Heeding the Voices of our Ancestors: Kahnawake Mohawk Politics and the Rise of Native Nationalism.* Oxford UP, 1999.

———. *Peace, Power, Righteousness: An Indigenous Manifesto.* 2nd ed., Oxford UP, 2009.

———. *Wasáse: Indigenous Pathways of Action and Freedom.* Broadview, 2005.

Tarrant, Shira, and Marjorie Jolles, editors. *Fashion Talks: Undressing the Power of Style.* SUNY P, 2012.

Trujillo, Simon. "USA is Trespassing in New Mexico: Indo-Hispano Mestizaje." *Chicano Studies Reader: An Anthology of Aztlán,* edited by Eric Avila et al., UCLA Chicano Studies Research Center, 2017.

Viesca, Victor Hugo. "The Battle of Los Angeles: The Cultural Politics of Chicana/o Music in the Greater Eastside." *American Quarterly,* vol. 56, no. 3, 2004, pp. 719–739.

Vizenor, Gerald. *Manifest Manners: Narratives on Postindian Survivance.* Wesleyan UP, 1999.

Warrior, Robert. "Native American Scholarship and the Transnational Turn." *Cultural Studies Review,* vol. 15, no. 2, 2009, pp. 119–130.

Wolfe, Patrick. "Settler Colonialism and the Elimination of the Native." *Journal of Genocide Research,* vol. 8, no. 4, 2006, pp. 387–409.

———. *Settler Colonialism and the Transformation of Anthropology: The Politics and Poetics of an Ethnographic Event.* Cassell, 1999.

Yosso, Tara J., and Daniel Solórzano. "Critical Race Methodology: Counter-Storytelling as an Analytical Framework for Education Research." *Qualitative Inquiry,* vol. 8, no. 1, 2002, pp. 23–44.

Contributors

NORMA ELIA CANTÚ is the Norine R. and T. Frank Murchison Endowed Professor in Humanities at Trinity University. She is professor emerita of English and US Latina/o literature at the University of Texas at San Antonio and the author of *Canícula*, which chronicles her childhood experiences on the border. She edits the Rio Grande / Rio Bravo Culture and Traditions book series for Texas A&M University Press.

MICAELA DÍAZ-SÁNCHEZ is an assistant professor in the Department of Chicana and Chicano Studies at the University of California, Santa Barbara. She is currently working on a manuscript entitled "Between Nation and Diaspora: Chicana and Mexicana Feminist Performance."

AMBER ROSE GONZÁLEZ (Indé/Xicana) is an educator, organizer, and associate professor and chair of the Ethnic Studies Department at Fullerton College. Her research focuses on the juncture between Chicanx studies, critical Indigenous studies, and womxn of Color feminisms. She is currently working on a co-edited anthology that chronicles the spiritual artivism of Mujeres de Maiz.

RACHEL VALENTINA GONZÁLEZ-MARTIN is an assistant professor of Mexican American and Latina/o studies at the University of Texas at Austin. She is currently working on a manuscript titled "Quinceañera Style: Social Belonging and Latinx Consumer Identities" (forthcoming from the University of Texas Press).

GABRIELLA GUTIÉRREZ Y MUHS is a poet, cultural worker, and professor at Seattle University. She conducts poetry readings, keynote speeches, diversity trainings, and motivational work throughout the world. Her poetry has been anthologized in Latin@ journals. As the child of migrant farm workers, she moved around northern Mexico and the southwestern United States. She published her first poems at eighteen while in France as a college student. Gutiérrez y Muhs worked as a teacher and counselor in central California, where she was one of the recurring participants of the unique breast cancer fundraising readings "In Celebration of the Muse." She came to Washington in July 2000 to begin a career as an assistant professor. Her writing focuses on the recovery of subjectivity through the works of Chican@/Latin@ authors. Her edited book *Rebozos de Palabras: An Helena María Viramontes Critical Reader* (University of Arizona Press) was published in 2013. She is first editor of *Presumed Incompetent: The Intersections of Race and Class for Women in Academia* (Utah University Press, 2012). She represented the United States in India as one of the three American poets to be invited to attend the 2011 Krytia International Poetry Festival. Gutiérrez y Muhs's most recent edited book is *Word Images: A Norma E. Cantú Reader* (University of Arizona Press, 2017). She has authored multiple articles, poetry collections, and encyclopedia entries, and in 2015 she was awarded the Provost's Inaugural Award for Scholarship, Research, and Creativity at Seattle University. In addition, she was recently selected as the university's director for the Center for the Study of Justice in Society. Her collection *¿How Many Indians Can We Be?* is forthcoming from Mango Press. Her book *The Runaway Poems* was published in 2017 (Finishing Line Press). Gutíerrez y Muhs has been named the Theiline Pigott McCone Chair for 2018–2020, one of two chairs in Arts and Sciences.

AÍDA HURTADO is the Luis Leal Endowed Professor and a faculty member in the Department of Chicana and Chicano Studies at the University of California, Santa Barbara. She is past chair of the National Association for Chicana/Chicano Studies. Dr. Hurtado's research focuses on intersectional theory, Latinos' educational achievement, and media representations of race. Her books include *Voicing Chicana Feminisms: Young Women Speak Out on Sexuality and Identity* (New York University Press, 2003), which received an honorable mention for the Myers Outstanding Book Awards given by the Gustavus Myers Center for the Study of Bigotry and Human Rights in North America; and *Chicana/o Identity in a Changing U.S. Society. ¿Quién soy? ¿Quiénes somos?* (coauthored with Patricia Gurin, University of Arizona Press, 2004). She is a co-editor (with Pedro Noguera and Edward Fergus) of the book *Invisible No More:*

Understanding the Disenfranchisement of Latino Men and Boys (Routledge, 2012). Her most recent book, *Beyond Machismo: Intersectional Latino Masculinities* (cowritten with Mrinal Sinha, University of Texas Press, 2016), received the Book of the Year Award from the American Association of Hispanics in Higher Education. Hurtado was also the recipient of the SAGE Award for Distinguished Contributions to Gender Equity in Education Research, granted by the American Educational Research Association (AERA), and the 2014 Outstanding Latino/a Faculty in Higher Education: Research/Teaching in Higher Education (Research Institutions) Award granted by the American Association of Hispanics in Higher Education.

STACY I. MACÍAS earned her PhD from UCLA in women's studies. She is currently an assistant professor in the Department of Women's, Gender, and Sexuality Studies at California State University, Long Beach. Her research and teaching are in the areas of Chicana/Latina studies, women of Color feminist theories, feminist transnational praxis, and queer of Color studies.

MARCI R. MCMAHON is an associate professor at the University of Texas at Rio Grande Valley. Her work has appeared in *The Chicano Studies Reader*, 3rd ed.; *Aztlán*; *Chicana/Latina Studies*; *Frontiers*; *Journal of Equity and Excellence in Education*; and *Text and Performance Quarterly*. She is the author of *Domestic Negotiations: Gender, Nation, and Self-Fashioning in US Mexicana and Chicana Literature and Art* (Rutgers University Press, 2013). Her current manuscript, "Sounding Cultural Citizenship: Latinx Dramaturgy in Times of Crises," explores critical moments in US history when citizenship has been redefined by Latinx communities and has been in crisis, arguing that citizenship is performed through sound, with aurality and listening as vital to performances of citizenship.

JOSIE MÉNDEZ-NEGRETE, a professor of Mexican American studies at the University of Texas at San Antonio, received her PhD at the University of California, Santa Cruz. The University of New Mexico Press published her most recent book, *A Life on Hold: Living with Schizophrenia* (2015). From 2009 to 2014, Méndez-Negrete served as lead editor of *Chicana/Latina Studies: The Journal of MALCS* and has been the chair of the National Association for Chicana and Chicano Studies (NACCS) and Mujeres Activas en Letras y Cambio Social (MALCS).

FELICIA "FE" MONTES is a Xicana Indigenous artist, activist, community and event organizer, educator, FEmcee, designer, poet, performer,
and professor living and working in the East Los Angeles area. Known
throughout the area as an established Xicana cultural worker of a new
generation, she is the cofounder and coordinator of Mujeres de Maíz,
In Lak Ech, Urban Xic, and La Botánica del Barrio and has worked on
various transnational art and organizing efforts, including work with
the Zapatistas, Peace & Dignity Journeys, and La Red Xicana Indígena.
Montes graduated with a BA from UCLA in world arts and cultures with
a minor in Chicanx studies, an MA in Chicanx studies from Cal State
Northridge, and an MFA from Otis College of Art and Design in public
practice art. Visit her at feliciamontes.com.

DOMINO RENEE PEREZ is an associate professor in the Department of
English and the Center for Mexican American Studies at the University
of Texas at Austin, where she regularly teaches courses in literature, film,
popular culture, and cultural studies. Her book *There Was a Woman: La
Llorona from Folklore to Popular Culture* (University of Texas Press, 2008)
examines one of the most famous figures in Mexican folklore, plotting
her movement from post-conquest oral narratives into contemporary
cultural productions. Perez has coedited the book *Race and Cultural Practice in Popular Culture* (Rutgers University Press, 2018) and has published numerous book chapters and articles on topics ranging from film
and Indigeneity in Mexican American studies to young adult fiction and
folklore.

LAURA PÉREZ is a professor of Chicano/Latino studies at the University
of California at Berkeley and is the author of *Chicana Art: The Politics of
Spiritual and Aesthetic Altarities* (Duke University Press, 2007). Her most
recent book is *Ero-Ideologies: Writings on Art, Spirituality, and the Decolonial* (Duke University Press, 2019).

JADE D. PETERMON is a visiting assistant professor of interdisciplinary
and communication studies at Miami University. She received her PhD in
film and media studies from the University of California, Santa Barbara
in 2014. She is currently working on a book to be titled "Hyper(in)visi-
bility: Reading Race and Representation in the Neoliberal Era," which
will trace the visibility of radicalized subjectivities across several media
platforms in the era of neoliberalism.

SONIA ALEJANDRA RODRÍGUEZ is an assistant professor of English at LaGuardia Community College, CUNY, where she teaches composition, literature, and creative writing. Her research focuses on decolonial healing practices in Latinx children's and young adult literature. She received her doctorate in English literature from the University of California, Riverside.

CHELA SANDOVAL (Genízar@ Abiquiu, Cañones, Medanales) is a trickster professor at the University of California, Santa Barbara in the department of Chicana/o/x studies. She is writing a book about how SWAPA (storytelling-witnessing/world art/performance as activism) and the nahuala-witness-nahuala ceremony teach the principles of the *Metodología de la Emancipación* (2018, UNAM Press).

Index

Note: Numbers in *italics* refer to images and tables.